AMERICAN STUDIES
OF CONTEMPORARY
CHINA

An East Gate Book

Studies on Contemporary China

AMERICAN STUDIES OF CONTEMPORARY CHINA

DAVID SHAMBAUGH
editor

Mary Brown Bullock
Thomas Fingar
Paul H.B. Godwin
Thomas B. Gold
Nina P. Halpern
Harry Harding
Anthony J. Kane
Terrill E. Lautz
Timothy Light

Richard Madsen
Jay Mathews
Linda Mathews
Michel C. Oksenberg
Penelope B. Prime
Thomas W. Robinson
Robert S. Ross
David Shambaugh
Eugene W. Wu

Woodrow Wilson Center Press

M.E. Sharpe

An East Gate Book

© Woodrow Wilson International Center for Scholars 1993

First published 1993

Editorial Offices:
The Woodrow Wilson Center Press
370 L'Enfant Promenade, SW, Suite 704
Washington, D.C. 20024-2518

Order from:
M. E. Sharpe
80 Business Park Drive
Armonk, New York 10504

Library of Congress Cataloging-in-Publication Data

American studies of contemporary China/David Shambaugh, editor.
p. cm.—(Studies on contemporary China)
"An East Gate Book"
Includes index
ISBN 1-56324-266-4.—ISBN 1-56324-267-2 (pbk.)
1. China—Research—United States. 2. Sinologists—United States.
I. Shambaugh, David L. II. Series.
DS734.97.U6A46   1993
951'.0072073--dc20
93-5618
CIP

Printed in the United States of America

The paper used in this publication meets the minimum requirements of
American National Standard for Information Sciences—
Permanence of Paper for Printed Library Materials,
ANSI Z39.48–1984.

∞

| BM (c) | 10 | 9 | 8 | 7 | 6 | 5 | 4 | 3 | 2 | 1 |
| BM (p) | 10 | 9 | 8 | 7 | 6 | 5 | 4 | 3 | 2 | 1 |

To the memory of John King Fairbank, Father of the Field

Contents

Acknowledgments

This volume has its origins in my long-standing interest in the images the United States and China hold of each other. It equally derives from an interest in the impact that opportunities for field research in China have had on contemporary China studies in the United States. This volume will, it is hoped, contribute to our understanding of both of these issues.

In organizing the conference that led to this volume, and during the lengthy process of producing the book, I have benefited from the intellectual and practical assistance of many individuals. Above all, I would like to express my gratitude to Mary Brown Bullock. As my successor as director of the Asia Program at the Woodrow Wilson International Center for Scholars, Mary has provided considerable time and assistance in guiding this project to fruition. Without her help the book may not have seen the light of day. Ronald Morse also deserves much credit for helping conceptualize the project initially. Terrill Lautz of the Luce Foundation was also quite helpful in the initial planning stages.

At the conference, several senior sinological scholars contributed their wisdom, although their input is not recorded directly in these pages: A. Doak Barnett, Stanley Lubman, Benjamin Schwartz, and Allen S. Whiting. To each I owe an intellectual debt. Also due gratitude are the editorial committee that assisted me in compiling and conceptualizing this volume—Allen Whiting, Steven Goldstein, Harry Harding, and G. William Skinner—and two external readers, Nicholas Lardy and Martin King Whyte, for their critical readings of the manuscript. At the Woodrow Wilson Center Press, particular thanks go to Joe Brinley, who has shepherded the book from inception to publication. Doug Merwin at M.E. Sharpe is also due a debt of thanks for recognizing the significance of this book and taking the project on board. Finally, sincere thanks go to Debra E. Soled, the manuscript copyeditor, whose professional skill considerably improved the product.

To all of these individuals I am personally indebted. Editing and producing conference volumes are lengthy and often tedious affairs, and they require assistance from many quarters. Ultimate thanks are expressed to the contributors, who in the case of this volume have demonstrated undue patience and considerable effort in revising their chapters. Hopefully, all of the work that has been put into this volume is adequately reflected in its pages.

David Shambaugh
London, England

Part I
The Evolution of
Contemporary China
Studies in the United States

1

Introduction

David Shambaugh

In 1971, on the eve of the Sino-American opening, Professor John Lindbeck surveyed contemporary China studies in the United States and lamented the impact of the Cold War on scholarly understanding of the post-1949 China.[1] Isolation had produced ignorance, he argued. Lindbeck admonished the China studies community for:

> the superficial and abstract quality of much research. Less than full interpretive use is made of available data. Virtually no American scholars who are not of Chinese origin are bilingual; not more than two or three can write a scholarly article in Chinese for a Chinese publication; less than a handful have been students in a Chinese academic institution working in competition with Chinese students; and few have any sense of ease in a wholly Chinese environment.[2]

Professor Lindbeck unfortunately did not live to witness the dramatic opening of a new era of Sino-American relations in 1971–72, nor the extensive development of scholarly exchange between China and the United States following diplomatic recognition in 1979, even though he had been centrally involved in laying the institutional groundwork for those exchanges in anticipation of an eventual change in the diplomatic climate. His assessment of China studies in the United States today would no doubt be quite different, since published research is now more interpretive and grounded in primary data drawn from field research; a majority of American scholars of non-Chinese origin can claim competence in Mandarin Chinese and some in regional dialects; many have published in Chinese learned journals; every year American students study in Chinese universities and American sinologists conduct advanced scholarly research in situ; and most China specialists now live and move with relative ease in Chinese society.

This volume is testimony to the dramatic development of contemporary (i.e., post-1949) China studies in the United States since Lindbeck's earlier assessment. The essays in this volume reflect the growth and maturation of the field between the 1970s and the 1980s, and in a real sense represent the harvest of efforts undertaken by Lindbeck, John King Fairbank, A. Doak Barnett, Benjamin Schwartz, Alexander Eckstein, Robert Scalapino, John Lewis, Allen S. Whiting, G. William Skinner, and other senior scholars to build the field of contemporary China studies in the United States—at a time when domestic and international politics were often inhospitable to the study of "Communist China." Many of the contributors to this volume, in fact, personify the impact of these pioneers insofar as many were trained by them directly or by their students.

Contemporary China Studies in the United States is the product of a multiyear project that began with the conference "Perspectives on the American Study of Contemporary China," which was generously supported by the Henry Luce Foundation and Woodrow Wilson International Center for Scholars. The conference was sponsored by the Asia Program of the Woodrow Wilson Center and convened at the Aspen Institute for Humanistic Studies, Wye Woods Conference Center, in July 1988. More than thirty leading scholars and professionals in the China field participated in three days of provocative and reflective discussion at the conference. Subsequently, others were invited to contribute to this volume, and all the chapters contained herein reflect prodigious effort and multiple drafts by the contributors.

This volume is far from the first effort to take stock of trends and the state of the China field in the United States.[3] Some previous discussions were highly polemical and critical of scholars and scholarship on modern and contemporary China. Members of the field were taken to task for excessive political bias—for being either too sympathetic toward Chinese socialism or condemnatory of the Communist regime and its many shortcomings. To be certain, postwar Chinese studies in the United States germinated in a political hothouse; the Korean War, Vietnam War, and the entire Cold War provided a highly charged atmosphere that had direct and far-reaching impact on the field.

Many previous surveys also debated paradigmatic tendencies in the field. Paradigms and politics became intertwined. Several observers sharply criticized American ethnocentrism in the analysis of China and the exaggeration of the Western "impact" on China. Some believed that American values were inappropriately applied to China, while others saw a failure to subject China to vigorous standards of international behavior. In the wake of the 1989 Beijing demonstrations and killings, as part of the general introspective gestalt sweeping the field, many China specialists were accused of wishful thinking about the chances for reform and reformers in China, a sympathy that supposedly blinded them to recognizing either the pent-up frustrations in society or the brutal nature of the regime.

Then there are those critics who believe the academic field of Chinese studies in the United States to be a self-perpetuating elite, an elitism supposedly sustained by an informal conspiracy of leading professors and the principal funding and scholarly exchange organizations. The impact that China specialists have had on American polity toward Asia has also long been a subject of speculation and a target of criticism.

In short, there has been no dearth of criticism, introspection, and hyperbole in the field of contemporary China studies in the United States. This volume does not seek to evaluate the field in such terms. Rather, it seeks a dispassionate examination of the historical evolution of contemporary China studies in the United States, to take stock of the state of the field in the 1990s, and assess the future trends and challenges for development toward the twenty-first century.

Specifically, *Contemporary China Studies in the United States* addresses five principal areas of inquiry: 1) the overall evolution of scholarship on contemporary China; 2) disciplinary surveys of the state of the field in the social sciences and humanities; 3) the professional community of contemporary China specialists in the United States; 4) aspects of infrastructural development; and 5) the future challenges to the field. The volume is organized according to these principal foci of inquiry and each raises particular themes, which are summarized below.

Thematic Highlights

Harry Harding opens with an essay on the postwar evolution of contemporary China studies in the United States that helps to place subsequent chapters— particularly those in Part II—in historical perspective. Harding clearly conveys the institutional growth and intellectual maturation of the academic study of China. He notes that the field has now acquired the empirical rigor and analytical perspective that Lindbeck previously found lacking. He writes that despite considerable cross-fertilization between area specialists and academic disciplines in the United States, and the placing of China in comparative perspective, a deep-seated tension between China area studies and parent disciplines still lingers. Despite Harding's generally upbeat diagnosis of contemporary China studies in the United States, he cautions that the field's increased empiricism and focus on increasingly smaller units of analysis may have resulted in the loss of a cumulative, syncretic, and macro perspective on a rapidly changing China. He warns that increased specificity ought not to come at the cost of novel interpretation and the ability to generalize. Harding concludes by calling for increased collaborative research and scholarly cooperation across disciplines, between countries (including with Chinese scholars), and with those in public policy circles.

The five chapters that comprise Part II of the volume offer state-of-the-field assessments of research trends in key disciplines related to contemporary China studies. Each is real testimony to the enormous impact that the opening of China has had on American studies of Chinese society, the humanities, economy, politics, and foreign and defense policy. All the contributors to this section take note of how the increased amount and variety of data available, and the opportunities for field research in situ, have affected positively their areas of study. Thus field research opportunities have resulted in an enriched sense of China's diversity and complexity; consequently each discipline reflects increased nuance and empiricism. To be sure, securing research access in China has not been an easy process and continues to be fraught with problems that do not necessarily confront scholars working in other countries. No sooner had China opened to American researchers than the Mosher incident resulted in a four-year-long moratorium on rural fieldwork.[4] Opportunities for rural fieldwork subsequently resumed and have produced some path-breaking studies on rural social change.[5] Archival research on the contemporary period remains impossible for foreign scholars because the archives of the Communist Party, the State Council, the military, and the provinces remain off-limits. Even scholars of the Republican period continue to have only partial access to the No. 2 Historical Archive in Nanjing. And post-Tiananmen policies of the State Education Commission cast much doubt over the potential for collaborative research between American and Chinese scholars.[6] A wide variety of collaborative social science projects involving millions of dollars of research funding were brought to a halt in 1990 after the intervention of the State Educational Commission (and certain Politburo members). Still, the overall impact that the opening of China and opportunities for field research have had on American scholarship has been profound and extensive. This is reflected in each chapter in Part II.

Thomas B. Gold surveys sociological and anthropological studies of Chinese society and finds that while these disciplines have perhaps benefited most from field research, they have concomitantly been particularly vulnerable to the political vagaries that too often govern such access. Participant observation, interviewing, survey research, and other socioanthropological methods previously utilized in other developing societies were, after 1979, extended to the Chinese mainland and have informed many significant studies of rural, urban, and non-Han China. In some cases (particularly demography) unprecedented data have been collected and analyzed by foreign scholars, often in collaboration with Chinese colleagues. The impact of reform policies on different social strata has been studied extensively, and in general all the social sciences have become more involved in understanding the nexus between state and society. As sociologists, demographers, and anthropologists explore the Chinese countryside and urban neighborhoods, one of the principal findings has been that of *continuity* with presocialist society. In all fields of twentieth-century China, the 1949 divide is proving an increasingly artificial one. To be sure, in Chinese society the unique features of socialist organization have produced new social norms and behavior,[7] but the tenacity of traditional Chinese social hierarchies, ethnic identity, and religiosity have been a striking conclusion for many social scientists studying Chinese society. Gold also notes the long-standing (and continuing) importance of informant-based research in Hong Kong, as well as the need to compare social change in "Greater China."

Anthony J. Kane focuses primarily on the American study of Chinese literature, but he also addresses research on China's intelligentsia more generally. He aptly identifies the resurgence of less-political literary expression in the post-Mao era and the impact that this literature has had on foreign understanding of Chinese society during and after Mao's lifetime. Kane takes note of the shortage of work on contemporary Chinese philosophy and thought, but is heartened by new work on Chinese art, drama, and film.

Penelope B. Prime offers an extensive, critical survey of studies of the Chinese economy. China has always occupied a precarious position in the economic sciences. Prime tells us why this has been the case historically and offers evidence that the gulf is narrowing. As in other disciplines, newly available data are pushing the study of the Chinese economy forward, both theoretically and empirically. Prime demonstrates how economists working on China (who reside not only at the universities, but also in the U.S. government, private think tanks, and international organizations) have been increasingly able to test and refine general economic theories and models in the China case; have sketched out in considerable detail how the Chinese economy functions—or does not function—and the key formal and informal actors; have ascertained an enriched empirical sense of performance levels; and better understand intersectoral and international linkages in economic behavior.

Nina P. Halpern's contribution reveals both continuity and change in the study of Chinese domestic politics. She sees continued influence of the pluralist paradigm in an emphasis on elite conflict and the relative importance of social groups in the policy-making process. And, like Harry Harding, Halpern takes note of the increased attention to local-level politics. But she sees emerging a new emphasis on institutions and the structural constraints on policy-making and implementation in China. This "new institutionalism," Halpern argues, is stimulated by a parallel resurgence in the broader discipline of political science for "bringing the state back in." In so doing, studies of Chinese politics are increasingly studying bargaining procedures, bureaucratic politics, institutional sabotage of policy initiatives, patron-client networks, coalition formation, and so on. A second major thrust of current research on Chinese politics is in the realm of state-society relations, most notably the study of intermediate organizations—ranging from county government to the *danwei* (work unit)—in fashioning this relationship. Halpern concludes that the field of Chinese politics is alive and fluid, responding to new departures as much in political science as in China itself.

As China became more globally engaged during the decade of the 1980s, studies of China's foreign relations and defense policies have grown apace, though perhaps somewhat slower than in other social sciences. A bona fide secondary literature, anchored in primary case study data and field research, has now emerged to provide the field with an independent identity within international relations studies. This is signified by the slowly increasing number of faculty positions in American universities separate from those who teach Chinese domestic politics. **Robert S. Ross** and **Paul H.B. Godwin** have collaborated to provide a cogent analysis of the evolution of the study of China's foreign relations, particularly its strategic dimension. Despite the continued sensitivity of the subject and limited access for foreign researchers in China, the once-impenetrable sphere of national security policy-making has now become more accessible than ever before. Ross and Godwin examine the newly emergent literature that has capitalized on this recent and unprecedented access to China's military, intelligence, and foreign policy circles. They find that the field has produced important studies at the global systemic, regional subsystemic, nation-state interactive, governmental and subgovernmental, and idiosyncratic levels of analysis. A notable feature of the new generation of writing is its emphasis on the domestic sources—particularly perceptions and decision-making processes—that give rise to China's external behavior. They conclude that opportunities now exist to explore the input side (decision-making) of Chinese national security and foreign policy, as well as to study systematically China's dyadic and multilateral interactions over time.

Part III of the book delineates the community of professional China specialists in the United States today. China-watching is no longer the sole preserve of academics and government intelligence analysts. Today academic and government analysts are joined by those in the journalistic community and a wide array of private sector organizations. **Richard Madsen** and **Thomas Fingar** begin by addressing, respectively, the China studies profession in the Academy and the U.S. government. Both define and assess the professional missions and the interrelationships—often conflictual—between the two communities.

Richard Madsen does not catalogue the university community of China specialists per se, but rather offers a stimulating sociological essay on what it means to be a China specialist in the ivory tower. Madsen considers many of the criticisms laid at the doorstep of the academic China specialists—ethnocentrism, cultural imperialism, political bias, and the elitist exclusivity of the profession. He notes that China specialists, like governmental China policy, have frequently become the victims of political witch-hunts and self-imposed angst within the profession. Madsen perceptively argues that academic sinologists, while in essence a sectlike social grouping, are very much influenced by broader social trends in American as well as Chinese society.

Thomas Fingar has experienced both the academic and the government China communities firsthand. He contributes here a unique study on the daily life of a China policymaker or intelligence analyst in the U.S. government. In detail never before published Fingar depicts the processes, pressures, demands, and analytical perspectives of a large cohort of China hands mostly hidden from public view. Fingar makes a strong case for the high quality of China specialists in the U.S. government and argues forcefully for increased interaction between the governmental and nongovernmental China communities.

While academe and government have long anchored the China field, it no longer remains their private domain. In recent years significant expertise on China has taken root in banks, corporations, consultancies, research institutes ("think tanks"), international organizations, law firms, nonacademic training institutes, nonprofit foundations, and public affairs organizations. China specialists in these bodies have become a repository of considerable knowledge and unique sources of information and primary data, and they gain access to sectors of Chinese society and officialdom often unavailable to other segments of the China studies community. It is this important realm of private sector China specialists that is the subject of the chapter by **Thomas W. Robinson,** who offers a personal and extensively researched glimpse into this community.

Newspapers and newsmagazines have long employed journalists to watch China and, through their writing, interpret it for the American and international public. For three decades after the Communists came to power, most China journalists—like other China specialists—plied their trade from the "listening post" of Hong Kong. However, beginning in 1979 (after the normalization of Sino-American diplomatic relations) the American media opened bureaus and took up residence in China. The results have been manifold, but the key impact has been that foreign correspondents bring events in China to international attention on a daily basis. This was perhaps most dramatically demonstrated by the live coverage of the 1989 demonstrations and their suppression—which so riveted the attention of the world. While sensational, such events are not the staple of the journalist's China beat. On a daily basis journalists in China collect and disseminate information on China that helps to inform not only the public, but other China specialists as well.

What is it like to be a foreign correspondent in China? **Jay** and **Linda Mathews** know better than most since they opened Beijing bureaus for the *Washington Post* and the *Los Angeles Times,* respectively, in 1979 and thus belong to the first generation of American journalists in China. As in the three previous chapters in Part III, the Mathews explore the professional mission of the journalist and what it means to work the China beat.

Part IV is devoted to the infrastructure of China studies in the United States. The chapters in this section address four topics: Chinese language training, library resources, scholarly exchanges, and funding for contemporary China studies in the United States. The infrastructure is deemed essentially sound by each contributor (except, perhaps, Mary Brown Bullock, who notes the dramatic erosion of U.S. government funding for scholarly exchange), but new challenges in these four critical areas augur increased attention to them all. Each area constitutes a vital part of the foundation on which the entire superstructure of the academic China community in the United States depends. **Timothy Light's** contribution on Chinese language training catalogues the current situation with respect to enrollment, faculty training, teaching materials and methods, and the requirements for language competence in an era of increased demand for linguistic proficiency. **Eugene W. Wu** looks at the bibliographical implications for American libraries of the publishing explosion in mainland China, Hong Kong, and Taiwan over the last decade. **Mary Brown Bullock's** chapter is a reflective and firsthand account of the growth (and decline?) of U.S. scholarly exchange programs with the People's Republic that takes account of the underlying premises guiding exchanges with China, as well as the many problems and accomplishments encountered along the way. Bullock argues that, for a number of reasons, the time has come to re-examine the national infrastructure of the China studies field and the role that exchanges play in furthering national understanding of China and Sino-American relations. In this regard, Bullock notes the alarming implications of the contraction of U.S. government funding for the National Program for Advanced Study and Research in China, administered by the Committee on Scholarly Communication with China (formerly the Committee on Scholarly Communication with the People's Republic of China). **Terrill E. Lautz** contributes a vital chapter on the evolution of public and private sector funding for China studies in the United States, and he examines the implications for the field of the shifting funding base.

The final contribution to the volume by **Michel C. Oksenberg** looks ahead at the development of contemporary China studies as the field approaches the next millennium. Drawing on the foregoing chapters and his own sense of the American understanding of China over time, Oksenberg is optimistic about the future of the field. He makes a strong case for placing contemporary China studies in a broadened comparative and interdisciplinary perspective, as well as rooting it firmly in the China area studies and historical traditions. Oksenberg correctly argues that "contemporary China studies" will increasingly fade in importance in the scholarly study of China, as many in the field learn to appreciate the continuities of post-1949 China with its Republican and imperial past. Oksenberg also argues for increased attention to "Greater China" and the mutual influence among the territorial entities that comprise it, in addition to noting the increased influence that émigrés from the mainland are having on the China studies field in the United States. He concludes with a discussion of potential research topics and "conceptual opportunities" that will challenge the field in years to come.

Retrospect and Prospect

John Lindbeck's study of the state of the contemporary China field two decades ago, discussed at the outset of this Introduction, set forth ten recommendations for the further development of the field.[8] At the risk of oversimplification they were:

1. Strengthen existing key training and research centers.
2. Open these key university centers to faculty and students from smaller programs.
3. Radically improve the quality of training and increase the numbers of graduate trainees to offset retirements from the field.
4. Expansion of national research funds.
5. Improve Chinese language capability.
6. Utilize Hong Kong for field research in lieu of access to the mainland.

7. Channel resources into training graduate students in underutilized social science disciplines: economics, anthropology, demography, social psychology, sociology, etc.
8. Increase contact and collaboration with China specialists from other countries.
9. Improve research collections of primary materials.
10. Improve public education on China.

Lindbeck would be proud that virtually all his recommendations were met. Recommendation number 6 was obviated by the opening of China to American scholars in 1979, though Hong Kong (and particularly the Universities Services Center) remains an important site for certain types of research and serves as a supplement to research on the mainland. Recommendation number 8 was met during the 1960s when American scholars often convened joint conferences with their European and Japanese counterparts, but such has rarely been the case since the mid-1970s (and needs funding and attention). The other eight areas have been largely resolved by concerted national, institutional, and individual efforts over two decades.

The net result is that, as the field of contemporary China studies in the United States proceeds into its fifth decade of development, it must be diagnosed as intellectually healthy and thriving. This situation provides clear testimony to what concerted effort and vision by key individuals and organizations, backed by sustained funding from the public and private sectors, can do for an academic field. Chapters 2–7 and 16 illustrate the exciting new frontiers that American scholars are probing and the important impetus for development that the opening of China has provided. John Lindbeck would no doubt be stunned by the depth and detail of knowledge about the Chinese system and society today. Certainly China remains a complex and difficult entity to study, but it is not the enigma it once was. Chapters 8–11 are further testimony to expansion of the China field and the considerable expertise that resides in each of these four professional sectors. Chapters 12–15 on the infrastructure of China studies also speak to the expansion and health of the field, but do point up pressing problems that require attention. Not to underestimate these problems (because they are real and have reverberating effects throughout the field), but there will always exist infrastructural imbalances so long as funding is finite.

There does, however, appear to be a general contraction of funding precisely at the time of the field's quantitative and qualitative expansion. This contraction poses serious national security dangers for the United States in an era when China's power is inexorably expanding in all dimensions while American power is declining relatively. By virtue of its economic and military growth, and its central geographic location, China will be the central and dominant actor in East Asia as we move into the twenty-first century. There are many indications that China is becoming more assertive in flexing its new-found muscle and power in the Asian region—a part of the world in which the United States has vital national security concerns.[9] It is therefore of vital national interest that the United States continue to build and cultivate future generations of specialists on contemporary China in all its facets. The erosion of government funding for American China studies therefore puts the nation at some risk. It is a source of deep concern to the entire profession. This volume is concrete evidence of what a systematic national effort, underwritten by sustained and generous public and private funding, can do for the expansion of an academic field. To a certain extent the field now has a more diversified funding base and is more self-sustaining, but without *expanded* funding from U.S. government agencies and private foundations a reversal of the progress over three decades witnessed in this volume is a distinct possibility (the early signs are already apparent). As is clearly the case in Great Britain, an erosion of national funding for modern China studies can cause the field to atrophy.

Notwithstanding pressing concerns about funding—which will always exist—the following chapters portray a profession generally in good stead. As the twenty-first century approaches, the importance of China to Americans increases steadily and the challenge to the professional China community in the United States to understand and interpret this large and multifaceted society and its impact on the United States will grow accordingly. In future years another study can be undertaken to measure the progress of the field since the publication of this volume, to ascertain whether the challenges of the 1990s have been met, and to further appreciate the pioneering efforts of Lindbeck and his colleagues.

Notes

This Introduction draws on discussions at the conference "Perspectives on the American Study of Contemporary China" and the rapporteur's report by Steven F. Jackson, assistant professor of political science at Rollins College.

1. John M. H. Lindbeck, *Understanding China: An Assessment of American Scholarly Resources* (New York: Praeger, 1971).

2. Ibid., p. 97.

3. See, for example, Paul M. Evans, *John Fairbank and the American Understanding of Modern China* (Oxford: Basil Blackwell, 1988); Ta-Chun Kuo and Ramon H. Myers, *Understanding Communist China: Communist China Studies in the United States and the Republic of China, 1949–1978* (Palo Alto, Calif.: Hoover Institution Press, 1986); Paul Cohen, *Discovering History in China* (New York: Columbia University Press, 1986); Colin Mackerras, *Western Images of China* (Oxford: Oxford University Press, 1989); Robert Marks, "The State of the China Field: Or, the China and the State," *Modern China* (October 1985): 461–509; Ramon H. Myers and Thomas A. Metzger, "Sinological Shadows: The State of Modern China Studies in the United States," *Washington Quarterly* (Spring 1980): 87–114; Michel Oksenberg, "Can Scholarship Flourish When Intertwined with Politics?" *ACLS Newsletter* (Winter–Spring 1986): 48–59; Michel Oksenberg, "Politics Takes Command: An Essay on the Study of Post-'49 China," *The Cambridge History of China,* Vol. 14 (Cambridge: Cambridge University Press, 1987), 543–90; Harry Harding, "From China, with Disdain: New Trends in the Study of China,"

Asian Survey (October 1982): 934–58; Andrew J. Nathan, "Americans Look at China: The New Optimism and Some Historical Perspectives," in *China's Crisis* (New York: Columbia University Press, 1990); Edward Friedman, "In Defense of China Studies," *Pacific Affairs* (Summer 1982): 252–66; Tang Tsou, "Western Concepts and China's Historical Experience," *World Politics* (July 1969): 665–91; Richard Wilson, "China Studies in Crisis," *World Politics* 23 (January 1971): 295–317.

For more discipline-based surveys, see Chalmers Johnson, "What's Wrong with Chinese Political Studies?" *Asian Survey* 22 (October 1982): 919–33; Harry Harding, "Competing Political Models of the Chinese Political Process: Towards a Sorting and Evaluation," *Issues and Studies* (February 1984): 13–36; Harry Harding, "The Study of Chinese Politics: Towards a Third Generation of Scholarship," *World Politics* (January 1984): 284–307; Kjeld Erik Brodsgaard, *Studies of Chinese Politics: A Survey*, Copenhagen Discussion Papers, No. 8 (Copenhagen: University of Copenhagen Center for East and Southeast Asian Studies, 1989); Elizabeth Perry, "State and Society in Contemporary China," *World Politics* (July 1989): 579–91; Andrew Walder, "Chinese Communist Society: The State of the Field," *Issues and Studies* (October 1982): 934–58; Lucian W. Pye, *The Mandarin and the Cadre* (Ann Arbor: Michigan Monographs in Chinese Studies, 1989), chapter 1; Victor Falkenheim, "Rational Choice Models and the Study of Citizen Politics in China," *Contemporary China* (Summer 1979): 93–101.

4. Steven Mosher was a Ph.D. candidate in anthropology at Stanford University who conducted rural field research in Guangdong province during the early 1980s. Mosher's transgressions of Chinese laws and norms of international scholarly research resulted in his expulsion from both China and his doctoral program at Stanford. While the Mosher case became a *cause célèbre* among conservatives in the United States (both because Mosher had graphically exposed widespread female infanticide in the Chinese countryside and because he was apparently being expelled from Stanford after pressure from the Chinese authorities), his transgressions—which went far beyond the exposure of female infanticide—had a very negative and lasting impact on American field research in China.

5. See, for example, the symposium on rural family change in *China Quarterly*, no. 130 (June 1992).

6. See Guojia jiaoyu weiyuanhui wenjian (State Educational Commission Documents), "Guanyu yu guowai renyuan hezuo zai guonei jinxing shehui diaocha youguan wenti de zhidao" (Directive concerning certain problems of collaboration with foreign personnel conducting social investigation in the country), Secret Document No. 598, December 19, 1990.

7. See, for example, Andrew G. Walder, *Communist Neo-Traditionalism: Work and Authority in Chinese Industry* (Berkeley: University of California Press, 1986).

8. Lindbeck, *Understanding China*, 115–22.

9. For further elaboration see David Shambaugh, "China's Security Policy in the Post–Cold War Era," *Survival* (Summer 1992): 88–106.

2

The Evolution of American Scholarship on Contemporary China

Harry Harding

For those who study China, 1989 was a year rich in anniversaries. In September of that year, three major American universities (Harvard, California at Berkeley, and Michigan) jointly sponsored a conference to commemorate no fewer than four of them: the tenth anniversary of the inauguration of the post-Mao reforms, the fortieth anniversary of the establishment of the People's Republic, the seventieth anniversary of the May Fourth demonstrations of 1919, and the 150th anniversary of the beginning of the Opium War.[1]

Paradoxically, however, these great centers for American scholarship on China neglected to celebrate another occasion even closer to home: the thirtieth anniversary of contemporary Chinese studies in the United States. For it was in 1959 that the American Council of Learned Societies and the Social Science Research Council, with the financial support of the Ford Foundation, organized the Joint Committee on Contemporary China. The grants for faculty research and graduate training given by the Joint Committee, together with larger institutional grants made by the Ford Foundation and the U.S. government, helped stimulate the first wave of American research on the economy, political system, and society of contemporary China.

Subsequent American scholarship on contemporary China can, for the sake of convenience, be divided into three periods, each spanning a decade. One way of distinguishing among the three periods is on the basis of their research agendas: the questions scholars have asked about China, and the methods they have used to answer them. In the first decade, for example, American specialists on contemporary China produced broad overviews of Chinese politics and economics after the Communist revolution, based on careful scrutiny of the Chinese press and occasionally on interviews with Chinese refugees. In the 1970s, stimulated by new sources of information provided during the Red Guard movement, American researchers wrote much more specific studies of various issue areas, time periods, and parts of the country, with a particular eye to the causes and consequences of the Cultural Revolution. More recently, in the 1980s, American scholars used new opportunities for field research in China to gain a deeper understanding of life in Chinese villages, factories, and bureaucratic organizations, as well as to trace the origins and implications of the post-Mao economic and political reforms. Moreover, as will be shown in greater detail below, in these three periods American specialists employed different analytical paradigms in their study of China, and showed varying degrees of interest in disciplinary, comparative, and historical perspectives.

The different decades can also be demarcated with reference to the roles played by scholars of contemporary China, not only in the university community, but also outside the academy. Over the past three decades, American China specialists were engaged at various times in conducting their own academic research, building university research and teaching programs, facilitating public education on China, advocating changes in American policy toward China, advising governmental agencies and private corporations, and creating exchange programs with their Chinese counterparts. In the 1960s, China specialists were preoccupied primarily with constructing the academic infrastructure of their field but showed some subsidiary interest in sponsoring public education about China and stimulating public debate about American relations with China. During the 1970s, these larger purposes occupied an even more prominent position in the field, with some scholars actively involved in the antiwar movement early in the decade, others serving in China-related positions in government, and still others building the national organizations devoted to public education, cultural exchange, and academic cooperation with China. The 1980s witnessed a tighter focus on scholarly pursuits, with relatively less attention devoted to public education and policy debate but greater interest in forming collaborative academic relationships with Chinese colleagues.

The evolution of Chinese studies in the United States along these dimensions was driven by developments in both countries. The turbulent history of the People's Republic constantly presented American China specialists with new *explananda* for their research: a new Communist regime, the Great Leap Forward, the Cultural Revolution, the post-Mao reforms, and most recently the post-Tiananmen environment. At the same time, changes in the political climate in China, and in Sino-American relations, helped determine the sources of information available to the American academic community, with the normalization of U.S.-China relations and the liberalization of Chinese academic life being crucial prerequisites to conducting extensive field research on the Chinese mainland.

Developments in the United States were also significant in the evolution of the field. The growth and decline of government and foundation funding for Chinese studies in the United States was obviously one major factor influencing the pace of American scholarship, helping to explain the vigor with which the field emerged in the 1960s and 1970s, and the relative sluggishness with which it entered the 1980s and 1990s. Changes within American universities also affected the climate for Chinese studies in the United States. Scholarship on contemporary China benefited in periods when universities had many vacancies for new graduate students and faculty and when area studies occupied a central place in the social science disciplines. Conversely, Chinese studies suffered at times when graduate enrollments were limited, when faculty positions were filled, and when other intellectual approaches achieved dominance within academic departments.

This chapter provides a brief overview of the evolution of American scholarship on contemporary China since its birth in the late 1950s through the early 1990s. It will offer a survey of the research agenda for each decade, a description of the role played by American China specialists in the academic community and in the wider society around them, and an evaluation of the accomplishments and shortcomings of each period. It concludes with a preliminary assessment of the challenges and opportunities confronting the field as it enters its fourth decade.

The First Decade: The 1960s

Although the People's Republic of China was established in 1949, American scholarship on contemporary China was seriously inhibited throughout the 1950s. In part, this was because of shortages of funds and personnel, as well as the impossibility of visiting China to conduct field research. But the slow development of contemporary Chinese studies in the United States was also the result of a repressive political climate in which many research institutions, China scholars, and specialists on China in the Foreign Service were labeled "Communist sympathizers."[2] Although some outstanding work was produced in the 1950s on traditional Chinese philosophy, late imperial political institutions, the foreign relations of the Qing Dynasty, and the origins of the Chinese Communist movement, the scholarly analysis of post-1949 China was delayed for a full decade. The few significant studies of the People's Republic undertaken in those years were small oases in what remained an academic desert.[3]

The emergence of the study of contemporary China in the early 1960s was the result of several factors. The period was one of rapid growth for higher education in the United States, with colleges and universities expanding their faculties to make room for the large number of students born in the late 1940s and early 1950s. The decade also witnessed significant innovation and maturation in the social sciences, with particular attention paid to economic modernization and political development in the Third World. Perhaps most important, Chinese studies received a large infusion of funds, from both the federal government (beginning with the National Defense Education Act of 1958) and the Ford Foundation (starting with major grants to various academic institutions in 1959–60), to promote research and faculty development. As noted above, much of the funding for graduate training, research projects, and scholarly conferences was channeled through the Joint Committee on Contemporary China, which was established in 1959.

Stimulated by this infusion of funding, a new wave of scholarly analysis of the People's Republic of China appeared in print in the 1960s. The principal topic during this first decade of scholarship was the nature of the new Communist regime and its impact on Chinese society. Three broad areas of inquiry received particular attention: the structure and operation of the major bureaucratic institutions that now governed China, especially the Chinese Communist Party and the massive state bureaucracy; the content and policy implications of Chinese Communist doctrine; and the recurring shifts in economic development strategy that had marked the evolution of the People's Republic since 1949. Ideology and organization, transformation and consolidation, mobilization and relaxation—these were the key aspects of postrevolutionary China analyzed by this first generation of American scholars.

Since China remained closed to American researchers—as well as to American journalists, merchants, and government officials—these important questions had to be studied at a distance. The most important source of information during this period was the official Chinese press, analyzed through the techniques of Kremlinology and propaganda analysis that had been developed to study the Soviet Union and Nazi Germany in earlier years. But this staple of analysis had severe shortcomings. The national media and academic periodicals were often vapid and uninformative. Provincial newspapers, ministerial journals, and official economic data were largely unavailable to foreigners after the debacle of the Great Leap Forward. As a consequence, scholars in this period had to be inventive in finding additional sources of information. Monitored provincial radio broadcasts and classified documents captured by Nationalist Chinese agents on the mainland provided useful supplements to the official national media. American scholars also obtained invaluable information and interpretation from Chinese refugees in Hong Kong, and even scanned contemporary Chinese novels and short stories for clues as to the workings of Chinese society.[4]

Limited access to information and the relatively tight controls over Chinese society severely handicapped many areas of American research on contemporary China during this period. There was little work in the humanities, largely because few scholars saw much literary or artistic merit in the works being produced on the mainland during the 1950s and early 1960s. Anthropology languished from the lack of opportunities to conduct field work in China, though some scholars continued to undertake investigations of contemporary Chinese society in Hong Kong and Taiwan. Economics was hampered by the enormous effort required to compile and reconstruct official data so as to obtain reliable statistics on China's industrial and agricultural performance.

Despite these constraints, the first period of scholarship yielded an impressive overview of contemporary China, offering preliminary general mappings of the major institutions, policies, and doctrines of the Communist regime. Political scientists created pathbreaking studies of Communist ideology, the Chinese party and state bureaucracies, the citizen's involvement in politics, and contemporary Chinese political culture.[5] In legal studies, there was a landmark survey of the system of criminal justice in the People's Republic.[6] One sociologist wrote a comprehensive history of a single Chinese province between the Communist takeover in 1949 and the onset of the Cultural Revolution in 1966; another produced in a single volume a sweeping institutional analysis of the party, the government, industrial enterprises, cities, and villages.[7] Similarly broad studies appeared on China's domestic economy, international economic relations, and foreign policy.[8]

The prevailing paradigm during this first decade of scholarship was totalitarianism, which stressed the mechanisms of political control over China's economy and society, and the purposes to which those mechanisms were put. Research focused on the use of ideology and political education to obtain support and compliance, the utilization of elections and mass organizations to guide political participation, the exercise of state planning over economic activity, the penetration of government agencies and industrial enterprises by party committees, and the control of intellectual life by continuous rectification campaigns against heterodox thinking.

This is not to say that there was no awareness of the limits to political control in China. One of the most influential works in this period was a model of "compliance cycles," which suggested that the party's efforts at mobilization and transformation produced such resentment and alienation that the regime was periodically forced to loosen its grip to regain support.[9] But this opposition to political control was depicted largely as passive resistance by relatively anomic social forces, rather than as active attempts to influence national policy; and the resulting changes in party programs were described primarily as the response of a unified elite to changing social and economic circumstances, rather than as the consequence of divisions within the leadership. On balance, even though American scholars acknowledged the constraints on political control, Chinese governance was still portrayed as essentially totalitarian.

The scholars at the forefront of research during this period were also engaged in other significant activities. Many of them served as academic entrepreneurs, using the federal funds and foundation grants available during the 1960s to build the institutional infrastructure that still shapes the field today. Some scholars founded major centers of contemporary Chinese studies at such universities as Harvard, Columbia, Michigan, Washington, California at Berkeley, and Stanford. Others, through their membership on the Joint Committee on Contemporary China, helped support promising graduate students, fund faculty research projects, and organize the research conferences that gave coherence and direction to the field. It was also during this period that three important institutions were created abroad with funding from the United States: *The China Quarterly*, the leading journal in the field, which is edited and published in England; the

Inter-University Program in Taipei, the major center for Chinese language studies overseas; and the Universities Services Center, the principal site for documentary research and refugee interviews in Hong Kong.

In addition to conducting scholarly research, the leading academic specialists on contemporary China in the 1960s also spoke to wider audiences. The Council on Foreign Relations, which had commissioned A. Doak Barnett's landmark study of Chinese foreign policy in the late 1950s, now sponsored an ambitious series on "The United States and China in World Affairs," in which leading American and foreign scholars sought to explain China's foreign relations to an informed elite public.[10] In 1966, Barnett joined Robert Scalapino, Lucian Pye, John Fairbank, Richard Walker, and other prominent China specialists in organizing the National Committee on U.S.-China Relations, which arranged a series of public programs on the prospects for the normalization of Sino-American relations and the management of the Taiwan issue.[11] Even a scholarly book such as Franz Schurmann's *Ideology and Organization in Communist China* received wide public attention through a front-page review in the Sunday book supplement of the *New York Times.*[12]

The principal works produced in this first decade of scholarship have had remarkable staying power. Doak Barnett's description of the Chinese bureaucracy remains a milestone in the study of contemporary Chinese political organizations. Ezra Vogel's history of Canton under communism is still a model for the study of local political institutions. Indeed, thirty years later, many of the analyses of the 1960s continue to shape the research agenda and analytical vocabulary of the field. The concept of cycles in Chinese development, introduced first by William Skinner and Edwin Winckler, has had a lasting impact on the analysis of the politics of the People's Republic. So have Schurmann's distinctions between "decentralization I" (decentralization to the enterprise) and "decentralization II" (decentralization to local government), and between "dual rule" and "vertical rule."

Despite its undeniable institutional legacy and its impressive academic accomplishments, this first decade of scholarship was marked by three major shortcomings. One was the high level of generality of most analysis, largely the result of the limited sources of information available to the field. Forced to rely primarily on the national Chinese press, scholars in the 1960s tended to write broad descriptions of the entire country, without adequate consideration of the possible variations from province to province, or from organization to organization. Even case studies of institutions and localities—such as Vogel's history of Canton and Barnett's analysis of a government ministry and a particular county—presented them not as unique entities but as examples of what could be found elsewhere in China.[13]

Second, given the heavy reliance on the Chinese press for information about contemporary China, the first decade of scholarship understandably tended to focus on the formal structure of political organizations, the tenets of official ideology, and the content of national policy, rather than on how key institutions actually worked, what individual leaders or ordinary Chinese truly thought, how policy was really made and implemented, or what impact it had on Chinese society. Compelled to study China from a distance, few China scholars were able to develop an intuitive feeling for the country, even though some scholars (such as Barnett and Vogel) engaged in extensive interviewing of refugees in Hong Kong in a valiant effort to overcome this problem.

And finally, the study of contemporary China remained largely divorced from the historical, comparative, or conceptual contexts that might have enhanced scholarly understanding. The influence of the Soviet Union on the First Five-Year Plan, and then the partial abandonment of the Soviet model during the Great Leap Forward, should have stimulated methodical comparison of China with other Communist countries. In the same way, the Communist Party's attempt at a revolutionary transformation of Chinese politics, economics, and society might also have inspired systematic comparison of post-1949 China with the pre-Communist period. The Chinese experience after 1949 could have been used to test emerging hypotheses in the social sciences about economic modernization, political development, totalitarianism, and postrevolutionary societies. But the efforts undertaken along these lines in the 1960s were woefully superficial. Compendia on comparative communism characteristically juxtaposed chapters on China alongside chapters on other Communist countries, without any attempt at rigorous contrast.[14] Historical comparison tended to focus on the similarities and differences between Communist ideology and other Chinese philosophical traditions, without examining change and continuity in concrete political or economic institutions before and after 1949. The one major conference devoted to placing Communist China in historical perspective offered excellent papers on the traditional period, but provided little systematic comparison between past and present.[15] Moreover, although the best works on contemporary China written during this period borrowed concepts from the social sciences fairly extensively, there was little attempt to use the Chinese case to challenge or confirm broader generalizations in the disciplines.[16]

In short, American scholarship on contemporary China made a good start in the 1960s. But, largely because of the limited sources of information available to researchers, it remained formalistic and shallow. Moreover, the prevailing paradigms overestimated the unity of the country's leadership, exaggerated their control over China's society and economy, and underestimated the grievances and cleavages in both rural and urban areas. The failure to anticipate the Cultural Revolution contributed to a sense by the end of the decade that China studies, like China itself, was in crisis.

The Second Decade: The 1970s

Several dramatic developments in China and the United States distinguished the scholarship of the 1970s from that of the previous decade. The Cultural Revolution in China, with its complex combination of elite conflict, mass turmoil, and utopian rhetoric, offered an exciting new reason for scholarship. Equally important, the loosening of controls over Chinese society during the Cultural Revolution produced a wave of new data about the country, revealing aspects of Chinese politics and society that previous sources had largely concealed.

These riveting developments in China occurred at a time of growth and ferment in academic life in the United States. The "baby boom" generation continued to swell enrollments in colleges and graduate schools in the United States—a trend encouraged by the draft deferments granted to those who chose to pursue university or postgraduate education. Both the government and private foundations continued to support the research and training programs in area studies that they had launched in the early 1960s. Perhaps most important, the agony of the war in Vietnam prompted younger scholars to undertake a critical reassessment of prevailing academic theories and assumptions, including those in Asian studies, seeking to understand how the United States could be engaged in what they passionately believed to be an unjust and unwise conflict.

The intellectual tumult and physical growth that characterized Chinese studies in the 1970s produced a new tide of essays, monographs, and books on many aspects of contemporary China. Some resulted from the large number of dissertations completed during the period. Others were the outcome of a critically important series of academic conferences that brought younger scholars together with their senior colleagues to address the intellectual issues raised by the Cultural Revolution.[17] Still others represented the attempts of senior researchers to come to grips with the new information and new analytical challenges produced by current developments in China. The principal focus of all these inquiries was a series of compelling questions: Why was China experiencing a Cultural Revolution? What were its origins within China's leadership? What was its basis in Chinese urban society? What impact was it having on China's political institutions, economy, and daily life? What lessons, if any, did it carry for the rest of the world?

In answering these questions, American scholars drew on significantly different sources of information than they had in the previous decade. At the height of the Cultural Revolution, most national periodicals stopped publication altogether, and those few that continued in operation adopted a highly didactic and polemical tone. But the dearth of useful data in official publications was counterbalanced by a flood of new information from unofficial sources. Between 1966 and 1968, Red Guard organizations published vast quantities of newspapers, pamphlets, and broadsides, carrying criticisms of central and provincial leaders, chronologies of debates on major policy issues since 1949, and accounts of factional struggle within various units and institutions. Moreover, as the violence in China increased, and especially after the Red Guards were dispersed to the countryside in late 1968, the flow of refugees into Hong Kong swelled, offering American scholars new information about the impact of Communist policies on grass-roots institutions and ordinary citizens both before and during the Cultural Revolution.

The new sources of information that became available during the Cultural Revolution made their greatest impact on political science and sociology. It was during this period, for example, that American scholars first learned about the central work conferences in which Chinese leaders made policy and the series of central party directives by which they conveyed their decisions to lower levels of the bureaucracy.[18] The revelations contained in the Red Guard documents also promoted an initial examination of leadership differences over foreign relations, economic development strategy, organizational management, and many other areas of national policy. The possibility of conducting interviews with large numbers of refugees made it possible to write the first comprehensive overviews of Chinese society in the 1970s, complementing the broad surveys of political structure that had been undertaken in the previous decade.[19]

Based on these new sources of data, political scientists and sociologists shifted their attention from the general to the specific and from the formal to the informal. Despite the important surveys of Chinese urban and rural society mentioned above, most students of China now eschewed the broad overviews characteristic of the 1960s in favor of more focused analyses. In this second decade of scholarship, the emphasis was on *disaggregation:* the effort to obtain a better understanding of the whole through a greater appreciation of its parts. The result was a plethora of case studies—some on particular areas of socioeconomic policy, some on specific cities and provinces, some on individual leaders, others on specific periods in contemporary Chinese history, and still others on particular sectors of society and their relationship to the state.[20]

At the same time, scholars in political science and sociology were able to use new sources of information to transcend their earlier descriptions of official ideology and formal organizational structure and to obtain a better understanding of the informal patterns and processes by which Chinese institutions actually worked. Sociologists could now write about marriage and divorce, holidays and rituals, personal relations and family life, welfare and inequality, and other aspects of life in urban and rural China. Political scientists engaged in a lively debate over competing models of the Chinese policy-making process, with scholars variously advocating tendency analysis, interest group analysis, factional analysis, and generational analysis as ways of describing and explaining the elite cleavages so dramatically revealed by the Cultural Revolution.[21] By the early 1980s, some scholars were attempting to combine these models into a single description of elite politics at the national level.[22]

In contrast to political science and sociology, other disciplines benefited less from the new materials that became available during the Cultural Revolution. The impossibility of conducting fieldwork in China continued to hamper anthropology, though sociologists gained an impressively comprehensive understanding of at least one village in South China through extensive interviews in Hong Kong.[23] The collapse of the Chinese statistical system and the atrophy of the legal order crippled the study of economics and law, so some American scholars turned to an analysis of Maoist theories of economic development and dispute resolution as a substitute for empirical research.[24] The persecution of Chinese intellectuals during the Cultural Revolution meant that there were even fewer works of literature and art to study in the 1970s than there had been in the 1960s. Like their counterparts in law and economics, therefore, American scholars interested in the humanities devoted more attention to Maoist theories of artistic creation than to actual practice.[25]

The large number of models of Chinese politics and society produced in the 1970s makes it difficult to identify a single dominant paradigm during this period. As a broad generalization, however, the prevailing images of China among American scholars were much less totalitarian than in the earlier decade. The Red Guard movement had revealed that the Chinese elite and Chinese society were not as monolithic as had previously been believed and that the political controls imposed on Chinese society in the 1950s had been severely weakened by the Cultural Revolution. As a result, American scholarship now focused on the divisions within the Chinese leadership and the opportunities for social groups to pursue their political and economic interests. All this promoted a view of China that was much more complex and diverse than in the past.

In developing this new interpretation of contemporary Chinese politics and society, American sinologists drew even more actively on social science concepts and methodology than they had in the 1960s. Some used concepts of political participation, political development, organizational theory, and patron-client relationships in their analyses of various aspects of Chinese life.[26] Others applied thematic apperception tests, Guttman scales, content analysis, aggregate elite data, and semiotics to their study of contemporary China.[27] More generally, they wrote in the language of modern social science, referring more frequently to their "hypotheses," "propositions," "models," and "variables."

As in the previous decade, American China specialists remained extensively involved in activities other than their own scholarly research. But now their activism had a different focus from the academic institution-building of the 1960s. Particularly in the early 1970s, many younger scholars participated in the activities of the Committee of Concerned Asian Scholars, holding teach-ins, publishing journals, and writing books not only to criticize American policy in Asia, but also to expose the financial and organizational connections among the pre-eminent university programs in Asian studies, the U.S. government, and major American foundations.[28] At their best, these activities helped stimulate a useful reassessment of the intellectual and institutional underpinnings of the field. At their worst, however, they involved ad hominem attacks on the character and motivations of senior China specialists in the United States that verged at times on McCarthyism from the Left.

Somewhat later in the decade, especially as American involvement in Vietnam came to an end and as Sino-American relations began to improve, scholars devoted their attention to the work of increasing public awareness of China and building exchange relationships with the Chinese. The China Council of the Asia Society, which absorbed the educational activities of the National Committee on U.S.-China Relations in the mid-1970s, sponsored two major compendia of essays designed for the informed general public, one on Chinese values and institutions, and the other on U.S.-China relations.[29] The Council on Foreign Relations, the American Assembly, and the Atlantic Council all sponsored analyses of Sino-American relations around the time of the normalization of relations between the two countries.[30] The National Committee, now concentrating almost exclusively on organizing cultural and political exchanges with China, provided opportunities for some American scholars to accompany American delegations on short-term visits to China, or to host Chinese delegations during their tours of the United States. All these organizations were able to draw liberally on the energies and talents of the best of the American sinological community.

Obviously, these two strands of academic activism differed significantly in political standpoint. The Committee of Concerned Asian Scholars took a critical stance toward both American policy and the mainstream of American scholarship, whereas the China Council and the National Committee seemed more comfortable in working together with the American academic and political establishments. But, at a more basic level, they shared with each other, and with comparable activities in the 1960s, the desire to enhance public awareness of conditions in contemporary China and to contribute to an improvement in U.S.-China relations. This orientation, an inheritance from the 1960s, would become less prominent in the field during the third decade of scholarship.

The research of the 1970s made major contributions to American understanding of China, primarily by adding greater depth and detail to earlier generalizations about the People's Republic, by providing preliminary assessments of the origins and consequences of the Cultural Revolution, and by discovering some of the informal mechanisms by which decisions were made by China's political leadership.

But this second period of scholarship also had several significant shortcomings. One was the lack of interest in placing contemporary China in a comparative or historical perspective. Despite their greater methodological and conceptual sophistication, China specialists did not appear much more interested in viewing China from a comparative or historical perspective than they had been in the 1960s. There were two major conferences during this period that placed China's economic development in a historical and comparative context, and there was a large collaborative project at Princeton that brought the same perspectives to bear on China's social and political modernization,[31] but a more common assumption in the 1970s was that the Cultural Revolution was so unique an experience as to make China, in a literal sense, incomparable to other countries. China was studied with the same techniques used to analyze other societies, but the field was pervaded by a sense of Chinese exceptionalism. Few scholars attempted to find precedents for the Cultural Revolution in China's own past, or to compare Mao's utopian vision with other radical tendencies in the international Communist movement.

A second problem, more unique to the 1970s, was the unfortunate tendency toward an uncritical acceptance of Maoist interpretations of the origins, goals, and outcomes of the Cultural Revolution. Much American scholarship on China during the period adopted a naive and idealistic attitude toward the Cultural Revolution that took official rhetoric at face value and that ignored or underplayed evidence of a more sordid reality.[32] All too often, American scholars took pains to explain, particularly to public audiences, that the Cultural Revolution was not an act of madness, as it was originally portrayed in the Western press, but rather a laudable effort to preserve revolutionary values in the face of seemingly inexorable trends toward stratification, bureaucratization, and routinization. All too seldom did they offer a critical evaluation of the goals of the Cultural Revolution, the methods that Mao employed in launching it, or the costs that both party officials and ordinary citizens endured during the course of the movement. Occasionally, they even implied that the Chinese revolutionary experience, including the Cultural Revolution, might provide salutary lessons for the United States.[33] The utopian rhetoric of the Cultural Revolution clearly encouraged this approach to the study of China. But the radical criticism of established institutions that pervaded American universities during the Vietnam War period helped ensure that official Chinese justifications would receive a sympathetic hearing. Our interpretations of China in these years came perilously close to apology.

A third weakness of the scholarship of the 1970s stemmed from the nature of the information available during the decade. Red Guard sources provided insights about two levels of the Chinese political system: the central and provincial elites, and the mass organizations of the Cultural Revolution. In particular, the documentation of the Red Guard era emphasized the contention within the elite, the conflicts among competing mass organizations, and the efforts of central and provincial leaders to mobilize and manipulate the mass movement in their struggle for power. What was less evident from the available sources of information was the operation of the intermediate social and political organizations in Chinese society—the party and state bureaucracies, the state enterprises, the communes—which provided the environment in which ordinary citizens lived, set the context in which mass organizations operated, and structured the policy options available to both national and provincial leaders. As Vivienne Shue and Nina Halpern have noted, rediscovering the middle levels of the Chinese political and economic systems would become one of the primary tasks of the third decade of scholarship.[34]

The Third Decade: The 1980s

Just as changes in China were one of the major factors demarcating the second decade of American scholarship from the first, so too did they help push the field from the second decade into the third. The Cultural Revolution was the great watershed separating the scholarship of the 1970s from that of the 1960s. In similar fashion, the post-Mao reform movement spearheaded by Deng Xiaoping was the stimulus that helped create a new generation of scholarship in the 1980s.

Like the Cultural Revolution, the post-Mao reforms played this catalytic role in two ways. First of all, they provided a new *explanandum* for the field, suggesting a demanding and exciting new research agenda. One task was simply to chronicle, catalogue, and analyze the sweeping political and economic reform measures adopted under Deng Xiaoping. An even more daunting challenge was to understand the origins of the reform program, its base of support, the obstacles it would encounter, and the prospects for its success.

Secondly, China's political liberalization in the post-Mao era, together with its opening to the outside world, made new sources of information available to foreign scholars. As in the past, fresh data from China strongly influenced the questions that would now be asked about the country, as well as the answers that American scholarship would provide. The economic data now released by the Chinese government were vastly superior in quality and quantity to those published at any other time since 1949. Chinese publications, long the principal source of information about the country, became increasingly valuable, thanks to their greater volume, detail, and candor. Chinese officials began to make themselves available for interviews, and some senior leaders published their memoirs. Intellectuals in China, Chinese scholars and graduate students in the United States, and foreign businesspeople and government officials with extensive experience in China proved to be useful sources of information and insight. Perhaps most important, limited opportunities opened up for fieldwork in China, particularly for those American scholars who had institutional and personal contacts in the country, or who proposed projects that involved collaboration with Chinese colleagues. All these new sources of information made it possible not only to conduct research on the reforms of the post-Mao era, but also to examine in greater detail the middle-level institutions neglected in earlier scholarship.

The dramatic changes inside China and the availability of new sources of information did not have an immediate impact on published American analysis. Indeed, Chinese studies in the United States entered a period of relative stagnation in the early 1980s, in which few significant monographs on contemporary China appeared in print. This period of dormancy was the result not so much of political factors, as had been true in the 1950s, but rather of changes within the academic community itself.

In several ways, the academic environment for Chinese studies was less supportive in the early 1980s than it had been in earlier periods. Universities, no longer straining to absorb the "baby boom" generation, did not expand their faculties and student enrollments as rapidly as before. The great wave of financial support for the field, which had played so key a role in promoting its growth in the 1960s and 1970s, began to recede. Foundations now appeared much more eager to facilitate the training of a new generation of scholars *from* China than to support the emergence of a new generation of American scholars *of* China. The interest in the study of modernization and development, which had helped promote the study of China as well as the investigation of other Third World countries, began to wane in several disciplines. Indeed, research on China, like area studies more generally, faced a relatively inhospitable climate in many branches of social science. In economics, sociology, comparative politics, and international politics, all of which increasingly emphasized the formation of general theory rather than the intensive study of particular societies, China scholars found themselves denigrated as "geographers" or "real-estate specialists," with slimmer prospects for tenure than in previous decades.

As a result of these and other factors, scholarship on China no longer enjoyed the rapid growth that it had experienced in the 1960s and early 1970s. In Chinese studies, as in other fields, most university teaching positions were now filled, with few new professorships created and few senior scholars retiring. The number of graduate students entering the field fell sharply, meaning that there were fewer of the dissertations and "first books" that help define a new generation of scholarship. Accordingly, the number of scholarly conferences—which tend to be dependent on the contributions of younger academics—also declined. The Joint Committee on Contemporary China sponsored fewer academic meetings than in the 1970s, and those that were convened often failed to produce a timely conference volume.[35]

In a paradoxical way, however, China itself was partly responsible for the problem. If anything, the pace of reform in post-Mao China was so rapid that it was not susceptible to easy analysis. Understanding the complex character of the reforms required an interdisciplinary background that most scholars lacked. The explosive growth of published material from China was not accompanied by adequate bibliographic guides to its selection or utilization. Field work—which rapidly and understandably became the favored research technique for younger scholars—was time-consuming both to arrange and to conduct.

These handicaps retarded the development of Chinese studies in the United States through the mid-1980s. But by the end of the decade a new surge of scholarship on contemporary China began to appear, produced both by a new generation of younger scholars with extensive language training and field research in China and by more senior scholars who had taken advantage of new opportunities in China to continue their work. In contrast with earlier periods, in which some disciplines benefited from new sources of information more than others, the new access to China was a boon to all fields of scholarship. Areas of research that had been at a particular disadvantage in the past—such as economics, anthropology, and the humanities—began to catch up with political science and sociology, given that there were now more comprehensive and reliable series of statistical data, more opportunities for field research, and more works of Chinese literature and art of genuine creative value.

The scholarship of the 1980s continued the disaggregation of China into particular institutions, issues, localities, and time periods. Research in economics featured more detailed examinations of local industry, agriculture, and finance than was common in earlier years.[36] Anthropologists, sociologists, and political sociologists studied in greater detail than was previously possible particular groups in Chinese society, including peasants, workers, intellectuals, the elderly, and students and young people.[37] Political scientists investigated individual bureaucratic agencies, cities, and counties, as well as particular aspects of political life.[38] Analysts of foreign policy gained invaluable information about past Chinese decisions in foreign affairs, including the development of nuclear weapons and China's entry into key international economic institutions.[39] Humanists began to specialize on various aspects of intellectual and cultural life in China, producing detailed studies of music, film, literature, and popular culture.[40]

But while the scope of scholarship was similar to that of the previous decade, the prevailing paradigms were significantly different. In the 1970s, influenced by the "behavioral revolution" in the social sciences, the most prominent models of Chinese society focused on inputs, identifying leadership conflict and the pursuit of political interest by various social sectors as the major building blocks of Chinese social life, political affairs, and foreign policy. In the 1980s, in contrast, greater attention was paid to the structural constraints on the actions of both elites and masses. In political science and sociology, the emerging models emphasized the ways in which enduring middle-level institutions shape the perceptions and preferences of individuals and groups at all strata of the Chinese system.[41] In foreign policy, the prevailing paradigm was structuralism, with greater attention to the constraints that the international political and economic systems imposed on Chinese decisionmakers.[42] In the study of both domestic and foreign affairs, in other words, the behavioral revolution of the 1970s was followed by a structural counterrevolution in the 1980s.

These new themes not only highlighted aspects of China that were overlooked in the past, but also promoted the further integration of Chinese studies with the social science disciplines. In previous decades, China scholars had been content to borrow from the social sciences concepts and methodologies that could illuminate the Chinese experience. By the late 1980s, however, many younger scholars realized that they were unlikely to receive tenure in their departments unless they made theoretical contributions to the disciplines in return. Thus economists were forced to study China not just to better understand the structure of the Chinese economy, but to learn more about privatization and deregulation; political scientists examined the role of state institutions and local systems in shaping political action; and foreign affairs specialists investigated China to better understand the impact of the international system on a country's foreign policies. Social scientists and humanists not specializing in China also began to incorporate Chinese materials into their scholarship, and some actually conducted research in China. Although the integration of Chinese studies into the disciplines was by no means complete, it was further advanced in the 1980s than in any previous decade of scholarship.

Relatedly, American scholarship on China in the late 1980s was more likely than before to be informed by comparative and historical concerns. Whereas the Cultural Revolution was widely regarded as *sui generis,* the post-Mao reforms could be fruitfully compared with other economic and political reform efforts in other Communist countries.[43] Mainland China's experiments with political liberalization, integration with the world economy, and economic restructuring stimulated comparisons with Taiwan.[44] And the rediscovery of the resilience, persistence, and influence of middle-level institutions in contemporary China encouraged comparisons with the past. Political scientists interested in rural political institutions and in urban political protest started to trace the roots of those phenomena before 1949.[45] Similarly, at least one historian of the Republican period began to trace the legacy of Nationalist economic planning mechanisms within the Communist period.[46]

The growing involvement of China specialists with their disciplines may have contributed to reducing their role in the broader worlds of public policy, public education, and intellectual discourse. The 1980s witnessed what might be described as the academicization of Chinese studies in the United States, with China specialists concentrating more completely on their scholarly research and identifying themselves more fully with their academic disciplines. This process of academicization was stimulated by the greater specialization and maturity of Chinese studies itself, but in the post-Mao period scholars were forced to spend greater amounts of their time keeping up with recent developments in their field. This trend was also encouraged by the norms of American research universities, which value advanced scholarly research much more highly than either undergraduate teaching or community service. And, as suggested above, it was further promoted by the declining fortunes of traditional area studies within most academic disciplines.

To some degree, the academicization of Chinese studies came at the expense of the earlier roles that scholars of China played as policy advocates or public educators. Fewer academic China specialists were involved in debating issues of American policy toward China than was true in the 1960s or 1970s, when first the Vietnam War and then the prospects for normalizing relations with China attracted considerable passion and attention. As the Tiananmen crisis of 1989 amply demonstrated, this was not because the outstanding issues in Sino-American relations had been resolved. Instead, it was because of the competing demands of purely academic research and because the U.S. government had fewer funds available to support contract research or to sponsor policy conferences. Similarly, there was less involvement in public education, though this may have been as much the result of declining funding for such activities as of declining interest in the academic community. Books by China scholars were less apt to be read by the informed general public or appear in major review media; instead, nonspecialists were more likely to draw their understanding of China from books by journalists, essayists, émigrés, and travelers.

China specialists continued to be active, however, as institution builders. Some helped to organize new academic programs on East Asia at institutions such as the University of California at San Diego or to enlarge and strengthen existing programs at such universities as Harvard. Considerable effort was also devoted to the creation of collaborative activities in China. Some of these were research programs housed at major universities, such as those based at Michigan and Stanford; others were training programs, such as the one at Nanjing University organized by Johns Hopkins; and still others were national fellowship programs for Chinese students and scholars, such as the committees on economics, law, and international studies supported by the Ford Foundation.

It is far too early to offer a final evaluation of the scholarship of this third generation, if only because much of it is just now beginning to appear in print. Clearly, it has had many achievements: notably a more sober and objective reappraisal of the origins, development, and outcomes of the Cultural Revolution; an initial understanding of the successes and failures of the post-Mao reforms; a better appreciation of the internal mechanisms of the Chinese bureaucracy and the foreign policy-making process; and a deeper awareness of the interaction among citizens, local institutions, and the state at the grass-roots level in both rural and urban China.

But a preliminary assessment of the scholarship of the 1980s suggests several shortcomings. First, there remained important gaps in coverage. There were relatively few book-length treatments of China's geopolitical posture, foreign economic relations in the post-Mao era, or Sino-Soviet or Sino-American relations.[47] This may largely have been because comparative foreign policy studies did not have a secure and established place within the discipline of political science, thus discouraging younger scholars from embarking on this particular line of research. Several aspects of the post-Mao reforms—especially the composition of the new party and government elites, the content and attractiveness of official ideology, the changing role of the party relative to government agencies and productive enterprises, the extent and consequences of marketization and price reform, and the relationship between central and provincial government—did not receive adequate attention, in some cases because they were not readily studied through field research. Nor, despite a wealth of new information about developments in China between 1949 and 1966, was there much new work on the history of the early Maoist period. This happened in large part because economists and political scientists were preoccupied with more recent events and because few historians moved beyond 1949 to examine the evolution of the early People's Republic.

Second, the level of synthesis and integration in the study of contemporary China lagged far behind the production of detailed scholarship on particular aspects of Chinese society. The field's knowledge of the parts outstripped its understanding of the whole. Broad reassessments of the history and structure of the People's Republic are necessary if the field is to convey a sound general understanding of China to a broader audience, or if scholars of China are to relate the Chinese case to broader disciplinary and intellectual concerns. Perhaps most important, the selection of topics for detailed study is often stimulated by the unresolved puzzles, discrepant details, and deviant cases suggested by attempts at broader generalization. And yet, despite all the new insights gained as a result of more direct access to China, there were few fresh overviews of the general structure and operation of the Chinese political or economic systems. Nor were there more than a handful of single-authored books assessing the overall course and outcomes of the Chinese reform program.

Finally, although the structural approaches to China characteristic of the scholarship of the 1980s offered useful correctives to the paradigms of earlier decades, they too had their shortcomings. As the events of 1989 made clear, the tight focus on middle-level organizations characteristic of much research in the 1980s presupposed a level of stability and institutionalization in China that does not yet exist.[48] An institutional analysis, for example, may be able to explain policy in specific issue areas, such as energy or education, but it is less helpful in understanding the choice among competing packages of political and economic reform. For this, the models of policy-making produced in the 1970s may still be of considerable value. Similarly, the new emphasis on structures failed to anticipate the rapid development of popular protest in the late 1980s, or the intense conflict within the party elite. To understand these developments, some insights from the models of the 1970s remain relevant.

In short, the third generation of American scholarship on China was slow to emerge, constrained as it was by conditions in both the United States and China. Once it did appear, however, it proved more detailed, more intricate, and more penetrating than any of its predecessors. The principal weaknesses were the tendency of American China specialists to study only what the new opportunities for fieldwork readily revealed, to lose their grasp of the general pattern of developments in China, and to set aside too quickly the valuable legacy of earlier analytical paradigms. In a sense, the rapidity and complexity of change in post-Mao China, and the new insights gained through direct access, may have been more than the field could readily digest.

Conclusion and Prospects for the 1990s

This review of scholarship on contemporary China over the past three decades reveals a wavelike pattern of development, with periods of physical growth and intellectual excitement punctuated by intervals of relative retrenchment and lethargy. Each of the three periods of growth was stimulated by new developments in China and generated a dominant paradigm to try to explain them. In the 1960s, a totalitarian model was the prevailing way of understanding the operation of the new Communist political system and its efforts at a restructuring of the Chinese society and economy. In the 1970s, a plurality of models seemed appropriate for analyzing the origins and development of the Cultural Revolution. The resistance to, or distortion of, the economic and political reforms in the 1980s prompted American scholars to examine the role of middle-level and grass-roots institutions in Chinese political, economic, and social life.

Over these three decades, American scholarship on China grew and matured. American specialists supplemented the limited official sources available in the 1960s with refugee interviews, Cultural Revolution materials, and then with direct access to China. As David Shambaugh notes in the Introduction, the new generation of scholars acquired a better "feel" for the country, and their work gained more insight, balance, and objectivity. As the number of scholars working on contemporary China grew, and as the opportunities to conduct field research increased, China specialists gained more detailed knowledge of various aspects of Chinese life, particularly at the grass roots.

Scholarship on China also gradually acquired a broader analytic perspective over the last three decades. Chinese studies are more closely linked with the academic disciplines now than was the case thirty years ago. From borrowing concepts from the disciplines so as better to understand China, as they did during the 1960s, China specialists are beginning to show how China can be used to test and modify general models of structures, processes, and change. There is an emerging interest in systematically comparing the society, political system, and economy of the People's Republic with those of other states in East Asia, Communist countries, and in the developing world. And there is a growing awareness of the continuities and contrast between the Communist system in China and its prerevolutionary forebears.

As this chapter shows, these developments did not occur to the same extent or at the same time across all disciplines in contemporary Chinese studies. The differences among disciplines have been based largely on their varying degrees of access to relevant sources of information about post-1949 China. The qualitative breakthroughs in understanding occurred first in political science (which was best able to tap the official sources of the 1950s and 1960s and the Red Guard materials of the 1970s), then in sociology (which could utilize refugee interviews in the 1970s), then in economics and the humanities (as new statistical data and works of art appeared in the early post-Mao era), and most recently in anthropology (as opportunities for field work became available in the mid-1980s). The study of law and foreign policy lagged behind the others, in part because of the lack of sources of information that go beyond official documents and in part because of the tenuous place of Chinese studies in these two disciplines.

Although we can justifiably celebrate what has been gained from the evolution of Chinese studies over the last thirty years, we should also be aware of what may have been lost as a result of the greater empirical detail and theoretical sophistication. As noted above, as we learn more about the minutiae of life in China, it is becoming more difficult to comprehend the broad patterns of change and structure. Relatedly, the growing depth and sophistication of our work means that the preparation and publication of research findings lag ever farther behind a rapidly evolving China, so that the field is forever learning about a country that has already changed.

As a result of these developments, we may be losing the ability to communicate our understanding of China to broader audiences. The rapid shift in American attitudes about China after the suppression of the popular protests in Beijing in June 1989 and the sense of disillusionment that many Americans expressed about the use of military force against civilian demonstrators suggest that the Chinese studies community had not adequately informed the American public of the ambiguities of the situation in China or the fragility of certain reforms. Nor did China specialists· play a central role in the subsequent debates over the renewal of China's most-favored-nation status since 1989.

In the 1990s we may also be on the threshold of a new stage in the American study of China. As with past transitions from one period of scholarship to another, the immediate stimulus is being provided by developments in China itself. The tragic events of 1989—the massive demonstrations across the country, the imposition of martial law, the violent suppression of the protests, and the subsequent tightening of restrictions against political dissent—are but symptoms of a deeper problem. By the end of the 1980s it had become evident that the post-Mao reforms had entered a much more delicate period, when the prospects for instability, repression, and even disintegration were much greater than before. These developments require American China specialists to begin a thorough reevaluation of the post-Mao reforms, seeking to understand the flaws in the reform program, the weaknesses in its political base, the cleavages within the reform coalition, and the sources of distortion of various reform initiatives.

Moreover, if China should enter an enduring period of repression and instability, then field research, interviews, and scholarly collaboration with Chinese colleagues, while not entirely impossible, will be much more difficult than they were during the 1980s. If that happens, American scholars will have to resurrect some of the research methods and sources of information that were previously employed to study China from a distance. This will greatly obstruct the investigation of middle-level and grass-roots organizations, the understanding of which benefited enormously from direct access to China in the 1980s. However, the restriction of research opportunities in China may paradoxically reinvigorate study of other important subjects—such as the history of the People's Republic, the structure and operation of the party, and the role of the military in civilian politics—that are less easily examined through direct observation.

Even less dire developments in China could have a deleterious impact on American scholarship. Economic reform is affecting all aspects of life in China, including academic research. Facing reduced government subsidies, Chinese academic institutions are already asking visiting scholars to pay higher fees for research assistance, access to materials, and field research. Moreover, American researchers may also find it more difficult to find able collaborators in China, as some of the country's most promising younger scholars, dismayed by the low salaries and political shackles in academic life, abandon teaching and research for less constrained and more lucrative careers in business. Indeed, there is some reason to fear that some of the country's academic infrastructure, especially the provincial academies of social science, is on the verge of disintegration. This, too, will make it significantly more difficult for American scholars to conduct in-country research.

Whatever the course of events in China itself, American scholars of contemporary China will face additional challenges in the 1990s. Perhaps the most basic will be to preserve and improve the infrastructure of the field. Lack of financial support has endangered two key institutions in the China field—the Universities Services Center in Hong Kong and the Center for Chinese Research Materials in Washington, D.C.—just at a time when refugee interviews and documentary research may play an even more important role in contemporary China studies. There is a critical need for better bibliographic control over the flood of publications that have been produced in China since 1976. *For these and other reasons, the decline in funding for advanced research on China needs to be halted and reversed.*

A second challenge confronting the field is that of cumulation. We need to identify and fill the gaps in our understanding of both the Maoist period and the post-Mao reforms. In particular, the study of contemporary China would greatly benefit from the decision of modern historians to move beyond 1949 and reconstruct the history of the People's Republic from 1949 to at least 1966, if not to the death of Mao in 1976, taking advantage of the new materials made available in the last ten years. There is also a pressing need for work that synthesizes the results of the detailed, specialized scholarship of the last twenty years into comprehensive reinterpretations of the politics, economics, society, and foreign relations of contemporary China. In so doing, one task will be to integrate the insights of the totalitarian, pluralist, and institutional paradigms, recognizing that although each has illuminated important aspects of Chinese society, none has provided a comprehensive model of how China works. Nina Halpern's contribution to this volume begins to address this problem. Another assignment will be to reach a more systematic understanding of the variations in social, economic, and political structures and processes across space, sector, and issue.

The challenge of cumulation can often be met most effectively through various forms of academic collaboration. Interdisciplinary research can benefit from cooperation among scholars from different branches of the humanities and social sciences. The integration of China studies with the disciplines can be promoted by collaboration between China specialists and scholars interested in theoretical and comparative issues. Dialogue with scholars of Chinese affairs in Europe and Asia—a feature of the field in its earliest decades that has unfortunately been allowed to lapse—should be resumed. And, political conditions permitting, American understanding of China can be greatly improved by cooperation with

Chinese colleagues, through both academic conferences and collaborative research projects.

Finally, there is the challenge of communicating this new understanding of China to those outside the world of scholarship. The academic community must always weigh two responsibilities: that of developing new knowledge and that of disseminating it. One of the field's most valuable legacies has been its tradition of active involvement in public education and policy debate. The academicization of American China studies has led to the neglect of this tradition in the 1980s. Yet the complexities of economic and political change in China and the importance of China in the management of international economic, strategic, and environmental problems make it imperative that the United States, as a society, gain the most objective, comprehensive, and accurate understanding of China possible. American China specialists in the 1990s will therefore need to devote greater energy and resources to reaching an audience wider than just each other.

Alongside these challenges, American sinology is also facing a significant new opportunity of a sort not experienced since the 1970s. The generation of senior scholars that entered the field in the 1950s and 1960s is now beginning to retire. Although not all these vacancies will be filled, the retirements are nevertheless creating a large number of openings for more junior specialists on contemporary China. They, in turn, will reinvigorate the field as they first publish their dissertations and then embark on new research agendas. What is more, a large proportion of the newly hired faculty is being drawn from the wave of students from mainland China who entered U.S. doctoral programs in the 1980s, received their degrees in the early 1990s, and have now been permitted, as a result of the Tiananmen crisis, to seek employment in the United States. Their fluency in Chinese language, understanding of grass-roots Chinese society, and training in the concepts and methods of Western social science should enable them to make a significant contribution to the fourth decade of American scholarship on contemporary China.

Notes

This paper draws, to a degree, on some of my previous essays on the state of Chinese studies in the United States: "Reappraising the Cultural Revolution," *Wilson Quarterly* 4 (Autumn 1980): 132–41; "From China, With Disdain: New Trends in the Study of China," *Asian Survey* 22 (October 1982): 934–58; "The Study of Chinese Politics: Toward a Third Generation of Scholarship," *World Politics* 36 (January 1984): 284–307; and "Competing Models of the Chinese Communist Policy Process: Toward a Sorting and Evaluation," *Issues and Studies* 20 (February 1984): 13–36. It has also benefited greatly from the other papers in this volume and from the comments of the participants at the Wye Conference, especially David Shambaugh and Anthony Kane.

1. The volume to emerge from the conference is Kenneth Lieberthal, Joyce Kallgren, Roderick MacFarquhar, and Frederic Wakeman, Jr., eds., *Perspectives on Modern China: Four Anniversaries* (Armonk, N.Y.: M.E. Sharpe, 1991).

2. For a short but useful summary of this "blank decade" of scholarship on contemporary China, see Michel Oksenberg, "Can Scholarship Flourish When Intertwined with Politics?" *ACLS Newsletter* 37 (Winter–Spring 1986): 48–59.

3. These studies include S.B. Thomas, *Government and Administration in Communist China* (New York: Institute of Pacific Relations, 1953); Richard L. Walker, *China under Communism: The First Five Years* (New Haven: Yale University Press, 1955); H. Arthur Steiner, *The International Position of Communist China* (New York: Institute of Pacific Relations, 1958); Choh-Ming Li, *Economic Development of Communist China* (Berkeley: University of California Press, 1959); C.K. Yang, *Chinese Communist Society: The Family and the Village* (Cambridge, Mass.: MIT Press, 1959); A. Doak Barnett, *Communist China and Asia: A Challenge to American Policy* (New York: Vintage Books, 1960); and Allen S. Whiting, *China Crosses the Yalu: The Decision to Enter the Korean War* (New York: Macmillan, 1960).

4. For a contemporary discussion of sources on China, see Michel Oksenberg, "Sources and Methodological Problems in the Study of Contemporary China," in *Chinese Communist Politics in Action,* ed. A. Doak Barnett (Seattle: University of Washington Press, 1969), 577–606.

5. John Wilson Lewis, *Leadership in Communist China* (Ithaca: Cornell University Press, 1963); A. Doak Barnett, *Cadres, Bureaucracy, and Political Power in Communist China* (New York: Columbia University Press, 1967); James R. Townsend, *Political Participation in Communist China* (Berkeley: University of California Press, 1967); and Lucian W. Pye, *The Spirit of Chinese Politics: A Psychocultural Study of the Authority Crisis in Political Development* (Cambridge, Mass.: MIT Press, 1968).

6. Jerome Alan Cohen, *The Criminal Process in the People's Republic of China, 1949–1963* (Cambridge, Mass.: Harvard University Press, 1968).

7. Ezra Vogel, *Canton under Communism: Programs and Politics in a Provincial Capital, 1949–1968* (Cambridge, Mass.: Harvard University Press, 1969); and Franz Schurmann, *Ideology and Organization in Communist China* (Berkeley: University of California Press, 1966).

8. On China's domestic economics and international economic relations, see Chao Kang, *The Rate and Pattern of Industrial Growth in Communist China* (Ann Arbor: University of Michigan Press, 1965); Alexander Eckstein, *Communist China's Economic Growth and Foreign Trade* (New York: McGraw-Hill, 1966); and Nai-ruenn Chen and Walter Galenson, *The Chinese Economy under Communism* (Chicago: Aldine, 1969). In foreign relations, see Harold Hinton, *Communist China in World Politics* (New York: Houghton Mifflin, 1966).

9. G. William Skinner and Edwin A. Winckler, "Compliance Succession in Communist China: A Cyclical Theory," in *A Sociological Reader on Complex Organizations,* ed. Amitai Etzioni (New York: Holt, Rinehart, and Winston, 1969), 410–38.

10. The series included A.M. Halpern, ed., *Policies toward China: Views from Six Continents* (New York: McGraw-Hill, 1966); A.T. Steele, *The American People and China* (New York: McGraw-Hill, 1966); Eckstein, *Communist China's Economic Growth and Foreign Trade;* Robert Blum, *The United States and China in World Affairs,* ed. A. Doak Barnett (New York: McGraw-Hill, 1966); Samuel B. Griffith, Jr., *The Chinese People's Liberation Army* (New York: McGraw-Hill, 1967); and Kenneth T. Young, *Negotiating with the Chinese Communists: The United States Experience, 1953–1967* (New York: McGraw Hill, 1968).

11. A. Doak Barnett and Edwin O. Reischauer, eds., *The United States and China: The Next Decade* (New York: Praeger, 1970); and Jerome Alan Cohen et al., *Taiwan and American Policy: The Dilemma in U.S.-China Relations* (New York: Praeger, 1971).

12. *New York Times,* July 17, 1966, sect. 7, p. 1.

13. For a contemporary critique of the tendency to "talk about 'China' as a holistic entity," see John K. Fairbank, "The State That Mao Built," *World Politics* 19 (July 1967): 664–767.

14. See, for example, Donald W. Treadgold, ed., *Soviet and Chinese Communism: Similarities and Differences* (Seattle: University of Washington Press, 1967); and Chalmers Johnson, ed., *Change in Communist Systems* (Palo Alto, Calif.: Stanford University Press, 1970). One exception was Richard Lowenthal's seminal contribution to the Johnson volume, which compared the origin and evolution of "utopian" and "developmental" tendencies in China, the Soviet Union, and Yugoslavia. Richard Lowenthal, "Development vs. Utopia in Communist Policy," ibid., 33–116.

15. Ping-ti Ho and Tang Tsou, eds., *China in Crisis,* 2 vols. (Chicago: University of Chicago Press, 1968).

16. This criticism was first made in Richard Wilson, "Chinese Studies in Crisis," *World Politics* 23 (January 1971): 295–317.

17. Some of the most important conference volumes produced during this period include Barnett, *Chinese Communist Politics in Action;* John Wilson Lewis, ed., *Party Leadership and Revolutionary Power in China* (Cambridge: Cambridge University Press, 1970); John M.H. Lindbeck, ed., *China: Management of a Revolutionary Society* (Seattle: University of Washington Press, 1971); Robert A. Scalapino, ed., *Elites in the People's Republic of China* (Seattle: University of Washington Press, 1972); Chalmers A. Johnson, ed., *Ideology and Politics in Contemporary China* (Seattle: University of Washington Press, 1973); Dwight H. Perkins, ed., *China's Modern Economy in Historical Perspective* (Palo Alto, Calif.: Stanford University Press, 1975); and Robert F. Dernberger, ed., *China's Development Experience in Comparative Perspective* (Cambridge, Mass.: Harvard University Press, 1980).

18. Parris H. Chang, "Research Notes on the Changing Loci of Decision in the CCP," *China Quarterly,* no. 44 (October–December 1970): 169–94; Kenneth Lieberthal, *A Research Guide to Central Party and Government Meetings in China, 1949–1975* (White Plains, N.Y.: International Arts and Sciences Press, 1976); idem, *Central Documents and Politburo Politics in China,* Michigan Papers in Chinese Studies, no. 33 (Ann Arbor: Center for Chinese Studies, University of Michigan, 1978); Michel C. Oksenberg, "Policy Making under Mao: An Overview," in Lindbeck, ed., *China: Management of a Revolutionary Society,* 79–115; and idem, "Methods of Communication within the Chinese Bureaucracy," *China Quarterly,* no. 57 (January–March 1974): 1–39.

19. William L. Parish and Martin King Whyte, *Village and Family in Contemporary China* (Chicago: University of Chicago Press, 1978); and idem, *Urban Life in Contemporary China* (Chicago: University of Chicago Press, 1984).

20. For a list of representative works on various issue-areas, individual cities and provinces, and particular historical periods, see Harding, "The Study of Chinese Politics," 292–93, nn. 13, 14, and 17. Important biographies produced during the period include Lucian Pye, *Mao Tse-tung: The Man in the Leader* (New York: Basic Books, 1976); Lowell Dittmer, *Liu Shao-ch'i and the Chinese Cultural Revolution: The Politics of Mass Criticism* (Berkeley: University of California Press, 1974); and Roxane Witke, *Comrade Chiang Ch'ing* (Boston: Little, Brown, 1977). On social sectors and their relationship to the state, see Hong Yung Lee, *The Politics of the Chinese Cultural Revolution: A Case Study* (Berkeley: University of California Press, 1978); Stanley Rosen, *Red Guard Factionalism and the Cultural Revolution in Guangzhou (Canton).* (Boulder, Colo.: Westview Press, 1982); Victor C. Falkenheim, ed., *Citizens and Groups in Contemporary China,* Michigan Monographs in Chinese Studies, vol. 56 (Ann Arbor: Center for Chinese Studies, University of Michigan, 1987); and Merle Goldman, *China's Intellectuals: Advise and Dissent* (Cambridge, Mass.: Harvard University Press, 1981).

21. For a review of these models, see Harry Harding, "Competing Models of the Chinese Communist Policy Process: Toward a Sorting and Evaluation," *Issues and Studies* 20 (February 1984): 13–36; and John Bryan Starr, "From the 10th Party Congress to the Premiership of Hua Kuo-feng: The Significance of the Colour of the Cat," *China Quarterly*, no. 67 (September 1976): 457–88.

22. Lucian Pye, *The Dynamics of Chinese Politics* (Cambridge, Mass.: Oelgeschlager, Gunn, and Hain, 1981); and Frederick C. Teiwes, *Politics and Purges in China* (White Plains, N.Y.: M.E. Sharpe, 1979). In an earlier essay (Harding, "The Study of Chinese Politics"), I described these as representatives of an emerging third generation of scholarship in the early 1980s. In retrospect, however, they are better regarded as part of the second period.

23. Richard Madsen, *Morality and Power in a Chinese Village* (Berkeley: University of California Press, 1984); and Anita Chan, Richard Madsen, and Jonathan Unger, *Chen Village: The Recent History of a Peasant Community in Mao's China* (Berkeley: University of California Press, 1984).

24. John G. Gurley, *China's Economy and the Maoist Strategy* (New York: Monthly Review Press, 1976); and Victor H. Li, *Law without Lawyers* (Palo Alto, Calif.: Stanford Alumni Association, 1977).

25. See Chapter 4 by Anthony Kane in this volume.

26. Harding, "The Study of Chinese Politics," 295, n. 21.

27. Ibid., 295, n. 22.

28. Examples of books published by those associated with the Committee of Concerned Asian Scholars are Edward Friedman and Mark Selden, eds., *America's Asia: Dissenting Essays on Asian-American Relations* (New York: Vintage Books, 1971); Committee of Concerned Asian Scholars, *China! Inside the People's Republic* (New York: Bantam Books, 1972); and Victor Nee and James Peck, eds., *China's Uninterrupted Revolution: From 1840 to the Present* (New York: Pantheon Books, 1975).

29. Michel Oksenberg and Robert B. Oxnam, eds., *Dragon and Eagle: United States-China Relations, Past and Future* (New York: Basic Books, 1978); and Ross Terrill, ed., *The China Difference* (New York: Harper and Row, 1979).

30. William J. Barnds, ed., *China and America: The Search for a New Relationship* (New York: New York University Press, 1977); Richard H. Solomon, ed., *The China Factor: Sino-American Relations and the Global Scene* (Englewood Cliffs, N.J.: Prentice-Hall, 1981); and U. Alexis Johnson, George Packard, and Alfred D. Wilhelm, Jr., eds., *China Policy for the Next Decade* (Cambridge, Mass.: Oelgeschlager, Gunn, and Hain, 1984).

31. Perkins, *China's Modern Economy in Historical Perspective;* Dernberger, *China's Development Experience in Comparative Perspective;* and Gilbert Rozman, ed., *The Modernization of China* (New York: Free Press, 1981).

32. For details, see Harding, "Reappraising the Cultural Revolution"; and idem, "From China, with Disdain."

33. See Michel Oksenberg, ed., *China's Developmental Experience* (New York: Praeger, 1973), esp. Oksenberg's introductory chapter, "On Learning from China" (1–16).

34. See Vivienne Shue, *The Reach of the State: Sketches of the Chinese Body Politic* (Palo Alto, Calif.: Stanford University Press, 1988); and Chapter 6 by Nina Halpern in this volume.

35. In political science, for example, a workshop on Chinese foreign policy, held at the University of Michigan in 1976, was never intended to result in a conference volume. A full-fledged conference on the pursuit of political interest in the People's Republic, held in Ann Arbor the following year, did not produce a conference volume until 1987. (Falkenheim, *Citizens and Groups in Contemporary China.*) No conferences on Chinese politics were held under Joint Committee sponsorship for seven years thereafter.

36. On economics, see Nicholas R. Lardy, *Agriculture in China's Modern Economic Development* (Cambridge: Cambridge University Press, 1983); Barry Naughton, "False Starts and Second Wind: Financial Reforms in China's Industrial System," in *The Political Economy of Reform in Post-Mao China,* ed. Elizabeth J. Perry and Christine Wong, Harvard Contemporary China Series, No. 2 (Cambridge, Mass.: Council on East Asian Studies, Harvard University, 1985), 223–52; idem, "The Decline of Central Control Over Investment in Post-Mao China," in *Policy Implementation in Post-Mao China,* ed. David M. Lampton (Berkeley: University of California Press, 1987), 51–80; idem, "Finance and Planning Reforms in Industry," in U.S. Congress, Joint Economic Committee, *China's Economy Looks toward the Year 2000, vol. 1: The Four Modernizations* (Washington, D.C.: GPO, 1986), 604–29; Christine Wong, "Material Allocation and Decentralization: Impact of the Local Sector on Industrial Reform," in *The Political Economy of Reform in Post-Mao China,* ed. Perry and Wong, 253–80; idem, "Ownership and Control in Chinese Industry: The Maoist Legacy and Prospects for the 1980s," in U.S. Congress, Joint Economic Committee, *China's Economy Looks toward the Year 2000,* vol. 1, 571–603; and Katherine Huang Hsiao, *The Government Budget and Fiscal Policy in Mainland China* (Seattle: University of Washington Press, 1988).

37. See, for example, Andrew G. Walder, *Communist Neotraditionalism: Work and Authority in Chinese Industry* (Berkeley: University of California Press, 1986); Carol Lee Hamrin and Timothy Cheek, eds., *China's Establishment Intellectuals* (Armonk, N.Y.: M.E. Sharpe, 1986); Merle Goldman, Timothy Cheek, and Carol Lee Hamrin, eds., *China's Intellectuals and the State: In Search of a New Relationship,* Harvard Contemporary China Series, No. 3 (Cambridge, Mass.: Council on East Asian Studies, Harvard University, 1987); Anne F. Thurston, *Enemies of the People* (New York: Alfred A. Knopf, 1987); Emily Honig and Gail Hershatter, *Personal Views: Chinese Women in the 1980's* (Palo Alto, Calif.: Stanford University Press, 1988); Jean C. Oi, *State and Peasant in Contemporary China: The Political Economy of Village Government* (Berkeley: University of California Press, 1989); Helen F. Siu, *Agents and Victims in South China* (New Haven: Yale University Press, 1989); David Zweig, *Agrarian Radicalism in China, 1968–1981* (Cambridge, Mass.: Harvard University Press, 1989); Susan L. Shirk, *Competitive Comrades: Career Incentives and Student Strategies in China* (Berkeley: University of California Press, 1982); Anita Chan, *Children of Mao: Personality Development and Political Activism in the Red Guard Generation* (Seattle: University of Washington Press, 1985); and Deborah Davis-Friedmann, *Long Lives: Chinese Elderly and the Communist Revolution* (Cambridge, Mass.: Harvard University Press, 1983).

38. See, for example, David M. Lampton, *Paths to Power: Elite Mobility in Contemporary China,* Michigan Monographs in Chinese Studies, vol. 55 (Ann Arbor: Center for Chinese Studies, University of Michigan, 1986); idem, *Policy Implementation in Post-Mao China;* John P. Burns, *Political Participation in Rural China* (Berkeley: University of California Press, 1988); Kenneth Lieberthal and Michel Oksenberg, *Policy Making in China: Leaders, Structures, and Processes* (Princeton: Princeton University Press, 1988); John P. Burns, "China's *Nomenklatura* System," *Problems of Communism* 36 (September–October 1987): 36–51; and Melanie Manion, "The Cadre Management System, Post-Mao: The Appointment, Promotion, Transfer, and Removal of Party and State Leaders," *China Quarterly,* no. 102 (June 1985): 203–33.

39. A. Doak Barnett, *The Making of Foreign Policy in China: Structure and Process* (Boulder, Colo.: Westview Press, 1985); David L. Shambaugh, "China's National Security Research Bureaucracy," *China Quarterly,* no. 110 (June 1987): 276–304; John Wilson Lewis and Xue Litai, *China Builds the Bomb* (Palo Alto, Calif.: Stanford University Press, 1988); and Harold K. Jacobson and Michel Oksenberg, *China's Participation in the IMF, the World Bank, and GATT* (Ann Arbor: University of Michigan Press, 1990).

40. See Chapter 4 by Anthony Kane in this volume.

41. See especially Shue, *The Reach of the State;* Walder, *Communist Neo-Traditionalism;* and Lieberthal and Oksenberg, *Bureaucratic Politics and Chinese Energy Development.*

42. See, for example, Robert Ross, "International Bargaining and Domestic Politics: Conflict in U.S.-China Relations since 1972," *World Politics* 30 (January 1986): 255–87.

43. See, for example, Gail W. Lapidus and Jonathan Haslam, eds., *Reforming Socialist Systems: The Chinese and Soviet Experiences: A Conference Report* (Berkeley: Berkeley-Stanford Program on Soviet International Behavior, 1987); Victor Nee and David Stark, eds., *Remaking the Economic Institutions of Socialism: China and Eastern Europe* (Palo Alto, Calif.: Stanford University Press, 1989); and Jan S. Prybyla, *Market and Plan Under Socialism: The Bird in the Cage* (Palo Alto, Calif.: Hoover Institution Press, 1987).

44. Alan P.L. Liu, *The Phoenix and the Lame Lion: Modernization in Taiwan and Mainland China, 1950–1980* (Palo Alto, Calif.: Hoover Institution Press, 1987); and Alvin Rabushka, *The New China: Comparative Economic Development in Mainland China, Taiwan, and Hong Kong* (Boulder, Colo.: Westview Press, 1987).

45. Shue, *The Reach of the State,* ch. 3; and Andrew J. Nathan, *Chinese Democracy* (New York: Alfred A. Knopf, 1985).

46. William Kirby, "Continuity and Change in Modern China: Chinese Economic Planning on the Mainland and on Taiwan, 1943–58" (paper presented to the annual meeting of the Association for Asian Studies, Washington, D.C., March 1989.)

47. Recent exceptions to this generalization are Nicholas R. Lardy, *Foreign Trade and Economic Reform in China, 1978–1990* (Cambridge: Cambridge University Press, 1992); George T. Crane, *The Political Economy of China's Special Economic Zones* (Armonk, N.Y.: M.E. Sharpe, 1990); and Harry Harding, *A Fragile Relationship: The United States and China Since 1972* (Washington, D.C.: Brookings Institution, 1992).

48. On these points, see Steven M. Goldstein, "Reforming Socialist Systems: Some Lessons of the Chinese Experience," *Studies in Comparative Communism* 21 (Summer 1988): 221–37; and Elizabeth J. Perry, "State and Society in Contemporary China," *World Politics* 41 (July 1989): 579–91.

Part II
Disciplinary Surveys

3

The Study of Chinese Society

Thomas B. Gold

Before 1979, lack of access to the field and a dearth of reliable data dissuaded many American scholars from studying Chinese society. With the restoration of academic exchanges and the availability of many kinds of data, scholars from a number of disciplines, including many non-China experts, embarked on numerous research projects conducted in China on various aspects of contemporary Chinese society. Their diverse methods and analytical perspectives are contributing to our understanding of the continuities and changes in Chinese society, in particular since the reform program began in 1979. They are also increasingly bridging the gap between the disciplines and area studies.

This chapter first reviews the evolution of the field up to 1979, then looks at developments since China opened its doors to foreign social scientists. It evaluates how access to China has affected our knowledge and approaches in five areas: lived experience, construction of identities, gender, historical continuities, and the collection and use of statistical data.

The topic of "Chinese society" is impossibly broad. To specify somewhat, under that rubric are included studies of social structure and process at the macro level as well as within organizations; communities; occupational groups; social categories such as women, elderly, youth, and minority nationalities; institutions; and social movements. Most of the works cited will be by card-carrying sociologists and anthropologists, but the nature of the field compels the inclusion also of publications by scholars from political science, economics, geography, and history.

Evolution of the Field

The study of Chinese society has been integral to the development of sociology as a discipline. In trying to explain Europe's unique experience, early sociologists such as Marx (1964) and Weber (1951) used China as a comparative case, even though neither of them visited China in the course of their work. Later sociologists who also have not had sinological training, such as Eisenstadt (1963), Goldstone (1991), Moore (1966), Moulder (1977), Parsons (1977),

Skocpol (1979), and Stacey (1983), have also incorporated the Chinese case in their efforts to build theories about general social processes.

The sociological study of Chinese society by Westerners probably dates to the work of the Europeans Granet (1975) and de Groot (1969) on religion, Burgess (1928) on Peking's guilds, and Gamble on Beijing and Ding county (1968). Largely anecdotal and subjective accounts by missionaries and travelers, such as Smith (1970), also provide useful material. Chinese sociologists and anthropologists, largely trained in Western schools in China or abroad, produced many valuable works, in particular community studies and ethnographies of minorities. Studies of the history of sociology and anthropology in China include Wong (1979) and Chiang (1986) (see also Freedman 1962). Publications in English by Fei Hsiao-tung (1945, 1953) and Lin Yue-hwa (1948) received wide circulation in the West and became indispensable contributions to the field.[1] As is well known, sociology and anthropology virtually disappeared in China after the reorganization of higher education in 1952 and especially the Anti-Rightist Movement of 1957. Subsequently, Fei Hsiao-tung (Fei Xiaotong) and others concentrated on the study of minority nationalities. Their assigned task was to determine the location of these nationalities in a progression of Marxist development stages. This was the primary type of anthropological research permitted for over two decades; sociology atrophied in name and practice (Rossi 1984).

A very few Chinese sociologist-anthropologists left the mainland and continued their work elsewhere, such as Martin Yang (1945) in Taiwan, Francis L. K. Hsu (1953) at Northwestern University, and C.K. Yang (1959) at the University of Pittsburgh. Some non-Chinese who had conducted fieldwork on the mainland before the Communist victory published works using their data. Major contributions include Lang's (1946) and Levy's (1949) volumes on the family, Eberhard's (1965) on social forces and minorities, and Skinner's (1963, 1964) work on rural marketing and social structure.

This mainland experience and possession of firsthand data differentiated these scholars from the succeeding cohort, which was denied access to mainland China. The inaccessibility of the mainland for fieldwork contributed to the unwillingness of many potential China-oriented sociologists and anthropologists even to enter the field, as discussed in Lindbeck (1971).

Hoping to redress this state of affairs, the federal government and private foundations (the Ford Foundation in particular) provided funds to train a new generation of China scholars beginning in the late 1950s. Much of this assistance supported social scientists, especially for graduate training.[2]

The American Council of Learned Societies and the Social Science Research Council's Joint Committee on Contemporary China (JCCC) set up a Subcommittee on Research on Chinese Society in 1962, which funded a number of conferences and sponsored the eight-volume Studies in Chinese Society series published by Stanford University Press. Although the social sciences themselves were becoming increasingly specialized and differentiated at that time, the JCCC

conferences consciously involved scholars from many disciplines, brought historians together with specialists on contemporary China, and included people engaged in studying Taiwan and Hong Kong society. In this way, the JCCC tried to
strengthen the links between area studies and numerous fields of expertise, while
bolstering Chinese area studies as well.

Hong Kong became the major research site for scholars of contemporary
Chinese society.[3] Based at the Universities Services Center (established in 1963),
researchers utilized the USC's unmatched collection of mainland publications, as
well as translation services such as the Foreign Broadcast Information Service
and the British Broadcasting Corporation's *Summary of World Broadcasts*. Hong
Kong–based researchers also used the Centre's services to arrange interviews
with recent Chinese émigrés from the mainland. This combination of official
publications supplemented by interviews comprised the primary source of data for
many years. (See Parish and Whyte 1978, Whyte and Parish 1984, and Walder 1986
for excellent discussions of the Hong Kong methodology. Also see Whyte, Vogel,
and Parish 1977 for a more general discussion of methods of research on China
through 1976.) Many scholars felt that access to fieldwork on the mainland made the
USC redundant. It moved to the Chinese University of Hong Kong in 1989. China's
post–June 4, 1989, crackdown demonstrated that the USC (and Hong Kong) retains
an extremely useful function as a backup site as well as a repository of printed
materials. What impact Hong Kong's scheduled 1997 reversion to Chinese control
will have on its ability to continue to play this role remains to be seen.

Hong Kong–based American sociologists produced a number of outstanding
works well into the 1980s. Two pioneering and still valuable books are Franz
Schurmann's *Ideology and Organization in Communist China* (1968) and Ezra
Vogel's *Canton under Communism* (1969). In their studies of Communist China
up to the early years of the Cultural Revolution, Schurmann and Vogel addressed
issues central to the discipline as a whole, including bureaucracy, social control,
large-scale organizations, rationalization, and so on.

These interests reflected the larger context of Communist studies and of
the social sciences. In the 1950s, the totalitarian paradigm dominated Communist studies, with scholars investigating the means by which Marxist-Leninist
parties restructured the societies they ruled, atomizing individuals and inserting
party control over most areas of life. Recent essays by Walder (1986), Shue
(1988), and Nee and Stark (1989) trace the evolution of the paradigm for
studying Communist societies from the totalitarian paradigm of the 1950s to a
modernization-convergence-pluralism approach in the 1970s. At the same time,
Parsonian structural-functionalism enjoyed ascendancy in the social sciences,
and its offshoot, modernization theory, held a similar place in studies of underdeveloped nations. Within this paradigm, Vogel and Schurmann demonstrated
how the Chinese Communists' Soviet-influenced strategy for economic development and form of political domination differed from the rational, universalistic,
modern path advocated by modernization theorists.

Then China veered away from the Soviet model during the Great Leap Forward and subsequent Cultural Revolution, calling into question many of the assumptions of scholars and practitioners about communism and economic development more generally. China's revolutionary experiments, understood primarily through official Communist publications—though as a by-product of the Cultural Revolution including exposés of political battles over the correct road to communism—inspired some sympathetic younger scholars such as Andors (1977), Cell (1977), and Nee and Peck (1975) to hold the Chinese experience up both as an alternative model of development, social organization, and authority, as well as a challenge to many cherished assumptions of bourgeois social science.[4]

Whereas sociologists utilized the Hong Kong sources and, beginning in the 1970s, short visits to the mainland in their research, anthropologists interested in Chinese society had to follow a different route. A handful conducted fieldwork at various sites in Hong Kong's New Territories, and an even smaller number went to Southeast Asia to study Chinese communities in that region. The much larger contingent went to Taiwan, seen in some eyes as more authentically "Chinese" than Hong Kong. Afforded exceptional access to a range of sites, Taiwan-based scholars produced a stellar array of works, including ethnographies and studies of women, folk religion, the family, industrial workers, peasants, minorities, and large and small-scale enterprises. The publications from Taiwan and Hong Kong have great value in their own right, while also providing a baseline for comparative research with the mainland and the burgeoning field of studies of a "Greater China."[5] The fieldworkers' experiences there proved invaluable for the work most of them later did on the mainland.

China Opens to American Social Scientists

The inauguration of Sino-American academic exchanges in the fall of 1979, at the time of the Democracy Wall Movement, followed by the landmark Third Plenum of the Eleventh Central Committee and subsequent establishment of diplomatic relations, raised hopes of a new age of access for extended fieldwork on the mainland for American social scientists. As a clear sign of this, the first four research scholars selected by the Committee on Scholarly Communication with the People's Republic of China (CSCPRC) included sociologist Deborah Davis-Friedmann (1991) and anthropologists Sulamith Heins Potter and Jack Potter (1990). Sociologist Thomas Gold was one of the seven graduate students selected in the first group. The CSCPRC has served as the main conduit for sociologists and anthropologists conducting fieldwork in China, but it lost its monopoly very soon after its exchanges began. For instance, Gail Henderson, then a doctoral candidate at the University of Michigan, accompanied her physician-research scientist husband, Myron Cohen, on a pilot program arranged by the Section of Infectious Disease, the Yale-China Association, and the University of Michigan Center for Chinese Studies (Henderson and Cohen 1984, xii).

At the teaching hospital attached to the Hubei Provincial Medical College, they used interviews and participant observation to collect the data used in their book, *The Chinese Hospital*. Steven Mosher (1983) also went to China under non-CSCPRC auspices in 1979 to engage in fieldwork in a Guangdong commune.

Some Overseas Chinese sociologists, led by C. K. Yang, began to teach and initiate contacts in China. Many of them, such as Lin Nan, had not initially studied China. Like their fellow Chinese-Americans in the natural sciences, they became a natural bridge between the Chinese and American scholarly communities. They conducted classes in China, brought Chinese students to the United States for graduate training, and established collaborative projects with Chinese colleagues.

Many non–sinologically trained Americans have gone to China under the CSCPRC or other exchange programs to teach and have ended up doing social research on China. For example, Alex Inkeles, a noted scholar of Soviet society and of modernization, embarked on a major project to apply his modernity scale in China in collaboration with Chinese colleagues.[6] Another example is Anthony Oberschall of North Carolina, who taught as a Fulbright visitor, wrote a paper on China (1987), and then undertook a life course study of Shanghai in collaboration with Gail Henderson and Glen Elder (both of UNC) and several Chinese.[7] Peter Blau's household survey in Tianjin, in collaboration with Andrew Walder and Chinese colleagues (1989), is another instance, as is Tamara Hareven's (1987) research on the Chinese family. Craig Calhoun, a specialist on social movements, happened to be lecturing in Beijing in the spring of 1989. He spent a great deal of time at Tiananmen Square, conducted a survey of participants, and published a series of articles on his findings (1989a, b, c).

Formal exchange programs offer access to data, libraries, sites, colleagues, and government officials, but China's openness and removal of most travel restrictions provided numerous informal channels for collecting firsthand data useful for sociological analysis, which I refer to as "guerrilla interviewing" (Gold 1989). When successful, it allows participant observation and interviewing without the possible tension that accompanies formally arranged interviews, though it lacks the extended time and replicability of the latter. (See Link, Madsen, and Pickowicz [1989] for essays on the range of data sources and examples of their use.)

Anthropology has followed a more torturous course. Though the facts and motives remain contentious, the Chinese authorities used Steven Mosher's alleged misbehavior while engaged in fieldwork in a Guangdong village as a pretext to radically restrict foreign access to rural fieldsites. Field research did not cease after the Mosher affair despite the official moratorium imposed in 1983. Some scholars went on multisite escorted research trips where they could only stay at any site for a brief period of time. Margery Wolf's (1985) analysis of the incomplete liberation of Chinese women resulted from this type of research. In collaboration with the Nanjing University History Department, a National

Endowment for the Humanities–funded group comprising Joseph Esherick, Linda Grove, Philip Huang (1990), and Elizabeth Perry conducted a complete household survey of four villages and a township seat in Songjiang county outside Shanghai over five summers from 1982 to 1986. One aspect of the project was the opportunity offered for comparison with the Mantetsu data collected from the same sites in 1941–42. Victor Nee (1989b, 1991) and Huang Shu-min (1992) combined teaching at Xiamen University with research at rural fieldsites to gather data on farm family entrepreneurship and the extended family respectively. Norma Diamond (1983) taught at Shandong University in Jinan while conducting a study of Taitou village to update Martin Yang's 1945 work.[8]

Urban fieldwork continued as well, with Mayfair Yang (1989a, b) residing in a Beijing factory and Lisa Rofel (1989) studying the cultural construction of the division of labor, including the sexual division of labor, in the Hangzhou silk industry.

Anthropological research on minority nationalities has flourished, with American field workers placed in Yunnan, Guizhou, Tibet, Inner Mongolia, Xinjiang, and elsewhere. See Harrell (1988), for example, for a discussion of fieldwork among minorities in Sichuan.

To compensate for Chinese-imposed restrictions on long-term rural fieldwork, the CSCPRC negotiated access to Fengjiacun, a village in Zouping county, Shandong. The CSCPRC selected a team of scholars from several disciplines, including the natural sciences, for a multiyear, multiple-visit program. The Chinese initially insisted that research be limited to one village and the county town, but then permitted increased access to other villages. Some in the American scholarly community were skeptical about what they disparagingly labeled a Potemkin village, though others argued that much could be learned there about rural life and its transformation (Smith 1989).[9]

Important changes within China since 1979 have also facilitated research on Chinese society. The revival of sociology and, to a lesser extent, anthropology, in China has facilitated American research. (See Cheng and So 1983; Chu 1984; Thurston and Parker 1980; Thurston and Pasternak 1983; Rossi 1984; *Shehui Yanjiu* Bianjibu 1986; Wong 1979; and the special issue of *Social Research* from Winter 1987, especially Guldin 1987.) Foreign scholars may gain institutional bases and colleagues in their fields. There is an annual pool of visiting scholars and graduate students to American institutions. Most of the latter write dissertations about China, some with data they brought with them. They provide a bridge to their home institutions, professors, and colleagues, though most began their professional careers outside China. In fact, much of the "American" study of contemporary China is now being conducted by expatriate Chinese studying and teaching at American institutions.

China's reforms have made a range of other types of data available. In addition to census data, income and social statistics,[10] and published academic research, the Chinese media have been much more forthright about social problems. The rapid growth of the field of Chinese demography is without question one of the breakthroughs in the post-1979 study of Chinese society. For a full discussion, see Greenhalgh (1990), and Lavely, Lee, and Wang (1990); on rural income, see Rozelle (1993). The party itself has produced revisionist histories, but one must be as careful about using today's dogma as about trusting yesterday's. Literary works, in particular the "literature of the wounded," the "literature that delves into reality," reportage and compilations of vignettes (e.g., Zhang and Sang 1986) have provided fresh insights into Chinese life. Many Chinese who have come abroad have written autobiographies that are particularly useful for longitudinal studies of the Communist period (Cheng 1986; Gao 1987; Hua 1987; Li 1990; Liang and Shapiro 1983; Liu 1990; Lo 1989; Lo and Kinderman 1980; Luo 1990; Shen and Yen 1990). The post–June 4 diaspora of former high-level Chinese also provides a new source of data.

As other contributions to this book illustrate, China's opening to the outside world similarly opened the door for numerous foreign journalists, businessmen, lawyers, and experts to live and work for extended periods. Many of them have intimate knowledge of otherwise off-limits aspects of Chinese society, which some have written about (Barlow and Lowe 1987; Bauer 1986; Bernstein 1982; Bonavia 1980; Butterfield 1982; Fraser 1980; Gargan 1990; Garside 1981; Liang and Shapiro 1986; MacLeod 1988; Mahoney 1990; Mann 1989; Mathews 1983; Salzman 1986; Schell 1986, 1988; Terrill 1990; Woodruff 1989) or privately shared with academics.

The status of the social sciences in China and research opportunities for Americans there in the wake of June 4 remains uncertain. Graduate programs in sociology did not admit new students in 1989. Some have revived only slowly, with reduced numbers of students and circumscribed approved research topics. Some collaborative research projects with foreigners were postponed. However, Chinese colleagues stress their eagerness to maintain linkages. Students and scholars continue to go abroad, and many American fieldworkers have returned to conduct continuing and new research projects. Circumstances apparently improve in inverse proportion to distance from Beijing.[11] Privately, Chinese scholars indicate that they are conducting research on a variety of sensitive issues, translating foreign works, and keeping up with global trends such as the discussion on civil society, although the official research climate has not been conducive to these topics.

Document 598 of the State Education Commission, issued on December 29, 1990, called the United States a "hostile nation," and ordered restrictions on collaborative projects and on access to social surveys, especially those trying to gauge Chinese public opinion. Two joint projects under way between Beijing University and the University of Michigan—one on marital issues and one on local politics—were suspended.[12] But the Luce Foundation inaugurated a second round of grants for U.S.-China Cooperative Research in 1991. Funded proposals included studies of aspects of contemporary Chinese society such as labor, welfare, and urban life, all involving collaboration with Chinese colleagues.

The Impact on American Scholarship

How have long-term access to the field, the explosion of data collected by Chinese and foreigners, the increased frankness of the Chinese media, the opportunities to collaborate with Chinese colleagues, the freedom to travel widely, and the ability to talk with Chinese outside official interviews since 1979 affected the American study of contemporary Chinese society? In this section, I will examine some areas where, in my judgment, these changes have significantly improved our knowledge of and approaches to the study of Chinese society over the past fifteen years. The areas and approaches covered include: lived experience; construction of identities; gender; historical continuities; and the collection and use of statistical data. There is obviously much overlap across some of these broad categories. Space limitations allow me to cite only a few examples; I apologize to my colleagues for any and all omissions. Further, this is an essay on the evolution of the field and not on research findings, so the focus in what follows will be on the former to the neglect of the latter. It is also limited to work done primarily in China.

Understanding Lived Experience

Surely, the major achievement from access to China has been an exponential improvement in our understanding of daily life. Because the fieldwork on which this understanding is based is usually conducted at one or at most a handful of sites, it is nearly impossible to generalize beyond one's cases. Nonetheless, for a wide variety of geographical locations (south and north, coastal and interior, core and periphery of macroregions), settings (rural villages, grasslands, plains, urban *danwei* [work units]), social categories (minorities, women, workers, farmers, entrepreneurs, intellectuals, cadres, youth, students, elderly), and activities (personal relations, mate choice, exercise of power, work), we have a rich accumulation of data on the lived experience in China. If nothing else, it empirically illustrates the tremendous diversity that, not surprisingly, still characterizes this continent-sized country.

Creative use of interviews conducted in Hong Kong, in some cases supplemented by short visits to the mainland, gave us a fairly sound understanding of many aspects of daily life in China, including rural society. It is hard to believe that an ethnography such as *Chen Village* (Chan, Madsen, and Unger 1984) was written without any of the authors actually ever setting foot in their fieldsite. (Chan, Madsen, and Unger [1992] includes data from a subsequent visit to the village.) Likewise, a comprehensive study such as Parish and Whyte (1978) is by no means "reduced to [a] historical curiosit[y]" (Whyte 1992a) as a result of decollectivization. In fact, scholarship of this sort will provide important data for the continued longitudinal study of Chinese society.

But there is no doubt that our understanding of rural society has deepened considerably through extended fieldwork. Potter and Potter (1990), based on years of repeat visits of long and short duration to their fieldsite, is the sort of solid comprehensive ethnography we take for granted from Taiwan but have not had from mainland China since well before 1949.

In spite of its excessively negative tone, doubts about its representativeness, and serious ethical concerns, Mosher (1983) provides a vital and intimate look at rural life in one Guangdong village at the inception of the reforms. The chapter on family planning, which opens with Mosher's chilling firsthand account of a family planning meeting where the cadres coerce the women to "volunteer" for abortions, even well into their third trimester, offers a devastating look at how the state can exercise power over relatively powerless individuals.

The study of minority nationalities has also benefited greatly from fieldwork, including access to some extremely remote areas. Goldstein and Beall (1990) lived and traveled with a community of 265 nomads across the *Changtang*, the northern plateau of western Tibet, for sixteen months between 1986 and 1988. They published an exceptional combination of photographs and text offering unprecedented insights into the history, customs, and daily life of these people.

Scholars of Chinese society trained before the opening of the country for field research had learned how to read between the lines of official pronouncements for clues as to the "real" thought, beliefs, motivations, and behavior of ordinary people. There was an assumption behind the research, but little direct hard evidence of a reality different from, though not necessarily the opposite of or hostile to, the presentation in official outlets. Fieldwork in China has permitted scholars to collect data from many hitherto inaccessible sources to apprehend more directly this "unofficial" China (equated with "popular culture") and gauge its relation to "official" China (Link, Madsen, and Pickowicz 1989).[13]

Combining this new knowledge of lived experience with the study of elite politics and policy shifts now permits us to establish linkages between the micro and macro levels, and provide an empirical basis for understanding the state-society nexus. Research conducted in rural China offers illustrative examples.

Huang Shu-min's (1989) extensive interviews with the party secretary of Lin village near Xiamen turned into a detailed chronicle of the village's political history through the eyes of one of its key players. Eighteen visits conducted over a decade to Wugong in Hebei province provided the multidisciplinary team of Friedman, Pickowicz, Selden, and Johnson (1991) with a diachronic analysis of the interplay of state policy and local society in one north China locale from the 1930s to the early 1960s. They were able to tease out the "socialist networks" among officials. In addition to extensive interviews, they utilized archives, village records, their own household surveys, and documents in their research. The authors reveal how the changing policies over the course of ten years influenced their research work. For example, whereas in 1978 they could not meet with the sole surviving landlord, from 1980 they could interview anyone. They talked with winners and losers in power struggles to get both sides of a story. They showed an early draft of the manuscript to some officials and villagers to correct certain factual errors, resisting efforts to amend analytical conclusions as well.

Another example is Siu (1989a), where multiple visits over six years permitted the researcher to compile a detailed ethnography of a rural site, and also to understand the activities of local elites functioning as brokers in the shifting relationship between state and society over time. Oi's (1990, 1991) interviews in various mainland locations and Hong Kong have helped us understand the difficult situation rural cadres face with the necessity of introducing market reforms into their collectives. In particular, she has gathered data on corruption. These findings on the rural political economy permit scholars to test hypotheses about the role of local elites such as those of Shue (1988) and Skinner (1963–64).

Extended fieldwork over the course of the post-Mao reform era has enabled scholars to gain understanding of the social consequences of the reforms. Sensitive scholars tried to understand the situation before the reforms in order to better comprehend what they were observing in situ. The demonstrations of 1989 brought these consequences into focus, but collections such as Baum (1991, a revised and updated version of a special edition of *Studies in Comparative Communism* from Summer/Autumn 1989) and Davis and Vogel (1990) were well under way before those events.

Related to the state-society and macro-micro approaches is the issue of civil society in China. The concept had been applied to the democratization process under way during the 1980s in Eastern Europe (Ash 1990; Pelczynski 1988). Only a few scholars assayed its relevance to reform-era China before the spring of 1989. However, the wave of popular protests and the emergence seemingly from nowhere of a wide range of self-styled "autonomous associations" attracted the attention of some China scholars to the concept. Historians have debated whether China had sprouts of civil society and a public sphere during the late Imperial and early Republican eras (e.g., Rankin 1986; Rowe 1990; Schoppa 1982; Strand 1989). But scholars of contemporary society have concentrated more on the separate issue of the emergence of something that might be labeled "civil society" as one consequence of the reforms (Gold 1990; Solinger 1991; Strand 1990; Sullivan 1990; Wank 1991; Whyte 1992b; Yang 1989b). In looking at workers, a group that played a central role in creating civil society in Poland, Walder, for instance, concludes that 1989 revealed that "small groups of committed workers" contemplated organizing independently and leading a political movement (1991, 492) even though they had not done so in 1989. Perry and Fuller (1991) evaluate the role of several social groups in China's emerging civil society.

Construction of Identity

Anthropologists, primarily younger ones, have utilized their fieldwork experiences to ask questions about the construction of identities. Deeply influenced by postmodernism and the work of Michel Foucault and his concepts of power, scholars have sought to establish the means by which particular groups create meaning and identities within the confines established by the state. This involves deconstructing the "discourse" on values, cultural meanings, practices, and so on.

Scholars have not used Foucault uncritically. Yang (1989a, 26–27) for instance, notes that Foucault's conception of power lacks "institutional specificity" and sensitivity to "internal contradictions" within power orders.

One of the most impressive achievements in this area is Gladney's (1991) study of the creation of ethnic nationalism among Muslim Chinese. Other examples based on the study of minorities include Diamond (1988), Harrell (1990), Jankowiak (1992), Mueggler (1991), Schein (1989), and Wu (1990). From 1982 to 1990 he conducted a total of three years of fieldwork among the Hui throughout China. The book's four ethnographic chapters are based on research in Ningxia, Beijing, Hebei, and Fujian, and he traveled extensively among other Hui communities scattered throughout the country. Using Benedict Anderson's concept of "imagined communities," Gladney argues that Hui and other minority ethnic identities in China derive from the "dynamic, even dialectical interaction of culture, socioeconomics, and the state" (1991, x). The book includes an insightful deconstruction of the author's own efforts to define exactly whom he was studying (98–111).

Gladney raises the issue of the construction of a "Han identity" as well. Honig (1989) has gone more deeply into this with her exploration of the status of "Subei people" in Shanghai. By interviewing Subei people (immigrants from north of the Yangzi River) and non-Subei people in Shanghai, she dissects the way in which a variety of social and economic structures reproduce historical prejudice and discrimination against this subethnic Han group.[14] Other Han identity-related studies include Davis's (1989b) analysis of how women use the private space of their apartments to create a private space reflecting their family roles, and Madsen's (1989) inquiry into the interrelation of Catholic belief and filial piety in the maintenance of a Catholic identity against extended severe persecution.

The role of the work unit in creating identities has also drawn the attention of American scholars. Yang (1989b) uses her three-month field study in a collectively-owned Beijing printing factory to speculate about "the construction of corporateness" and the implications of this for the formation of civil society. Rofel (1989) conducted fieldwork in the Hangzhou silk industry over the course of twenty months from 1984 to 1986. She starts from the frequently used slogan of "raising workers' productivity" to explore the ways in which workers and managers interpret "productivity" and other reformist policies, and how the state's ideological hegemony shapes the process of creating values and practices.

Gender

Certainly related to the category of identity construction is the expanding area of gender studies, which in the China case has meant women's studies exclusively.

(Stacey [1983], for instance, written by a non-sinologist based on secondary sources, is a sophisticated and critical application of a range of feminist theories to the Chinese experience.) Sensitized by the growth of women's studies in the United States, many works address the subject of gender as part of a larger project, though much still needs to be done. Andors (1983), Johnson (1983), and Wolf (1985) have debunked notions that socialism has liberated Chinese women to any great degree. The most comprehensive fieldwork-based book-length study to date is Honig and Hershatter's *Personal Voices* (1988). The authors note that when they went to China in 1979 to conduct research, they "did not intend to write a book about contemporary women" (v). But through roommates, classmates, and contacts within society, they began to collect data systematically on how women's roles were changing (or not) in the course of the reforms. The result is a compendium of interviews, history, and published documents touching on virtually every aspect of women's lives. The very personal nature of much of it results from the extensive experience of the authors over the course of many research stints and travels.

Historical Continuities

Although historians have been stressing this for some time, and ethnographies trace the history of their sites, other social scientists conducting fieldwork in China on contemporary society have begun increasingly to emphasize the porousness of the 1949 timeline. This is part of a general process of the debunking and demystification.

Friedman, Pickowicz, Selden, and Johnson (1991) is one of the more explicit and extended works in this category. They open with Raoyang county in the mid-eighteenth century, then focus on the decades from the 1930s to the early 1960s, tracing the manner in which the growing socialist power transformed or failed to transform social relations, life changes, and politics in one village. A central theme in this book and Siu (1989a) is the continuing role of local elites in a Janus-faced position between the outside and their locality.

Siu (1989a, b) raises another important issue: the significance of the revival of popular rituals in rural China. Based on her observations primarily of life-cycle rituals, she concludes that while their form may be similar to pre-Communist practices, their content and meaning have changed, revealing the extent to which "the power of the socialist state has long been internalized" (1989b, 134). Connecting "cultural change and political economy," Siu proposes that what she observed were "cultural fragments" being "recycled" in the reform era.

Scholars have been able to trace the impact of Communist policies on Chinese rural family structure. Cohen (1990), using Hebei findings, addresses the issue of lineage organization in North China, in comparison to southern China, the source of most of our data until now, as well as pre-Communist structures. Huang (1992), based in Fujian, asks not only about the fate of the traditional extended family under communism, but also the prevalence of this type before 1949—was it, in fact, more common than had previously been thought?

Statistics

The availability of statistics collected and published by the Chinese and the ability of foreign scholars to collect data in China have had a dramatic effect on the evolution of the field (see Lavely, Lee, and Wang 1990). First, we now have solid empirical data for a wide range of social phenomena. Second, the ability to create tables and employ sophisticated statistical techniques has made the study of China more acceptable to many scholars in the disciplines who are skeptical of the way area studies experts in general, and China scholars in particular, conduct research and analysis. Third, empirical data permits comparisons with other societies. Fourth, based on statistical analysis, some scholars have begun to offer theoretical generalizations about processes in China and, by extension, other similar cases.

In their studies of Chinese rural (Parish and Whyte 1978) and urban life (Whyte and Parish 1984), Parish and Whyte constructed "samples" based on their Hong Kong interviews and then employed a gamma test, which is an ordinal measure of association, to determine relations among the characteristics they determined to be independent and dependent variables (Parish and Whyte 1978, 341–43). Since then, the explosion in Chinese and foreign-collected data has permitted more reliable means of random sampling and the application of more sophisticated analysis.

Surveys conducted in Tianjin have provided a detailed look at many aspects of life in that very large metropolis. Teh-wei Hu and his Chinese colleagues (Hu, Bai, and Shi 1987; Hu, Li, and Shi 1988) utilized a survey conducted annually by the Bureau of Statistics, Tianjin Municipal Government, of five hundred randomly selected households to analyze household expenditure patterns in 1982 and 1984, and how wages and bonuses of urban workers are determined. They argue that "although the survey data are limited to one city, the overall Chinese Government guidelines prevail throughout the country. The results from one major city may reflect general patterns of the wage and bonus systems in China" (1988, 77).

Walder (1990) and colleagues randomly sampled 1,011 households in Tianjin in 1986 to analyze the effect of the reforms on income distribution. They structured their research so that the findings could be compared with the experience of other socialist and developing countries. Based on surveys conducted in Tianjin as part of an ongoing joint project on Work and Social Life in Urban China between the Sociology Institute of the Tianjin Academy of Social Sciences and the Sociology Department of Columbia University, their group (Ruan, Zhou, Blau, and Walder 1990) also examined social networks. Again, the work is explicitly comparative, this time with social networks in American cities. Whyte (1990) conducted collaborative surveys in Chengdu over several years to gather the data used in his comparison of mate choice in that city and Detroit.

Much of the numerical data has been used to understand aspects of stratification in China. Some of the authors have explicitly tested Whyte's (1986) hypothesis that late Maoist China was not so egalitarian as it was often portrayed, and Dengist China is not necessarily moving in the direction of inequality. For instance, Walder (1990) performs a variety of tests on his 1986 Tianjin data and agrees that the trend was in the direction of "marked further equalization of incomes" (138). However, using Chinese data, Davis (1989a) found that, in the area of social welfare goods, at least, there had been an increase in inequality. Combining data she collected in collaboration with Chinese colleagues with official figures, Henderson (1990) argues that the reform era has seen increased inequality in access to health-care services. Davis (1988), Ikels (1990), and Kallgren (1992) have examined generation-based inequality, an extremely important topic given the increasing numbers of elderly in China combined with the rising percentage of single-child families.

American scholars have also utilized data collected in China to understand other aspects of stratification in China: Davis (1990) used a survey she conducted in 1987 in Shanghai to reveal aspects of China's low rates of urban mobility that are specific to that country. Lin and Xie's (1988) representative sample of 1,632 adults in Beijing provided data for them to construct a ranking of occupational prestige. They compared their findings with five Western occupational scales and with ratings from other countries/societies. Lin and Bian (1991) administered a questionnaire to a stratified random sample of 1,000 employed adults in Tianjin to test their hypothesis that the segmentation theory of social stratification and social mobilization derived from capitalist societies would also apply to nonmarket, complex societies such as China. They had to introduce work-unit sector as a meaningful status criterion for the China case in order to determine more accurately the effect of parental intergenerational status transmission. Also using Tianjin survey data, Walder (1992) proposes an institutional theory of stratification for socialist economies based on property rights.

Among the boldest in proposing theories based on data collected in China is Victor Nee (1989a, 1991). For his theory of market transition, he explicitly situates China in the literature on institutional change in state socialist economies undergoing market reforms. Using data collected in 1985 from the Fujian Rural Survey Project jointly sponsored by Xiamen University and the University of California at Santa Barbara, Nee tests ten hypotheses from three market transition theses as to why the transition benefits direct producers relative to cadre redistributors.

Another example of the use of Chinese statistics is provided by Rosen (1989, 1991; Rosen and Chu 1987). He has made use of the explosion of Chinese public opinion polling of the 1980s, in particular to understand the attitudes of youth to a wide range of issues.

Conclusion

This chapter highlights some of the areas where access to China since 1979 has improved our knowledge of and ability to study Chinese society. We are able to generate questions and find empirically verifiable answers to ones previously not even on the research agenda. This is not to say that there is not still a long way to go. Our research is still vulnerable to China's domestic political vagaries. Data are incomplete and often of dubious reliability and validity. There are numerous areas where our knowledge is still very slim, for example, the rhythms of daily life in an urban neighborhood or urban work unit; activity on a shop floor in various kinds of enterprises; whether Walder's (1986) theory of Communist neotraditionalism applies outside of the state sector, and how the ongoing reforms of that sector have affected the organizational culture; the "embeddedness" of mainland economic and management practices in traditional Chinese culture comparable to the work of Hamilton and Biggart (1988) on capitalist East Asia; the construction of a Han identity and sub-identities; the construction of a male identity (identities); from a life course perspective, how membership in a birth cohort affects behavior and attitudes to certain issues such as corruption, political participation, and foreign influence; popular religion and the tenacity of Christianity; deviance; the emergence of voluntary associations; the social consequences of China's incorporation into the world capitalist system. We have vastly improved our micro knowledge, and the time for a synthesis of numerous case studies and theoretical generalizations is on the horizon. Close collaboration with scholars from Taiwan and Hong Kong, and use of data from sites in those two Chinese societies can be very helpful in this endeavor.

The events of 1989 revealed a number of fissures in Chinese society that have attracted attention from American scholars. However, there is a risk that research will become overly timebound, focusing too much on either 1989 or the preceding decade of reform to the neglect of the study of historical continuities discussed earlier. There may also be a misguided notion that social change stopped on June 4, 1989.

The old issue of area studies versus the disciplines continues to raise its head (see Freedman 1962; Lambert 1991; Schwartz 1980; and Skinner 1964). Although not everyone finds this something to celebrate, scholars of Chinese society are now more able to engage in discourse with the colleagues in their disciplines. If for no other reason, the realities of the job market and requirements for tenure dictate that this must be done. Ideally, a balance will be found where paradigms and methods from the disciplines can help to illuminate structures and processes in Chinese society, and data from China can contribute to constructing general social theories.

Notes

1. Fei's 1948 *Xiangtu Zhongguo* was not published in English until 1992, as *From the Soil: The Foundations of Chinese Society* (Berkeley: University of California Press).
2. In 1991 the Ford Foundation initiated a similar program, through the Social Science Research Council, to attract graduate students in the social sciences to area studies generally.
3. During the 1970s, Victor Nee conducted research while studying at Beijing Univer-

sity, and a group comprising Edward Friedman, Paul Pickowicz, Mark Selden, and Kay Ann Johnson gained access to a county in Hebei for an extended multivisit project (1991). Kessen (1975) grew out of an official delegation on early childhood that spent three weeks in China in 1973. Sidel (1974) was based on a short visit.

4. Their perspective and debates with mainstream China experts were published primarily in *The Bulletin of Concerned Asian Scholars,* the journal of the Committee of Concerned Asian Scholars.

5. After conducting fieldwork in Hebei, Cohen (1990), who had done extensive research in Taiwan, raises the important issue of the applicability of studies of Taiwan and Hong Kong to regions on the mainland outside of Fujian and Guangdong.

6. On the measurement of individual modernity, see Alex Inkeles and David Smith, *Becoming Modern: Individual Change in Six Developing Countries* (Cambridge, Mass.: Harvard University Press, 1974). Although criticized in the West, especially by adherents of the Marxist-inspired dependency school, Inkeles has enjoyed great prominence in China.

7. On life course, see Glen H. Elder, Jr., "Perspectives on the Life Course," *Life Course Dynamics,* ed. Glen H. Elder, Jr. (Ithaca: Cornell University Press, 1985), 23–49. This project subsequently collapsed because of data problems.

8. "A Symposium on Rural Family Change," *China Quarterly,* no. 130 (June 1992), provides examples of fieldwork-based research in diverse rural areas of China.

9. The project was terminated by the CSCPRC in 1991. The same year, a new long-term, multidisciplinary project on the Mongolian grasslands was inaugurated.

10. The State Statistical Bureau has published a great deal of detailed data, including a yearly survey of self-reported expenditure and income data for 30,000 rural and 20,000 urban households. It covers 700 counties and 100 cities. There is much data on per capita income and other quality of life indicators.

11. *China Exchange News* (Spring 1991), 36, reports that "anthropological fieldwork in Yunnan and Sichuan flourished" in 1990.

12. *San Francisco Chronicle,* May 20, 1991, p. 9, and June 25, 1991, p. 9. CASS was said to be preparing a comparable document. Many local units reportedly ignored the policies and research was proceeding as before.

13. The determined search for some "authentic" China, by definition different from the official portrayal, risks the imposition by the foreign observer of his/her own wishes on the "evidence" collected, and the very process of data gathering. This is another form of orientalism, or turning China into the "Other." The upcoming cohort of scholars in most cases began its training in China and is less burdened by the sense of two realities and the compulsion to debunk everything. The discovery of an "unofficial" China, something they have known about all along, may not strike them as newsworthy.

14. The relationship between some larger Han identity and local identities offers interesting research possibilities. Some scholars have been examining the conscious construction of a Taiwanese identity over the course of the 1980s, especially as relations with the mainland have intensified.

References

Andors, Phyllis. 1983. *The Unfinished Liberation of Chinese Women, 1949–1980.* Bloomington: Indiana University Press.

Andors, Stephen. 1977. *China's Industrial Revolution.* New York: Pantheon.

Ash, Timothy Garton. 1990. *The Uses of Adversity.* New York: Vintage.

Barlow, Tani E., and Donald M. Lowe. 1987. *Teaching China's Lost Generation.* San Francisco: China Books and Periodicals.

Bauer, E.E. 1986. *China Takes Off.* Seattle: University of Washington Press.

Baum, Richard, ed. 1991. *Reform and Reaction in Post-Mao China: The Road to Tiananmen.* New York: Routledge.

Bernstein, Richard. 1982. *From the Center of the Earth.* Boston: Little, Brown.

Blau, Peter M., and Danqing Ruan. 1989. "Social Mobility in Urban China and America." Paper presented at the annual meeting of the American Sociological Association, San Francisco, August 9–13.

Bonavia, David. 1980. *The Chinese.* New York: Lippincott and Crowell.

Burgess, J.S. 1928. *The Guilds of Peking.* New York: Columbia University Press.

Butterfield, Fox. 1982. *China: Alive in the Bitter Sea.* New York: Times Books.

Calhoun, Craig. 1989a. "The Beijing Spring, 1989." *Dissent* (Fall), 435–47.

——. 1989b. "Protest in Beijing: The Conditions and Importance of the Chinese Student Movement." *Partisan Review* 56, no. 4 (Fall): 563–80.

——. 1989c. "Revolution and Repression in Tiananmen Square." *Society* 26, no. 6 (September–October): 21–38.

Cell, Charles. 1977. *Revolution and Work: Mobilization Campaigns in China.* New York: Academic Press.

Chan, Anita, Richard Madsen, and Jonathan Unger. 1984. *Chen Village.* Berkeley: University of California Press.

——. 1992. *Chen Village Under Mao and Deng.* Berkeley: University of California Press.

Cheng, L., and A. So. 1983. "The Reestablishment of Sociology in the PRC: Toward the Sinification of Marxian Sociology." *Annual Review of Sociology* 9: 471–98.

Cheng, Nien. 1986. *Life and Death in Shanghai.* New York: Grove Press.

Chiang, Yung-chen. 1986. *Social Engineering and the Social Sciences in China, 1898–1949.* Ph.D. diss., Harvard University.

Chu, David S., ed. 1984. *Sociology and Society in Contemporary China, 1979–83.* Armonk, N.Y.: M.E. Sharpe.

Cohen, Myron L. 1990. "Lineage Organization in North China." *Journal of Asian Studies* 49, no. 3 (August): 509–34.

Davis, Deborah. 1988. "Unequal Chances, Unequal Outcomes: Pension Reform and Urban Inequality." *China Quarterly* no. 114 (June): 223–42.

——. 1989a. "China's Social Welfare: Politics and Outcomes." *China Quarterly* no. 119 (September): 577–97.

——. 1989b. "My Mother's House." In Link et al., eds., 1989, 88–100.

——. 1990. "Urban Job Mobility." In Davis and Vogel, eds., 1990, 85–108.

——, and Ezra F. Vogel, eds. 1990. *Chinese Society on the Eve of Tiananmen: The Impact of Reform.* Cambridge: Harvard University Press.

Davis-Friedmann, Deborah. 1991. *Long Lives: Chinese Elderly and the Communist Revolution.* Expanded ed. Stanford: Stanford University Press.

deGroot, Jan Jakob Maria. 1969. *The Religious System of China.* New York: Paragon Press.

Diamond, Norma. 1983. "Taitou Revisited: Prospects for Community Restudies." In Thurston and Pasternak, eds., 1983, 123–42.

——. 1988. "The Miao and Poison: Interactions of China's Frontier." *Ethnology* 27, no. 1 (January): 1–25.

Eberhard, Wolfram. 1965. *Conquerors and Rulers: Social Forces in Medieval China,* 2nd ed. Leiden: Brill.

Eisenstadt, S.N. 1963. *The Political Systems of Empires.* New York: Free Press.

Fei, Hsiao-tung. 1945. *Earthbound China.* Chicago: University of Chicago Press.

——. 1953. *China's Gentry.* Chicago: University of Chicago Press.

Fraser, John. 1980. *The Chinese: Portrait of a People.* New York: Summit.

Freedman, Maurice. 1962. "Sociology in and of China." *British Journal of Sociology* 12, no. 2 (June): 106–16.

Friedman, Edward, Paul G. Pickowicz, and Mark Selden, with Kay Ann Johnson. 1991. *Chinese Village: Socialist State*. New Haven: Yale University Press.

Gamble, Sidney D. 1968. *Ting Hsien, A North China Rural Community*. Stanford: Stanford University Press.

Gao Yuan. 1987. *Born Red*. Stanford: Stanford University Press.

Gargan, Edward. 1990. *China's Fate*. New York: Doubleday.

Garside, Roger. 1981. *Coming Alive: China After Mao*. New York: McGraw-Hill.

Gladney, Dru C. 1991. *Muslim Chinese: Ethnic Nationalism in the People's Republic*. Cambridge: Harvard University Press.

Gold, Thomas B. 1989. "Guerrilla Interviewing Among the Getihu." In Link et al., eds., 1989, 175–92.

————. 1990. "Party-State versus Society in China." In *Building a Nation-State: China After Forty Years*, ed. Joyce K. Kallgren, 125–52. Berkeley: Institute of East Asian Studies.

————. 1991. "Youth and the State." *China Quarterly* no. 127 (September): 594–612.

Goldstein, Melvyn C., and Cynthia M. Beall. 1990. *Nomads of Western Tibet*. Berkeley: University of California Press.

Goldstone, Jack. 1991. *Revolution and Rebellion in the Early Modern World*. Berkeley: University of California Press.

Granet, Marcel. 1975. *The Religion of the Chinese People*. New York: Harper and Row.

Greenhalgh, Susan. 1990. "Population Studies in China: Privileged Past, Anxious Future." *Australian Journal of Chinese Affairs* 24: 357–84.

Guldin, Gregory Eliyu. 1987. "Anthropology in the PRC: The Winds of Change." *Social Research* 54, no. 4 (Winter): 757–78.

Hamilton, Gary G., and Nicole W. Biggart. 1988. "Market, Culture and Authority: A Comparative Analysis of Management and Organization in the Far East." *American Journal of Sociology* 94 (Supplement): S52–94.

Hareven, Tamara. 1987. "Divorce, Chinese Style." *Atlantic Monthly* (April), 70–76.

Harrell, Stevan. 1988. "Joint Ethnographic Fieldwork in Southern Sichuan." *China Exchange News* 16, no. 3 (September): 8–14.

————. 1990. "Ethnicity, Local Interests, and the State: Yi Communities in Southwest China." *Comparative Studies in Society and History* 32, no. 3 (July): 515–48.

Henderson, Gail. 1990. "Increased Inequality in Health Care." In Davis and Vogel, eds., 1990, 263–82.

————, and Myron S. Cohen. 1984. *The Chinese Hospital*. New Haven: Yale University Press.

Honig, Emily. 1989. "Pride and Prejudice: Subei People in Contemporary China." In Link et al., eds., 1989, 138–55.

————, and Gail Hershatter. 1988. *Personal Voices: Chinese Women in the 1980s*. Stanford: Stanford University Press.

Hsu, Francis L.K. 1953. *Americans and Chinese: Two Ways of Life*. New York: Henry Schuman.

Hu, Teh-wei, Jushan Bai, and Shuzhong Shi. 1987. "Household Expenditure Patterns in Tianjin, 1982 and 1984." *China Quarterly* no. 110 (June): 179–95.

Hu, Teh-wei, Ming Li, and Shuzhong Shi. 1988. "Analysis of Wages and Bonus Payments Among Tianjin Urban Workers." *China Quarterly* no. 113 (March): 77–93.

Hua, Linshan. 1987. *Les Années Rouges*. (The Red Years). Paris: Editions du Seuil.

Huang, Philip C.C. 1990. *The Peasant Family and Rural Development in the Yangzi Delta, 1350–1988*. Stanford: Stanford University Press.

Huang, Shu-min. 1989. *The Spiral Road*. Boulder: Westview Press.
————. 1992. "Re-examining the Extended Family in Chinese Peasant Society: Findings from a Fujian Village." *Australian Journal of Chinese Affairs* 27 (January): 25–38.
Ikels, Charlotte. 1990. "The Resolution of Intergenerational Conflict: Perspectives of Elders and Their Family Members." *Modern China* 16, no. 4 (October): 379–406.
Jankowiak, William R. 1992. *Sex, Death, and Hierarchy in a Chinese City: An Anthropological Account*. New York: Columbia University Press.
Johnson, Kay Ann. 1983. *Women, the Family, and Peasant Revolution in China*. Chicago: University of Chicago Press.
Kallgren, Joyce K. 1992. *Strategies for Support of the Rural Elderly in China: A Research and Policy Agenda*. Hong Kong: Hong Kong Institute of Asia-Pacific Studies, Chinese University of Hong Kong.
Kessen, William, ed. 1975. *Childhood in China*. New Haven: Yale University Press.
Lambert, Richard D. 1991. "Blurring the Disciplinary Boundaries: Area Studies in the United States." In *Divided Knowledge*, ed. David Easton and Corinne S. Schelling, 171–94. Newbury Park, Calif.: Sage Publications.
Lang, Olga. 1946. *Chinese Family and Society*. New Haven: Yale University Press.
Lavely, William R., James Lee, and Wang Feng. 1990. "Chinese Demography: The State of the Field." *Journal of Asian Studies* 49, no. 4 (November): 807–34.
Levy, Marion, Jr. 1949. *The Family Revolution in Modern China*. New York: Atheneum.
Li Lu. 1990. *Moving the Mountain: My Life in China from the Cultural Revolution to Tiananmen Square*. London: Macmillan.
Liang Heng, and Judith Shapiro. 1983. *Son of the Revolution*. New York: Knopf.
————. 1986. *After the Nightmare*. New York: Knopf.
Lin Nan and Yanjie Bian. 1991. "Getting Ahead in Urban China." *American Journal of Sociology* 97, no. 3 (November): 657–88.
———— and Wen Xie. 1988. "Occupational Prestige in Urban China." *American Journal of Sociology* 93, no. 4 (January): 793–832.
Lin, Yueh-hwa. 1948. *The Golden Wing: Sociological Study of Chinese Familism*. London: K. Paul, Trench, Trubner.
Lindbeck, John M.H. 1971. *Understanding China*. New York: Praeger.
Link, Perry, Richard Madsen, and Paul G. Pickowicz, eds. 1989. *Unofficial China: Popular Culture and Thought in the People's Republic*. Boulder, Colo.: Westview Press.
Liu Binyan. 1990. *A Higher Kind of Loyalty*. New York: Pantheon.
Lo Fulang. 1989. *Morning Breeze*. San Francisco: China Books and Periodicals.
Lo, Ruth Earnshaw, and Katherine S. Kinderman. 1980. *In the Eye of the Typhoon*. New York: Harcourt Brace Jovanovich.
Luo Zi-ping. 1990. *A Generation Lost*. New York: Henry Holt.
MacLeod, Roderick. 1988. *China, Inc.* Toronto: Bantam.
Madsen, Richard. 1989. "The Catholic Church in China: Cultural Contradictions, Institutional Survival and Religious Renewal." In Link et al., eds., 1989, 103–20.
Mahoney, Rosemary. 1990. *The Early Arrival of Dreams*. New York: Fawcett Columbia.
Mann, Jim. 1989. *Beijing Jeep*. New York: Simon and Schuster.
Marx, Karl. 1964. *Pre-Capitalist Economic Formations*. New York: International Publishers.
Mathews, Jay and Linda. 1983. *One Billion*. New York: Ballantine.
Moore, Barrington, Jr.. 1966. *Social Origins of Dictatorship and Democracy*. Boston: Beacon Press.
Mosher, Steven W. 1983. *Broken Earth: The Rural Chinese*. New York: Free Press.
Moulder, Frances V. 1977. *Japan, China and the Modern World Economy*. Cambridge: Cambridge University Press.

Mueggler, Erik. 1991. "Money, the Mountain and State Power in a Naxi Village." *Modern China* 17, no. 2 (April): 188–226.

Nee, Victor. 1989a. "A Theory of Market Transition: From Redistribution to Markets in State Socialism." *American Sociological Review* 54, no. 5 (October): 663–81.

————. 1989b. "Peasant Entrepreneurship and the Politics of Regulation in China." In *Remaking the Economic Institutions of Socialism: China and Eastern Europe,* ed. Victor Nee and David Stark, 169–207. Stanford: Stanford University Press.

————. 1991. "Social Inequalities in Reforming State Socialism: Between Redistribution and Markets in China." *American Sociological Review* 56, no. 3 (June): 267–82.

————, and James Peck, eds. 1975. *China's Uninterrupted Revolution.* New York: Pantheon.

————, and David Stark. 1989. "Toward an Institutional Analysis of State Socialism." *Remaking the Economic Institutions of Socialism: China and Eastern Europe,* ed. Victor Nee and David Stark, 1–31. Stanford: Stanford University Press.

Oberschall, Anthony. 1987. "The Personal Influence System in China: A Complement of Chinese Social Organization." Paper presented at the annual meeting of the American Sociological Association, Chicago, August.

Oi, Jean C. 1990. "The Fate of the Collective after the Commune." In Davis and Vogel, eds., 1990, 15–36.

————. 1991. "Partial Market Reform and Corruption in Rural China." In Baum, ed., 1991, 143–61.

Parish, William L., and Martin King Whyte. 1978. *Village and Family in Contemporary China.* Chicago: University of Chicago Press.

Parsons, Talcott. 1977. *The Evolution of Societies.* Englewood Cliffs, N.J.: Prentice-Hall.

Pelczynski, Z.A. 1988. "Solidarity and 'The Rebirth of Civil Society.'" In *Civil Society and the State,* ed. John Keane, 361–80. London: Verso.

Perry, Elizabeth J., and Ellen V. Fuller. 1991. "China's Long March to Democracy." *World Policy Journal* (Fall), 663–85.

Potter, Sulamith Heins, and Jack M. Potter. 1990. *China's Peasants: The Anthropology of a Revolution.* Cambridge: Cambridge University Press.

Rankin, Mary Backus. 1986. *Elite Activism and Political Transformation in China: Zhejiang Province, 1865–1911.* Stanford: Stanford University Press.

Rofel, Lisa. 1989. "Hegemony and Productivity: Workers in Post-Mao China." In *Marxism and the Chinese Experience,* ed. Arif Dirlik and Maurice Meisner, 235–52. Armonk, N.Y.: M.E. Sharpe.

Rosen, Stanley. 1989. "Value Change Among Post-Mao Youth: The Evidence from Survey Data." In Link et al., eds., 1989, 193–216.

————. 1991. "The Rise (and Fall) of Public Opinion in Post-Mao China." In Baum, ed., 1991, 60–83.

————, and David Chu. 1987. *Survey Research in the People's Republic of China.* Washington, D.C.: United States Information Agency.

Rossi, Alice S. 1984. *Sociology and Anthropology in the People's Republic of China.* Washington, D.C.: National Academy of Sciences.

Rowe, William T. 1990. "The Public Sphere in Modern China." *Modern China* 16, no. 3 (July): 309–29.

Rozelle, Scott. 1993. "Grain Policy in Chinese Villages: Simulating the Response of Grain Yields to Price, Procurement and Loan Policies." *American Journal of Agricultural Economics.*

Ruan Danqing, Zhou Lu, Peter M. Blau, and Andrew G. Walder. 1990. "A Preliminary Analysis of the Social Network of Residents in Tianjin and a Comparison with Social Networks in America." *Social Sciences in China* 3 (September): 68–89.

Salzman, Mark. 1986. *Iron and Silk*. New York: Random House.

Schein, Louisa. 1989. "The Dynamics of Cultural Revival Among the Miao in Guizhou." In *Ethnicity and Ethnic Groups in China*, ed. Chien Chiao and Nicholas Tapp, 199–212. Hong Kong: New Asia College, Chinese University of Hong Kong.

Schell, Orville. 1986. *To Get Rich Is Glorious*. Rev. ed. New York: New American Library.

————. 1988. *Discos and Democracy: China in the Throes of Reform*. New York: Pantheon.

Schoppa, Keith. 1982. *Chinese Elites and Political Change: Zhejiang Province in the Early Twentieth Century*. Cambridge: Harvard University Press.

Schurmann, Franz. 1968. *Ideology and Organization in Communist China*, 2d ed. Berkeley: University of California Press.

Schwartz, Benjamin I. 1980. "Presidential Address: Area Studies as a Critical Discipline." *Journal of Asian Studies* 40, no. 1 (November): 15–25.

Shehui Yanjiu Bianjibu [*Social Research* Editorial Department]. 1986. *Shehuixue Jicheng, 1979–85* (Sociological Records, 1979–85). Beijing: Zhongguo Zhanwang Press.

Shen Tong and Marianne Yen. 1990. *Almost a Revolution*. Boston: Houghton Mifflin.

Shue, Vivienne. 1988. *The Reach of the State*. Stanford: Stanford University Press.

Sidel, Ruth. 1974. *Families of Fengsheng*. Baltimore: Penguin Books.

Siu, Helen F. 1989a. *Agents and Victims in South China: Accomplices in Rural Revolution*. New Haven: Yale University Press.

————. 1989b. "Recycling Rituals: Politics and Popular Culture in Contemporary Rural China." In Link et al., eds., 1989, 121–37.

Skinner, G.W. 1963. "Marketing and Social Structure in Rural China." Part 1. *Journal of Asian Studies* 24, no. 1 (November): 3–43.

————. 1964. "What the Study of China Can Do for Social Science." *Journal of Asian Studies* 23, no. 4 (August): 518–22.

Skocpol, Theda. 1979. *States and Social Revolutions*. Cambridge: Cambridge University Press.

Smith, Arthur H. 1970. *Chinese Characteristics*. Port Washington, N.Y.: Kennikat.

Smith, Kathlin. 1989. "Shandong Field Research: Report on Work in Zouping County." *China Exchange News* 17, no. 1 (March): 18–22.

Solinger, Dorothy J. 1991. "The Floating Population as a Form of Civil Society?" Paper presented at the annual meeting of the Association for Asian Studies, New Orleans, April 11–14.

Stacey, Judith. 1983. *Patriarchy and Socialist Revolution in China*. Berkeley: University of California Press.

Strand, David. 1989. *Rickshaw Beijing*. Berkeley: University of California Press.

————. 1990. "Protest in Beijing: Civil Society and Public Sphere in China." *Problems of Communism* 39, no. 3 (May–June): 1–19.

Sullivan, Lawrence R. 1990. "The Emergence of Civil Society in China, Spring 1989." In *The Chinese People's Movement*, ed. Tony Saich, 126–44. Armonk: M.E. Sharpe.

Terrill, Richard. 1990. *Saturday Night in Baoding*. Fayetteville: University of Arkansas Press.

Thurston, Anne F., and Jason H. Parker, eds.. 1980. *Humanistic and Social Science Research in China*. New York: Social Science Research Council.

————, and Burton Pasternak, eds. 1983. *The Social Sciences and Fieldwork in China: Views from the Field*. Boulder, Colo.: Westview Press.

Vogel, Ezra. 1969. *Canton Under Communism*. Cambridge: Harvard University Press.

Walder, Andrew G. 1986. *Communist Neo-Traditionalism: Work and Authority in Chinese Industry*. Berkeley: University of California Press.

————. 1990. "Economic Reform and Income Distribution in Tianjin, 1976–1986." In Davis and Vogel, eds., 1990, 135–56.

————. 1991. "Workers, Managers and the State: The Reform Era and the Political Crisis of 1989." *China Quarterly* no. 127 (September): 467–92.

————. 1992. "Property Rights and Stratification in Socialist Redistributive Economies." *American Sociological Review* 57, no. 4 (August): 524–39.

Wank, David L. 1991. "Merchant Entrepreneurs and the Development of Civil Society: The Impact of Private Sector Expansion on State/Society Relations in a Chinese City." Paper presented at the annual meeting of the Association for Asian Studies, New Orleans, April 11–14.

Weber, Max. 1951. *The Religion of China.* New York: The Free Press.

Whyte, Martin King. 1983. "On Studying China at a Distance." In Thurston and Pasternak, eds., 1983, 63–80.

————. 1986. "Social Trends in China: The Triumph of Inequality?" *Modernizing China,* ed. A. Doak Barnett and Ralph Clough, 103–23. Boulder, Colo.: Westview Press.

————. 1990. "Changes in Mate Choice in Chengdu." In Davis and Vogel, eds., 1990, 181–214.

————. 1992a. "Introduction: Rural Economic Reforms and Chinese Family Patterns." *China Quarterly* no. 130 (June): 317–22.

————. 1992b. "Urban China: A Civil Society in the Making?" *State and Society in China: The Consequences of Reform,* ed. Arthur Lewis Rosenbaum, 77–101. Boulder, Colo.: Westview Press.

————, and William L. Parish. 1984. *Urban Life in Contemporary China.* Chicago: University of Chicago Press.

————, Ezra F. Vogel, and William L. Parish, Jr. 1977. "Social Structure of World Regions: Mainland China." *Annual Review of Sociology, 1977* 3:179–207.

Wolf, Margery. 1985. *Revolution Postpones.* Stanford: Stanford University Press.

Wong, Siu-lun. 1979. *Sociology and Socialism in Contemporary China.* London: Routledge and Kegan Paul.

Woodruff, John. 1989. *China in Search of Its Future.* Seattle: University of Washington Press.

Wu, David. 1990. "Chinese Minority Policy and the Meaning of Minority Culture: The Example of Bai in Yunnan, China." *Human Organization* 49, no. 1 (Spring): 1–14.

Yang, C.K. 1959. *Chinese Communist Society: The Family and the Village.* Cambridge, Mass.: MIT Press.

Yang, Martin C. 1945. *A Chinese Village: Taitou, Shantung Province.* New York: Columbia University Press.

Yang, Mayfair Mei-hui. 1989a. "The Gift Economy and State Power in China." *Comparative Studies in Society and History* 31, no. 1 (January): 25–54.

————. 1989b. "Between State and Society: The Construction of Corporateness in a Chinese Socialist Factory." *Australian Journal of Chinese Affairs* 22 (July): 31–59.

Zhang Xinxin and Sang Ye. 1986. *Chinese Profiles.* Beijing: Panda Books.

4

The Humanities in Contemporary China Studies: An Uncomfortable Tradition

Anthony J. Kane

Sinology was once a largely humanistic endeavor. It was the philosophers of the Hundred Schools and the poets of the Tang Dynasty who attracted Western scholars to the study of China; there they found a civilization in which education was revered and officials were drawn from the literati.

During World War II a small group of career Foreign Service officers and scholars-turned-"China hands" had seen what was coming and urged the United States to work with the Communists, but they were first ignored and later accused of having delivered China into Stalin's hands. Many of those same scholars returned to their universities after the war with a new set of priorities. They created the field of modern Chinese studies because they perceived it to be, in John King Fairbank's words, "a national necessity to help the American public accept the facts of life in [post-1949] China."[1] Fairbank and Benjamin Schwartz tried to put a human face on the Chinese revolution, arguing that Mao Zedong was at heart a Chinese nationalist and not at all a Soviet puppet.[2] But scholars who tried to maintain an air of academic detachment were frequently overwhelmed by the passions of McCarthyist charges and countercharges. The debate was emotional and often reflected America's sense of trauma more than it revealed Chinese realities now largely locked away from Americans' view.

In this environment a few students of the Chinese humanities remained the purest of sinologists: translators and transmitters of a great tradition to the rest of the field and to the public at large. But their enthusiasm did not extend to post-1949 China. The work of contemporary Chinese in the humanities, be it literature, art, music, film, philosophy, or history, paled beside the work of earlier generations. Traditional sinology seemed to have less and less to say to a field whose focus was increasingly the present, not the distant past.

China studies received another shock, but also a significant boost, with the outbreak of the Cultural Revolution. People were again drawn to the study of China in large numbers because of their interest in the contemporary scene. Against the backdrop of disillusionment with U.S. policy in Vietnam, younger scholars exchanged their advisers' stance of academic detachment for political activism, an activism that often spilled over into their scholarship. By the early 1970s there was at least a perceived preponderance of modernists in the field and a preponderance of social scientists studying the post-1949 period within that group. That trend was only reinforced by the general ascendance of the social sciences over the humanities on American campuses.

After the death of Mao Zedong and the end of the Cultural Revolution, the field was transformed once again, this time by two simultaneous events: the normalization of Sino-American relations and the introduction of Deng Xiaoping's reforms. The former provided more direct access to the PRC for American researchers, allowing scholars to meet and learn more about the people whose works they were studying. The latter often produced dramatic changes in China as a whole, and those changes were reflected in the country's literature, art, and humanistic scholarship. Not only was more being produced, but there was also a greater variety in both form and content as more room was allowed for individual creativity and initiative. Once again, American China scholars found themselves enjoying the material they were writing about. At the same time that the complexities of context were being better understood and analyzed by researchers, the texts themselves were being better appreciated and, as a result, more closely examined. The result was a welcome upsurge in studies of the contemporary Chinese humanities that continues today despite the serious blow dealt to literature and art in China after the crackdown in Tiananmen Square on June 4, 1989. How long this newest chill will last and what effect it will have on foreign scholarship in the humanities remain to be seen.

This chapter seeks to provide an overview of the study of the contemporary Chinese humanities over the last four decades, beginning with literature, the largest field of study within the Chinese humanities, because it is the one with which I am most familiar. It then briefly examines trends in other fields of the humanities, including oral history and contemporary Chinese thought, and concludes with a look at what we might expect to see in the future in these areas and others. A number of specific works are cited, but no attempt has been made to be comprehensive. The conclusions are at best impressionistic.

The Literature of Mao's China

The founding of the People's Republic of China in 1949 represented the dropping of a "second shoe" for Chinese writers. The first was the delivery of Mao Zedong's "Talks at the Yan'an Forum on Literature and Art" in May 1942, an event that marks the beginning of a thirty-five-year period in which politics took precedence over aesthetics in the world of Chinese culture. There were ighs (like the brief Hundred Flowers campaign in 1956–57) and lows (like the Cultural

Revolution) within the period, but one can for the most part take it as a whole.

The initial response of American scholars in this period was to examine the largely negative impact of Chinese Communist Party (CCP) cultural bureaucrats on the lives and works of the people they attempted to control. In August 1962, *The China Quarterly* sponsored a conference on Chinese Communist literature at Ditchley Park near Oxford, England, and published a special issue based on the conference the following year.[3] In his introductory essay for the volume, Cyril Birch asked, "How is a group of men whose inclinations and commitments are to literature as art to approach a literature which is ideological in inspiration and intent?"[4] This is a fair statement of the general problem confronting students of Chinese culture in the Maoist period. Artistic quality proved hard to find for all the Ditchley conferees, but they insisted on its importance. They consoled themselves, as Birch described it, with a passage from Boris Pasternak's novel *Doctor Zhivago:*

> We may take encouragement in our search from a statement confided by Zhivago to his diary in Varykino. The passage bears repetition here in that, cited during the opening session of the Ditchley discussions, it proved prophetic of the approach most characteristic of those present: the search for the particle of art:
>
> "I have always thought that art is . . . something concentrated, strictly limited. It is a principle that is present in every work of art, a force applied to it and a truth worked out in it . . . .
>
> You can call it an idea, a statement about life, so all-embracing that it can't be split up into separate words: and if there is so much as a particle of it in any work that includes other things as well, it outweighs all the other ingredients in significance and turns out to be the essence, the heart and soul of the work."

Thus the words of the best-known Soviet writer of the day were used to support a conclusion that art must be the paramount consideration: "If we study problems of literature at all, we must concentrate on works of art as the essence or basis. After we have done enough close observation of this essence, we may expatiate on the social significance and political connotations of the work."[5]

One might expect that humanistic scholars who were drawn to the study of China because of their love of the traditional culture would be horrified at the CCP's effort to label (and thereby negate) the country's entire heritage as "feudal," but that was not the only issue. Even the problematic and iconoclastic literature of the May Fourth generation looked good when compared with post-1949 Chinese literature. As Howard Boorman noted in his contribution to the Ditchley Park volume, despite Nationalist government repression in the Republican period, a repression often credited with driving writers into the Communist camp, "a genuine literature of social protest—a literature which served as a sort of national conscience—did emerge." Boorman noted,

> the authorities at Peking have erected a new control system designed to inhibit the production of imaginative writing as that term is conventionally used in the West. Aware of the function of literature as an instrument of social stimulus,

the Communist leaders now emphasise the production of what appear to the bourgeois mind to be essentially propaganda and educational materials cast in the forms traditionally employed by literature: fiction, drama and verse.[6]

In other words, as difficult as the Nationalists made it to write, the Communists made it worse. Boorman could find no value in the literature itself, as either art or social documentation. He could find significance only in the party's policy toward literature, because "the attitudes which Communist China displays toward its writers and artists, and the views which it holds of the proper position of art and literature in the life of the society affords important insights into China's deeper aspirations."

Some scholars were so repelled by the politicization of contemporary Chinese literature that they reacted by making heroes of those whom the authorities condemned. The best known work in the field, Merle Goldman's *Literary Dissent in Communist China,* was concerned primarily not with literature but dissent. Thus the author took Boorman a step further in her concluding assertion: "The lives of the revolutionary writers in Communist China have more importance than their literary works."[7] The struggle was always cast as party versus writer; little acknowledgment was made of the often strong differences *among* writers, and the writers' views on literature were neither analyzed nor evaluated. The negative impact of the party's attempt to control literature became the complete focus of scholarship—all that mattered was that writers were seeking freedom and it was being denied. Of those who shared Boorman's and Goldman's concern with the writers' fate, only C.T. Hsia attempted to analyze the literary quality of the writings themselves in his brief sections on Communist fiction in *A History of Modern Chinese Fiction.*[8]

The status of China's professional writers was a continuing cause for concern in the first fifteen years of the People's Republic, but their situation became nearly hopeless with the outbreak of the Cultural Revolution. Nevertheless, in the 1970s there emerged a number of mostly younger, leftist scholars who, inspired by the rhetoric of the period, mounted a defense of the Maoist attempt to produce a people's literature. In a review of "The Development of Modern Chinese Literature Studies in the West" for *Modern China,* for example, Michael Gotz wrote:

The best approach to Chinese literature is, I believe, one which takes into account the nature and function of literature in prerevolutionary or socialist Chinese society. It should be an attempt to come to terms with the literature on the basis of an understanding of the Chinese theory and practice of a particular period. Such an approach will preclude, therefore, the application of culture-bound method of analysis and criteria for evaluation. There are no universals in literary praxis, and Western literature cannot stand as a world model. The approach of many Western scholars undertaking the study of modern Chinese literature reflects only an interest in those aspects most closely corresponding to Western literary taste.

Gotz could find few examples of his preferred approach among American stud-ies of contemporary Chinese literature, citing only Kai-yu Hsu's *The Chinese Literary Scene* and Joseph C. Huang's *Heroes and Villains in Communist China.*[9]

These scholars acknowledged the low quality of the literature being produced, but preferred to join Mao in looking past China's present difficulties to what everyone hoped would be a brighter future. Kai-yu Hsu, for example, suggested, "Perhaps Mao Tse-tung's prophecy will prove correct that as the literary experi-ence of the proletariat progresses, it will demand works of higher quality."[10] This allowed Hsu to overlook his earlier observation that when he visited the model "East is Red" tractor factory in Luoyang, "the reading room . . . was dusty and rarely used," evidence that the people's literature was not successfully appealing to the people. Joseph Huang read the masses' indifference to the literature as a positive reflection on the people's improved taste, predicting that an increasingly sophisticated public would demand better works and that therefore "a cultural renaissance may bloom sooner than expected."[11] John Berninghausen and Ted Huters were even more optimistic in their introduction to a special issue on Chinese revolutionary literature of the *Bulletin of Concerned Asian Scholars,* inferring that despite the pervasive interference of bureaucrats, the literary re-naissance might already be under way: "There probably are unknown writers currently producing highly interesting and artistically advanced works of revolu-tionary literature in China of which we are still unaware."[12]

Gotz's call to overcome culture-bound values, underscored by the fact that both of the scholars he cited were ethnic Chinese, sprang from a passionate belief in the ideals of the Cultural Revolution. Birch's insistence on the search for artistic quality was often cited directly by those seeking to develop other criteria with which to evaluate the PRC's literary output. But what they were really defending was the *politics* of contemporary Chinese literature and art while simply positing the existence of the literature and art itself. In the years since the death of Mao and the fall of the Gang of Four, the false optimism of the early 1970s has become the cause of much soul-searching and embarrassment, acknowledged and unacknowledged. Why, many wonder, were many in the field so determined to defend something that in retrospect seems so completely inde-fensible? It is a mistake that most are determined not to make again.

Is the answer that American values should be universalized? Is "the particle of art" the same everywhere? Is the lesson of the Cultural Revolution period that we need not worry about our own cultural blinders when evaluating works produced in China? Not at all. Had the scholars who claimed to be examining China's new socialist culture "on the basis of an understanding of the Chinese theory and practice" of the period really done so, they might well have come up with some very different conclusions. The mistake was not in trying to avoid being culture-bound; rather it was that in the process scholars suspended their disbelief to a point where they lost the ability to analyze critically. They joined

Boorman and Goldman in looking exclusively at the *function* of literature in the new society without analyzing its *nature*. In the process, they became so enamored of the theory that they totally ignored the practice, the disastrous reality of what was happening to Chinese culture under the structures of Mao's dictums and the interference of the cultural bureaucrats who sought so clumsily to enforce them.

In the end, it was politics more than scholarship that left the field so divided. In scholarly terms, there may have been less difference than there appeared at the time between those like Birch, who seemed to believe that the quality of the literature was the only point, and those like Gotz, who responded by seeking to establish new criteria by which to measure the revolution's success. In retrospect it can be said that each side was correct in its own way, but because of the nature of the "two-line struggle" neither could acknowledge the validity of the other's argument. One group of scholars, dismayed by the results of Maoist policy, refused to take the theory seriously or credit the sincerity of those who were trying to make it work. The next group reacted by going to the opposite extreme. In fact, everyone agreed that the literature and art of the Maoist period was generally of low quality and that the party's handling of cultural affairs contributed to the situation.

Party policy was not the only problem facing contemporary literature. The cultural problems inherent in trying to adapt Western forms in order to produce a modern Chinese literature, problems readily acknowledged in studies of the pre-1949 period, had not suddenly disappeared. Even when these issues were discussed, however, as they were in the Berninghausen and Huters introduction noted above, the discussion was for the most part in the debate over the political issues that dominated the Maoist literary scene. In 1973, Perry Link noted that even Zhou Enlai had chided American journalists for shifting "too abruptly from all-bad to all-good descriptions of China, thereby blithely skipping over the truth."[13] One might have wished to ask the premier how one could discern the truth from the small amount of tightly controlled information made available to foreigners at the time. American scholars could not really begin to understand the complexities of Chinese life and its reflection in literature and art until the Chinese authorities began to open their society more fully to the critical scrutiny of outsiders.

Normalization and Reform

The effects of Mao's death and the fall of the Gang of Four on Chinese humanists was profound, but not immediate. Writers and artists responded cautiously at first, waiting to see if the winds would continue to blow alternately hot and cold. American scholars were even more cautious, praising each liberalization but reacting strongly to each setback. Despite the underlying caution of Chinese humanists, there was a discernible, mounting enthusiasm among American scholars for contemporary Chinese literature and art. The volume of publication on literature alone increased dramatically, ranging from conference volumes to thematic anthologies to studies of individual writers. In addition, as art, music, and film became more accessible, more scholars began looking at these aspects of contemporary Chinese culture in the 1980s.

One source of the field's renewal was a turn away from policy studies and toward an increasing interest in examining the texts themselves, territory more comfortable for the humanist scholar. In her "Report on the Workshop on Contemporary Chinese Literature and the Performing Arts at Harvard, June 13–20, 1979," Bonnie McDougall wrote:

> At the present workshop, there was more concern with the examination of the text as autonomous or semi-autonomous phenomenon, and a greater variety of critical techniques, including linguistic, semiotic and mythic analysis, was employed. . . . While the specific political and biographical circumstances under which the works were produced cannot be ignored, the primacy of text, at this stage of research, is necessary for the development of contemporary Chinese literature and performing arts as an independent field of studies.[14]

Like other conference reports of the period, McDougall's still explicitly rejected the anti-Communist bias of the Ditchley conferees, noting, "If the Ditchley [sic] conference was generally agreed on the threat to literature posed by a communist state, several of the participants at this workshop were inclined to regard the establishment of the People's Republic of China as having had a positive effect on cultural development." Yet in returning to an emphasis on text, McDougall and her colleagues tacitly acknowledged the validity (at least in part) of the stance taken by Birch and his colleagues seventeen years earlier, that one must examine the text in search of a "particle of art."

One of the first volumes published in the wake of the Harvard conference was McDougall's own retranslation of and commentary on Mao Zedong's "Talks at the Yanan Conference on Literature and Art." The stated purpose of this excellent commentary was "to draw attention to those of Mao's comments whose significance is primarily literary, as distinguished from political or historical." Among her arguments is that "Mao's 'talks' read in the context of modern Western literary criticism provides an alternative to the 'essence' or 'particle of art' approach . . . [of the Ditchley group]." She also argues that the "Talks" had many positive effects on contemporary literature but that they were not the dominant force in the literary scene of the 1940s and the 1950s. She acknowledges in fact that "the periods of greatest circulation of the 'Talks' have coincided with the most intense censorship and persecution of individual writers."[15] Thus McDougall's study forms a kind of bridge to a new era of scholarship: it is a balanced, well-argued analysis of Maoist literary theory, probably the last to take that theory seriously.

For the most part, scholars have been losing interest in the theory of revolutionary literature and focusing more on its practice. This is not to say that the emphasis on literary texts has meant that scholars in the field are taking a purely "particle of art" approach to contemporary Chinese literature. Textual analysis can serve other ends than the search for literary quality. For example, Michael S. Duke argues that "it is . . . extremely important that we study the literary works of the immediate Post-Mao Era in order to understand the problematic nature of life in the PRC as it is presented by its own writers to its own citizens."[16] Duke's assertion was reflective of a growing awareness and recognition of the importance of politics and the social role of literature not just to party bureaucrats, but to the writers themselves. This awareness was made possible not just by methodological changes introduced by American scholars, but by changes occurring in China as well.

The changes are noted, for example, in Perry Link's introduction to his anthology *Stubborn Weeds,* a meditation on the "scope" allowed to writers in the years covered, 1979–80. He writes that "these two years stand out clearly since 1949 in terms of the relaxation of controls on writers and the frankness with which writers were able to reveal some of the profound and complex problems in Chinese society and in recent Chinese history." Making no apology for the fact that these years were not "banner years artistically," Link instead seeks to understand why:

> First we need to remind ourselves that . . . the distinction between art and outspokenness has for a long time been less clear in China than in the modern West. In China, candor in behalf of one's people and country has long been considered a primary duty of intellectuals and therefore a literary value in itself. Not surprisingly, the traditional sense of a responsibility to speak out has in recent years been magnified by the very fact of controls on expression. It thus can happen, ironically, that when the controls are eased and writers have more leeway to shape their artistic intuitions, they are impelled instead to use their new freedom to complain about control. Thus when we think of the artistic harm done by the "scope" that writers must stay within, we are mistaken to think only about the fertile areas for inspiration that the scope rules out of bounds. More insidious, and ultimately more damaging, is the simple presence of the "scope" itself, which, even at its broadest, irritates writers enough to draw their attention away from art.[17]

Link adds that Chinese readers share this preoccupation with the question of scope, leading to the phenomenon that "works that are highly praised by Chinese readers can seem quite dull to an outsider."

This lengthy passage is included here because it reveals so much about evolution in the field over the last decade. First, rather than apologizing for or attempting to justify the relatively low quality of contemporary literature, the author provides an analysis of the context that allows the reader to understand why these works read the way they do. Link stresses the differences in the priorities of Chinese writers, but he does not argue that artistic quality is a Western and therefore irrelevant yardstick by which to measure literature. Whereas previously it was argued that writers had given up aesthetic considerations either voluntarily or under duress in the process of following the party line, Link points out that priorities were also rearranged in the quest for autonomy. Furthermore, the quest itself is more than a fight for the right to write "literature for literature's sake"; just as often it is an attempt to assert a social role for literature that differs from the narrow role assigned to it by the authorities.

Link's analysis explains why the Ditchley group found it so difficult to locate the "particle of art" in the literature they were reading. It is not that Chinese writers ignore questions of literary quality or even that they uniformly disdain what might have once been labeled "bourgeois" literary values. The recent Chinese obsession with winning a Nobel prize for literature provides ample evidence of their desire to achieve recognition in the West. As the "scope" allowed to Chinese writers expands, more and more of them are writing in ways more familiar to the Western reader. But few write with no thought of the social and political implications of their work. If one is to read contemporary Chinese literature with the kind of understanding that leads to appreciation, one must understand the sense of *social* (not just literary) mission felt by its creators and their reaction to the constraints they work against in attempting to fulfill that mission.

Both Duke and Link reflect another important trend in post-Mao studies of contemporary culture: the return to a discussion of questions of historical continuity. In the Maoist period the culture of the People's Republic was seen as a nearly complete break with the past. The Right and the Left agreed on this point, but the Right bemoaned it while the Left celebrated it. Now we see agreement that there is in fact a great deal of continuity with the past, both in the attitudes of the writers and artists and in the authorities' attitude toward them. The social mission felt by Chinese writers and reflected in their work is not simply a function of Mao's dictum that art is political. As Chow Tse-tsung pointed out more than twenty years ago, it is a reflection of a traditional view of literature as a "vehicle for moral principles" that even the iconoclasm of the May Fourth movement could not overcome. It was not the concept that changed; it was the moral principles that were modified to fit the needs of the revolution. Thus we now see that while the Yan'an Talks may have represented an important change in the party's attitude toward literature and art, in the end they had little impact on the attitude of the writers and the artists toward their work. The forces of political change have been overwhelmed by forces of cultural continuity, a phenomenon increasingly recognized by (and itself a point of considerable interest to) scholars in all fields of Chinese studies.

The theme of historical continuity is even more apparent in studies of the cultural bureaucracy than in studies of cultural works themselves. For example, just in the title of Merle Goldman's *China's Intellectuals: Advise and Dissent* we see a significant change from her earlier book: an interest not just in the negative, dissenting role played by intellectuals but in the active advisory role they have traditionally played and are increasingly playing once again. Even on the dissent side Goldman's analysis is more sophisticated, seeing beyond Western-style creative spirits rebelling against party control to a literati tradition of *gingyi* (pure opinion) that dates back to Imperial China. The greatest difference, however, is in Goldman's attitude toward people in the cultural bureaucracy itself. Most striking is the inclusion of Zhou Yang, the chief villain of *Literary Dissent,* in the roaster of "Liberals' Political Patrons" in *Advise and Dissent.* And it is not simply that Zhou Yang changed in the wake of his purge in the Cultural Revolution. In the second book Goldman recognizes changes in Zhou's attitude dating back to the early 1960s, changes already alluded to during the Cultural Revolution but certainly not easily discernible to Western scholars at the time.[18]

The appearance of Goldman's book portended a revival of writers' and artists' participation in government seen most clearly in the 1986 appointment of Wang Meng as minister of culture and the selection of the actor Ying Ruocheng as vice-minister. (Some might argue that these are simply ambitious people willing to sacrifice principle for career, but both men remained practicing artists with significant support among many of their colleagues after leaving office following Tiananmen.) It also signaled a renewed interest among scholars in the political careers of Chinese intellectuals. Subsequent studies have looked at specific individuals, both artist and bureaucrat, who have played leading advisory or dissenting roles in the PRC. A number of these are contained in *China's Establishment Intellectuals* and *China's Intellectuals and the State: In Search of a New Relationship.*[19]

Nevertheless, the greatest interest remains with the literature itself. The 1980s witnessed a great increase in the number of anthologies (with translations being done by scholars on both sides of the Pacific) and in studies of the literature. The latter include conference volumes like *After Mao,* edited by Jeffrey Kinkley, and studies by individual scholars like Michael Duke's, cited above. The theme of continuity is reflected in anthologies like *Born of the Same Roots,* edited by Vivian Ling Hsu, and *Literature of the Hundred Flowers,* edited by Nieh Hualing.[20] The former combines stories from before and after 1949 and includes authors from Taiwan as well as some now living in the United States. The latter combines literature of the 1956–57 period with similar works from the 1930s and 1940s. Hsu is particularly assertive in defending the quality of the literature, arguing in the preface that

> Chinese literature of the twentieth century has often been unfairly criticized for its immaturity, crudity, and lack of sophistication. The fact is, the best fiction by Chinese writers of the past fifty years rivals the best in the West. However, alongside the gems ... there exists a huge bulk of second- and third-rate products, some of which have for one reason or another gained sizeable readerships, misleading the nondiscriminating Western critic to form an erroneous low opinion of modern Chinese fiction.[21]

In focusing on the last fifty years Hsu begs the question of whether literature suffered a particular setback under CCP control, but she is clearly willing to let the literature speak for itself. In defending the past quality of Chinese literature, she implies a degree of faith that future works will be of equal if not higher quality.

Oral Histories

Along with the resurgence of literary studies, other fields of the humanities have also blossomed in the last decade, aided again by the openness that has characterized the period. Perhaps the best example is the subfield of oral history, which has proved to be a rich vein for American scholars with improved access to China and its people. Jan Myrdal's classic study, *Report from a Chinese Village,* was a precursor to these studies, but comes from a time when only part of the story was being told.[22] The short interviews in that book give us a sense of why people supported the Communists in the 1940s and early 1950s, but the enthusiasm voiced by the villagers was presented with no real attempt to measure its depth. Only toward the end does one get a sense of the fatigue and confusion created by a relentless series of movements in which land was first distributed to the peasants and then in a sense taken away again through the process of collectivization. But given what we know now of the disastrous failures of the Great Leap Forward, it is difficult to understand how such a largely positive picture could have come from a series of interviews conducted in 1962.

The other side of the story was fully revealed only after the death of Mao and the fall of the Gang of Four led to the reexamination of the Maoist legacy. The "literature of the wounded" coming out of China in the late 1970s exposed much of the suffering of the Maoist years but did little to explain either how it could happen or how it could have been so well concealed from Myrdal and other Westerners who had access to the country during those troubled years (including, of course, Americans with the opportunity to go to China in the early 1970s who returned with largely glowing reports). The answer to those questions awaited the publication of books like *Mao's People,* B. Michael Frolic's superb collection of sixteen longer oral histories. Frolic's interviews exposed the gulf between the lofty ideals of the Cultural Revolution and the often frustrating realities of peoples' lives. As he noted in the introduction:

> Daily life goes on, regardless of the big political campaigns of the moment. Individuals have enough trouble coping with the small things of life, and they are weary of big solutions. Most individuals are more concerned with personal survival, both in political and in economic terms. Consequently, they externalize acceptance of the current line and political ideology, in order to remain politically "safe."[23]

Frolic's study was itself based on refugee interviews done in Hong Kong, but the skepticism that led him to it was based on the experience of having lived in China. And while the observations he made may now seem obvious and almost trite, they were startlingly fresh in 1980 when Frolic's book first appeared.

Oral histories have filled in the gaps left by analytical studies done by social scientists. They have provided us with a profoundly humanistic picture of life in revolutionary China, ranging from the dark tones of Anne Thurston's *Enemies of the People,* about intellectuals destroyed in the Cultural Revolution, to Ann-ping Chin's *Children of China,* which gives voice to China's future. Oral histories are also valuable for studies that focus on specific social groups, as they were for Emily Honig and Gail Hershatter in *Personal Voices: Chinese Women in the 1980s.* The genre has really come full circle with the publication of *Chinese Lives,* an English translation of the Chinese oral history *Beijing ren.* Authors Zhang Xinxin and Sang Ye were inspired by the work of an American, Studs Terkel, who in turn was inspired by Myrdal's original *Report from a Chinese Village.*[24]

Full-length biography is of course another important tool of the humanist scholar, and two recent ones stand out as having further rounded out the picture. Interestingly, both are part autobiography and part oral history in that they are collaborations between the Chinese subject and a Western coauthor. The first is *Son of the Revolution,* the account of an individual (not a cadre) growing up in the People's Republic. Its subject, Liang Heng, was the child of intellectuals, and he watched uncomprehendingly as a succession of political campaigns destroyed his parents' marriage and disrupted his own life irretrievably.[25] Even more compelling is *To the Storm,* whose subject, Yue Daiyun, was herself an adult and a committed revolutionary when the Cultural Revolution broke out. Having believed herself to be on the side of the leftists, Yue only found the events more bewildering when she herself was swept into the maelstrom. She and coauthor Carolyn Wakeman present an unforgettable picture of a Kafkaesque world in which standards of truth and falsehood are sacrificed to the demands of necessity and circumstance.[26] It is a story now being told with chilling frequency of passionate commitment and great potential ground to dust in the zeal of revolutionary excess.

Studies of Chinese Thought

A more disappointing field in the humanities has been philosophy, or studies of contemporary thought. Like the Chinese, American scholars have focused largely on the thought of Mao Zedong, from Stuart Schram's pathbreaking work *The Political Thought of Mao Tse-tung* to John Bryan Starr's more focused *Continuing the Revolution.*[27] No one has yet published an analysis of the complete works of Mao in the years since his death, and perhaps it is still too early to attempt such a feat. What seem to be missing are works of larger scope like

Donald Munro's *The Concept of Man in Contemporary China*. Much discussion of the subject has emerged on the topic of human nature in China since the publication of that book more than a decade ago, but nothing has been published analyzing the results beyond David A. Kelly's brief treatment of the debate on humanism and alienation led by Wang Ruoshui and others in the early 1980s.[28] One hopes that new studies of thinkers ranging from the Marxist Su Shaozhi to the iconoclastic Fang Lizhi will emerge in the not-too-distant future.

A possible model for more theoretical studies of contemporary Chinese culture is Andrew Nathan's *Chinese Democracy*. A study of political culture that might best be categorized as intellectual history, Nathan's book represents an important attempt to understand a concept that intrudes into all studies of Chinese culture. For the writer and artist, democracy means autonomy, and even in the Maoist period it was recognized that ultimately the "season for the blossom of a hundred flowers can be ushered in by a recognition of the respective autonomy of art and ideology."[29] Nathan returns us to the question of cultural values, noting in his preface that

> I am not a believer in the kind of analysis of other societies that tires to avoid issues on the grounds that different societies' values are not the same. Discussing another society's values seriously is a sign of respect, not cultural arrogance. Not to do so means either pretending that differences do not exist or—disrespectfully to our own values—acting as if we do not consider them important.[30]

The point Nathan is making about a specific value—democracy—is equally applicable to others. Eventually, students of the contemporary Chinese humanities will have to address other questions concerning cultural values in the same fashion. As the Chinese themselves seek respect for their contemporary culture, it will become increasingly important for American scholars to assess their own cultural values and decide which are fundamental to their beliefs about humanism and humanistic scholarship. Perhaps in working with Chinese colleagues humanists from both sides of the Pacific can begin to agree on which values are distinctively culture-bound and which, if any, are universal.

A Look Ahead

What does the future hold for American studies of the contemporary Chinese humanities? The crackdown in Tiananmen Square on June 4, 1989, put a chill on literary, artistic, and scholarly endeavors in China that remains in force at the time of this writing. In other words, the circumstances that led to the limited blossoming of Chinese culture after 1978 and to American scholars' ability to do research in China no longer pertain. Many of China's best and most creative minds have been forced into exile, and foreign soil has proved unfertile ground for most of them. One must wait for a new generation of voices to emerge before the reactions of foreign scholars can be gauged.

Nevertheless, some important trends in the field have begun to emerge as studies begun in the 1980s come to press. Perhaps most important is that scholars in increasing numbers are diversifying beyond literature proper (i.e., short stories and fiction) to diverse areas of the arts and the humanities. In one sense the new openness in China was both a blessing and a curse to scholars working in the field, because the explosion of available material made it impossible for a single individual to keep up with everything being published. But it was precisely that boom that made it possible to specialize in new, previously understudied subfields. One of the first indications of this phenomenon was the publication of a conference volume on popular culture edited by Bonnie McDougall, a direct outgrowth of the 1979 conference on which she reported earlier.[31] It represents an effort to understand popular (as opposed to elite) culture that continues in a research project based at the University of California today. The reemergence of popular customs after a hiatus of nearly four decades is a phenomenon of great interest that should fuel both humanistic and social science scholarship on China for a long time to come.

Specialization and diversification have resulted in greater sophistication of scholarship, a trend that will also certainly continue. For example, both a recent conference volume on drama and the popular culture volume just cited contain studies of both the performing arts and film at a level considerably more profound than the best-known studies of the Maoist period by Lois Wheeler Snow and Jay Leyda.[32] In addition we have new studies of the world of contemporary art by Joan Lebold Cohen and Ellen Johnston Laing. Even music has received attention in recent books by political scientist Richard Kraus. Interestingly, these studies share a focus on context (the world of the Chinese painter and musician) rather than text; perhaps these kinds of studies are necessary to clear the way for interest in those analyzing the works themselves.[33]

Beyond bringing a richness and depth to the field, the overall blossoming of contemporary Chinese culture in the 1980s promises to keep the field in general good health for a while despite present conditions. The anti-Spiritual Pollution Campaign of 1983 put a damper on literary production that was apparent in a falloff of studies of literature in the second half of the decade. However, as the literary flowering subsided, the Chinese film industry seemed to explode with new energy, and scholars followed along by turning their attention to it in increasing numbers. A major symposium on film was held in 1989 at UCLA, and one can expect increased publication in the field to follow. Similarly, interest in contemporary Chinese art (among consumers as well as scholars) has increased dramatically in recent years; the two works mentioned are likely to be followed by others. Thus scholars were able to follow trends in the field and diversify along with the culture itself.

It is impossible to judge how long it will take for the present chill to pass, and there is certainly cause for concern. Howard Goldblatt has argued that "the highs of one period seem always to fall short of those that preceded them, and the corrosive forces of cynicism, distrust, and despair eat deeply into the fabric of cultural life."[34] But while the ups and downs of Chinese politics are troublesome, there is evidence that the swings are becoming less dramatic and less intrusive in the lives of cultural workers.

As the best of the younger generation of Chinese writers and artists develop track records and lasting reputations, American scholars will undoubtedly look more critically at the corpus of their work, as has only recently been done for writers of the May Fourth generation.[35] At the 1988 annual conference of the Association for Asian Studies, for example, an entire panel was devoted to the works of Gao Xiaosheng, with Gao himself serving as discussant. Panel chair Yi-tsi Mei Feuerwerker noted the historic nature of this event, which is indicative of the impact of access to the object of study. The effect of the writer's participation in the process of analyzing his work remains to be seen.

One difficult but crucial mission for the future of Chinese studies in the humanities, not limited to studies of the contemporary scene, is to transmit our own improved appreciation of Chinese culture to our colleagues. The increasingly theoretical focus of the traditionally humanistic disciplines in imitation of the social sciences presents some serious obstacles to such an effort. But the problem goes beyond questions of disciplinary methodology in an age when "area specialist" is used as a pejorative. As debates rage in the schools, in the press, and in Washington, D.C., about the nature of core curricula and the importance of appreciating our Western heritage, it behooves us all to assert the value of studying non-Western culture as well.

The definition of the humanities has narrowed to a point where it is often described as an appreciation of our own cultural heritage, rather than appreciation of what it means to be human. American scholars of China must not be afraid to argue that teaching Americans to have an equal respect and appreciation of other cultures does not imply disrespect for their own. The perspective provided by greater understanding is a necessity, not a luxury, in this ever-shrinking world.

Notes

1. John King Fairbank, *Chinabound: A Fifty-Year Memoir* (New York: Harper and Row, 1982), xiv.
2. John King Fairbank, *The United States and China* (Cambridge, Mass.: Harvard University Press, 1948), and Benjamin Schwartz, *Chinese Communism and the Rise of Mao* (Cambridge, Mass.: Harvard University Press, 1951).
3. *China Quarterly* 13 (January–March 1963). Henceforth referred to as *CQ* 13.
4. Cyril Birch, "The Particle of Art," *CQ* 13:3.
5. Birch, *CQ* 13:4.
6. Howard Boorman, "The Literary World of Mao Tse-tung," *CQ* 13:16.

7. Merle Goldman, *Literary Dissent in Communist China* (Cambridge, Mass.: Harvard University Press, 1967), 272.

8. C.T. Hsia, *A History of Modern Chinese Fiction* (New Haven: Yale University Press, 1971, 1961), 469–95, 509–32.

9. *Modern China* 2 (July 1976): 397–416. Cited passage on p. 398.

10. Kai-yu Hsu, *The Chinese Literary Scene* (New York: Vintage, 1975), Foreword, ix–x.

11. Joseph C. Huang, *Heroes and Villains in Communist China* (New York: Pica Press, 1973), 327.

12. John Berninghausen and Ted Huters, "Introductory Essay," *Bulletin of Concerned Asian Scholars, Special Issue: Chinese Revolutionary Literature,* Part 1 (January–March 1976): 12. Parts 1 and 2 were later published together as *Revolutionary Literature in China: An Anthology* (Armonk, N.Y.: M.E. Sharpe, 1976). "Too much control . . . has been a big problem in China and continues to be one. On the other hand, we must recognize the revolutionary logic and potential impact of China's choice, one which has been to stress increased participation of ordinary people in the creation and appreciation of art and literature and to seek to 'de-professionalize' the production of art and literature as much as possible."

13. Perry Link, "Li Hsi-fan on Modern Chinese Literature," *China Quarterly* 58 (April–June 1974): 349.

14. Bonnie S. McDougall, "Report on the Workshop on Contemporary Chinese Literature and the Performing Arts at Harvard, June 13–20, 1979," *Modern Chinese Literature Newsletter* 5 (Spring–Fall 1979): 28–29. In a review of *Essays in Modern Chinese Literature and Literary Criticism: Papers of the Berlin Conference 1978,* Leo Ou-fan Lee notes the difference in attitude between participants in the Berlin Conference and the Ditchley group. See *China Quarterly* 96 (December 1983): 736–37.

15. Bonnie S. McDougall, *Mao Zedong's "Talks at the Yan'an Conference on Literature and Art": A Translation of the 1943 Text with Commentary* (Ann Arbor: Michigan Papers in Chinese Studies 39, 1980), 3, 7.

16. Michael S. Duke, *Blooming and Contending: Chinese Literature in the Post-Mao Era* (Bloomington: Indiana University Press, 1985), ix.

17. Perry Link, *Stubborn Weeds: Popular and Controversial Literature after the Cultural Revolution* (Bloomington: Indiana University Press, 1983), 24.

18. Merle Goldman, *China's Intellectuals: Advise and Dissent* (Cambridge, Mass.: Harvard University Press, 1981).

19. Carol Lee Hamrin and Timothy Cheek, eds., *China's Establishment Intellectuals* (Armonk, N.Y.: M.E. Sharpe, 1986); Merle Goldman, Carol Lee Hamrin, and Timothy Cheek, eds., *China's Intellectuals and the State: In Search of a New Relationship* (Cambridge, Mass.: Council on East Asian Studies, Harvard University, 1987).

20. Jeffrey C. Kinkley, ed., *After Mao: Chinese Literature and Society, 1978–81* (Cambridge, Mass.: Council on East Asian Studies, Harvard University, 1985); Vivian Ling Hsu, ed., *Born of the Same Roots: Stories of Modern Chinese Women* (Bloomington: Indiana University Press, 1981); Nieh Hualing, ed., *Literature of the Hundred Flowers* (New York: Columbia University Press, 1981).

21. Hsu, *Born of the Same Roots,* vii.

22. Jan Myrdal, *Report from a Chinese Village* (London: Heinemann, 1965).

23. B. Michael Frolic, *Mao's People: Sixteen Portraits of Life in Revolutionary China* (Cambridge, Mass.: Harvard University Press, 1980), 6.

24. Anne F. Thurston, *Enemies of the People: The Ordeal of the Intellectuals in China's Great Cultural Revolution* (New York: Alfred A. Knopf, 1987); Ann-ping Chin, *Children of China: Voices from Recent Years* (New York: Alfred A. Knopf, 1988); Emily

Honig and Gail Hershatter, *Personal Voices: Chinese Women in the 1980s* (Palo Alto, Calif.: Stanford University Press, 1988); Zhang Xinxin and Sang Ye, *Chinese Lives: An Oral History of Contemporary China,* ed. W.J.F. Jenner and Delia Davin, trans. the editors and Cheng Lingfang, Gladys Yang, Judy Burrows, Jeffrey C. Kinkley, Carol Murray, and Geremie Barme (New York: Pantheon Books, 1987).

25. Liang Heng and Judith Shapiro, *Son of the Revolution* (New York: Alfred A. Knopf, 1983).

26. Yue Daiyun and Carolyn Wakeman, *To the Storm: The Odyssey of a Revolutionary Chinese Woman* (Berkeley: University of California Press, 1985).

27. Stuart Schram, *The Political Thought of Mao Tse-tung* (New York: Praeger, 1969, 1963); John Bryan Starr, *Continuing the Revolution: The Political Thought of Mao* (Princeton: Princeton University Press, 1979). I do not mention here works by Frederic Wakeman or Raymond Wylie that look at the pre-1949 origins of Mao's thought in Europe and China, nor do I treat the "Symposium on Mao and Marx" that ran in the pages of volumes 2 and 3 (1976–77) of *Modern China*. The former fall outside the scope of this discussion, and the latter parallels the debates in literature already described above.

28. Donald J. Munro, *The Concept of Man in Contemporary China* (Ann Arbor: University of Michigan Press, 1977); David A. Kelly, "The Emergence of Humanism: Wang Ruoshui and the Critique of Socialist Alienation," in *China's Intellectuals and the State,* ed. Goldman, Hamrin, and Cheek, 159–82.

29. Bonnie S. McDougall, ed., *Popular Chinese Literature and Performing Arts in the People's Republic of China, 1949–1979* (Berkeley: University of California Press, 1984).

30. Constantine Tung and Colin Mackerras, eds., *Drama in the People's Republic of China* (Albany, N.Y.: State University of New York Press, 1987); Lois Wheeler Snow, *China on Stage: An American Actress in the People's Republic* (New York: Random House, 1972); Jay Leyda, *Dianying (Electric Shadows): An Account of Films and the Film Audience in China* (Cambridge, Mass.: MIT Press, 1972).

31. Joan Lebold Cohen, *The New Chinese Painting: 1949–1986* (New York: Harry N. Abrams, 1987); Ellen Johnston Laing, *The Winking Owl: Painting in the People's Republic of China* (Berkeley: University of California Press, 1988); Richard Kraus, *Pianos and Politics in China: Middle Class Ambitions and the Struggle over Western Culture* (New York: Oxford University Press, 1989).

32. Howard Goldblatt, "Back Where We Started: Culture in 1987," in *China Briefing, 1988,* ed. Anthony J. Kane (Boulder, Colo.: Westview Press, 1988), 63.

33. See, for example, Yi-tsi Mei Feurwerker, *Ding Ling's Fiction: Ideology and Narrative in Modern Chinese Literature* (Cambridge, Mass.: Harvard University Press, 1982), and Yu-shih Chen, *Realism and Allegory in the Early Fiction of Mao Tun* (Bloomington: Indiana University Press, 1986).

5

The Study of the
Chinese Economy

Penelope B. Prime

In recent years there has been an explosion in the quantity of research done on China's economy by economists in the United States.[1] There are several reasons for this. With Deng Xiaoping's reform initiative, China became a fascinating example of a developing economy, an economy radically changing its economic system, and an economy entering the world system. In addition, China's reforms opened the country to investigation by foreign scholars and paved the way for Chinese scholars to be trained in the field. Finally, and perhaps most important for the economics discipline, the reforms allowed for systematic data collection on unprecedented levels for that country. Since data are essential to economic analysis, the change in data access has had an enormous influence on the study of China's economy.

The purpose of this chapter is to provide an overview of the issues, approaches, and problems of American economists who have studied China's economy in recent decades, beginning with research done before the 1980s.[2] Data access problems defined the field at that time. New research opportunities that emerged in conjunction with reform in China and improved U.S.-China relations are discussed next. The impact these changes had on the field are then seen from a review of research done since 1980. This review underscores the importance of data in allowing a variety of methods and issues, but it also suggests that data problems are far from over. The chapter concludes with a discussion of the study of the Chinese economy as it relates to Chinese area studies and to the economics discipline generally.

Past Research: Studying from a Distance

The establishment in 1979 of formal U.S.-China diplomatic relations, together with reform in China, allowed U.S. citizens to travel to China and to engage in many types of exchanges. Before these events, studying China's economy was a radically different endeavor. (This was also true of other disciplines to varying degrees. See Chapter 2 by Harry Harding in this volume.) The following discussion of research on China's economy carried out before the 1980s is divided into two periods: before 1972 and between 1972 and the 1980s.

Before the early 1970s the way people studied China's economy was largely shaped by the paucity of data. Most data that were available were for the First Five-Year Plan period (1953–57). Other information was obtained from the Central Intelligence Agency or interviewees in Hong Kong, and by extrapolating from policy statements printed in the official Chinese press. Walter Galenson, in a review of the field in 1967, described the situation this way:

> The Chinese have gone far beyond the Russians (in data suppression), and, indeed beyond any major nation in modern times. Most books, journals, and newspapers have been embargoed, so effectively that they are not even available in Hong Kong. Those few that still come through contain almost no economic data. There is an occasional statement about the success of an individual enterprise in raising its output, and a few percentage increase claims have been released. . . . Visitors have been given an odd figure or two. But there is nothing of a systematic character; not even plan targets. Indeed, we do not know whether China is actually operating under a 5-year plan. (Galenson 1967, 4)

From this distant vantage point, few standard economic theories seemed relevant to the Chinese case. Throughout the 1950s agriculture was being collectivized and industry and commerce were being nationalized, following the example of the Soviet Union. With the Great Leap Forward, China diverted from the Soviet path, but in a way that did not fit the experience of other developing countries. These factors, combined with studying China from a distance, influenced the type of research that was done on China by U.S. scholars at the time.

If standard theories were not useful, developing new ones applicable to China was an option. This was discouraged, however, by the lack of data needed to test the theories. As a result, few people spent time on theoretical research applicable to China. The little work of this nature that was done raised insightful questions, but delivered only general answers that could have been achieved just as well using other methods. (See Dwight Perkins's [1983, 349] review of economic research on China.)

Not surprisingly, under these circumstances most economic research done before the mid-1970s described institutions and policy, or measured economic performance. Even within this type of research, methods were limited because many techniques were inappropriate to use with such a crude database. Reconstruction of basic statistical series, for example, resulted in a wide range of performance estimates because of the necessity of making numerous fundamental assumptions (Perkins 1983, 349–51; Chao 1980). To their credit, researchers were very sensitive to data problems and spent much time reconstructing official

Chinese figures as well as dealing with the problems of converting these data for international comparisons. (See Chao 1974; N. Chen 1967; Chin 1968; Eckstein 1961, 1980; Field et al. 1975, 1976; Hollister 1967; Liu and Yeh 1965.) This careful work provided the foundation for what was known about China's economy by those on the outside looking in.

Interdisciplinary approaches also characterized research on China's economy at that time. Economists generally found it useful to consider non-economic variables and constraints, especially in the political realm. (See Dernberger 1980; Eckstein 1966, 1976, 1977; Perkins 1966, 1969, 1975; Prybyla 1970, 1981a; Rawski 1980; Riskin 1978.) With a planned system and socialist goals, economic decisions were explicitly influenced by politics. Further, the lack of consistent economic data meant that economists had to search for other types of information to understand the problems they were dealing with. This approach provided a richness for understanding China but not for advancing knowledge of general economic relations per se. Hence at that time the study of China was only tangential to the economics discipline in the United States.

The importance of non-economic phenomena carried over into the focus of research as well. Harry Harding, in Chapter 2 in this volume, discusses the importance of totalitarianism as a paradigm during these early years of scholarship on China. For economists, the corollary was central planning. While political scientists were addressing the mechanisms of social control, economists were studying the means, extent, and results of economic control. The general conclusion was that while planning might not be successful in achieving efficiency or quality goods, it appeared to be effective in putting control of the economy in the hands of central elites.

In the 1970s the situation with respect to economic data began to change, albeit slowly. The United States had not yet established diplomatic relations with China, but Richard Nixon's visit in 1972 had opened the way for U.S. citizens to travel to China. Researchers obtained access to Chinese publications containing more than just rhetoric about socialist economic policy. The State Statistical Bureau began to function again after being essentially closed down during the Cultural Revolution. The reconstruction of figures for missed years was undertaken, as well as reestablishing the system for collecting national and subnational economic data. All these changes allowed renewed work on the economy with more choice with respect to approaches. In this period important studies by Nicholas Lardy (1978), Thomas Rawski (1980), and others were produced.

Along with new information came reevaluation of the effectiveness of central planning. Lardy and Audrey Donnithorne initiated a lively (and continuing) debate over the effect of several waves of decentralization on resource allocation and decision-making (Donnithorne 1976a, 1976b; Lardy 1975, 1976). As the 1970s progressed, many studied how planning was changing as a result of the combined effects of worsening economic performance and the disarray of key institutions as a result of the Cultural Revolution (Field et al. 1975, 1976; Kravis

1981; Lardy 1978; Prybyla 1981a, 1981b; Wiens 1982a; C. Wong 1982). This work provided the basis for understanding that economic reform was needed in China. It did not, however, capture the extent of the problems or anticipate the magnitude of the reform program that would be undertaken.

New Opportunities in the 1980s

Important as the effect of expanded information was in the 1970s, it paled compared with what followed. In the 1980s access to information and statistical data on China's economy changed dramatically. This included data for the reform period as well as new information about the entire post-1949 period and even the pre-1949 economy. The improvement included both the quantity and quality of information and the ease with which it could be obtained. Researchers no longer had to comb press releases for every piece of information. Statistical yearbooks for the country, provinces, cities, and individual sectors have become widely available. Moreover, on-site surveys, interviews, and collaborative work with Chinese colleagues also became possible.

Simultaneously China was rapidly changing. This opened the field to a myriad of new, pressing questions. Before these could be addressed, the first task was to learn what was happening and to share this with non-China specialists as well as with others in the field.

Many Economies, Many Players

Change in China also significantly altered the types of research done and who was doing research on China's economy. There are three aspects of special importance. The first is that micro and regional case studies, including surveys, have changed the way economists do research in China and the way they view the economy generally. Not long ago economic research on China was largely done at the national level. There were only a few provincial-level studies (Field et al. 1975, 1976; Lardy 1978) and work on micro units and the linkages between them relied heavily on anecdotal evidence. (At least one earlier study was based on enterprise interviews, Richman 1969.) In the 1980s analyses of subnational units became not only possible but perhaps essential to understanding economic change in China. (Some examples are economic studies of provinces: Denny 1991; Lyons 1991; Prime 1987, 1992a, 1992b; Sicular 1986b; Walker 1989; World Bank 1988c; counties and cities: Byrd 1988b; Byrd and Lin 1990; Jefferson 1989, 1991a; Kueh 1983; Lavely 1984; Pannell 1986; Pannell and Welch 1980; Wiens 1982a; C. Wong 1986b; Wortzel 1983; state enterprises: Byrd et al. 1984; Granick 1990; Jefferson 1990; rural collectives: Lin 1987, 1988; Putterman 1987, 1988a, 1990a; Sicular 1986a; and urban households: Hu et al. 1988; Veeck and Pannell 1989.) The possibilities abound; for example, surveys of enterprises and households; case studies of provinces, cities, counties, villages, households, and enterprises; and extensive interviews with leaders as well as people working and living in a variety of situations. Chinese scholars in China are also actively conducting surveys, collecting data, and researching China's economy. And since joining the International Monetary Fund and the World Bank in 1980, China has provided data and other information as required by these institutions.

As these data become available, many interesting questions can be explored. Work already done has shown significant variations between and within provinces, between urban and rural areas, and by type of enterprise. County-level data make it possible to study regions defined by economic variables rather than administrative boundaries. Micro studies have also revealed complex relationships between levels of government administration and economic actors. Analyzing these relations is crucial for explaining China's pattern of economic development.

Although a full evaluation of this work for broad implications for the field and for China's economy is premature, one result does stand out. The notion that there is one Chinese economy may be gone forever. Researchers have discovered that what is relevant for one part of China may not be relevant at all for another part. The variations apply to policy, performance, institutions, and how things actually get done. This raises a question for further research: Is the extent of regional variation primarily a result of China's reforms, or is it an accurate characterization of earlier decades as well?

Generalists Join the Field

A second way in which the study of China's economy has changed in the last decade is that economists with little or no previous experience with China have begun to address their particular issues using the Chinese case. For example, David Granick (1990) applied a property-rights framework to China, a framework that he developed over many years within the context of the Soviet Union and central Europe. (Examples of other U.S. economists who have not specialized in China but who have recently engaged in research on China's economy are Adelman and Sunding 1987; Anderson and Tyers 1987; Bahl 1988; Bahl and Zhang 1989; Balassa 1987; Feder et al. 1989; Gordon 1988; Johnson 1982, 1988, 1990; Polenske and Chen 1991; Srinivasan 1990; and Svejnar 1990.) One strength of works by scholars with varied backgrounds is the ability to identify China's similarities and differences with other economies—characteristics and relationships that are less obvious to those who concentrate primarily on the Chinese economy. Many of the projects that these people have been involved with have been the result of some form of collaboration with Chinese scholars. Such collaboration is one way to overcome the language and data interpretation challenges that face students of China.

The Next Generation of Scholars of China's Economy

The third significant way in which China's opening and reform has affected the study of China's economy is the training of Chinese scholars, working both inside and outside of China, who are concerned with their own economy. Many of these scholars studied at universities in other countries, while others benefited from programs such as the Committee on Economics Education and Research in China,[3] Fulbright, and others that arrange for foreign professors to teach in China.

This group of scholars is just emerging since some of them have only recently been awarded their Ph.D.'s. Nonetheless, these researchers have already made major contributions to the study of China's economy and will no doubt transform it appreciably.[4] In the United States the China Economists Society was formed in 1984 to support students from China studying China's economic problems. This group supports its own journal dedicated to publishing research on China's economy.[5]

Economic Research on China since 1980

To look more specifically at what type of research was done in the 1980s and early 1990s it is helpful to organize recent work according to the following categories: 1) theory; 2) institutions, policy, and performance; 3) China in the world economy; and 4) interdisciplinary work on China's economy.[6] Since some of the works fit into more than one category, the choice of where to discuss or reference a work was based on each work's primary purpose. In some cases works are referenced more than once.

Applying General Economic Theories to the China Case

With the opening of China to American scholars, there has been a renewed interest in understanding China using applicable theoretical frameworks. This type of research has concentrated on planning, planning with markets, and input-output models: Byrd (1987a, 1989); Chang (1989); Fung (1987); B. Reynlds (1987b); Sicular (1983, 1988c); macroeconomic relationships: Chow (1985b, 1987b); Feltenstein and Ha (1991); Naughton (1986b, 1987b); Portes and Santorum (1987); and labor allocation and incentives within agriculture: Chinn (1979, 1980); Lin (1985, 1987, 1988, 1991); Putterman (1985b, 1987, 1990, 1992); Sicular (1986c). Another aspect has been the inclusion of China in multiple-country economic models: Baumol (1986); Baumol and Wolff (1988); S. Brown (1989); Perkins and Syrquin (1988–89); and Waelbroeck (1976). China can serve as a non-Western, developing country case study for many questions of broad interest. This type of work is valuable for exposing the often subtle interrelationships between sectors, resource and institutional constraints, and individual or group behavior. It also brings China research into the economics discipline by utilizing the discipline's tools and addressing its concerns.

For example, Terry Sicular (1988c) has developed a general equilibrium model for agriculture incorporating markets with planning to ask whether a mixed system like the one emerging in China is theoretically feasible. She uses the standard neoclassical profit and utility maximization assumptions for producers and consumers, but incorporates quotas, rationing, and price constraints of China's state plan.

Despite the simplicity of Sicular's model relative to the complexities of how market and planning decisions are actually made in China, the results of the model are generally consistent with what has been happening in the agricultural sector. The model is therefore extremely helpful in identifying fundamental variables and constraints. Sicular's results suggest that market signals and not the state plan are directing economic behavior because state prices are in fact constrained by market prices, and not the other way around. As a result, the efficiency and distribution function of planning is improved with this system, while the plan's ability to influence production and consumption directly is reduced.

William Byrd (1987a, 1989, 1991) has developed a general equilibrium model of a dual plan-market system for state industry. This model allows for an array of equilibria from some or all markets being constrained by the plan to a fully unconstrained situation that results in a market solution overriding all plan variables. Byrd's formulation of the constraints differs from Sicular's and others in that all enterprises have planned targets, but some choose, if "unconstrained," also to buy inputs or sell outputs on the market, depending on market prices and planned target levels. When constrained, an enterprise chooses not to participate in markets, rather than being prevented from doing so, in order to maximize profits. The results are that the unconstrained equilibrium is efficient and optimal, while the constrained equilibrium is not. Byrd hypothesizes that in the constrained case, plan adjustments could be made to move the economy to a more efficient position.

One implication of Sicular's and Byrd's models is that theoretically China's mixed system is economically sustainable. Their work also suggests that introducing markets into the planned system has facilitated further reform by forcing prices to reflect scarcity more accurately and allowing enterprises to respond to these prices. Sustainability and momentum are, of course, critical if China is to succeed with economic reform. Even more important, China is reforming the economy from within. Also, in marked contrast to the former Soviet Union and central Europe, living standards have risen on average during the reform period. These models provide explanations about how that process is working.

Significantly, Barry Naughton (1986b, 1987b) comes to similar conclusions in his analysis of macro policy, despite China's experience with periodically having to back off from certain reform measures because growth has been too rapid and imbalanced. Naughton first links the behavior of actors in the economy through a series of general financial flow identities for centrally planned economies and then applies this framework to China using carefully adjusted data from the banking system. By looking at savings and investment measures, he concludes that the responses of households and enterprises to reform measures have offset the state budget problem to some extent. In this way budgetary allocations, which in themselves help to minimize opposition to reform, can continue without having to alter the fundamental directions of reform.

Naughton's research nonetheless points to serious problems of macro imbalances that must be managed. After this work was completed, the budgetary imbalance worsened. The revenue and inflationary consequences caused the central government to impose austerity beginning in the fall of 1988. The student demonstrations in the spring of 1989 added political tension to the already severe economic concerns. By the early 1990s the worse economic restrictions had been eased and reform was again going forward, but the budget situation continued to worsen. Some analysts argue that these disruptive economic cycles are evidence that China's mix of plan and market is not sustainable after all (Prybyla 1990).

Another example of research that adapts economic theory to the Chinese case is Louis Putterman's (1987, 1990) and Justin Lin's (1987, 1988) work on incentives in collective agricultural production. While incentives are the basis for most explanations of the apparent success of the household responsibility system, Putterman and Lin make explicit the assumptions and conditions that would actually lead to this result. Putterman shows that incentive problems need not be the result of collective production per se and that other problems such as measuring labor input for the purpose of compensation play a critical role. Lin's research focuses on the relationship between supervision and supervision costs, and work incentives. Again in these studies the application of theory clarifies the complexities and subtleties of the issues involved.

The development and application of economic theories and models to China can now be tested empirically. Until recently even the use of standard planning methodologies such as input-output tables was frustrated by insufficient data. Again, the possibilities of new contributions of this type are now more promising. But some caution is in order. While the amount of data has increased substantially, there are many pitfalls in using these data. For example, prices may not reflect choices made on the basis of utility or profit maximization, and many categories of data have changed over time. Without careful consideration of these data issues, applications of theory could be misleading.

Understanding China's Economic Institutions, Policy, and Performance

Two tasks fall into this category: reevaluating the past, and evaluating the post-1978 reform period itself.

Research reevaluating the past continues to be central to understanding the pressures that existed—and continue to exist—for reform; which reform policies, institutions, and strategies were chosen; and economic performance in the reform period. Dominant themes include decentralization and self-reliance in the 1970s, changes in industrial productivity, income distribution, behavior of cooperatives, socialist theory and practice, as well as broader studies exemplified by Lardy's and Perkin's chapters in the Cambridge history series (MacFarquhar and Fairbank). (For example, decentralization and self-reliance: Field 1986; Naughton, Prime, Riskin, and C. Wong in Joseph et al. 1991; Lardy 1983a; Lyons 1985, 1986, 1987a, 1987b; Naughton 1988b, 1991b; C. Wong 1982, 1985b, 1986c; changes in industrial productivity: Chen et al. "New Estimates" 1988, "Productivity Change".1988; Field 1983; Jefferson and Xu 1988; Prime 1987, 1992a; Tidrick 1986; income distribution: Adelman and Sunding 1987; Ashton et al. 1984; Hsiung and Putterman 1989; Lyons 1991; behavior of cooperatives: Putterman 1987, 1988c, 1990; socialist theory and practice: Dirlik and Meisner 1989; Gurley 1979; Lippit 1987; Lippit and Selden 1982.)

One question addressed by these works taken collectively is in what ways the economy was succeeding or failing before the reform period. On the one hand, if the current Chinese leaders are to be believed, the reaction against the past as expressed in the radical reform measures is the result of an economy in extreme disarray; on the other hand, if the economic problems were this severe, how were any gains achieved and why did the system not collapse sooner? In addressing these questions recent work has tried to understand the extent of central control over the economy in different periods, the process by which this control weakened, and the implications of central-local control for the economic system and performance. Clearly both the central government and localities played important economic roles, but the balance between them and their implications continue to be debated.

Recent research on institutions, policy, and performance for the reform period has been extensive, especially in the late 1980s and early 1990s. For ease of presentation, these works are grouped into the following subject areas: agriculture, industrial productivity, intersectoral linkages, income distribution, comparative, and general.

Agriculture

Because increases in surplus output in agriculture are fundamental to the growth potential of the rest of the economy, much recent research on agriculture has focused on how reforms have affected agricultural growth and efficiency. While it is agreed that output has risen substantially with reforms, the reasons for these increases, and their sustainability, have been debated.

For example, Nicholas Lardy's study (1983a) of agriculture attributes much of this increase to improved comparative advantage in cropping patterns, but suggests that these were primarily one-time improvements. He argues that major investment in agriculture, and further increases in marketing and specialization, will be essential for continued progress (see also 1986a, 1986b). Thomas Lyons (1988) also looks at these issues using interprovincial comparisons through 1985. He finds substantial change in regional output patterns, reversing the pre-1979 trend toward provincial self-sufficiency. However, Lyons also concludes with the caveat that it is too early to know whether these changes toward specialization are temporary or permanent. Clifton Pannell, working in economic geography (1985, 1987–88), also reaches similar conclusions.

A related approach to studying China's agricultural reforms focuses on the development of markets, which would encourage more accurate price signals as well as household incentives to produce surplus for sale. The general picture these works give is one of increasing market activity pushing prices to reflect scarcity, with significant household response but with many remaining problems, including continued bureaucratic interference. Other works relevant to this issue are: Hsu (1984); Kueh (1984); Rada (1983); Sicular (1985a, 1985b, 1986b, 1988a, 1988b); Wiens (1981, 1982c, 1983, 1985, 1987).

Another line of inquiry concerns the response of production to new incentives resulting from institutional changes allowing rural households decision-making power and therefore also allowing them to bear the risk of losses and benefits of profits. One aspect of this research has been to understand what these institutional changes have been and their significance (Crook 1986; Hsu 1982; Nee and Young 1991; Stone 1986; Surls 1984, 1986; Wiens 1983); a second has been to understand what incentives are working and why (Aslanbeigui and Summerfield 1989; Chinn 1979, 1980; Cremer 1982; Koo 1990; Lin 1987, 1988; Putterman 1985b, 1988b; Sicular 1986c); and a third has been to measure agricultural output and productivity (Field 1988; McMillan et al. 1989; L. Wong 1987).

Industry

Industrial output has also grown quickly, though questions have been raised with respect to the accuracy of industrial output data (Rawski 1991; Taylor and Banister 1989a; C. Wong 1988b) and the role of productivity in industry's performance.

Some productivity estimates have used partial output per input measures (Field and Noyes 1981; Field 1983), or growth accounting using arbitrary input elasticities as weights to measure total factor productivity (Dernberger and Eckaus 1988; Field 1983, 1984; Lardy 1987d; Perkins 1986, 1988; Perkins and Yusuf 1984; Prime 1987; Tidrick 1986). While these measures continue to be useful, with new data sets use of other techniques that allow estimation of input elasticities is now possible (Chen et al. "New Estimates" 1988, "Productivity Change" 1988; Dollar 1990; Gordon and Li 1990; Jefferson 1989, 1990, 1991a, 1991b; Jefferson et al. 1992; Prime 1992a).

One reason for the progress in productivity estimates is that the ability to reconstruct disaggregated, annual series of input and output data is now feasible. One example is the recent work of Chen et al. ("New Estimates" 1988, "Productivity Change" 1988). This work is based on careful reconstruction of capital data in China's state industry to take out residential construction and to put the series in constant price indices. With these changes estimates of capital stock growth are revised downward. When the revised capital series are used to estimate partial and total factor productivity, productivity change appears more favorable than with earlier estimates using unrevised data.

The Chen et al. estimates, albeit based on better data, still rely on several critical assumptions, and therefore are likely to be revised with further study. For example, the share of housing in state industrial capital stock is unknown, so the proportion for the whole state sector is used. More important, there are many difficulties in reconstructing the components of fixed capital in constant prices (Chen et al. "New Estimates," 1988, 247–50), including estimating how prices have changed and knowing what parts of the official data were reported in current or other prices in order to deflate them (Lardy 1987d, 10–11).

Aside from affecting how China's past performance is viewed, input estimates affect measures of whether or not reforms are improving efficiency. Although there is some debate over the treatment of the data, most estimates have shown improvements in productivity consequent with reforms. Nonetheless recent work also suggests that productivity performance has varied by industry, enterprise, and region (Jefferson and Xu 1991a; Naughton 1992). Next steps will be to separate the relative importance of technological and institutional change from growth in the factors of production, and to distinguish what types of inefficiencies exist (Jefferson 1990, 1991b; Jefferson and Xu 1991b).

Intersectoral Linkages

Before the reform period in China the most important determinant of linkages was the plan. One notable earlier work dealing with the relevance of markets in a centrally planned economy is Perkins (1966). With reforms, numerous non-plan linkages have developed, creating a new area of interest for research. For example, new work has been done on the role of factor markets, pricing, and allocation in enterprise behavior and performance: Byrd (1983b, 1985); Byrd and Tidrick (1987); Chang (1984); K. Chen (1990); Grub and Sudweeks (1988); Jefferson and Xu (1991a, 1991b); Naughton (1988a); Perkins (1991); Rawski (1982a); Rehn and Simon (1988); Stepanek (1991); Stone and Zhong (1989); Wiemer (1992); Wiemer and Liu (1989); inter-provincial linkages: Denny (1991); Lardy (1990); Lyons (1987c, 1990); Prime (1992a); Tao and Holton (1989); labor flows: Emerson (1983); Orleans and Burnham (1984); Taylor (1985, 1986b, 1986c, 1988); Taylor and Banister (1989b); distribution networks: Holton and Sicular (1991); Kung (1992); Lyons (1992); the role of demand: Bowen (1992); Taylor and Hardee (1986); Theil and Seale (1987); the interaction of markets, plans, and bureaucracy: Byrd (1987a, 1987b, 1987c, 1988a, 1989, 1991); Chinn (1984); Hsu (1984); Naughton (1990a, 1991a); Perkins and Yusuf (1984); Prybyla (1985); Sicular (1983, 1985b, 1988a, 1988c); C. Wong (1987, 1988a, 1989); Yeh (1984); economic cycles: Keidel (1991); Zinser (1991); and foreign sector links: B. Reynolds (1983), Taylor (1989).

The primary focus of this research is trying to understand how these linkages work, how they have developed, and their consequences and problems. For example, as discussed in conjunction with theory, William Byrd has focused on the introduction of markets into China's planned system, which has taken the form of enterprises producing and selling some output within a plan and some without. Byrd's analysis suggests that under certain circumstances the incentives involved in this system predict that the market sector will grow while the planned sector will shrink, in an almost natural, if not assured, way. Even where the dual system would remain, prices and resource allocation would be influenced primarily by the market portion. These conclusions are consistent with the model developed by Sicular (1988c) and imply that the direction of the system changes being experienced in China is feasible and sustainable, and even reinforcing, at least in theory.

In contrast, Christine Wong's research (1986a) suggests a much more important, and perhaps destabilizing, role for Kornai's "soft budget constraint" phenomenon, which mitigates against the potential benefits of introducing markets into a planned system. Wong argues that increased funds under the control of localities and enterprises without proper macro guidance in their use, combined with enterprises' ability to negotiate key parameters such as prices and taxes, have led to overexpansion, worsened inefficiencies, and exacerbated macro imbalances. She argues further that while the second phase of reforms saw some improvements in the policies being attempted, the incentives countering the "softening" tendencies were weak and too late. This version of what is happening in China's industrial sector, especially state industry, suggests that the dynamic of partial reforms is self-destabilizing both economically and politically, rather than progressively reinforcing.

Tidrick's chapter on planning and supply in Tidrick and Chen (1987) also raises questions about the efficacy of a dual system. Based on extensive interviews with twenty enterprises, Tidrick describes pervasive bargaining between enterprises and supervising bodies, and a weakening of links between plan targets and incentives, to the point that "bonus and welfare payments determine profit retention and plan targets, not the reverse" (p. 184). Both Tidrick's and Wong's research raise the question of whether the results of the simple theoretical models are actually useful in the face of the complexity of China's economic and political system.

Income Distribution

Income distribution is a key issue with respect to the process and performance of development, and one to which Chinese policymakers have been particularly sensitive. Nonetheless the conclusions of research on this question range from characterizing China's degree of inequality in the pre-1978 period from substantial to low by international standards. (See Adelman and Sunding 1987; Hare 1991; Hsiung and Putterman 1988; Hu et al. 1988; Lardy 1984; Perkins and Yusuf 1984, chap. 6; Rawski 1982b; Riskin 1987, chap. 10; Travers 1984, 1985, 1986.) Research results on the reform period are equally contradictory, for some suggest that inequalities are increasing while others suggest the opposite. Part of the problem is the varying units of analysis investigated, and part is the existence of major problems and gaps in the available data, despite a substantial increase in information in the form of case studies, surveys, and macro indicators.

For example, for the first time an estimate of China's national distribution of income is possible and has been done by Irma Adelman and David Sunding (1987) for the years 1952 to 1983. They combine various data sources for the rural and urban size distribution to estimate the national distribution for 1952, 1978, and 1983. They conclude that rural inequality remained the same between 1952 and 1978, and increased between 1978 and 1983. National income inequality, however, fell in the reform period because of rising peasant incomes and a decreasing rural-urban income differential.

These conclusions conform to what might be expected a priori, and are consistent with reports from local units (e.g., Hsiung and Putterman 1989). These results need to be viewed with caution, however, because the estimates are based on a number of critical assumptions that make their conclusions questionable. For example, since there are no size distributions for urban areas in 1952 and 1978, Adelman and Sunding assume that the distribution in these two years had the same shape as in 1981. A second example is that estimates of average income in each class in rural areas are based on estimates of the relationship of household size and per capita income, while data are available for the urban sector eliminating the intermediate step. Further problems with this study arise with respect to measuring subsidies, and whether the categories of "rural" and "urban" have changed over time affecting the corresponding measures of income and population. So even though Adelman and Sunding's work represents a step forward in what can be attempted in research on income distribution in China, their conclusions are still tentative.

Comparative Studies

Comparisons between China's economic system and development and those of other countries are often made, but formal comparisons are less numerous. Some examples of recent work are comparisons of China with other planned or market socialist economies: Balassa (1987); Granick (1987); Hewett (1989); Prybyla (1990); Van Ness (1989); Wiens (1985); with developing countries: Dernberger (1980); Dernberger and Eckaus (1988); Lyons (1987a); Malenbaum (1982, 1985, 1990); Perkins (1986, 1988); Putterman (1980, 1985a); Rosen (1990a, 1990b);

Sicular (1989); Srinivasan (1987, 1990); L. Wong (1987); and with Taiwan: Meyers (1991); Prime (1986). Much of this work simply puts studies of two or more countries together in one volume, or uses examples from other countries to enhance the discussion of China. So far few studies actually attempt to explain similarities and differences analytically.

The importance of such studies works both ways; that is, China could benefit from knowing which experiences of other countries are relevant, just as other countries could benefit by learning from China. The success of such an exchange of knowledge, however, depends on a full understanding of what is relevant, and why, and what results particular policies or institutions have achieved. Problems of data comparability are immense. Much comparative work suffers from using unadjusted data for China and therefore distorting the comparative picture.

Wilfred Malenbaum's work (1982) comparing India and China is one example where the comparability of data is carefully examined. He argues that if China's data problems are explicitly considered, China's past economic performance is not substantially different from that of India. Double-counting, valuation, and coverage are particularly troublesome in the Chinese data. Unfortunately because of the timing of Malenbaum's study, he was not able to take advantage of the substantial increase in official statistical information that was published in China after his research was completed.

General Studies

There has been a plethora of books and articles written on China's current economic change generally. These primarily describe policy, point out problems, and try to decipher functions of institutions (Bahl 1989; Chen et al. 1992; Chow 1987a; Dernberger 1986, 1987, 1991; Fei and Reynolds 1987; Griffin 1984; Lee 1990; Myers 1988; Naughton 1987a, 1990b, 1991c, 1991d; Perry and Wong 1985; Prime 1991b; Prybyla 1982, 1991; Putterman 1989; B. Reynolds 1982, 1987a; Rothenberg 1987; Schmidt 1987; Sicular 1990; Tidrick 1987; C. Wong 1985a, 1985c). There are also numerous sectoral studies dealing, for example, with international trade and investment, agriculture, finance, energy, technology, and macroeconomic issues such as inflation and unemployment. Before the 1980s numerous sectoral studies were done (Perkins 1983, 360). More recent work has been done on international trade and investment: Kamath (1990); Noyes (1986); Prybyla (1984); Svejnar and Smith (1982); Taylor (1989); Tsao (1987); World Bank (1988a); agriculture: Lardy (1983a); Perkins and Yusuf (1984); Walker (1984a, 1984b); finance: Bahl (1988); Bahl and Zhang (1989); Byrd (1983a); Carver (1986); Dernberger and Eckaus (1988); Gordon (1988); Hsiao (1984, 1987); Lyons and Yan (1988); Naughton (1985, 1986a); Prime (1991a, 1991c, 1992b); P. Reynolds (1982); C. Wong (1990, 1991); World Bank (1988b, 1990b); energy: W. Brown (1986); Keidel (1986); Lewik (1986); technology: Simon (1986a, 1986b, 1986c); Rehn and Simon (1988); Stone (1988);

transport: Rawski (1986); and macroeconomic topics: Chen and Hou (1986); Chow (1987b); Jefferson and Rawski (1992); Naughton (1991c, 1991e); Taylor (1985); World Bank (1990a); Yeh (1984).

There are few up-to-date, comprehensive overviews of China's economy, however. The periodic collections of articles published by the Joint Economic Committee (see U.S. Congress) are important in this respect. Cheng (1982) and Riskin (1987) concentrate on the pre-reform period; Chow's book (1985a) was written primarily for a Chinese audience; the World Bank's various studies are primarily sector studies, except for the 1985 World Bank study, which projects future growth paths. Johnson's book (1990) is a brief overview of the reform period, with a short summary of the pre-reform years.

Understanding China in the World Economy

Academia

Academic research has only begun to deal with the impact of changes in China on the international economy (Anderson and Tyers 1987; Carter and Zhong 1991; Lardy 1987a, 1992; Melvin and Zhou 1989; Perkins 1986; B. Reynolds 1985). Many new questions have suddenly become more relevant, for example: how China's export growth and demand for imports will affect other countries' trade flows; what difference China's opening to foreign investment will make to capital flows to Latin America; and the credit consequences for other countries of China's membership in the World Bank and as a recipient of other public and private financing.

Anderson and Tyers (1987) investigate some of these issues using a global dynamic simulation model for grain, livestock, and sugar to predict production, consumption, and trade trends for China into the 1990s. Their results suggest that China's comparative advantage in agriculture will decline, and if allowed to affect trade flows, would lead China to become a net importer of food even if increases in agricultural productivity continue. Lardy's analysis (1987b) is consistent with these results. He argues that China's future economic progress crucially depends on furthering its integration into world markets, which in turn will depend on domestic changes including pursuing their comparative advantage in labor-intensive manufactured goods. Lardy does not speculate explicitly on the impact this would have on food production and trade, but Perkins (1986) suggests that China will not be willing to allow food imports to grow too large, and therefore may have to accept lower productivity growth than other countries in East Asia.

Government and Business

Understanding China in the world economy is essential for government and business. In government, publications such as the Joint Economic Committee series (see U.S. Congress) and government department staff papers make timely information and analyses available to legislators.[7] Another format begun in the U.S. Department of Agriculture is a newsletter (see Crook and Tuan) whose purpose is to improve communications among economists working on China's agricultural situation. Formal Congressional briefings, seminars, and panels (e.g., Dernberger 1988) are other ways that promote informed decision-making. As Chapter 9 by Tom Fingar in this volume makes clear, however, much more could be done.

Interaction between the U.S. business community and researchers of China's economy is even less developed. Some examples of work relevant to businesses are: Fisher (1986a, 1986b); Grow (1986, 1987); Grub and Lin (1988); Pegels (1987); Szuprowicz and Szuprowicz (1978); Tung (1980, 1982). Perhaps the most effective publication in this regard is *The China Business Review,* published by the U.S.-China Business Council), which often includes articles by academic researchers as well as its own staff. The Asia Society's annual publication of *China Briefing* (Goldstein 1984; Kane 1988; Major 1986; Major and Kane 1987) also serves the business community as well as academia and government. When compared with Japan's support for China research to help Japanese business, however, these efforts seem small indeed (Lardy 1987a, 54).

Incorporating Economics into Interdisciplinary Studies of Contemporary China

To answer questions such as what impact China is likely to have on the world economy, and to predict events such as the student demonstrations in 1989, factors other than economics must be considered. Research on China's economy is read and used by other disciplines, and vice versa, but given the potential for cross-fertilization, much more interdisciplinary or collaborative work could be done. Collections of essays drawn from various disciplines are numerous, but work on China's economy that attempts interdisciplinary approaches and methodologies is rare. Research on the changing power of political cadre under economic reforms, for example, could potentially benefit from rent-seeking, principal agent, or interest group theories in economics, just as economic work could benefit from formally incorporating non-economic power relationships into models of allocation and decision-making in China. Generally, scholars from other disciplines, especially political science and sociology, have attempted to use and explain economic phenomena in their analyses more than economists have incorporated the work of other disciplines. (See, for example, Halpern 1985; Liu 1992; Pearson 1991; Tong 1989, 1991; Walder 1986a, 1986b, 1989; Zweig 1991. See also Chapters 3 by Tom Gold and 6 by Nina Halpern in this volume.) With the extent of economic change in China in recent years, there have been some concerted efforts to encourage collaborative work that includes economists. The support from the Luce Foundation for collaborative, interdisciplinary projects is one example.

There are a few areas within economics that tend to be more interdisciplinary than others. These are research on socialism in China, which explicitly deals with historical and political factors; ideology and economic development (Dirlik and Meisner 1989; Lippit 1987; Lippit and Selden 1982; Michael et al. 1990; Prybyla 1990; Raichur 1981; *World Development* 11 [1983]); economic demography (Ashton et al. 1984; Lavely 1984); economic geography (Pannell 1980, 1981, 1985, 1988; Pannell and Ma 1983; Pannell and Welch 1980; Veeck 1991; Veeck and Pannell 1989); and economic history (Brandt 1985, 1987, 1989; Brandt and Sargent 1989; Chao 1983; Gottschang 1987; Myers 1980; Myers and Sands 1986; Rawski 1989; Weins 1982b). Recent research on China's economic history—by both economists and historians—is a good example of integrating economics with other research on China. This research has led to serious debate over the degree of commercialization and its effect on living standards and income distribution historically. These questions have important implications for understanding the possible effects of market reforms now, as well as for reevaluating the post-1949 years in light of the history situation.

However, the more economists publish their China research in economic journals, the less likely it is that integration or cross-fertilization with other China research will occur. This is partly because of the technical way in which much economic research is presented and because these journals are not typically followed by the China specialist audience. One possible solution is for economists to publish their technical results in economics journals, and then to rewrite them for China studies journals or as monographs aimed at wider audiences. In cases where results cannot be adequately explained without the methodology that generated them, technical aspects of the argument and data issues could be presented in appendices.

The Data Dilemma

While research on China's economy expanded with the changed data situation in the 1980s, many of the problems raised in the discussion thus far have in one way or another touched on the formidable obstacles in interpreting the data. First, we must understand what these data mean. There are many unanswered questions: the coverage of data categories; how categories have changed over time; what information is not being collected; how samples are taken; how variables are defined; what interest rates, price deflators, and depreciation rates have been used; what prices mean; and in what ways China's data are comparable with data from other countries. One example of the significance of these data problems is that despite releasing infinitely richer data in the 1980s as compared with the 1970s, economic system and data category changes make these data inappropriate for meaningful time-series estimation.

Second, more could be done to make these data and their interpretations available to other people who want to work on China's economy. The last attempt at a statistical handbook was based on a conference held in 1976 (Eckstein 1980). Easy access to both data issues and thorough overviews of various sectors in China's economy would improve the feasibility and quality of research by economists who are not China specialists. The availability of such materials would also help China specialists themselves, since no one person can productively cover all the areas single-handedly anymore. No matter how sophisticated the questions or methods applied to the field become, until these tasks are taken seriously, many of the results will be questionable and much effort will be wasted. Recent studies that have focused on such data problems are Chen et al. ("New Estimates" 1988); Chow (1986); Crook (1988); Field et al. (1975, 1976); Jefferson (1988); Kravis (1981); Lardy (1983b); Le Gall (1986); Rawski (1983, 1991); Stone (1984); Taylor (1983, 1984, 1986a, 1987); Taylor and Banister (1989a); and C. Wong (1988b).

Collaborative research between U.S. and Chinese scholars is one way to help with these tasks, the K. Chen et al. ("New Estimates" 1988, "Productivity Change" 1988) work being a good example. Some collaborative research has been published, and numerous others are in progress (Bahl and Zhang 1989; Byrd and Lin 1990; Byrd et al. 1984; Chen et al. "New Estimates" 1988, "Productivity Change" 1988; Feder et al. 1989; Hu et al. 1988; Tidrick and Chen 1987; Wu and Reynolds 1988).

Fortunately Chinese scholars at economic institutions in China are also working on these problems in the process of doing their own data collection, modeling, and research. The contribution of this work will increasingly aid foreign scholars doing research on China. Unless a scholar can read Chinese, however, this contribution will be limited by the few formats in which Chinese work appears in English. Chinese scholars who have studied and published in the United States will also bridge the two academic communities.

The Contributions, Pitfalls, and Opportunities of New Research on China's Economy

Since the late 1970s, China has questioned many aspects of its economic system and policies, and has experimented with major changes. At the same time, access to information and statistical data on China's economy has increased dramatically for both the reform period and the historical data. How has economic research on China reflected these significant changes?

First, there have been renewed attempts to model theoretically how China's economic system works. Reasons for the attempts include a better understanding of the institutions and relationships within the economy, opportunities to test theoretical models, and the fact that with reform China's system has more market elements and therefore is more suited to standard assumptions used in economic theory.

Second, research is now able to capture rich detail and deal with many units of analyses, expanding the general knowledge about China's economy in a way that was not possible before. Research on households, enterprises, and farms, as well as by counties, cities, and provinces, has added new perspectives and questions, and has enabled reinvestigation of commonly held beliefs.

Third, both the number of those interested in doing economic research on China and the audiences this research serves have expanded. Evidence of this is seen in the increased variety of journals and presses publishing economic research on China. This reflects increased access to China for scholars and businesses, and China's growing economic and political importance in regional and world affairs.

While substantial contributions are evident, taking this body of research as a whole one might ask why more has not already been done. For example, there are obvious gaps in overviews of China's economy, studies related to business, and those explaining the relationship between reform and development. There also continues to be major discrepancies in conclusions concerning basic economic phenomena. For example, debates are ongoing concerning the extent to which planning functions, whether state enterprises have improved their performance, and how the reforms are affecting the distribution of income.

Part of the problem is simply one of timing. First, much of the work included in this survey that was published in the early 1980s was based on research carried out in the 1970s. Second, some work published even in the late 1980s was basically earlier research that the authors tried to revise as new information became available. Since great change was occurring within China's economy as well, the question of when to stop revising was a difficult one. And third, there is a lengthy lag between research and publication. However, the large amount of research by economists that has been published since 1990 is an indication that these timing problems have become less serious.

Another part of the problem is that there are too few economists doing research on China's economy. Just keeping abreast of changes occurring in China is itself an enormous task—one that must precede any serious attempt to build or test economic models. The entrance of generalists working on China and the new generation of Chinese scholars trained in Western methods will help in this regard.[8]

Serious pitfalls still remain, however. Data limitations and inconsistencies must be taken seriously, or results will be misleading. Further, with market reforms and more informal market activity, it is tempting to apply economic theories developed for market economies. While in some cases these theories may be appropriate and provide useful insights, their appropriateness should not be taken for granted. (See Badgett [1988, 5–11] for a discussion of the problem of applying economic theory applicable to market economies in economic research on the Soviet Union.) While much of the new research suggests relatively strong market results, it is helpful to recall the extent to which the assumptions and methodology may be shaping those results. Incorporating more of China's particular institutions and goals, as well as studying the reform period in light of the past, may be essential for accurately understanding the economy and predicting future performance.

Another potential pitfall is a tendency to draw conclusions that on balance are consistent with the interpretations of those in power in China, that overestimate the extent to whichpolicy intentions have been implemented, or that let data availability decide which questions are asked. Before the reform period, researchers pointed out problems that existed in China's economy, but few stressed the extent of the problems that have been acknowledged in hindsight. Likewise, evaluations of progress during the reform period have sometimes been more laudatory than perhaps was merited. While overall balance in perspective has generally been maintained, it is useful to be aware of the factors shaping the available information. (See the Introduction by David Shambaugh in this volume.)

Keeping these caveats in mind, however, opportunities abound. The Chinese case could add new understanding to a whole range of issues. For example, if regional variations are so marked, what factors determine these variations? What has been the relative importance of modern inputs, organizational change in production and commerce, and technological change in recent increases in agricultural output? What are the sources of growth, and constraints, in state industry? What are the linkages between rural industry and agriculture, and rural and state industry, that might explain China's recent rapid growth?

Under what conditions could China become the next East Asian NIC (Newly Industrialized Country)?

Comparing work done earlier with research done since 1980 suggests that the lack of specific economic data motivated people to think more in broad ways that cut across disciplines, but marginalized China vis-à-vis the economics discipline. It is now possible to tackle more specific economic problems for the first time to fill in the numerous gaps that have remained guesswork or assumptions. Further, work on China is becoming part of the mainstream within the discipline.

This can be seen in scholarly journals publishing economic research, especially in the areas of comparative economic systems and development. The *Economic Literature Index,* which covers all major economics journals, reported that the number of articles on China published between 1980 and March 1991 was 1,381.[9] This compares with only 279 articles on China published between 1969 and 1979. Compared with the total number of articles published, these numbers represent an increase from 0.4 percent to 0.9 percent.

Within specific fields, *Economic Development and Cultural Change* published eighteen articles on China between 1980 and March 1991, compared with only nine between 1969 and 1979. The *Journal of Comparative Economics* published thirty-four articles dealing with China's economy between 1980 and March 1991.[10]

Interestingly, however, there has been virtually no change in the contribution of China research to general economic theory as represented by two of the main theory journals in the discipline. The *American Economic Review* published eleven articles on China between 1980 and 1991, and the same number during the decade before. The *Journal of Political Economy* published five China articles since 1980 and four in the period before.

Since the dominant economic theories are most applicable to advanced market economies, the fact that China research has been a minor contributor in these areas is not surprising. More important is the fact that China research is playing a significant and growing role in understanding questions of system transition and developing economies.

But the potential also exists for a generalizable economic theory to be developed out of the Chinese experience that is comparable to, for example, Janos Kornai's theory of the soft budget constraint based on the Hungarian experience. China is currently an important case for studying the process of reform in a planned economy—one to which even Kornai has turned (Kornai 1989; Kornai and Daniel 1986). But so far even Kornai's theory has not been tested for China. When his theory is used, it is assumed to be relevant, even though the reasons why it appears relevant in China may be very different than why it is so in Hungary.

China research could also lead to a generalizable theory of economic systems reforming with continuity of political system and living standards. China's experience with privatization, for example, is wholly different than that of other formerly centrally planned economies. In China, private enterprises have grown up around, in conjunction with, or in spite of, the state-owned sector. Simultaneously, state enterprises have begun to behave more like private firms. (See, for example, Rawski 1992. For one attempt to develop the elements of a theory of reform, see Jefferson and Rawski 1991.) While not smooth by many measures, reform in China has so far been carried out without the devastation of economic life that has occurred in the former Soviet Union.

All these questions make China an interesting case, which might contribute to the frontiers of various aspects of economic theory. And with systematic empirical work now possible, much previous understanding about China's economy will be questioned and expanded. By taking care with methodology, data, and perspective, China research can bring the China case into the economics discipline.

But a tradeoff may be occurring. Economists may tend to ignore the larger, interrelated questions about Chinese society. This could happen more readily than with researchers in other disciplines because of the pressure to address questions relevant primarily to economics and to publish in a particular type of economics journal for tenure and promotion. In fact, in many American economics departments publications in area studies journals do not count for tenure and promotion. This could be the price that the field will pay. The gain could be more rigorous and generalizable research that is readily accepted within the discipline of economics.

Notes

1. In preparing this paper I have benefited greatly from discussions and correspondence with Tom Bouye, Loren Brandt, William Byrd, Robert Dernberger, Nicholas Lardy, Barry Naughton, Dwight Perkins, Louis Putterman, Thomas Rawski, David Shambaugh,

and Christine Wong. I have not, however, tried to present a consensus, and I am responsible for the interpretations and any mistakes.

2. In the interests of space and focus, the scope of this chapter is limited in at least four ways. First, many students from China are working on, or have finished, economics graduate work in the United States. These scholars are currently doing important work on China's economy using methods that fall into the mainstream of the economics discipline. Some of this work has been included in this review but not all. In addition, at the time of this writing, many research projects are at the dissertation stage and not yet published.

Second, much important work on China's economy has been done by scholars outside the United States, for example, in Europe, Japan, Australia, and, of course, in China. Again, for practical reasons, this review focuses primarily on work by U.S. scholars.

Third, this chapter surveys work dealing with mainland China only. Obviously much important work has been done on Hong Kong, Taiwan, and other Chinese communities, but this work is beyond the scope of this review.

Finally, this review focuses on the work of scholars trained as economists. Scholars in other disciplines have contributed greatly to issues pertaining to China's economy. This work cannot be adequately reviewed in this chapter, although it is mentioned in the section on interdisciplinary research.

3. This committee is administrated under the Committee on Scholarly Communication with China.

4. They have also made substantial contributions to the field of economics generally.

5. This journal is currently edited by Bruce Reynolds at Union College. Another group of China economists is the Chinese Economic Association in North America (CEANA). This association has a large number of members from Taiwan and accepts non-Chinese members. CEANA's goal is to promote its members in the economics profession generally, not necessarily as researchers of China's economy, though some members are engaged in research on China.

6. The works discussed in this section are ones that primarily use information that has become recently available. In the interests of space and focus, I have chosen to leave out work on intellectual and policy-oriented economic thought. I do not intend to be comprehensive, since the focus of this chapter is research on China's post-1949 economy by U.S. economists.

7. These staff papers are often available to the general public. For example, the China Section, Centrally Planned Economies Branch, Economic Research Service, Washington, D.C., and the China Branch, Bureau of Census, U.S. Department of Commerce, Washington, D.C., have staff paper series and newsletters that can be obtained by writing directly.

8. A counter tendency, however, is that many potential researchers of China's economy have turned their attention to other parts of the world where extraordinary change is also occurring, such as the former Soviet Union, central Europe, and Vietnam.

9. These numbers are based on a computer search of the *Economic Literature Index* database counting articles that had "China" or "Chinese" in the title or as key words. To the extent that these articles deal with the Republic of China (and have "China" in the title), these numbers overestimate the amount of research on the People's Republic of China per se. Importantly, however, *China Quarterly,* the leading journal in the China field that publishes articles on the Chinese economy, is not considered a bonafide economics journal by the compilers of the *Economic Literature Index* and thus does not include *China Quarterly* articles in the *Index.*

10. Only three articles on China were published in the *Journal of Comparative Economics* before 1980, but this is misleading because the journal began publication in 1977.

References

Adelman, Irma, and David Sunding. 1987. "Economic Policy and Income Distribution in China." *Journal of Comparative Economics* 11:444–61.

Anderson, K., and R. Tyers. 1987. "Economic Growth and Market Liberalization in China: Implications for Agricultural Trade." *Developing Economies* 25:124–47.

Ashton, Basil, Kenneth Hill, Alan Piazza, and Robin Zeitz. 1984. "Famine in China, 1958–61." *Population and Development Review* 10:613–46.

Aslanbeigui, Nahid, and Gale Summerfield. 1989. "Impact of the Responsibility System on Women in Rural China: An Application of Sen's Theory of Entitlements." *World Development* 17:343–50.

Badgett, Lee D. 1988. "Defeated by a Maze: The Soviet Economy and its Defense-Industrial Sector." Santa Monica, Calif.: Rand Corporation (October).

Bahl, Roy. 1989. "Chinese Economic Policy." *Forum* (Summer).

———. 1988. "Local Government Finance and Intergovernmental Fiscal Relations in China." Washington, D.C.: World Bank.

Bahl, Roy, and Jun Zhang. 1989. *Taxing Urban Land in China*. Washington, D.C.: World Bank (March).

Balassa, Bela. 1987. "China's Economic Reforms in a Comparative Perspective." *Journal of Comparative Economics* 11:410–26.

Baumol, William J. 1986. "Productivity Growth, Convergence, and Welfare: What the Long-run Data Show." *American Economic Review* 76:1072–85.

Baumol, William J., and Edward N. Wolff. 1988. "Productivity Growth, Convergence, and Welfare: Reply." *American Economic Review* 78:1155–59.

Bowen, Ray. 1992. "A Model of Urban Household Nondurable Consumption in China's Economic Reform and Modernization Program." Ph.D. diss., University of Michigan, Ann Arbor.

Brandt, Loren. 1989. *Commercialization and Agricultural Development: Central and Eastern China, 1870s–1930s.* Cambridge: Cambridge University Press.

———. 1987. "Farm Household Behavior, Factor Markets, and the Distributive Consequences of Commercialization in Early Twentieth-Century China. *Journal of Economic History* 42:711–37.

———. 1985. "Chinese Agriculture in the International Economy, 1870s–1930s: A Reassessment." *Explorations in Economic History* 22:168–93.

Brandt, Loren, and Thomas J. Sargent. 1989. "Interpreting New Evidence about China and U.S. Silver Purchases." *Journal of Monetary Economics* 23:31–51.

Brown, Stuart S. 1989. "Export Uncertainty in Centrally Planned Economies and Administered Protection." *Journal of Comparative Economics* 13:553–65.

Brown, William B. 1986. "China: Energy and Economic Growth." In U.S. Congress 1986, vol. 2, 22–59.

Byrd, William A. 1991. *The Market Mechanism and Economic Reforms in China.* Armonk, N.Y.: M.E. Sharpe.

———. 1989. "Plan and Market in the Chinese Economy: A Simple General Equilibrium Model." *Journal of Comparative Economics* 13:177–204.

———. 1988a. "Market Prices for Industrial Producer Goods in China: Structure, Trends, and Efficiency." Paper presented at the annual meeting of the American Economic Association and the Chinese Economic Association in North America. New York, December 28–30.

———. 1988b. "Rural Industrialization and Ownership in China." Paper presented at the annual meeting of the American Economic Association. New York, December 28–30.

————. 1987a. "The Market Mechanism and Economic Reforms in Chinese Industry." Ph.D. diss., Harvard University.

————. 1987b. "The Role and Impact of Markets." In Tidrick and Chen 1987, 237–276.

————. 1987c. "Two-Tier Plan/Market System in Chinese Industry." *Journal of Comparative Economics* 11:295–308.

————. 1985. "The Shanghai Market for the Means of Production: A Case Study of Reform in China's Material Supply System." *Comparative Economic Studies* 27:1–30.

————. 1983a. *China's Financial System: The Changing Role of Banks.* Boulder, Colo.: Westview Press.

————. 1983b. "Enterprise-Level Reforms in Chinese State-Owned Industry." *American Economic Review* 73:329–32.

Byrd, William A., and Lin Qingsong, eds. 1990. *China's Rural Industry: Structure, Development, and Reform.* New York: Oxford University Press.

Byrd, William, and Gene Tidrick. 1987. "Factor Allocation and Enterprise Incentives." In Tidrick and Chen 1987, 60–102.

Byrd, William, Gene Tidrick, Chen Jiyuan, Xu Lu, Tang Zongkun, and Chen Lantong. 1984. "Recent Chinese Economic Reforms: Studies of Two Industrial Enterprises." World Bank Staff Working Paper no. 652. Washington, D.C.: World Bank.

Carter, Colin A., and Fu-Ning Zhong. 1991. "China's Past and Future Role in the Grain Trade." *Economic Development and Cultural Change* 39:792–814.

Carver, Dean. 1986. "China's Experiment with Fiscal and Monetary Policy." In U.S. Congress 1986, vol. 2, 110–31.

Chang, Hsin. 1989. "Shortage, Repressed Inflation, and Distorted Growth: A General Disequilibrium Model of Centrally Planned Economies." Department of Economics, University of Ohio, Toledo.

————. 1984. "The 1982–83 Overinvestment Crisis in China." *Asian Survey* 24:1275–1301.

Chao, Kang. 1983. "Tenure Systems in Traditional China." *Economic Development and Cultural Change* 31:295–314.

————. 1980. "The China-Watchers Tested." *China Quarterly*, no. 81:97–104.

————. 1974. *Capital Formation in Mainland China, 1952–1965.* Berkeley: University of California Press.

Chen, Kang. 1990. "The Failure of Recentralization in China: Interplays Among Enterprises, Local Governments and the Center." In *Markets and Politics*, ed. Arye Hillman, 209–29. Boston: Kluwer Academic.

Chen, Kang, G.H. Jefferson, T.G. Rawski, H.C. Wang, and Y.X. Zheng. 1988. "New Estimates of Fixed Investment and Capital Stock for Chinese State Industry." *China Quarterly*, no. 114:243–66.

Chen, Kang, Gary H. Jefferson, and Inderjit Singh. 1992. "Lessons From China's Economic Reform." *Journal of Comparative Economics* 16:201–25.

————. 1988. "Productivity Change in Chinese Industry: 1953–1985." *Journal of Comparative Economics* 12:570–91.

Chen, Nai-Ruenn. 1967. *Chinese Economic Statistics: A Handbook for Mainland China.* Chicago: Aldine.

Chen, Nai-Ruenn, and Chi-ming Hou. 1986. "China's Inflation, 1979–1983: Measurement and Analysis." *Economic Development and Cultural Change* 34:811–35.

Cheng, Chu-yuan. 1982. *China's Economic Development: Growth and Structural Change.* Boulder, Colo.: Westview Press.

Chin, Rockwood Q.P. 1968. "The Validity of Mainland China's Cotton Textile Statistics." *Southern Economic Journal* 34:319–34.

Chinn, Dennis L. 1984. "Research Note: Basic Commodity Distribution in the People's Republic of China." *China Quarterly*, no. 84:744–54.

————. 1980. "Diligence and Laziness in Chinese Agricultural Production Teams." *Journal of Development Economics* 7:331–44.

————. 1979. "Team Cohesion and Collective-labor Supply in Chinese Agriculture." *Journal of Comparative Economics* 3:375–94.

Chow, Gregory C. 1987a. "Development of a More Market-Oriented Economy in China." *Science* 16 (January): 295–99.

————. 1987b. "Money and Price Level Determination in China." *Journal of Comparative Economics* 11:319–33.

————. 1986. "Chinese Statistics." *American Statistician* 40:191–96.

————. 1985a. *The Chinese Economy.* New York: Harper and Row.

————. 1985b. "A Model of Chinese National Income Determination." *Journal of Political Economy* 93:782–92.

Cremer, Jacques. 1982. "On the Efficiency of a Chinese-Type Work-Point System." *Journal of Comparative Economics* 6:343–52.

Crook, Frederick W. 1988. *Agricultural Statistics of the People's Republic of China, 1949–86.* U.S. Department of Agriculture, Economic Research Service, Statistical Bulletin No. 764 (April).

————. 1986. "The Reform of the Commune System and the Rise of the Township-Collective-Household System." In U.S. Congress 1986, vol. 1, 354–86.

Crook, Frederick W., and Francis C. Tuan, comps. *China's Agricultural Economy: News Notes for Economists,* three issues annually, China Section, Centrally Planned Economies Branch, Economic Research Service. Washington, D.C.

Denny, David L. 1991. "Regional Economic Differences During the Decade of Reform." In U.S. Congress 1991, 186–208.

Dernberger, Robert F. 1991. "China's Mixed Economic System." In U.S. Congress 1991, 89–101.

————. 1988. "Reforms in China: Implications for U.S. Policy." *American Economic Review, Papers and Proceedings* 79:21–25.

————. 1987. "The Drive for Economic Modernization and Growth: Performance and Trends." Paper presented at the International Conference on a Decade of Reform Under Deng Xiaoping, Brown University, 4–7 November.

————. 1986. "Economic Policy and Performance." In U.S. Congress 1986, vol. 1, 15–48.

————, ed. 1980. *China's Development in Comparative Perspectives.* Cambridge: Harvard University Press.

Dernberger, Robert F., and Richard S. Eckaus. 1988. *Financing Asian Development: China and India.* Lanham, Md.: Asia Society, University Press of America.

Dirlik, Arif, and Maurice Meisner, eds. 1989. *Marxism and the Chinese Experience: Issues in Chinese Socialism.* Armonk, N.Y.: M.E. Sharpe.

Dollar, David. 1990. "Economic Reform and Allocative Efficiency in China's State-owned Industry." *Economic Development and Cultural Change* 39:89–105.

Donnithorn, Audrey. 1976a. "China's Cellular Economy: Some Economic Trends Since the Cultural Revolution." *China Quarterly,* no. 66:605–19.

————. 1976b. "Comment on 'Centralization and Decentralization in China's Fiscal Management.'" *China Quarterly,* no. 66:328–40.

Eckstein, Alexander, ed. 1980. *Quantitative Measures of China's Economic Output.* Ann Arbor: University of Michigan Press.

————. 1977. *China's Economic Revolution.* Cambridge: Cambridge University Press.

————. 1976. *China's Economic Development: The Interplay of Scarcity and Ideology.* Ann Arbor: University of Michigan Press.

————. 1966. *Communist China's Economic Growth and Foreign Trade.* New York: McGraw-Hill.

————. 1961. *The National Income of Communist China.* New York: Free Press.

Emerson, John Philip. 1983. "Urban School-leavers and Unemployment in China." *China Quarterly,* no. 93:1–16.

Feder, Gerson, Lawrence J. Lau, Justin Y. Lin, and Luo Xiaopeng. 1989. "Agricultural Credit and Farm Performance in China." *Journal of Comparative Economics* 13:508–26.

Fei, John, and Bruce Reynolds. 1987. "A Tentative Plan for the Rational Sequencing of Overall Reform in China's Economic System." *Journal of Comparative Economics* 11:490–502.

Feltenstein, Andrew, and Jiming Ha. 1991. "Measurement of Repressed Inflation in China: The Lack of Coordination Between Monetary Policy and Price Controls." *Journal of Development Economics* 36:279–94.

Field, Robert Michael. 1988. "Trends in the Value of Agricultural Output, 1978–86." *China Quarterly,* no. 116:556–91.

————. 1986. "China: The Changing Structure of Industry." In U.S. Congress 1986, vol. 1, 505–47.

————. 1984. "Changes in Chinese Industry Since 1978." *China Quarterly,* no. 100:742–61.

————. 1983. "Slow Growth of Labour Productivity in Chinese Industry, 1952–81." *China Quarterly,* no. 96:641–65.

Field, Robert Michael, Nicholas R. Lardy, and Jon Philip Emerson. 1976. "Provincial Output in the People's Republic of China: 1949–75." Foreign Economic Report no. 12. Washington, D.C.: U.S. Department of Commerce (September).

————. 1975. "A Reconstruction of the Gross Value of Industrial Output by Province in the People's Republic of China: 1949–73." Foreign Economic Report no.7. Washington, D.C.: U.S. Department of Commerce (July).

Field, Robert Michael, and Helen Louise Noyes. 1981. "Prospects for Chinese Industry in 1981." *China Quarterly,* no. 85:96–106.

Fisher, William A. 1986a. "Chinese Industrial Management: Outlook for the Eighties." In U.S. Congress 1986, vol. 1, 548–70.

————. 1986b. "The Transfer of Managerial Knowledge to China." Office of Technology Assessment, Contract no. 633–1670.0 (May).

Fung, K.K. 1987. "Surplus Seeking and Rent Seeking through Back-Door Deals in Mainland China: Price Control and Central Planning Fix Prices Below Market Clearance, Creating a Contrived Surplus." *American Journal of Economics and Society* 46:299–317.

Galenson, Walter. 1967. "The Current State of Chinese Economic Studies." In U.S. Congress 1967, vol. 1, 3–13.

Goldstein, Steven. 1984. *China Briefing, 1984.* Boulder, Colo.: Westview Press and the Asia Society.

Gordon, Roger. 1988. "Perverse Incentives Faced by Local Governments in the People's Republic of China." Paper presented at the annual meeting of the American Economics Association, New York, December 27–30.

Gordon, Roger H., and Wei Li. 1990. "The Change in Productivity of Chinese State Enterprises, 1983–1987." University of Michigan, Ann Arbor.

Gottschang, Thomas R. 1987. "Economic Change, Disasters, and Migration: The Historical Case of Manchuria." *Economic Development and Cultural Change* 35:461–90.

Granick, David. 1990. *Chinese State Enterprises: A Regional Property Rights Analysis.* Chicago: University of Chicago Press.

————. 1987. "The Industrial Environment in China and the CMEA Countries." In Tidrick and Chen 1987, 103–31.

Griffin, Keith. 1984. *Institutional Reform and Economic Development in the Chinese Countryside.* Armonk, N.Y.: M.E. Sharpe.

Grow, Roy F. 1987. "Reconsidering the China Market: Guidelines for Success." *Euro-Asia Business Review* 6:9–14.

———. 1986. "Japanese and American Firms in China: Lessons of a New Market." *Columbia Journal of World Business* 21:5–25.

Grub, Phillip D., and Jian Hai Lin. 1988. "Foreign Investment in China: Myths and Realities." *Journal of Economic Development* 13:17–40.

Grub, Phillip D., and B.L. Sudweeks. 1988. "Securities Markets and the People's Republic of China." *Journal of Economic Development* 13:51–69.

Gurley, John G. 1979. "Rural Development in China 1949–75, and the Lessons to be Learned from It." In *China's Road to Development,* 2d ed., ed. Neville Maxwell, 5–26. Oxford: Pergamon Press.

Halpern, Nina. 1985. "China's Industrial Economic Reforms: The Question of Strategy." *Asian Survey* 25:998–1112.

Hare, Dennis. 1991. "Rural Non-Agricultural Activities and Their Impact on the Distribution of Income: Evidence from Farm Households in Southern China." Discussion draft. Reed College, Portland, Oreg.

Hewett, Ed A. 1989. "Economic Reform in the USSR, Eastern Europe, and China: The Politics of Reform." *American Economic Review* 79:21–25.

Hollister, William W. 1967. "Trends in Capital Formation in Communist China." In U.S. Congress 1967, 122–53.

Holton, Richard H., and Terry Sicular. 1991. "Economic Reform of the Distribution Sector in China." *American Economic Review,* Papers and Proceedings 82:212–17.

Hsiao, Katharine H.Y. Huang. 1987. *The Government Budget and Fiscal Policy in Mainland China.* Taipei: Chung-hua Institution for Economic Research.

———. 1984. *Money and Banking in the Chinese Mainland.* Seattle: University of Washington Press.

Hsiung Bingyuan and Louis Putterman. 1989. "Pre- and Post-Reform Income Distribution in a Chinese Commune: The Case of Dahe Township in Hebei Province." *Journal of Comparative Economics* 13.

Hsu, Robert C. 1984. "Grain Procurement and Distribution in China's Rural Areas: Post-Mao Policies and Problems." *Asian Survey* 24:1229–46.

———. 1982. "Agricultural Financial Policies in China." *Asian Survey* 22:638–58.

Hu, Teh-wei, Ming Li, and Shuzhong Shi. 1988. "Analysis of Wages and Bonus Payments Among Tianjin Urban Workers." *China Quarterly,* no. 113:77–93.

Jefferson, Gary H. 1991a. "Urban and Rural Chinese Industry: A Preliminary Investigation of the Dispersion of Inter-and Intra-Regional Factor Returns." In *China's Economic Reforms,* ed. M.J. Dutta and Z.L. Zhang, 93–109. American Committee on Asian Economic Studies monograph series. Greenwich, Conn.: JAI Press.

———. 1991b. "Decomposing Sources of Changes in the Dispersion of Factor Returns: An Evaluation of Chinese Industry." Research Paper Series, no. 3. Washington, D.C.: World Bank.

———. 1990. "China's Iron and Steel Industry: Sources of Enterprise Efficiency and the Impact of Reform." *Journal of Development Economics* 33:329–55.

———. 1989. "Potential Sources of Productivity Growth within Chinese Industry." *World Development* 17:45–57.

———. 1988. "A Decade of Chinese Reform: Pitfalls and Lessons in Evaluating Industrial Productivity." Paper presented at the annual meeting of the American Economic Association, New York, December 27–30.

Jefferson, Gary H., and Thomas G. Rawski. 1992. "Unemployment, Underemployment, and Employment Policy in China's Cities." *Modern China* 18:42–71.

———. 1991. "A Theory of Economic Reform." Working Paper no. 245. Department of Economics, Brandeis University, Waltham, Mass.

Jefferson, Gary H., Thomas Rawski, and Y.X. Zheng. 1992. "Growth, Efficiency and Convergence in Chinese Industry: A Comparative Evaluation of the State and Collective Sectors." *Economic Development and Cultural Change* 40:239–65.

Jefferson, Gary H., and Xu Wenyi. 1991a. "The Impact of Reforms on Social Enterprises in Transition: Structure, Conduct and Performance in Chinese Industry." *Journal of Comparative Economics* 15:45–64.

———. 1991b. "Assessing Gains in Efficient Production Among China's Industrial Enterprises." Research Paper Series, no. 4. Socialist Economies Unit, Country Economics Department, World Bank.

———. 1988. "China's State and Collective-Owned Industry in Comparative Perspective: 1953–1987." Working Paper no. 200, Department of Economics, Brandeis University, Waltham, Mass.

Johnson, D. Gale. 1990. *The People's Republic of China: 1978–1990.* San Francisco: ICS Press.

———. 1988. "Economic Reforms in the People's Republic of China." *Economic Development and Cultural Change* 36 Supplement:S225–45.

———. 1982. *Progress of Economic Reform in the People's Republic of China.* Washington, D.C.: American Enterprise Institute.

Joseph, William, Christine Wong, and David Zweig, eds. 1991. *New Perspectives on the Cultural Revolution.* Cambridge: Harvard University Press and the Council on East Asian Studies.

Kamath, Shyam J. 1990. "Foreign Direct Investment in a Centrally Planned Developing Economy: The Chinese Case." *Economic Development and Cultural Change* 39:107–30.

Kane, Anthony J., ed. 1988. *China Briefing, 1988.* Boulder, Colo.: Westview Press and the Asia Society.

Keidel, Albert, III. 1991. "The Cyclical Future of China's Economic Reforms." In U.S. Congress 1991, 119–34.

———. 1986. "China's Coal Industry." In U.S. Congress 1986, vol. 2, 60–86.

Koo, Anthony Y.C. 1990. "The Contract Responsibility System: Transition from a Planned to a Market Economy." *Economic Development and Cultural Change* 38:797–820.

Kornai, Janos. 1989. "Some Lessons from the Hungarian Experience for Chinese Reformers: A Comment." In Van Ness 1989, 75–106.

Kornai, Janos, and Z. Daniel. 1986. "The Chinese Economic Reforms as Seen by Hungarian Economists." *Acta Oeconomica* 36:289–305.

Kravis, Irving B. 1981. "An Approximation of the Relative Real per Capita GDP of the People's Republic of China." *Journal of Comparative Economics* 5:60–78.

Kueh, Y.Y. 1984. "China's New Agricultural Policy Program: Major Economic Consequences, 1979–1983." *Journal of Comparative Economics* 8:353–75.

———. 1983. "Economic Reform in China at the 'Xian' Level." *China Quarterly,* no. 96:665–88.

Kung, James Kaisung. 1992. "Food and Agriculture in Post-Reform China: The Marketed Surplus Problem Revisited." *Modern China* 18:138–70.

Lardy, Nicholas R. 1992. *Foreign Trade and Economic Reform in China, 1978–1990.* New York: Cambridge University Press.

———. 1990. *China's Interprovincial Grain Marketing and Import Demand.* U.S.D.A. Economic Research Service, Agriculture and Trade Analysis Division, Staff Report no. AGES 9059. Washington, D.C.: GPO.

————. 1987a. *China's Entry into the World Economy: Implications for Northeast Asia and the United States.* Lanham, Md.: University Press of America.

————. 1987b. "The Chinese Economy Under Stress, 1958–1965." In MacFarquhar and Fairbank 1987, Vol. 14, 360–97.

————. 1987c. "Economic Recovery in the First Five Year Plan." In MacFarquhar and Fairbank, 1987, Vol. 14, 144–84.

————. 1987d. "Technical Change and Economic Reform in China: A Tale of Two Sectors." Jackson School of International Studies, University of Washington, Seattle.

————. 1986a. "Overview: Agricultural Reform and the Rural Economy." U.S. Congress 1986, vol. 1, 325–35.

————. 1986b. "Prospects and Some Policy Problems of Agricultural Development in China." *American Journal of Agricultural Economics* 68:451–57.

————. 1984. "Consumption and Living Standards in China, 1978–83." *China Quarterly,* no. 100:849–65.

————. 1983a. *Agriculture in China's Modern Economic Development.* Cambridge: Cambridge University Press.

————. 1983b. "Agricultural Prices in China." World Bank Staff Working Paper no. 606. Washington, D.C.: World Bank.

————. 1978. *Economic Growth and Distribution in China.* New York: Cambridge University Press.

————. 1976. "Reply." *China Quarterly,* no. 66:340–54.

————. 1975. "Centralization and Decentralization in China's Fiscal Management." *China Quarterly,* no. 61:25–60.

Lavely, W.R. 1984. "The Rural Chinese Fertility Transition: A Report from Shifang Xian, Sichuan." *Population Studies* 38:365–84.

Lee, Keun. 1990. "The Chinese Model of the Socialist Enterprise: An Assessment of Its Organization and Performance." *Journal of Comparative Economics* 14:384–400.

Le Gall, Françoise. 1986. "An Analysis of Price Dynamics in China, 1952–1982." Ph.D. diss., University of Michigan, Ann Arbor.

Lewik, Jim. 1986. "China's Electric Power Industry." In U.S. Congress 1986, vol. 2, 104–22.

Lin, Justin Yifu. 1991. "Public Research Resource Allocation in Chinese Agriculture: A Test of Induced Technological Innovation Hypothesis." *Economic Development and Cultural Change* 40:55–73.

————. 1988. "The Household Responsibility System in China's Agricultural Reform: A Theoretical and Empirical Study." *Economic Development and Cultural Change* 36 Supplement:S199–S224.

————. 1987. "The Household Responsibility System Reform in China: A Peasant's Institutional Choice." *American Journal of Agricultural Economics* 69:410–15.

————. 1985. "Supervision, the Household Responsibility System, and Agricultural Reform in China." Ph.D. diss., University of Chicago.

Lippit, Victor. 1987. *The Economic Development of China.* Armonk, N.Y.: M.E. Sharpe.

Lippit, Victor, and Mark Selden, eds. 1982. *The Transition to Socialism in China.* Armonk, N.Y.: M.E. Sharpe.

Liu, Ta-chung, and Kung-chia Yeh. 1965. *The Economy of the Chinese Mainland: National Income and Economic Development, 1933–1959.* Princeton: Princeton University Press.

Liu, Yia-Ling. 1992. "Reform From Below: The Private Economy and Local Politics in the Rural Industrialization of Wenzhou." *China Quarterly,* no. 130:293–316.

Lyons, Thomas P. 1992. "Grain in Fujian: Intra-Provincial Patterns of Production and Trade, 1952–1988." *China Quarterly,* no. 129:184–215.

————. 1991. "Interprovincial Disparities in China: Output and Consumption, 1952–1987." *Economic Development and Cultural Change* 39:471–506.

————. 1990. "Planning and Interprovincial Coordination in Maoist China." *China Quarterly*, no. 121:36–60.

————. 1988. "Concentration and Specialization in Chinese Agriculture, 1979–1985." *Journal of Developing Areas* 22:437–56.

————. 1987a. *Economic Integration and Planning in Maoist China.* New York: Columbia University Press.

————. 1987b. "Interprovincial Trade and Development in China, 1957–1979." *Economic Development and Cultural Change* 35:223–56.

————. 1987c. "Spatial Aspects of Development in China: The Motor Vehicle Industry, 1956–1985." *International Regional Science Review* 11:75–96.

————. 1986. "Explaining Economic Fragmentation in China: A Systems Approach." *Journal of Comparative Economics* 10:209–36.

————. 1985. "China's Cellular Economy: A Test of the Fragmentation Hypothesis." *Journal of Comparative Economics* 9:125–44.

Lyons, Thomas P., and Wang Yan. 1988. "Planning and Finance in China's Economic Reforms." Cornell University East Asian Papers no. 46.

MacFarquhar, Roderick, and John King Fairbank, eds. 1991, 1987. *The Cambridge History of China*, vols. 14–15. Cambridge: Cambridge University Press.

McMillan, John, John Whalley, and Zhu Lijing. 1989. "The Impact of China's Economic Reforms on Agricultural Productivity Growth." *Journal of Political Economy* 97:781–807.

Major, John S., ed. 1986. *China Briefing, 1985.* Boulder, Colo,: Westview Press and the Asia Society.

Major, John S., and Anthony J. Kane, eds. 1987. *China Briefing, 1987.* Boulder, Colo.: Westview Press and the Asia Society.

Malenbaum, Wilfred. 1990. "A Gloomy Portrayal of Development Achievements and Prospects: China and India: Review Article." *Economic Development and Cultural Change* 38:391–406.

————. 1985. "Modern Economic Growth in India and China: Reply." *Economic Development and Cultural Change* 34:161–66.

————. 1982. "Modern Economic Growth in India and China: The Comparison Revisited, 1950–1980." *Economic Development and Cultural Change* 31:45–84.

Melvin, Michael, and Zhou Su. 1989. "Do Centrally Planned Exchange Rates Behave Differently from Capitalist Rates?" *Journal of Comparative Economics* 13:325–34.

Michael, Franz, Carl Linden, Jan Prybyla, and Jurgen Domes. 1990. *China and the Crisis of Marxism-Leninism.* Boulder, Colo.: Westview Press.

Myers, Ramon H. 1991. *Two Societies in Opposition: The Republic of China and the People's Republic of China after Forty Years.* Stanford: Hoover Institution Press.

————. 1988. "Review Article: Land and Labor in China." *Economic Development and Cultural Change* 36:797–806.

————. 1980. *The Chinese Economy Past and Present.* Belmont, Calif.: Wadsworth.

Myers, Ramon H., and Barbara Sands. 1986. "The Spatial Approach to Chinese History." *Journal of Asian Studies* 45:721–43.

Naughton, Barry. 1992. "Implications of the State Monopoly over Industry and Its Relaxation." *Modern China* 18:14–41.

————. 1991a. "Hierarchy and the Bargaining Economy: Government and Enterprise in the Reform Period." In *Bureaucratic Politics and Decision-making in Post-Mao China*, ed. David Lampton and Kenneth Lieberthal, 245–79. Berkeley: University of California Press.

————. 1991b. "Industrial Policy During the Cultural Revolution: Military Preparation,

Decentralization, and Leaps Forward." In Joseph et al. 1991, 153–81.

———. 1991c. "Inflation: Patterns, Causes, and Cures." In U.S. Congress 1991, 135–59.

———. 1991d. "The Pattern and Legacy of Economic Growth in the Mao Era." In *Perspectives on Modern China: Four Anniversaries.* Ed. Joyce Kalgren, Kenneth Lieberthal, Roderick MacFarquhar, and Frederick Wakeman. Armonk, N.Y.: M.E. Sharpe.

———. 1991e. "Why Has Economic Reform Led to Inflation?" *American Economic Review, Papers and Proceedings* 81:207–11.

———. 1990a. "China's Experience with Guidance Planning." *Journal of Comparative Economics* 14:743–67.

———. 1990b. "Economic Reform and the Chinese Political Crisis of 1989." *Journal of Asian Economics,* no. 2:349–61.

———. 1988a. "Large and Small Enterprises in China's Reforms." Paper presented at the annual meeting of the American Economic Association, New York, December 27–30.

———. 1988b. "The Third Front: Defence Industrialization in the Chinese Interior." *China Quarterly,* no. 115:351–86.

———. 1987a. "The Decline of Central Control over Investment in Post-Mao China." In *Policy Implementation in Post-Mao China,* ed. David M. Lampton, Studies in China 7. Berkeley: University of California Press.

———. 1987b. "Macroeconomic Policy and Response in the Chinese Economy: The Impact of the Reform Process." *Journal of Comparative Economics* 11:334–53.

———. 1986a. "Finance and Planning Reforms in Industry." In U.S. Congress 1986, vol. 1, 604–29.

———. 1986b. "Saving and Investment in China: A Macroeconomic Analysis." Ph.D. diss., Yale University.

———. 1985. "False Starts and Second Wind: Financial Reforms in China's Industrial System." In Perry and Wong 1985, 223–52.

Nee, Victor, and Frank W. Young. 1991. "Peasant Entrepreneurs in China's 'Second Economy': An Institutional Analysis." *Economic Development and Cultural Change* 39:293–310.

Noyes, Helen Louise. 1986. "United States-China Trade." In U.S. Congress 1986, vol. 2, 335–47.

Orleans, Leo A., and Lynne Burnham. 1984. "The Enigma of China's Urban Population." *Asian Survey* 14:788–804.

Pannell, Clifton W. 1988. "Regional Shifts in China's Industrial Output." *Professional Geographer* 40:19–32.

———. 1987–88. "Economic Reforms and Readjustment in the People's Republic of China and Some Geographic Consequences." *Studies in Comparative International Development* 22:54–73.

———. 1986. "Recent Increase in Chinese Urbanization." *Urban Geography* 7:291–310.

———. 1985. "Recent Chinese Agriculture." *Geographical Review* 75:170–85.

———. 1981. "Recent Growth and Change in China's Urban System." In *Urban Development in Modern China,* ed. Laurence J.C. Ma and Edward Hanten, 91–113. Boulder, Colo.: Westview Press.

———. 1980. "Geography." In *Science in Contemporary China,* ed. Leo Orleans, 567–86. Stanford: Stanford University Press.

Pannell, Clifton W., and Laurence J.C. Ma. 1983. *China: The Geography of Development and Modernization.* London: V.H. Winston and Sons.

Pannell, Clifton W., and R. Welch. 1980. "Recent Growth and Structural Change in Chinese Cities." *Urban Geography* 1:68–80.

Pearson, Margaret M. 1991. *Joint Ventures in the People's Republic of China: The Control of Foreign Direct Investment under Socialism.* Princeton: Princeton University Press.

Pegels, C. Carl, ed. 1987. *Management and Industry in China.* New York: Praeger.

Perkins, Dwight Heald. 1991. "Price Reform vs. Enterprise Autonomy. Which Should Have Priority?" In U.S. Congress 1991, 160–69.

———. 1988. "Reforming China's Economic System." *Journal of Economic Literature* 26:601–45.

———. 1986. *China: Asia's Next Economic Giant?* Seattle: University of Washington Press.

———. 1983. "Research on the Economy of the People's Republic of China: A Survey of the Field." *Journal of Asian Studies* 42:345–72.

———, ed. 1975. *China's Modern Economy in Historical Perspective.* Stanford: Stanford University Press.

———. 1969. *Agricultural Development in China, 1368–1968.* Chicago: Aldine.

———. 1966. *Market Control and Planning in Communist China.* Cambridge: Harvard University Press.

Perkins, Dwight, and Moshe Syrquin. 1988–89. "The Development of Large Countries: The Influence of Size." In *Handbook of Development Economics,* ed. Hollis Burnley Chenery and T.N. Srinivasan. Amsterdam and New York: North Holland.

Perkins, Dwight, and Shahid Yusuf. 1984. *Rural Development in China.* Baltimore: Johns Hopkins University Press.

Perry, Elizabeth, and Christine Wong, eds. 1985. *The Political Economy of Reform in Post-Mao China.* Cambridge: Harvard University Press.

Polenske, Karen R., and Xikang Chen. 1991. *Chinese Economic Planning and Input-Output Analysis.* New York: Oxford University Press.

Portes, Richard, and Anita Santorum. 1987. "Money and the Consumption Goods Market in China." *Journal of Comparative Economics* 11:354–71.

Prime, Penelope B. 1992a. "Industry's Response to Market Liberalization in China: Evidence from Jiangsu Province." *Economic Development and Cultural Change* 41:27–50.

———. 1992b. "China's Fiscal Reform: A Cross-Provincial Analysis." Research Paper no. 24. Policy Research Center, Georgia State University, Atlanta.

———. 1991a. "Central-Provincial Investment and Finance: The Cultural Revolution and its Legacy in Jiangsu Province." In Joseph et al. 1991, 197–215.

———. 1991b. "The Spatial Implications for China's Economic Reforms, 1978 to 1988." In Veeck, ed. 1991.

———. 1991c. "Taxation Reform in China's Public Finance." In U.S. Congress 1991, 167–85.

———. 1987. "The Impact of Self-Sufficiency on Regional Industrial Growth and Productivity in post-1949 China: The Case of Jiangsu Province." Ph.D. diss., University of Michigan, Ann Arbor.

———. 1986. "A Comparison of Female Employment Patterns in Chinese Development Strategies: The Cases of Taiwan and Mainland China." Paper presented at the annual meeting of the American Economics Association, New Orleans, December 28–30.

Prybyla, Jan S. 1991. "A Systemic Analysis of Prospects for China's Economy." In U.S. Congress 1991, 209–25.

———. 1990. *Reform in China and Other Socialist Economies.* Washington, D.C.: American Enterprise Institute.

———. 1985. "The Chinese Economy: Adjustment of the System or Systemic Reform?" *Asian Survey* 25:553–86.

————. 1984. "China's Special Economic Zones." *ACES Bulletin* 26:1–24.

————. 1982. "Economic Problems of Communism: A Case Study of China." *Asian Survey* 22:1206–37.

————. 1981a. *The Chinese Economy: Problems and Policies.* 2d ed. Columbia: University of South Carolina Press.

————. 1981b. "Key Issues in the Chinese Economy." *Asian Survey* 21:925–46.

————. 1970. *The Political Economy of Communist China.* Scranton, Penn.: International Textbook Company.

Putterman, Louis. 1992. "Dualism and Reform in China." *Economic Development and Cultural Change* 40:467–94.

————. 1990. "Effort, Productivity, and Incentives in a 1970s Chinese People's Commune." *Journal of Comparative Economics* 14:88–104.

————. 1989. "Entering the Post-Collective Era in North China: Dahe Township." *Modern China* 15:275–320.

————. 1988a. "Group Farming and Work Incentives in Collective Era China." *Modern China* 14:419–50.

————. 1988b. "People's Republic of China: Systemic and Structural Change in a North China Township." *American Journal of Agricultural Economics* 70:423–30.

————. 1988c. "Ration Subsidies and Incentives in the Pre-Reform Chinese Commune. *Economica* 55:235–47.

————. 1987. "The Incentive Problem and the Demise of Team Farming in China. *Journal of Development Economics* 26:103–27.

————. 1985a. "Extrinsic versus Intrinsic Problems of Agricultural Cooperation: Anti-Incentivism in Tanzania and China." *Journal of Development Studies* 21:175–204.

————. 1985b. "The Restoration of the Peasant Household as Farm Production Unit in China: Some Incentive Theoretic Analysis." In Perry and Wong 1985, 63–82.

————. 1980. "Voluntary Collectivization: A Model of Producers' Institutional Choice." *Journal of Comparative Economics* 4:125–57.

Rada, Edward L. 1983. "Food Policy in China: Recent Efforts to Balance Supplies and Consumption Requirements." *Asian Survey* 23:518–35.

Raichur, Satish. 1981. "Economic 'Laws,' the Law of Value, and Chinese Socialism." Australian Economic Papers Series (December): 205–18. Adelaide: University of Adelaide and Flanders University of South Australia.

Rawski, Thomas G. 1992. "Progress Without Privatization: The Reform of China's State Industries." Working Paper no. 281. University of Pittsburgh, Pittsburgh.

————. 1991. "How Fast Has Chinese Industry Grown?" Research Paper Series No. 7. Washington, D.C.: World Bank.

————. 1989. *Economic Growth in Prewar China.* Berkeley: University of California Press.

————. 1986. "Overview: Industry and Transport." In U.S. Congress 1986, vol. 1, 497–504.

————. 1983. "New Sources for Studying China's Economy." *Journal of Economic History* 43:997–1002.

————. 1982a. "Agricultural Employment and Technology." In *The Chinese Agricultural Economy,* ed. Randolph Barker, Radha Sinha, and Beth Rose, 121–36. Boulder, Colo.: Westview Press.

————. 1982b. "The Simple Arithmetic of Chinese Income Distribution." *Jingji Yanjiu* [Economic Research] 33, no. 1:12–26.

————. 1980. *China's Transition to Industrialism: Producer Goods and Economic Development in the Twentieth Century.* Ann Arbor: University of Michigan Press.

Rehn, Detlef, and Denis Fred Simon. 1988. *Technological Innovation in China: The Case of the Shanghai Semiconductor Industry.* Cambridge, Mass.: Ballinger.

Reynolds, Bruce L., ed. 1988. *Chinese Economic Reform: How Far, How Fast?* San Diego, Calif.: Harcourt Brace Jovanovich, Academic Press.

―――, ed. 1987a. *Reform in China: Challenges and Choices.* Armonk, N.Y.: M.E. Sharpe.

―――. 1987b. "Trade, Employment, and Inequity in Post-Reform China." *Journal of Comparative Economics* 11:479–89.

―――. 1985. "China in the World Economy." In *International Relations in the 1980s,* ed. John Hardt, 71–106. New Haven: Yale University Press.

―――. 1983. "Economic Reforms and External Imbalance in China, 1978–81." *American Economic Review* 73:325–28.

―――. 1982. "Reform in Chinese Industrial Management." In U.S. Congress 1982, part 1, 119–37.

Reynolds, Paul D. 1982. *China's International Banking and Financial System.* New York: Praeger Publishers.

Richman, Barry M. 1969. *Industrial Society in Communist China.* New York: Random House.

Riskin, Carl. 1991. "Neither Plan nor Market: Mao's Political Economy." In Joseph et al. 1991, 133–52.

―――. 1987. *China's Political Economy: The Quest for Development Since 1949.* Oxford: Oxford University Press.

―――. 1978. "Political Conflict and Rural Industrialization in China." *World Development* 6:681–92.

Rosen, George. 1990a. "India and China: Contrasting Industrial Reform Styles." Occasional Paper no. 36, Asia Program, Woodrow Wilson International Center for Scholars, Washington, D.C.

―――. 1990b. "India and China: Perspectives on Contrasting Styles of Economic Reform." *Journal of Asian Economics* 1:273–90.

Rothenberg, Jerome. 1987. "Space, Interregional Economic Relations, and Structural Reform in China." *International Regional Science Review* 11:5–22.

Schmidt, Marlis. 1987. *Economic Reforms in the People's Republic of China Since 1979: A Bibliography of Articles and Publications in English-Language Magazines and Newspapers.* Locust Hill.

Sicular, Terry. 1990. "Ten Years of Reform: Progress and Setbacks in China's Agricultural Planning and Pricing." Harvard Institute for Economic Research Discussion Paper no. 1474 (March).

―――. 1989. *Food Price Policy in Asia: A Comparative Study.* Ithaca: Cornell University Press.

―――. 1988a. "Agricultural Planning and Pricing in the Post-Mao Period." *China Quarterly,* no. 116:671–705.

―――. 1988b. "Grain Pricing: A Key Link in Chinese Economic Policy." *Modern China* 14:451–86.

―――. 1988c. "Plan and Market in China's Agricultural Commerce." *Journal of Political Economy* 96:283–307.

―――. 1986a. "Agricultural Planning in China: The Case of Lee Willow Team No. 4." *Food Research Institute Studies* 20:1–24.

―――. 1986b. "Recent Agricultural Price Policies and Their Effects: The Case of Shandong." In U.S. Congress 1986, vol. 1, 407–30.

―――. 1986c. "Using a Farm-Household Model to Analyze Labor Allocation on a Chinese Collective Farm." In *Agricultural Household Models: Extensions, Applications, and Policy,* ed. Inderjit Singh, Lyn Squire, and John Strauss, 277–305. Baltimore: Johns Hopkins University Press.

————. 1985a. "China's Grain and Meat Economy: Recent Developments and Implications for Trade." *American Journal of Agricultural Economics* (December), 1063–66.

————. 1985b. "Rural Marketing and Exchange in the Wake of Recent Reforms." In Perry and Wong 1985, 83–110.

————. 1983. "Market Restrictions in Chinese Agriculture: A Microeconomic Analysis." Ph.D. diss., Yale University.

Simon, Denis Fred. 1986a. "The Challenge of Modernizing Industrial Technology in China: Implications for Sino-U.S. Relations." *Asian Survey* 26:420–39.

————. 1986b. "China's Evolving Computer Industry: The Role of Foreign Technology Transfers." Washington, D.C.: Office of Technology Assessment.

————. 1986c. "The Evolving Role of Technology Transfer in China's Modernization." In U.S. Congress 1986, vol. 1, 254–86.

Srinivasan, T.N. 1990. "External Sector in Development: China and India, 1950–89." *American Economic Review, Papers and Proceedings* 80:113–17.

————. 1987. "Economic Liberalization in China and India: Issues and an Analytical Framework." *Journal of Comparative Economics* 11:427–43.

Stepanek, James B. 1991. "China's Enduring State Factories: Why Ten Years of Reform Has Left China's Big State Factories Unchanged." In U.S. Congress 1991, 440–54.

Stone, Bruce. 1988. "Developments in Agricultural Technology." *China Quarterly*, no. 116:767–822.

————. 1986. "Chinese Fertilizer Application in the 1980s and 1990s: Issues of Growth, Balance, Allocation, Efficiency, and Response." In U.S. Congress 1986, vol. 1, 453–96.

————. 1984. "An Analysis of Chinese Data on Root and Tuber Crop Production." *China Quarterly*, no. 99:594–630.

Stone, Bruce, and Tong Zhong. 1989. "Changing Patterns of Variability in Chinese Cereal Production." In *Variability in Grain Yields: Implications for Agricultural Research and Policy in Developing Countries*, ed. J.R. Anderson and P.B.R. Hazell, 35–59. Baltimore: Johns Hopkins University Press.

Surls, Frederic M. 1986. "China's Agriculture in the Eighties." In U.S. Congress 1986, vol. 1, 336–53.

————. 1984. "Agricultural Policy and Growth." *China Quarterly*, no. 100:866–69.

Svejnar, Jan. 1990. "Productive Efficiency and Employment." In Byrd and Lin 1990, 243–54.

Svejnar, Jan, and Stephen C. Smith. 1982. "The Economics of Joint Ventures in Centrally Planned and Labor-Managed Economies." *Journal of Comparative Economics* 6:148–72.

Szuprowicz, Bohdan O., and Maria R. Szuprowicz. 1978. *Doing Business with the People's Republic of China*. New York: John Wiley and Sons.

Tao, Bei, and Richard H. Holton. 1989. "Interprovincial Trade and Economic Development in China." *China Economic Review* 1:23–32.

Taylor, Jeffrey R. 1989. "Trade Reform and Efficiency of Resource Use in China." Ph.D. diss., University of Michigan, Ann Arbor.

————. 1988. "Rural Employment Trends and the Legacy of Surplus Labour, 1978–86." *China Quarterly*, no. 116:736–66.

————. 1987. *China: Consumer Demand Statistical Update*. U.S. Census Bureau Center for International Research Staff Paper. Washington, D.C.

————. 1986a. *China's Price Structure in International Perspective*. U.S. Census Bureau Center for International Research Staff Paper. Washington, D.C.

————. 1986b. *Employment Outlook for China to the Year 2000*. U.S. Census Bureau Center for International Research Staff Paper. Washington, D.C.

————. 1986c. "Labor Force Developments in the People's Republic of China, 1952–

83." In U.S. Congress 1986, vol. 1, 222–62.

—————. 1985. *Occupation and Employment in China: Results from the Ten Percent Sample Tabulation of China's 1982 Population Census*. U.S. Census Bureau Foreign Economic Report. Washington, D.C.

—————. 1984. *Input-Output Tables for the People's Republic of China, 1956 and 1980*. U.S. Census Bureau Center for International Research Staff Paper. Washington, D.C.

—————. 1983. "Reestimation of Gross Value of Industrial Output by Branch of Production for the People's Republic of China,1952–1957." U.S. Census Bureau Center for International Research Staff Paper. Washington, D.C.

Taylor, Jeffrey R., and Judith Banister. 1989a. "Statistical Reliability in China." Paper presented at the annual meeting of the American Statistical Association.

—————. 1989b. *China: The Problem of Employing Surplus Rural Labor*. U.S. Census Bureau Center for International Research Staff Paper. Washington, D.C.

Taylor, Jeffrey R., and Karen Hardee. 1986. *Consumer Demand in China*. Boulder, Colo.: Westview Press.

Theil, Henri, and James L. Seale, Jr. 1987. "A Regional Analysis of Food Consumption in China." *Empirical Economics* 12:129–35.

Tidrick, Gene. 1987. "Planning and Supply." In Tidrick and Chen 1987, 175–209.

—————. 1986. "Productivity Growth and Technological Change in Chinese Industry." World Bank Staff Working Paper no. 761. Washington, D.C.: World Bank.

Tidrick, Gene, and Chen Jiyuan, eds. 1987. *China's Industrial Reform*. New York: Oxford University Press.

Tong, James. 1991. "Central-Provincial Fiscal Relations in Post-Mao China: A Principle-Agent Analysis." University of California, Los Angeles.

—————. 1989. "Fiscal Reform, Elite Turnover, and Central-Provincial Relations in Post-Mao China." *Australian Journal of Chinese Affairs* 22:1–28.

Travers, Lee. 1986. "Peasant Non-Agricultural Production in the People's Republic of China." In U.S. Congress 1986, vol. 1, 376–86.

—————. 1985. "Getting Rich through Diligence: Peasant Income after the Reforms." In Perry and Wong 1985, 111–30.

—————. 1984. "Post-1978 Rural Economic Policy and Peasant Income in China." *China Quarterly*, no. 98:241–59.

Tsao, James T.H. 1987. *China's Development Strategies and Foreign Trade*. Lexington, Mass.: D.C. Heath.

Tung, Rosalie L. 1982. *Chinese Industrial Society after Mao*. Lexington, Mass.: Lexington Books.

—————. 1980. *Management Practices in China*. New York: Pergamon Press.

U.S. Congress. Joint Economic Committee. 1991. *China's Economic Dilemmas in the 1990s: The Problems of Reforms, Modernization, and Interdependence*. 2 vols. Washington, D.C.: Government Printing Office.

—————. 1986. *China's Economy Looks Toward the Year 2000; Vol. 1: The Four Modernizations; Vol. 2: Economic Openness in Modernizing China*. Washington, D.C.: Government Printing Office.

—————. 1982. *China Under the Four Modernizations*. Washington, D.C.: Government Printing Office.

—————. 1967. *An Economic Profile of Mainland China*. Washington, D.C.: Government Printing Office.

Van Ness, Peter, ed. 1989. *Market Reforms in Socialist Societies: Comparing China and Hungary*. Boulder, Colo.: Lynne Rienner.

Veeck, Gregory, ed. 1991. *The Uneven Landscape: Geographic Studies in Post-Reform China*. Baton Rouge: Louisiana State University, Geoscience Publications.

Veeck, Gregory, and Clifton W. Pannell. 1989. "Rural Economic Restructuring and Farm Household Income in Jiangsu, People's Republic of China." Association of American Geographers, *Annals* 79:275–92.

Waelbroeck, Jean L., ed. 1976. *The Models of Project Link.* Amsterdam: North-Holland Publishing Co.

Walder, Andrew G. 1989. "Factory and Manager in an Era of Reform." *China Quarterly,* no. 118:242–64.

———. 1986a. *Communist Neo-traditionalism: Work and Authority in Chinese Industry.* Berkeley: University of California Press.

———. 1986b. "The Informal Dimension of Enterprise Financial Reforms." In U.S. Congress 1986, vol. 2, 630–45.

Walker, Kenneth R. 1989. "Forty Years On: Provincial Contrasts in China's Rural Economic Development." *China Quarterly,* no. 119:448–80.

———. 1984a. "Chinese Agriculture During the Period of the Readjustment, 1978–83." *China Quarterly,* no. 84:783–812.

———. 1984b. *Food Grain Procurement and Consumption in China.* Cambridge and New York: Cambridge University Press.

Wiemer, Calla. 1992. "Price Reform and Structural Change: Distribution Impediments to Allocative Gains." *Modern China* 18:171–96.

Wiemer, Calla, and Liu Xiaoxun. 1989. "Price Reform in China: The Transition to Rationality." In *China's Economic Revolution,* ed. M. Jan Dutta and Zhang Zhongli. Greenwich, Conn.: JAI Press.

Wiens, Thomas B. 1987. "Issues in the Structural Reform of Chinese Agriculture." *Journal of Comparative Economics* 11:372–84.

———. 1985. "Agriculture in the Soviet Union and China: Implications for Trade: Discussion." *American Journal of Agricultural Economics* (December), 1063–66.

———. 1983. "Price Adjustment, the Responsibility System, and Agricultural Productivity." *American Economic Review, Papers and Proceedings* 73:319–24.

———. 1982a. "The Limits to Agricultural Intensification: The Suzhou Experience." In U.S. Congress 1982, 462–74.

———. 1982b. *The Microeconomies of Peasant Economy: China, 1920–40.* New York: Garland.

———. 1982c. "Technological Change." In *The Chinese Agricultural Economy,* ed. R. Barker and R. Sinha, 99–120. Boulder, Colo.: Westview Press.

———. 1981. "Agriculture in the Four Modernizations." *China Geographer* no. 11:57–72.

Wong, Christine P.W. 1992. "Fiscal Reform and Local Industrialization: The Problematic Sequencing of Reform in Post-Mao China." *Modern China* 18:197–227.

———. 1991. "Maoism and Development: Local Self-Reliance and the Financing of Rural Industrialization." In Joseph et al. 1991, 183–96.

———. 1990. "Central-Local Relations in an Era of Fiscal Decline: The Paradox of Fiscal Decentralization in Post-Mao China." Working Paper no. 210 (September). University of California, Santa Cruz.

———. 1989. "Between Plan and Market: The Role of the Local Sector in Post-Mao Reforms." In *Economic Reforms in the Socialist World,* ed. S. Gomulka, Y. Ha, and C. Kim. London: Macmillan Press.

———. 1988a. "Between Plan and Market: The Role of the Local Sector in Post-Mao Reforms." In *Chinese Economic Reform: How Far, How Fast?*, ed. Bruce L. Reynolds, 95–108. Boston: Academic Press.

———. 1988b. "Interpreting Rural Industrial Growth in the Post-Mao Period." *Modern China* 14:3–30.

———. 1987. "Between Plan and Market: The Role of the Local Sector in Post-Mao

China." *Journal of Comparative Economics* 11:385–98.

———. 1986a. "The Economics of Shortage and Problems of Reform in Chinese Industry." *Journal of Comparative Economics* 10:363–87.

———. 1986b. "Intermediate Technology for Development: Small-scale Chemical Fertilizer Plants in China." *World Development* 14:1329–46.

———. 1986c. "Ownership and Control in Chinese Industry: The Maoist Legacy and Prospects for the 1980s." In U.S. Congress 1986, vol. 1, 571–603.

———. 1985a. "Economic Performance in Post-Mao China." In *China Briefing, 1984,* ed. S. Goldstein, 109–19. Boulder, Colo.: Westview Press.

———. 1985b. "Material Allocation and Decentralization: Impact of the Local Sector on Industrial Reform." In Perry and Wong 1985, 253–80.

———. 1985c. "The Second Phase of Reform in Chinese Industry." *Current History* (September).

———. 1982. "Rural Industrialization in the People's Republic of China: Lessons from the Cultural Revolution Decade." In U.S. Congress 1982, vol. 1, 394–418.

Wong, Lung-Fai. 1987. "Agricultural Productivity in China and India: A Comparative Analysis." Working Paper no. 87–3. Economic Development Center, University of Minnesota, Minneapolis-St. Paul.

World Bank. 1990a. *China: Macroeconomic Stability and Industrial Growth under Decentralized Socialism.* Washington, D.C.: World Bank.

———. 1990b. *China: Revenue Mobilization and Tax Policy.* Washington, D.C.: World Bank.

———. 1988a. *China: External Trade and Capital.* Washington, D.C.: World Bank.

———. 1988b. *China: Finance and Investment.* Washington, D.C.: World Bank.

———. 1988c. *China: Growth and Development in Gansu Province.* Washington, D.C.: World Bank.

———. 1985. *China: Long Term Issues and Options.* Washington, D.C.: World Bank.

———. 1983. *China: Socialist Economic Development.* Washington, D.C.: World Bank.

World Development. 1983, vol. 11.

Wortzel, Heidi Vernon. 1983. "Equity and Efficiency in the Distribution of Non-Food Consumption Goods in China: Shanghai as an Example." *Asian Survey* 23:845–57.

Wu Jinglian and Bruce L. Reynolds. 1988. "Choosing a Strategy for China's Economic Reform." *American Economic Review, Papers and Proceedings* 78:461–66.

Yeh, K.C. 1984. "Macroeconomic Changes in the Chinese Economy During the Readjustment." *China Quarterly,* no. 100:691–716.

Zinser, Lee. 1991. "The Performance of China's Economy." In U.S. Congress 1991, 102–18.

Zweig, David. 1991. "Internationalizing China's Countryside: The Political Economy of Exports from Rural Industry." *China Quarterly,* no. 128:716–41.

6

Studies of Chinese Politics

Nina P. Halpern

Studies of post-1949 Chinese politics have demonstrated some distinct trends. Several factors have influenced the way that scholars investigate and interpret Chinese politics: the sources of available data; current political events; and trends within the broader discipline of political science. In response to these factors, four interrelated characteristics of the field have changed over time: research topics; basic paradigms (sets of assumptions and conceptions); research puzzles; and emotional tone or normative evaluation.

The purpose of this chapter is to examine studies of Chinese politics since 1978 and contrast them with earlier ones. The analysis will demonstrate significant continuity in research topics, but the emergence of a new paradigm—institutionalism—has produced a new set of research puzzles. There has also been significant change in emotional tone, though less than is often believed within the scholarly community. The discussion concludes with a consideration of the new research puzzles arising from the dramatic events of 1989 in China and assesses their likely impact on the field.

Pre-1978 Writings

During the 1950s and 1960s, research on Chinese politics focused on the basic institutions of the party and state, including both structures and processes, but in a fairly descriptive fashion. Scholars such as Lewis (1963), Schurmann (1966), and Barnett (1967) greatly increased our understanding of the formal institutions of the party and government, exploring such aspects as organization, recruitment, and communications. Jerome Cohen (1968) mapped out the basic institutions and practices of the legal system, and Ellis Joffe (1965) analyzed the Chinese military and its relationship to the party. Donnithorne (1967) described the basic workings of the economic management system. Ideology also received much attention, both in the above-cited works by Schurmann and Lewis and in works by Schram (1963) and Schwartz (1968).

Although a few scholars studied other subjects (for example, Lucian Pye

[1968] directed our attention to the importance of traditional culture), the focus on formal institutions and ideology fit well with a dominant "totalitarian" paradigm that assumed a basically unified leadership able to implement its agreed-upon policies and effectively control the population. These assumptions were manifest even in Townsend's (1967) important study of political participation, which focused on formal mechanisms and argued that such participation primarily served the function of executing party policies. The research puzzles produced by this paradigm centered on how the leadership pursued its revolutionary goals and achieved compliance from the population. During this period, most scholars, in part because of the nature of their sources, saw the description of formal institutions and procedures, and official ideology, as the best way to address these puzzles.

Perhaps surprisingly, given the influence of this paradigm, the normative tone of this period was either neutral or quite positive; Townsend, for example, described the Chinese form of participation as different from, but not worse than, that in the West. Many have commented on the fact that China scholars, in contrast to scholars of the Soviet Union, appear to *like* the system they are studying.

The Cultural Revolution brought a major shift of scholarly effort to describing and interpreting the new upheavals and to analyzing the impact of these events on the workings of the system. As many have pointed out, these events and the new data sources they produced fundamentally altered our understanding of the system. They made dramatically clear the existence of elite conflict and social tensions, and thus the limitations of the totalitarian model. Accordingly, much of the field's attention became focused on trying to understand and model these conflicts and their impact on policy outcomes. Chang (1976), Ahn (1976), and MacFarquhar (1974) provided excellent analyses of policy-making from an elite perspective, while Nathan (1973), Tsou (1976), Oksenberg (1971), Teiwes (1979), and others discussed the structure and norms of elite interactions. Some authors accepted the "two-line struggle" model propagated by the Red Guards; others argued instead for a "Mao-in-Command," factional, bureaucratic, or generational model of elite politics. At the same time, the explosion of socially based activity led some scholars to pay more attention to the mass level, analyzing the social divisions reflected in the Red Guard movements (Lee 1978), or even arguing for the relevance of occupational groups to the policy process (Oksenberg 1968). Lampton's (1974) work also began to look at policy-making from a more organizational perspective, but this approach did not predominate at the time.

Most of the work produced during the early and mid-1970s, therefore, had three basic characteristics differentiating it from earlier work: acceptance of the existence of elite conflict; recognition of the importance of mass as well as elite actors; and a focus on informal processes as opposed to formal institutions. Without ever using the word, the field had moved in the direction of accepting a much more "pluralist" notion of Chinese politics: policy outcomes could be explained by identifying the major competing groups or "interests" and then discovering which set of actors was most powerful. The major research puzzles thus consisted of discerning the lines of elite or social cleavage and analyzing the relative power of different groups. To be sure, these studies did not uncover interest group behavior or power that much resembled that of such pluralist countries as the United States. But they did differ significantly from earlier works on Chinese politics in their assumption that differing interests and conflicts, especially within the elite, were a crucial subject of analysis in Chinese politics.

Together with this shift in paradigm and research topics came a shift in emotional tone: the evaluation of the Chinese system during the Cultural Revolution years was predominantly very favorable, reaching at times what Harry Harding (1982) has referred to as a "euphoria" about the Chinese political system. Authors began to refer to the Chinese or Maoist "model," sometimes meaning the term in its laudatory rather than analytical sense. At the time, many authors characterized the system as far more egalitarian, participatory, and ideologically committed than currently seems credible. This shift in tone was probably due both to the nature of the sources available from China and to a willingness to believe, particularly but not exclusively on the part of a younger generation disillusioned with American involvement in Vietnam. Nevertheless, this shift in emotional tone was not as great as sometimes believed; much scholarship continued to maintain a neutral tone, neither praising nor criticizing. All of the works discussed in this section fall into that category.

Trends in Post-Mao Research

Studies of contemporary Chinese politics written after the death of Mao have changed in certain important respects, but nevertheless demonstrate more continuity with past works than is sometimes believed. Some readers of Western writings have pointed to a much more negative emotional tone and normative evaluation of the Chinese political system. However, the shift in this regard was actually much greater among the journalistic community (e.g., Butterfield 1982) than the scholarly one. The more emotional rejections of the Chinese system cited by Harding (1982) are mostly journalistic or popular accounts. This is not to say that scholarly evaluations have not changed at all; new writings on the Cultural Revolution question the degree to which social transformation occurred or argue that the transformation was in a direction opposite to that earlier believed: toward a more *in*egalitarian, more elitist or totalitarian, system (Tsou 1983; Walder 1982). Likewise, attention has focused on understanding the more negative aspects of the movement, such as its violence (White 1989). But as with much of the earlier literature on the Cultural Revolution, these are neutral, scholarly accounts, not diatribes for or against the regime. Moreover, negativism about the Maoist regime soon evolved into a more positive, though often qualified, praise for the post-Mao leadership and its reforms.

The research topics of the post-Mao period represent somewhat of an amalgam of those of the earlier periods. Renewed attention has been directed to understanding basic institutions and processes. Melanie Manion (1985) and John Burns (1987) have shed new light on the personnel system, and Kenneth Lieberthal and Michel Oksenberg (1988) have produced a major study of the energy bureaucracy. An edited volume (Lieberthal and Lampton 1991) contains chapters discussing basic structures and authority relations at different levels of the bureaucracy. Although most of this work has focused on the government bureaucracy, Kevin O'Brien (1990) produced the first major study of China's National People's Congress, and articles have also discussed the party's control organs (Sullivan 1984; Young 1984) and relationship with enterprises (Chamberlain 1987) and the army (Johnston 1984; Shambaugh 1991). This work on institutions and governmental processes clearly reflects primarily new access to the bureaucracy, which permits an updating and further development of earlier work by Barnett and others.

But studies of formal structures are far from dominant. Scholars have continued to analyze the policy process and elite politics, often shedding new light on the development of policy in Maoist China. Harry Harding's (1981) work on organizational policy and Dorothy Solinger's (1984) on commercial policy trace the evolution of policy in these realms from 1949 to the post-Mao era, each describing competing elite views that have predominated at different times. John Lewis and Xue Litai (1988) studied the process by which China acquired nuclear weapons, detailing an evolving process involving symbiotic relations between leaders and experts. David Zweig (1989) analyzed elite conflict over agricultural policy and the impact on social interests, especially during the Cultural Revolution. David Bachman's work on the politics of the Great Leap Forward suggested that it resulted from "the day-to-day concerns of top leaders with protecting and extending the interests of their bureaucratic coalitions," coalitions formed on the basis of differing functional responsibilities (Bachman 1985, 137, and 1991).

A few works focused less on policy and implementation processes than on leadership methods of achieving social transformation or legitimation. Kenneth Lieberthal's (1980) study of Tianjin during the first three years of Communist rule explored the relative impact of organizational control and mass mobilization in promoting social change, concluding that the former method was more effective in undermining the traditional system of *guanxi* (personnel relations). William Joseph (1984) studied ideological campaigns against ultra-leftism in the 1958–81 period, and Lowell Dittmer (1987) examined post-1949 Chinese political development as a product of leadership efforts to legitimize itself by "continuing the revolution."

During the 1980s, responding to political developments within China, the post-Mao reforms became a major topic of analysis. In addition to many articles and several conference volumes (Barnett and Clough 1986; Baum 1991; Lampton 1987b; Morse 1983; Perry and Wong 1985), a small number of book-length studies have appeared. These include Harry Harding's (1987) excellent analysis of reform politics and policy, which focuses particularly on elite politics, and Benedict Stavis's (1988) and Barrett McCormick's (1990) studies of the post-Mao political reforms. Carol Hamrin, drawing on new documentary sources and extensive interviews, produced a detailed analysis of the political processes underlying the reform program of the 1980s, especially the interaction between elite and intellectuals. She concluded, "The decade of rapid economic reform from 1979 to 1989 under the leadership of Deng Xiaoping was a time of transition from rule by a tiny oligarchy of revolutionaries toward a new, more open, and inclusive type of politics" (Hamrin 1990, 210).

The research agenda emerging from the Cultural Revolution is reflected in a large number of studies focusing on mass participation (Burns 1988) and social groups (Falkenheim 1987; Goodman 1984; Rosen 1982). Susan Shirk's (1982) analysis of career incentives and student strategies reflects this interest in social actors. Andrew Nathan's (1985) study of "Chinese democracy" also fits within this category, though his cultural approach is somewhat distinct. Likewise, David Strand's (1989) study of social conflict in Beijing, though focused on the Republican era, concludes with some partial analogies with the present.

Consequently, other than shifting attention to the post-Mao reforms, the research topics of the post-Mao era—political institutions, the policy process, mass participation, and interest groups—mostly do not constitute a major break with the past. Many of these studies also reflect a continuing influence of the pluralist paradigm, with major research puzzles still concerning the nature of elite conflict and the relative importance of social groups in policy-making. This is true, for example, of both Harding's and Hamrin's excellent analyses of post-Mao reform politics, as well as Zweig's study of rural policy. One major alternative to this paradigm is the cultural approach adopted by Pye (1988), Nathan (1985), and Strand (1989). A more dominant departure from the pluralist paradigm, however, is one that I will label "institutionalist" or "structural." This emergent paradigm shifts attention away from particular elites or social groups per se, and directs it to the institutional or structural context of elite and mass behavior, thereby producing a somewhat different set of research questions.

The Institutionalist Paradigm

The emergence of this new approach results from a similar trend within the discipline of political science, borrowed largely from the adjoining discipline of sociology. The pluralist perspective dominating the China field in the past two decades was also absorbed mainly from the discipline, where it has held sway since the 1950s (cf. Shue 1988). Although in the field of American politics "pluralism" generally referred to competing social interests, as opposed to the competing elite interests often exclusively studied by China scholars, the fundamental assumption was the same: politics and policy are best explained by identifying the relevant competing interests and their relative political strengths.

The challenge to this perspective has emerged in the discipline under a number of rubrics: some refer to a "statist" perspective and call for "bringing the state back in" (Evans et al. 1985; Krasner 1984); others identify it as a "new institutionalism" (March and Olsen 1984). In the study of American politics, a focus on institutional constraints produced new attention to the importance of state structures in shaping political actions and outcomes: thus the call for "bringing the state back in." Although students of socialist systems are clearly far more aware than Americanists of the importance of the state, some of the more pluralist studies of China have tended to ignore the role of state *structures*, focusing instead on elite *actors*. In fact, these studies have not paid much attention to the Chinese state, and in this sense the China field also benefits from renewed attention to state structures. But as scholars such as Peter Hall (1986) have pointed out, social structures matter, too; the important questions concern how state *and* social structures together influence elite and mass actions and their results. Accordingly, studies adopting the institutionalist paradigm need not necessarily focus on the elite as opposed to social level. For example, Nee and Stark (1989), in an edited volume applying the institutionalist paradigm to reform efforts in China and Hungary, emphasize its relevance to understanding both state structures and the behavior of social actors.

The "new institutionalism" emerging in the field of Chinese politics shares the basic characteristics of such work in the broader discipline of political science. It, too, focuses on how institutions or structures—meaning enduring patterns of political authority, not simply formal institutions—shape political actors' interests, ideas, and resources. Policy outcomes are not explained as simple products of competing interests, with the more powerful actors or coalition of actors winning; instead, attention is being paid to how the institutional setting shapes political conflicts and their outcomes. These studies show that policy outcomes often fail to achieve the interests or intentions of any group or actor— even one as powerful as the Communist Party.

In a sense, these studies begin to combine the 1950s emphasis on formal structures with the Cultural Revolution focus on informal behavior and policy process. By looking at the interaction between elite and mass choices and institutions, they are providing us with a better understanding of the historical evolutions resulting in contemporary policies and behavior. In the China field, such studies examine the state bureaucracy, state-society relations, and mass participation. Works by Lieberthal and Oksenberg (1988) and Lampton (1987a, 1987b) illustrate the new approach as applied to studies of the bureaucratic policy process and policy implementation; Shue's (1988) work applies it to the relationship between the Chinese state and the peasantry; and Walder (1986, 1987) best exemplifies its application to the topics of social groups and mass participation. Although these works differ significantly, all adopt a basically institutionalist or structural interpretation of Chinese politics.

Studies of Policy-making and Implementation

Some post-Mao studies of the bureaucracy and the policy process differ from those of the Maoist period. The works of the 1950s and 1960s described the formal institutions; the early-to-mid-1970s studies of the policy process typically focused on conflict among competing elite groups. But recent works by Lieberthal and Oksenberg (1988) and Lampton (1987a, 1987b) begin to examine how the policy-making and implementation processes are shaped by the institutional contexts in which they are carried out. These studies present a very different —and more detailed—picture of the bureaucracy than we formerly possessed. They portray it as characterized by a fragmentation of authority among different units. Lieberthal and Oksenberg suggest a historical process by which Leninist bureaucracies gradually develop an increasing division of labor, agencies proliferate and central monitoring becomes more difficult, and different units develop almost proprietary "rights" to resources that they control. As a result of this structural evolution within the bureaucracy, the policy process becomes one in which the central leaders must "bargain" with subordinate units in order to carry out their policies. Policies are often reshaped dramatically in the process of implementation, and change is basically incremental. This view of the policy process is basically shared by David Lampton (1987a).

A major difference between this approach and works such as Solinger's (1984) and Harding's (1981), which reflect a more pluralist perspective, is the former's suggestion that the fragmented structure of authority may produce policies that fail to reflect the interests or ideas of any elite group. Both Solinger and Harding focus on competing elite views and generally attribute shifts in policy to changing power configurations. Solinger, for example, identifies three competing policy positions regarding commercial policy that have prevailed at different times since 1949. But this focus on elite conflict and competing ideas is problematic in two ways. First, it is in danger of becoming tautological: if policy shifts, we then assume that the power of the proponent of that position has shifted; no real test exists of whether changing power configurations actually produce changes in policy. Second, it ignores the possibility that policy, particularly as implemented, may not reflect the views of any particular actor or group. Lieberthal and Oksenberg suggest that at least in the current institutional context, policy-making becomes a difficult process of compromise and consensus-building within the bureaucracy; the result may not, therefore, reflect the views even of the most powerful elite actors.

Lieberthal and Oksenberg's picture of the bureaucratic structure of authority has not gone unchallenged; a subsequent conference on this subject produced a wide range of views about the adequacy of this portrayal (Lieberthal and Lampton 1991) and a review article has criticized it for its failure to take sufficient account of the importance of leadership in shaping policy outcomes (Goldstein 1988). Nevertheless, these challenges reflect the way in which the institutionalist approach has altered the nature of the field's research puzzles. The arguments here concern the *structure* of authority, not which elite group is more powerful. By recognizing that elite preferences alone provide a far from adequate prediction of policy choices, this approach advances us a step beyond the pluralist paradigm.

The gap between elite preferences and policy outcomes emerges even more clearly in studies of policy implementation. While Lieberthal and Oksenberg's book primarily demonstrates how the structure of authority shapes the process of policy *choice,* these studies illuminate how the institutional setting has a crucial impact on policy *outcomes.* The collection of articles in Lampton's (1987b) edited volume on policy implementation vary in their attention to institutional setting, but that setting (called the "context") emerges clearly as one crucial variable explaining policy outcomes. In some of her more recent work on the implementation of industrial reform, Solinger (1986) also shows clearly that existing institutions severely limit the leadership's ability to implement chosen policies. Her explanation of why so little has changed in the industrial economy despite the leadership's advocacy of market-oriented reform points to the influence of "customary ways of doing things ingrained by the planned economy— coupled with a generalized disinclination to upset power relationships fashioned by thirty years of following, or behaving as if following, a state plan" (Solinger 1986, 114). The behavior of the relevant actors—who may not necessarily be the most powerful ones—is explicable only with reference to the structures of the planned economy: that is, the institutional setting of reform. The influence of that institutional setting is seen not just in the pattern of "interests" that it creates, but more broadly in the pervasive attitudes and expectations which also shape the reaction to reform policies. In this work, Solinger moves a long way from her earlier focus on competing elite ideas.

As suggested above, the importance of the institutionalist perspective lies as much in posing new research puzzles as in specific empirical conclusions reached about the political system. Many research questions come to mind. How much does the structure of authority vary across regions, sectors, and levels of the system? How much has the system changed over time: Is the new picture of a fragmented authority structure due to the fact that we are asking new questions (learned in part from more reading in the literature on American politics), the availability of more data, or real change in the post-Mao period? If the post-Mao system is in fact more incremental and suffering from greater "implementation bias" (to use a term in Lampton 1987b) than during the Cultural Revolution, then how do we reconcile this fact with Lieberthal's (1980) earlier insight that the periods of greater and more anticipated change are ones of institutional strength, not weakness? What would account for the strength of bureaucratic institutions that came under such dramatic attack during the Cultural Revolution? Finally, Lieberthal and Oksenberg's account of the policy-making consequences—for example, incrementalism—of the bureaucratic structure of authority needs further analysis, particularly in comparison with other systems. How can one describe as "incremental" a policy process that has produced the dramatic reforms of the past decade? Is this process incremental only compared with our notions of revolutionary change—and perhaps our earlier understanding of the degree of change that occurred during the Cultural Revolution—or is it also incremental compared with other political systems?

In sum, the new vision of the Chinese political system as a "bargaining" and incremental one generates as many research questions as it answers. There is a vital need to explore further certain empirical questions, such as the extent and nature of bargaining within the bureaucracy, but even more, to pose these questions *comparatively*. Comparisons within China and with other systems will sharpen our empirical and analytical understanding of the system; comparisons over time will illuminate the degree of novelty of current patterns. In carrying out historical analysis, scholars must not only ask static comparative questions (how different is the current structure of authority from the Cultural Revolution or the 1950s?), but also process ones (how did bureaucrats come to feel that they have a right to control certain resources? Where did their understanding of their role come from? How is it changing, if at all?). These kinds of research questions will ultimately provide a more useful perspective on the current reforms than any simple investigation of competing elite preferences.

State-Society Relations

From a somewhat different angle, Vivienne Shue (1988) has recently presented an extremely thoughtful plea for moving away from the predominant pluralist perspective on Chinese politics and policy-making. While Lieberthal and Oksenberg's and Lampton's works focus primarily on the structure of the Chinese state and its implications for policy-making, Shue's examines the interactive process through which the Chinese state and rural society have gradually reshaped each other. Her analysis of the structure of rural society and its evolution over time produces a distinctive perspective on the current reform effort.

Shue describes a historical process in which Maoist rural policies since the 1950s paradoxically had the effect of strengthening preexisting localist tendencies in rural life, resulting in a "honeycomb" pattern of rural organization. Rural cadres operating in this social environment, particularly after the apparent betrayal by the central state during the Great Leap Forward, came to identify with their local units and to see their role as one of protecting their communities from state demands. The pattern of state-rural relations thus became one of rural localism in which local cadres bargained with higher authorities over which tasks they would accept and often distorted or ignored commands coming down from above. As a consequence, Shue suggests, the Maoist state suffered from a lack of power to implement its intended policies. Shue argues that the current marketizing reforms must be seen not as an attempt to lessen state power, but as an effort to break down these local sources of power and permit the central authorities thereby to expand the power of the state and its ability to strengthen the nation through economic growth.

Interestingly, Shue's depiction of state-society relations in many ways resembles Lieberthal and Oksenberg's and Lampton's. Each infers that central leaders are lacking in power to implement their desired policies because authority has become fragmented between the central leadership and bureaucratic or local units. Bargaining again emerges as a core feature of policy formulation and implementation. Shue, like Lieberthal and Oksenberg, believes that this pattern of authority is the product of a historical process in which leaders' efforts to achieve their policy goals, interacting with the existing institutional context, gradually produced a particular pattern of authority manifest in both structures and attitudes. Where they differ most is in their understanding of the current reforms: Lieberthal and Oksenberg and Lampton view the current reforms as greatly contributing to the fragmentation of authority and weakening of central state actors, while Shue sees them as breaking down the cadre buffer between peasant and state, thereby promoting the expansion of central state power. Their contrasting conclusions may well stem from their different levels of analysis: Lieberthal et al. are examining fragmentation *within* the state, while Shue is examining the relationship between the peasant and the bureaucratic state as a whole.

As in the case of the works discussed earlier, Shue's conclusions raise many new questions for research and analysis. Her empirical conclusions have been a subject of dispute. Many question whether in the past local forces in fact constituted such a barrier to central ability to enforce its policies as she suggests, and whether the marketizing reforms are actually enhancing that ability. Similarly, some dispute her picture of local cadres acting on behalf of "their" units and contend that these cadres should be seen either as agents of the state or as a corporate group with interests quite distinct from ordinary peasants. Either of these conclusions would call into question Shue's argument that the current reforms will expose peasants more to the force of the *central* state. Indeed, Jean Oi (1989) argues quite persuasively that peasants today suffer from continuing dependence on these same local cadres who have now found new ways to pursue their own interests at the expense of the peasants.

More work also needs to be done to explore the actual pattern of authority in the prereform rural setting: how was authority distributed among different levels, such as team, brigade, commune, and county? Did this vary across localities (Perry 1989, 583)? How do we explain variations in policy implementation, such as movement to the brigade level of accounting during the Cultural Revolution? Once these questions are addressed, further work can then be done to analyze how these patterns have changed since the reforms. We can ask, as does Thomas Bernstein, how we combine Shue's picture of an increasingly strong state in the post-Mao era with Beijing's "well-publicized troubles enforcing national policy at the local level" (Bernstein 1989, 374).

But again, the strength of Shue's analysis lies less in her empirical conclusions than in her demonstration of the utility of seeking to understand the evolving *structure* of relations between the state and rural society. She makes clear that local cadre interests and behavior (their responses to centrally determined policies) cannot be fully understood without analyzing the structural setting in which the cadres were located: that is, the preexisting pattern of rural organization that led cadres to identify their interests with defense of their localities. Those who disagree with her conclusions and suggest alternative views of cadre interests and behavior will need to ground their arguments in some equally persuasive picture of state and social structures. Indeed, Oi (1989) has already presented a quite different analysis of state-peasant relations, emphasizing their clientelist structure. Future studies will undoubtedly continue to dispute the actual structure of these relationships, and how they have changed in the post-Mao era. But as Shue demonstrates, rural policy and political relationships are most usefully understood as the products of a historical interaction between elite choices and state and social structures. This approach is as useful for understanding past rural policies as for analyzing the reform process currently under way.

Political Participation and Social Groups

A third set of studies demonstrates that a structural perspective can shed as much light on the nature and meaning of participation by social groups as it does on policy-making and implementation, or relations between the state and rural society. Walder's (1986, 1987) analyses of workers' politics also dissent from the pluralist perspective and use a structural approach to address his topic. Although Walder is a sociologist by training, his work has influenced our understanding of Chinese politics.

Like Shue, Walder analyzes how past elite policies produced particular—often unanticipated—structural arrangements that in turn shaped the interests and interactions of different actors. While most discussions of interest groups assume a fairly unified entity, Walder demonstrates that workers' interests are not uniform and depend greatly on their location within the industrial sector. More important, Walder shows how the differential embeddedness of different types of industrial settings in broader social and political structures further affects the interests of these different groups of workers and their manner of acting on them. Walder focuses most of his attention on the permanent workers in large state enterprises. He shows how state-imposed structures of surveillance, control, and reward shape the workers' strategy for pursuing their interests. These institutional features of the state industrial sector prevent workers from organizing to pursue their interests, and encourage workers, when in formal participatory settings, to pursue defensive strategies devoid of interest articulation. At the same time, they make the worker dependent on the workplace, and especially individuals dependent on authority figures. The result is the development of informal clientelist networks within which individual workers pursue their particularized interests in an unorganized fashion.

Walder's approach suggests that the questions encouraged by the pluralist perspective—whether workers as a group can achieve their interests—are at best of limited utility, and probably misleading. For him, the important focus of analysis is the way in which the Chinese state shapes the sociopolitical structure in which workers are located, and in turn affects both the interests of workers and the manner in which they pursue them. In contrast to Lieberthal and Oksenberg, and Shue, he describes a rather unified structure of authority, in which the power of the central party/state penetrates every unit. The clientelist networks he describes at best soften the impact of the state, without shifting real power into the hands of workers. The closest workers can come to exerting real influence on policy is through a form of "hidden bargaining" involving withholding of work effort. For this strategy to be effective, he suggests, national leaders must value labor productivity highly, and they must permit factory managers flexibility in determining incentive pay. Thus, unlike Shue, Walder suggests that the reforms are increasing the power of social actors vis-à-vis the state. Despite these changes, he argues, the basic structures creating worker dependence on their units have not changed; thus the increase in worker influence is only marginal.

Like the other authors who employ an institutionalist framework, Walder leaves us with an important new set of research questions. How well does his account of dependency and clientelism apply to other social groups? Oi's (1986, 1989) work asks similar questions about the peasantry, but suggests that particularly in the reform era, the issue of dependence on cadres is somewhat more complicated than in state industry. Her findings might also apply to operators of private or collective enterprises (as opposed to employees of state enterprises) who probably find themselves, like peasants today, operating in a nexus between state-controlled resources and market-allocated ones. Other important questions include: How might the fragmentation of authority among bureaucratic units affect authority patterns within the enterprise and the relative influence of workers? How will marketizing reforms affect these patterns? What relationship exists between such subgroup characteristics as age, experience, and status, and the formation of clientelist networks (Perry 1989, 588)? Future research efforts along these lines will need to illuminate further the interaction between elite policies, the state structures they create, their interaction with existing social institutions, and their ultimate impact on social actors. And, as Perry's (1989) thoughtful review essay argues, the legacy of the pre-1949 Chinese labor movement on post-1949 worker politics requires greater analysis.

The Impact of Tiananmen

Above it was suggested that a new paradigm emerging in the field of Chinese politics, borrowed from the broader discipline of political science, has begun to reshape our understanding of the central Chinese state, state-society relations, and social actors. Although research topics have not changed greatly in the post-Mao period—scholars still seek an understanding of basic political institutions, processes, and social groups—the perspective brought to bear on these topics has altered. As a consequence, new research puzzles have emerged, centering on understanding the source, evolution, and effects of political institutions on Chinese politics and society.

However, as in the past, political events in China have affected the field's focus and interpretations at least as much as developments within the discipline of political science. Not surprisingly, many scholars responded to the post-Mao reforms by trying to describe and interpret these reforms and the changes that they had introduced into the Chinese political system. The reforms' apparent success in moving China away from the destructive patterns of the Cultural Revolution produced a generally favorable normative evaluation of the post-Mao Chinese political system. Although a shift in tone had already begun to appear as problems with the reforms and elite conflict over them became increasingly obvious, by far the most important influences on the field at the current time and probably for years to come are the unprecedented and unanticipated mass demonstrations of the spring of 1989 and the Chinese government's violent response.

Scholars have only just begun to respond to these events, but one can already discern several components of their response. Apart from producing a flood of studies seeking to understand the actual events themselves, and a far more negative assessment of the post-Mao leadership and its accomplishments, the political events of 1989 seem likely to affect our analyses and interpretations of Chinese politics in at least three ways.

First, Tiananmen gives rise to questions about how well we have understood urban society: What were the wellsprings of the massive popular protests in Beijing and other cities? How well were urban residents integrated into—dependent on, in Walder's terms—their units if they could engage in such political action? Further study of the protests may find work units providing an important base for societal organization, or may even find that in some cases these units tacitly or explicitly encouraged popular protest. However, it might be that social actors have begun to mobilize and organize independently of these Communist-controlled work units. In this case, it might be relevant to speak, as Thomas Gold (1990) and Strand (1990) have done, of an emergent civil society. Neither set of empirical findings would negate the value of a structural approach; however, each would have very different implications for the nature of social institutions. The degree to which Maoist structures continue to be the most relevant ones for understanding and predicting social behavior in China, as opposed to new ones formed as a result of post-Mao reforms, will be a central research question in the future. And despite the relative quiescence of the rural population, similar questions will also be asked about the countryside—with a greater awareness now of the need to differentiate between rural and urban sectors in any conceptualization of state-society relations.

A second issue raised by the Tiananmen events is the nature of the current leadership and the reasons for its repressive response. Perhaps as striking as the use of violence, if not as immediately horrifying, is the leadership's return to methods of ideological indoctrination, political study, and self-criticism, which we had begun to identify largely with the Maoist past. The institutional perspective on the government bureaucracy and policy-making discussed above seems, on the surface, far less helpful in understanding these choices. However, even at the leadership level there are issues susceptible to a structural approach.

First, while we can readily agree that the leadership's response to the Tiananmen crisis was not determined by bureaucratic structure, it remains unclear how much this response to crisis reveals about the overall nature of policy-making and leadership behavior. We will now need to focus on differentiating spheres and contexts of policy-making to determine when a structural approach is relevant and when the attitudes of a small, relatively unconstrained set of elite actors are more important. Second, although it appears that leaders were relatively unconstrained structurally when they made their decision to use force against the demonstrators, further analysis might conclude that their choices were more influenced by the available structures for containing or controlling this unprecedented social mobilization than we at first thought. Indeed, McCormick (1990) comes to essentially this conclusion in his analysis of the post-Mao political reforms. In his interpretation, it was the *failure* of the post-Mao reforms to create new institutional mechanisms for effective mediation between state and society that led to the leaders' violent response (and, one might add, to their falling back on Maoist methods of political indoctrination). McCormick arrives at this conclusion by developing a structural framework for analyzing Leninist states that is quite similar to Walder's (and, like Walder's, much influenced by the work of Kenneth Jowitt [1983]).

McCormick also suggests how a structural analysis might address the third major puzzle raised by Tiananmen, one for which structural analysis would appear singularly unsuited—the issue of discontinuous political change. That is, structural approaches are typically regarded as useful for explaining political continuity, or, at best (as in Shue's approach) evolutionary change. Large discontinuities, such as the Tiananmen events, seem inherently out of reach of structural explanations.

Although I agree in many ways with this criticism of structural approaches, I also think that we might usefully analyze events like the Tiananmen crisis as resulting from a clash between evolving and contradictory structures—such as ones that produce a more active society without effective institutional channels for social action or elite response (this point was of course made long ago by Samuel Huntington [1968]). Also relevant is McCormick's suggestion that certain types of state structures might actually produce political instability and the appearance of discontinuity:

> This [the fact that Chinese politics is usually less stable than it appears] is because of the structure of the Chinese Leninist state. Comprehensive state organization and state domination of the means of communication create the illusion of unity and minimize opportunities to organize and articulate meaningful opposition. At the same time, the high relative autonomy of the state means that it is poorly rooted in society and that there is a very high potential for conflict between state and society. The possibility for confrontation increases as the Party's claim to virtue is diminished and as reforms marginally increase the autonomy of civil society. To the extent that unity in the Party's higher levels depends on personal relationships, there is a strong prospect for division and conflict among personal cliques and factions, which could at least immobilize the Party during periods of crisis and at worst lead to grave internal conflicts. (McCormick 1990, 200).

The above quotation illustrates two points about the current condition of studies of Chinese politics. First, despite the shock of the Tiananmen events, scholars have not stopped applying the structural paradigm to the analysis of Chinese politics, even though some will see Tiananmen as evidence of the limitations of such an approach. Second, Chinese politics remains sufficiently complex and opaque to Western scholars that new research puzzles are likely to emerge repeatedly both from actual Chinese political events and from our continuing effort to adopt and apply new paradigms providing answers to these puzzles. Accordingly, there is no more reason to anticipate future stability, much less stasis, in the study of Chinese politics than in Chinese politics itself.

References

Ahn, Byung-joon. 1976. *Chinese Politics and the Cultural Revolution.* Seattle: University of Washington Press.

Bachman, David M. 1985. *Chen Yun and the Chinese Political System.* Berkeley: Institute of East Asian Studies, University of California, Berkeley, Center For Chinese Studies.

———. 1991. *Bureaucracy, Economy, and Leadership in China.* Cambridge: Cambridge University Press.

Barnett, A. Doak. 1967. *Cadres, Bureaucracy, and Political Power in Communist China.* New York: Columbia University Press.

Barnett, A. Doak, and Ralph N. Clough, eds. 1986. *Modernizing China.* Boulder, Colo.: Westview Press.

Baum, Richard, ed. 1991. *Reform and Reaction in Post-Mao China.* New York and London: Routledge Press.

Bernstein, Thomas. 1989. Review of *The Reach of the State: Sketches of the Chinese Body Politic.* By Vivienne Shue. *Journal of Asian Studies* (May).

Burns, John P. 1987. China's *Nomenklatura* System. *Problems of Communism* 36 (September–October).

———. 1988. *Political Participation in Rural China.* Berkeley: University of California Press.

Butterfield, Fox. 1982. *Alive in the Bitter Sea.* New York: New York Times Books.

Chamberlain, Heath B. 1987. "Party-Army Relations in Chinese Industries: Some Political Dimensions of Economic Reform." *China Quarterly* 112 (December).

Chang, Parris. 1976. *Power and Policy in China.* University Park: Pennsylvania State Press.

Cohen, Jerome. 1968. *The Criminal System in Communist China*. Cambridge: Harvard University Press.

Dittmer, Lowell. 1987. *China's Continuous Revolution*. Berkeley: University of California Press.

Donnithorne, Audrey. 1967. *The Chinese Economic System*. New York: Praeger Publishers.

Evans, Peter B., Dietrich Rueschemeyer, and Theda Skocpol, eds. 1985. *Bringing the State Back In*. Cambridge: Cambridge University Press.

Falkenheim, Victor C., ed. 1987. *Citizens and Groups in Contemporary China*. Ann Arbor: University of Michigan Center for Chinese Studies.

Gold, Thomas B. 1990. "The Resurgence of Civil Society in China." *Journal of Democracy* 1 (Winter).

Goldstein, Steven M. 1988. "Reforming Socialist Systems: The Lessons of the Chinese Experience." *Studies in Comparative Communism* 21 (Summer).

Goodman, David S.G., ed. 1984. *Groups and Politics in the People's Republic of China*. Armonk, N.Y.: M.E. Sharpe.

Hall, Peter. 1986. *Governing the Economy*. New York: Oxford University Press.

Hamrin, Carol Lee. 1990. *China and the Challenge of the Future*. Boulder, Colo.: Westview Press.

Harding, Harry. 1981. *Organizing China*. Stanford: Stanford University Press.

———. 1982. "From China with Disdain: New Trends in the Study of China." *Asian Survey* 22 (October).

———. 1987. *China's Second Revolution*. Washington, D.C.: Brookings Institution.

Huntington, Samuel P. 1968. *Political Order in Changing Societies*. New Haven: Yale University Press.

Joffe, Ellis. 1965. *Party and Army: Professionalism and Political Control in the Chinese Officer Corps, 1949–1964*. Cambridge: East Asian Monographs Series no. 19, Harvard University Press.

Johnston, Alastair I. 1984. "Changing Party-Army Relations in China, 1979–1984." *Asian Survey* 24 (October).

Joseph, William A. 1984. *The Critique of Ultra-Leftism in China, 1958–1981*. Stanford: Stanford University Press.

Jowitt, Kenneth. 1983. "Soviet Neo-Traditionalism: The Political Corruption of a Leninist Regime." *Soviet Studies* 35 (July).

Krasner, Stephen D. 1984. "Approaches to the State: Alternative Conceptions and Historical Dynamics." *Comparative Politics* (January).

Lampton, David M. 1974. *Health, Conflict, and the Chinese Political System*. Ann Arbor: University of Michigan Center for Chinese Studies.

Lampton, David M. 1987a. "Chinese Politics: The Bargaining Treadmill." *Issues and Studies* 23 (March).

———, ed. 1987b. *Policy Implementation in Post-Mao China*. Berkeley: University of California Press.

Lee, Hong Yung. 1978. *The Politics of the Chinese Cultural Revolution*. Berkeley: University of California Press.

Lewis, John Wilson. 1963. *Leadership in Communist China*. Ithaca: Cornell University Press.

Lewis, John Wilson, and Xue Litai. 1988. *China Builds the Bomb*. Stanford: Stanford University Press.

Lieberthal, Kenneth G. 1980. *Revolution and Tradition in Tientsin, 1949–1952*. Stanford: Stanford University Press.

Lieberthal, Kenneth G., and David M. Lampton, eds. 1991. *Bureaucracy, Politics, and Decision Making in Post-Mao China*. Berkeley: University of California Press.

Lieberthal, Kenneth, and Michel Oksenberg. 1988. *Policy Making in China.* Princeton: Princeton University Press.

McCormick, Barrett L. 1990. *Political Reform in Post-Mao China.* Berkeley: University of California Press.

MacFarquhar, Roderick. 1974. *The Origins of the Chinese Cultural Revolution,* vol. I. New York: Columbia University Press.

Manion, Melanie. 1985. "The Cadre Management System, Post-Mao: The Appointment, Promotion, Transfer and Removal of Party and State Leaders." *China Quarterly* 102 (June).

March, James G., and Johan P. Olsen. 1984. "The New Institutionalism: Organizational Factors in Political Life." *American Political Science Review* 78 (September).

Morse, Ronald A., ed. 1983. *The Limits of Reform in China.* Boulder, Colo.: Westview Press.

Nathan, Andrew J. 1973. "A Factionalism Model for CCP Politics." *China Quarterly* 53 (January–March).

————. *Chinese Democracy.* Berkeley: University of California Press.

Nee, Victor, and David Stark, eds. 1989. *Remaking the Economic Institutions of Socialism: China and Eastern Europe.* Stanford: Stanford University Press.

O'Brien, Kevin J. 1990. *Reform Without Liberalization: China's National Congress and the Politics of Institutional Change.* New York: Cambridge University Press.

Oi, Jean C. 1986. "Commercializing China's Rural Cadres." *Problems of Communism* 35 (September–October).

————. 1989. *State and Peasant in Contemporary China.* Berkeley: University of California Press.

Oksenberg, Michel. 1968. "Occupations and Groups in Chinese Society and the Cultural Revolution." In *The Cultural Revolution: 1967 in Review,* ed. Michel Oksenberg et al., 1–44. Ann Arbor: University of Michigan Center for Chinese Studies.

————. 1971. "Policy Making Under Mao, 1949–68: An Overview." In *China: Management of a Revolutionary Society,* ed. John M.H. Lindbeck, 79–115. Seattle: University of Washington Press.

Perry, Elizabeth J. 1989. "State and Society in Contemporary China." *World Politics* 41 (July).

Perry, Elizabeth J., and Christine Wong, eds. 1985. *The Political Economy of Reform in Post-Mao China.* Cambridge: Harvard University Council on East Asian Studies.

Pye, Lucian W. 1968. *The Spirit of Chinese Politics.* Cambridge: MIT Press.

————. *The Mandarin and the Cadre: China's Political Culture.* Ann Arbor: University of Michigan Center for Chinese Studies.

Rosen, Stanley. 1982. *Red Guard Factionalism and the Cultural Revolution in Guangzhou (Canton).* Boulder, Colo.: Westview Press.

Schram, Stuart. 1963. *The Political Thought of Mao Tse-tung.* New York: Praeger.

Schurmann, Franz. 1966. *Ideology and Organization in Communist China.* Berkeley: University of California Press.

Schwartz, Benjamin. 1968. *Communism and China; Ideology and Flux.* Cambridge: Harvard University Press.

Shambaugh, David. 1991. "The Soldier and the State in China." *China Quarterly* 127 (September).

Shirk, Susan L. 1982. *Competitive Comrades.* Berkeley: University of California Press.

Shue, Vivienne. 1988. *The Reach of the State.* Stanford: Stanford University Press.

Solinger, Dorothy J. 1984. *Chinese Business under Socialism.* Berkeley: University of California Press.

————. 1986. "Industrial Reform: Decentralization, Differentiation, and the Difficulties." *Journal of International Affairs* 39 (Winter).

Stavis, Benedict. 1988. *China's Political Reforms*. New York: Praeger.

Strand, David. 1989. *Rickshaw Beijing: City People and Politics in the 1920s*. Berkeley: University of California Press.

————. 1990. "Protest in Beijing: Civil Society and Public Sphere in China." *Problems of Communism* 39 (May–June).

Sullivan, Lawrence R. 1984. "The Role of the Control Organs in the Chinese Communist Party, 1977–83." *Asian Survey* 24 (June).

Teiwes, Frederick. 1979. *Politics and Purges in China: Rectification and the Decline of Party Norms, 1950–1965*. White Plains, N.Y.: M.E. Sharpe.

Townsend, James. 1967. *Political Participation in Communist China*. Berkeley: University of California Press.

Tsou, Tang. 1976. "A Prolegomenon to the Study of Informal Groups in Chinese Communist Party Politics." *China Quarterly* 65 (March).

————. 1983. "Back From the Brink of Revolutionary-'Feudal' Totalitarianism." In *State and Society in Contemporary China*, ed. Victor Nee and David Mozingo, 53–88. Ithaca: Cornell University Press.

Walder, Andrew G. 1982. "Some Ironies of the Maoist Legacy in Industry." In *The Transition to Socialism in China*, ed. Mark Selden and Victor Lippit, 215–65. Armonk, N.Y.: M.E. Sharpe.

————. *Communist Neo-Traditionalism*. Berkeley: University of California Press.

————. "Communist Social Structure and Workers' Politics in China." In *Citizens and Groups in Contemporary China*, ed. Victor C. Falkenheim, 45–89. Ann Arbor: University of Michigan Center For Chinese Studies.

White, Lynn T., III. 1989. *Policies of Chaos: The Organizational Causes of Violence in China's Cultural Revolution*. Princeton: Princeton University Press.

Young, Graham. 1984. "Control and Style: Discipline Inspection Commissions Since the 11th Congress." *China Quarterly* 97 (March).

Zweig, David. 1989. *Agrarian Radicalism in China, 1968–1981*. Cambridge: Harvard University Press.

7

New Directions in Chinese Security Studies

Robert S. Ross and Paul H.B. Godwin

American scholarship on post-1949 Chinese security policy has developed into a number of subdisciplines. The most popular of these includes PRC policy toward the superpowers, regional security affairs, crisis behavior, defense policy, and international economic policy. Each area has developed a body of literature revealing rich and important insights into the sources of PRC unilateral and multilateral behavior aimed at protecting Chinese interests. Regarding the superpowers, a stimulating and productive scholarly debate has unfolded over the relative importance of domestic and international factors in influencing Chinese policy. In other areas, scholars have developed a consensus concerning patterns of PRC behavior. Nevertheless, throughout the foreign policy field, with only a few exceptions, there is but little evidence that scholars are venturing into new areas of research. Rather than further consolidate the existing consensus, the time has come to promote promising new areas of research and to seek new debates amid disharmony.

The purpose of this chapter is not to criticize the state of the field. On the contrary, the field of Chinese security studies merits praise for what it has accomplished in such a short period of time—the PRC itself is a young country, and it was only in 1960 that A. Doak Barnett published *China and Southeast Asia* and Allen Whiting published *China Crosses the Yalu,*[1] the first major works in the field. But the field also requires new directions. This chapter tries to show what has been accomplished and to point out some of the new directions for exploration, including new issues raised by the end of the Cold War. It examines the scholarship on policy-making in strategic and international economic affairs, the international sources of China's policy toward the United States and the former Soviet Union, China as a regional power, Chinese crisis behavior and use of force, and defense policy.

The Politics of Policy-making

The literature on the politics of policy-making covers a broad range of topics, including Chinese security policy, foreign economic strategy, and, in recent years, the foreign affairs bureaucracy. In each case, the issue is the extent to which domestic factors determine external policy. In the area of strategic policy, a debate exists, mirroring the larger domestic-international debate, concerning the importance of factions to the policy-making process.

The Foreign Policy of Domestic Turbulence

An important and influential portion of the policy-making literature links domestic politics with Chinese policy toward the United States and the Soviet Union and its successors. This scholarship argues that the outcome of political struggles among the Chinese elite fundamentally affects China's strategic posture, insofar as members of the elite hold different foreign policy preferences.

The early work on domestic linkage by Melvin Gurtov and Harry Harding, Uri Ra'anan, and Donald Zagoria focused on the struggle in Beijing over the appropriate PRC response to escalating U.S. involvement in the Vietnam War and the ensuing purge of Marshal Luo Ruiqing.[2] Although these authors differed over the substance of the debate, particularly concerning Sino-Soviet "united action" and the extent of PRC support for Vietnam, with Gurtov and Harding concentrating their attention on the narrower issue of China's defense posture, they all concluded that domestic politics could significantly alter China's strategic relations.

This first generation domestic-linkage literature was followed by research on the domestic origins of U.S.-China rapprochement. Thomas Gottlieb and John Garver argued that Zhou Enlai and Lin Biao differed over China's response to the escalating Soviet threat and that Mao Zedong ultimately sided with Zhou.[3] The two leaders then successfully pursued rapprochement with the United States, but only after they had significantly weakened the political base of Lin Biao and his colleagues. Garver further argued that the course of the Lin-Zhou struggle led to a PRC tilt toward the Soviet Union in 1970, just in the midst of probing rapprochement with the United States. Thus, these scholars found the origins of the U.S.-Soviet-China "strategic triangle" to lie in developments in Chinese domestic politics.[4] Kenneth Lieberthal carried this approach forward in time by addressing the dynamics of the strategic triangle in the mid-1970s before Mao's death. He also added greater nuance to our understanding of the policy debate in post–Lin Biao China by identifying three distinct policy preferences among the elite. Lieberthal argued that "soft moderates" in the Chinese elite, including Deng Xiaoping, favored moderating Sino-Soviet tension and that the ups and downs of particular Chinese leaders explain the rise and fall of Chinese overtures to the Soviet Union. Similarly, Harding perceived that there was strong disagreement in the leadership during this period regarding policy toward the Soviet Union, with moderate politicians using their brief ascendancy in 1974 and 1975 to take various initiatives suggesting PRC interest in improved Sino-Soviet relations. Harding suggested that Zhou Enlai occupied the middle position in the foreign policy debate between moderates and radicals. Similar to the earlier work on Beijing's response to escalating U.S.-Vietnamese conflict, Lieberthal's and Harding's conclusions were that developments in Chinese domestic politics could significantly affect China's position between the superpowers.[5]

Carol Hamrin extended this three-way domestic struggle approach to an analysis of China's security posture in the post-Mao era.[6] She argued that post-Mao competition focused on three distinct "policy packages," each of which included both domestic policy components and a preferred PRC policy toward the superpowers. In this context, the gradual emergence in the early 1980s of the Sino-Soviet rapprochement and of greater PRC distance from the United States, the key components of China's "independent foreign policy," reflected the weakening of Deng's authority and the resulting necessity for conciliation in the face of an opposition coalition composed of politicians having a stake in the status quo and politicians interested in expanded economic cooperation with Moscow, as well as Deng's vulnerability over the Taiwan issue—his "Achilles' heel." As with the literature concerning the Maoist period, Beijing's strategic posture under Deng's leadership was found to be significantly influenced by China's domestic political circumstances.

Strategic Consistency Amid Domestic Turbulence

In contrast to the domestic-focus literature, which finds in political instability and competing domestic institutions the bases for important foreign policy change, other scholarship on elite politics and the domestic-foreign linkage have tended to minimize the importance of elite instability on developments in PRC security policy. For these scholars, domestic political change cannot be ignored, but their writings on domestic politics emphasize the extent to which continuity persists in the face of political instability.

One interesting angle on this underscores the extent to which domestic policy has been a function of China's international position. Hence, Thomas Fingar has argued that the course of China's domestic economic development program after the three peak years of the Cultural Revolution reflected the leadership's interpretation of China's international situation. Fingar emphasizes that despite intense opposition from radical politicians, the stability in China's international circumstances vis-à-vis the superpowers throughout the 1970s ensured basic continuity in China's domestic development program and in its security policies.[7]

In a similar vein, Robert Ross has argued that the degree to which domestic opposition can influence security policy has been shaped by China's international circumstances. When Chinese leaders have perceived the PRC as relatively more secure, China's policy options have expanded, thus affording greater influence to politicians with alternative policy preferences. Ross further emphasizes that the preeminent leaders in Chinese politics, both Mao and Deng, have exercised such unique authority in the foreign policy realm that factionalism and policy debates among their lieutenants affect policy only tangentially. Nevertheless, in the absence of a preeminent leader, such as at the height of a succession crisis, policy can be held hostage to a leader's parochial political considerations.[8]

Allen Whiting's work on domestic politics and foreign policy falls into this category.[9] In his analysis of the media's treatment of the Taiwan issue in U.S.-China relations through the domestic turbulence of the 1970s, Whiting found that the most plausible explanation for greater salience of the Taiwan issue was not radical influence over media, but changing PRC interpretations of the U.S.-Soviet balance. Neither the shifting fortunes of radical and moderate leaders nor divergent bureaucratic interests served to explain the shifting importance of the Taiwan issue. Rather, Taiwan became a more prominent media issue when China observed new foreign policy opportunities in the international system.

Authors interested in civil-military relations and Chinese foreign policy-making have reached similar conclusions. Paul Godwin and Jonathan Pollack have shown that despite the opposition of the military elite to the civilian leadership's optimistic view of China's strategic environment and to its deemphasis of the military budget in the early 1980s, the reform coalition's Soviet policy and its defense modernization plans continued to reflect its reduced concern for the immediacy of the Soviet threat. Deng Xiaoping, China's preeminent leader, exercised his authority over his military colleagues.[10]

The Politics of Foreign Economic Policy

While there is debate over the domestic sources of Chinese security policy, there is much less disagreement concerning the impact of domestic politics on the development of China's international economic strategy.

An important 1974 article by Michel Oksenberg and Steven Goldstein offered a historical perspective on Chinese attitudes toward "self-reliance" and PRC participation in the international economy. They discussed four leadership conceptions of China's national interest over the previous hundred years, irrespective of ideology, and argued that the middle two options of relatively more or less participation have characterized actual policy through the contemporary era.[11] Since that article appeared, scholars have written more detailed studies of the politics of the PRC's international economic policy. In contrast to the limited evidence available for documenting leadership debates over foreign policy, in the 1970s and 1980s the Chinese media fully revealed the intense conflict in the leadership over the role of international trade and capital in China's development strategy. On this basis, Ann Fenwick documented the radical critique of China's growing involvement in international economics and examined the impact of factionalism and the 1976 "pi-Deng" (Criticize Deng) campaign on Chinese trade policy.[12]

One of the most recent and significant tangents to this approach concerns the domestic political economy of the evolution of China's open-door policy. As China's involvement in the international economy has significantly expanded and domestic China has become more permeable to international developments, scholars have explored the implications of expanded PRC trade and foreign investment for competing domestic institutions and the resulting impact on policy evolution. Moving beyond elite analysis, they have explored the societal implications of particular policy agendas. Lieberthal has examined the domestic consequences of China's increasing trade with the advanced market economies for various domestic institutions, arguing that in the battle between "all-round modernizers" and "eclectic modernizers," the latter have sought to protect their interests in conservative institutions by reducing the scope of Deng's open-door reforms. Susan Shirk's work has examined the importance of coalitions of interest-based societal institutions, revealing that the heavy industrial sector and the internal, more backward provinces, as relative "losers" in the battle for funding and in the pace of development within the open-door strategy, have protected their interests by trying to interfere with full implementation of Deng's foreign economic program. Successful implementation of the strategy depends on the influence of a coalition made up of various export industries and coastal provinces, which have developed a stake in the open-door policy.[13]

New Directions: The Domestic Politics of Foreign Policy

The issue of domestic politics and foreign policy and the debate over security policy have long occupied the attention of China scholars, with research beginning in the 1960s. These studies, however, were all framed within the Cold War context of Chinese hostility toward one or both of the superpowers, in which the constant threat to Chinese security framed the parameters of the domestic role in foreign policy. The end of the Cold War calls for research into the role of domestic politics in Chinese foreign policy during a period of reduced threat perception and for a historical comparative approach to the domestic-foreign linkage. Moreover, the combination in the early 1990s of the end of the Cold War and heightened succession politics in the aftermath of the June 1989 Beijing massacre provides an opportunity for examining the domestic-foreign linkage when domestic politics has a relatively more influential role on foreign policy.

In addition to asking recurring questions about a changing China, it is also appropriate to begin asking new questions about the impact of domestic politics on foreign policy. This is especially the case now that China is becoming more accessible to research and scholars can conduct interviews in various government organizations concerned with foreign policy.

The foreign affairs bureaucracy has become an exciting area of scholarship.

A. Doak Barnett's interviews have enabled him to discuss the roles of various domestic institutions in the decision-making process, including the military, the public security apparatus, universities, and think tanks. David Shambaugh has closely analyzed an important aspect of the foreign affairs bureaucracy: research institutions focusing on Chinese security policy. In great detail he has described their respective affiliations with particular leadership organizations and their research activities and publications. Shambaugh has also conducted in-depth interviews with foreign policy analysts at these institutions, revealing variegated approaches toward international affairs and the United States among China's community of foreign relations analysts.[14]

The next stage in this research on foreign policy institutions is to explore the process by which these various institutions interact to forge policies, if indeed they influence policy formation at all. One set of issues deals with the changing locus of authority in the day-to-day management of foreign affairs. To the extent that power resides in individuals and leadership changes periodically create new decision-making patterns, can we discuss with any certainty where decisions are made within the party, the government, and the military? The question here is how individuals are able to capture policy for their particular institutions. Similarly, is authority divided according to foreign policy arenas, and how fluid is any given distribution?

Of particular interest in this regard is the role of the military. As the state's security specialists, how do elite soldiers influence security policy? A 1981 essay by Gerald Segal succinctly outlined the issue in this area. He argued that when there have been debates on the appropriate military action in the face of a "threat," the division has not been between the civilian leadership and the military but between or among factions that cut across institutional lines. He thus suggests that the institutional role of the People's Liberation Army (PLA) in foreign policy is minimal.[15] This logic of cross-cutting factions calls into question an emphasis on civil-military relations drawn from the logic of military professionalism and institutional interests. Nevertheless, a major question for the future is whether or not the smaller, more professional military sought by Deng Xiaoping and withdrawn from civil affairs will seek greater influence in foreign policy and national security affairs.

A similar set of issues concerns the policy-analysis institutions. Are think tanks required to prepare policy statements in support of their particular leading institution's policy preferences, thus participating in the "bureaucratic struggle"? Alternatively, the burgeoning research community may play a more subtle role by educating the elite, thus ensuring that a range of policies is considered before decisions are reached. This may especially be the case for think tanks involved in foreign economic policy, where policy latitude is greater than it is in security affairs. Essentially, we still do not fully understand what role these various institutions play in shaping policy.

Alternatively, it may well be that in explaining PRC security policy a focus on a few elites rather than on institutions is sufficient to explain policy evolution. Similar to the issue of domestic politics and the role of the preeminent leader in policy-making, does foreign policy-making authority concerning key issues remain so highly concentrated within the elite that subordinate institutions can only influence policy at the narrow margins?

In addition to exploring the institutions of policy-making, research should consider the importance of domestic culture in foreign policy. If China is different than other countries, if looking inside the state is necessary to explain the state's behavior, then culture should be a major contributor to any uniqueness in Chinese foreign policy. One promising area concerns China's "strategic culture." Interviews with foreign affairs specialists and analysis of contemporary PRC writings on historical international events can yield important insights into Chinese conceptions of power and balance of power, and attitudes toward compromise and conciliatory behavior, domestic-foreign linkage, and the role of historical trends in determining political outcomes. Together, these questions, when related to actual practice, may yield an understanding of patterns in Chinese negotiating behavior and in its approach toward resolving bilateral conflicts of interest and toward participation in multilateral cooperation.[16]

China and the Great Powers: The International Perspective

In contrast to this focus on domestic politics and institutions, much of the scholarship on Chinese security policy, while recognizing the clear importance of domestic leadership debates and domestic institutions in policy-making, emphasizes the international sources of Chinese foreign policy. This literature considers China's foreign policy as a search for security in an environment in which its options are severely limited by international circumstances over which it has little control.

Work from this strategic perspective has examined important developments in China's policy as a reflection of change in PRC security developing from shifting trends in the balance of power between the superpowers. This work focuses on the impact of the bipolar world and superpower policies toward the PRC in explaining Chinese policy. Hence, as Robert Sutter has argued, the 1968 Soviet occupation of Czechoslovakia, U.S-Soviet détente during the Nixon and Carter administrations, Soviet gains in the Third World in the 1970s, the 1975 U.S. defeat in Indochina, heightened U.S.-Soviet tension following the 1979 Soviet invasion of Afghanistan, and other such international occurrences have been key events informing PRC behavior.[17]

In an effort to formalize their understanding of China's role between the superpowers, scholars have tried to generalize using such concepts as bipolarity and, alternatively, the U.S.-Soviet-China "triangle." Michael Ng-Quinn's work stresses the impact of bipolarity on the PRC. Emphasizing that China is not a superpower and that there is no triangular relationship between China and the superpowers, he argues that since 1949 there has been great continuity in Chinese behavior, reflecting the stability in superpower bipolarity.[18]

Other authors, including Lowell Dittmer, Banning Garrett and Bonnie Glaser, Jonathan Pollack, Robert Ross, and Franz Schurmann, albeit readily acknowledging that the world is bipolar and that China is not a superpower since it lacks the nuclear arsenal of the former Soviet Union and the United States, argue that China's potential superpower status, and its regional authority, size, and military power, grant it unique status among the world's second-rank powers during the Cold War. Aside from the superpowers, China's impact on the global balance of military power was greater than that of any other country since World War II. These scholars argue that changing relations between the United States and the Soviet Union, and between those two countries and China, created the circumstances in which Chinese leaders evaluated PRC security vis-à-vis its primary adversary. In this context, Beijing adapted its policies to reach its objectives. Thus these authors discuss such issues as the development and devolution of the Sino-Soviet alliance, the emergence of U.S.-China rapprochement, China's changing negotiating tactics since the 1970s regarding its objective of disengaging the United States from Taiwan, and the emergence of its "independent foreign policy" with reference to changes in U.S.-Soviet-PRC relations.[19]

New Directions: The International Sources of Foreign Policy

The above literature on China and the superpowers is partly a discussion of alliance politics, emphasizing China's utilitarian, rational-choice approach to security relationships. It leaves unanswered, however, other aspects of alliance politics, including "burden-sharing" and the importance of expectations regarding mutual obligations. During the heyday of Sino-Soviet relations, this issue was expressed as "proletarian internationalism."[20] To what extent did unrealized PRC expectations of Soviet "burden-sharing" obligations contribute to Beijing's disillusionment with the Sino-Soviet alliance? How have PRC attitudes changed since the demise of Sino-Soviet friendship and with what implications for the course of U.S.-China security cooperation? Is China now more cynical in its superpower relationships?

Related to this is the lack of analysis of the bilateral dynamics of China's relations with the superpowers. Only Su Chi's work explores the interactions of both Soviet and Chinese attitudes in order to reach a subtle understanding of Sino-Soviet relations. Similarly, in Sino-Japanese relations, only Chae-Jin Lee has utilized both Japanese and Chinese language sources. Concerning relations between China and the United States, Robert Ross has examined the dynamics of bargaining between the two countries during the 1970s and 1980s by examining the sources and interaction of Chinese and U.S. negotiating policy.[21] But these limited studies cannot begin to address the many issues involved in each of these important bilateral relationships. Indeed, there is little work using Chinese and

American sources to reexamine Sino-American interactions in the 1950s, including during the war in Korea and the various crises over Taiwan, despite considerably expanded access to Chinese materials concerning U.S.-China relations in the 1950s, the declassification of U.S. documents from the 1950s, and access to interviews with former U.S. officials. Chinese materials could also be used to better explain U.S.-China interactions during the Vietnam War. Indeed, such studies could benefit from greater use of Chinese scholarship and from collaborative efforts involving Chinese scholars using authoritative Chinese materials and interviews with former Chinese officials.[22]

Interaction analysis of China's involvement with other countries can address a number of important issues, including the role of misperceptions and mirror images in the development of heightened conflict and crisis escalation, and how different international and domestic circumstances between China and its counterparts have produced particular outcomes in China's relationships with both its allies and adversaries. Rarely is conflict or cooperation the result of just one country's action.

Another shortcoming of this literature is its excessive focus on Chinese security policy. As China has become more active in international affairs, its interaction with its security partners has extended beyond strategic considerations. Trade issues are now at the forefront of China's relations with the United States, Japan, and other advanced market economies, and China is now a member of various international economic organizations and seeks admittance to the General Agreement on Tariffs and Trade (GATT). Both in bilateral and in multinational contexts, China must reach agreements permitting it to reap the benefits of cooperation in international economics. Thus a central and unresearched area, with the exception of the important work by Samuel Kim on China's attitude toward world order principles,[23] and by Michel Oksenberg and Harold Jacobson on Chinese negotiations with the International Monetary Fund and the World Bank, is an explanation of Beijing's negotiating postures in bilateral and multilateral economic negotiations. What is the balance between economic and strategic leverage in bilateral Sino-American and Sino-Japanese trade negotiations? How does China relate the importance of its market to its need for exports? Are the strategic and economic "chessboards" kept separate in bilateral economic negotiations? If not, how do they interact and with what results?

Whereas the strategic approach argues that security considerations limit the importance of domestic politics in making policy toward the superpowers, domestic politics clearly plays a much greater role in developing foreign economic policies than in developing security policies. Nonetheless, except for work on the overall evolution of the open-door policy, this domestic-international linkage remains a largely unexplored subject. What is the interplay between international and domestic considerations when Chinese leaders make decisions regarding international economic conflicts of interest? How might domestic interests contribute to PRC adoption of a "hard" line versus a "soft" line in GATT negotiations, in textile talks with the United States, or in balance of trade discussions with Japan?

Finally, the demise of the Soviet Union and the ensuing fundamental changes in world politics have created an entirely new international context for Chinese policy-making and present a new set of issues for research. During the Cold War, Chinese policy was easily managed insofar as security threats created the imperative of cooperation. After the Cold War, China may be more secure, but policy-making is more difficult since there is not a primary security threat defining Chinese policy. How have China's willingness to compromise and its negotiating style changed now that it lacks the imperative of cooperation? Similar to post–Cold War research on domestic politics and foreign policy, a comparative approach to the international sources of Chinese foreign policy would reveal the impact of international politics on Chinese foreign policy by emphasizing the differences across historical periods.

China as a Regional Power

China may not be a superpower, but there is little disagreement that it is a regional power with important regional interests. It is widely recognized that the PRC plays an important role in maintenance of regional stability and it influences the vital security interests of nearly all the states from the Korean peninsula through Southeast and South Asia and, increasingly, into the Middle East. Given its increasingly pivotal role in Asia, understanding the sources of PRC regional behavior continues to interest scholars of PRC foreign policy.

The literature on China as a regional power continues to emphasize the importance of national interest in determining China's policies toward states other than the superpowers. The most influential book on this issue was Peter Van Ness's early work on China's support for national liberation movements.[24] Van Ness found that China supported subversive movements only when the host country adopted policies inimical to PRC interests, especially regarding diplomatic recognition and membership in the United Nations. Scholars focusing on China's Asian neighbors stress the role of threat perception in policy formation, underscoring the relationship between China's neighbors and Beijing's primary adversary in determining whether China treats its neighbor as friend or foe. Work on China's pre-1973 Vietnam policy by Jay Taylor, David Mozingo, Thomas Robinson, and others stressed that Beijing placed priority on management of its conflict with the United States over support for Hanoi's unification plans. Melvin Gurtov's work on Chinese policy toward Burma, Thailand, and Cambodia during the 1960s emphasized the importance of these countries' relations with the United States and their contribution to U.S. participation in the war in Vietnam on China's bilateral policy.[25]

Despite the significant changes in China's domestic scene after the death of Mao and the changes in Chinese relations with the superpowers in the 1970s and

1980s, including the emergence of the Soviet Union as China's primary adversary and the subsequent development of the "independent foreign policy," scholars still considered the security theme useful in explaining PRC behavior—as China's primary adversary changed, its attitudes toward its neighbors changed accordingly. Steven Levine pointed out that China in the late 1970s and early 1980s made "anti-Sovietism" the basis of its Asia policy, using a global perspective on regional issues. Similarly, Eugene Lawson found that China's concern over the Soviet threat intruded into Sino-Vietnamese relations as early as the 1960s. Robert Ross's examination of China's Vietnam policy after the fall of Saigon in 1975 argued that China tried to use various policy instruments to minimize Hanoi's incentive to cooperate with Moscow and that Beijing's enmity for Vietnam grew as PRC policy failed and Soviet-Vietnamese security relations expanded.[26]

Scholarship on PRC policy toward maritime Southeast Asia and South Asia follows this perspective. Mozingo stressed the importance of Indonesia's policy toward the United States on China's Indonesia policy. John Garver's work on Sino-Indian relations emphasizes the importance of developments in Soviet security policy and Soviet-Indian relations on China's changing policy toward India. Regarding Sino-Pakistani relations, Yaacov Vertzberger's work reveals the importance of strategic, multilateral considerations in Chinese policy-making.[27]

Thus scholarship on China's regional security policy has forged an important consensus that Chinese leaders look on its neighbors in the context of PRC security concerns vis-à-vis its superpower adversary. Having established that this significant pattern exists, creative scholarship is required to pursue unstudied areas and report new findings.

There has been little work examining Chinese expectations of its less powerful allies. Nowhere is this more the case than in Sino-Thai relations. After 1975, China assumed from the United States much of the burden of providing for Thai security. But how has this relationship developed and is it based merely on a consolidated military relationship, or are there other shared interests? Do Thailand and China have identical objectives for Cambodia, or has China tried to use its influence to inhibit Bangkok from developing an independent Vietnam policy? Has China's interest in Thailand been limited to opposition to Vietnam, or does Beijing also seek to influence Thai policy in other issues and in domestic affairs?

The issues raised by Sino-Thai relations can be extended to the search for patterns in China's policy toward other weaker states. Now that the Soviet withdrawal has made China the dominant political force in Indochina, what will it demand from Vietnam? How much control does China want and in what issue areas does it expect to be consulted? Are its expectations different today than they were in 1975, when the Soviet Union was a major actor in Indochina? These same questions should be asked concerning Chinese policy toward Pakistan, Cambodia, and North Korea. Essentially, what does China demand of its smaller neighbors? As a counterpart to China's expectations from alliance relationships with the superpowers, we need to know what kind of burdens China imposes on smaller states with which it has developed security ties.

Related to these questions is the issue of the instruments China has to expand its regional influence. It may be that China shares with the former Soviet Union an inability to cement ties with potential allies except through arms sales, for it has limited economic or ideological incentives to offer. This may be particularly the case concerning economic relations with the ASEAN countries. American Soviet specialists have argued that this created a destabilizing aspect to Soviet foreign policy, since arms sales helped escalate conflict. Can the same be said of Chinese policy and with what implications for regional stability? Does this pattern help to explain PRC arms sales to the Middle East? In addition to the work by John Lewis, Hua Di, and Xue Litai on the domestic politics of Chinese arms sales,[28] additional work can be done that draws on the more general literature on domestic politics and foreign policy, particularly concerning the decision-making authority of the highest civilian leaders concerning exports of particular weapons to particular countries. Research is also needed to determine whether Beijing has exercised any restraint in the interest of regional stability and how it has used the influence it has acquired as an arms supplier to the Third World.

One particularly pressing question concerns China's future role in Asia. There is general awareness throughout academia and the popular press that the geopolitical center of gravity is shifting toward Asia and that China is destined to be a more powerful and influential world actor. China specialists, however, have not begun to consider how the PRC is apt to use its developing authority. Despite the risks associated with prediction, scholarship can be useful in discussing China's future.

Economic projection can be used to evaluate various alternative economic futures for China, each with different political and military implications. Alternatively, scholarship can safely assume that China's future capabilities will surpass the requirements of its current regional role and thus it can begin to consider the demands that China will impose to make Asian alignments commensurate with its increased power. From this angle, as Asia evolves in the post–Cold War period, what are likely to be the future regional "hot spots" involving China? Will China seek to use its influence over its neighbors simply to deny their strategic value to its competitors, or will China seek actual control over its neighbors? How will Beijing's policy toward current but latent conflicts of interest likely change, including policy toward the Paracel and Spratly islands in the South China Sea, which are claimed by Vietnam, the Philippines, Malaysia, and Brunei, as well as by China and Taiwan?

In the post–Cold War era China's attention has turned to Japan and its potential as a political and military power in Asia. Allen Whiting has revealed Chinese ambivalence toward Japan. On the one hand, China needs friendly relations with Japan in order to attract Japanese investment and technology in order to modernize its economy and participate in a world increasingly characterized by technology-based competition. On the other hand, China's experience with Japanese occupation has led the leadership to exaggerate fears of Japanese "militarism" and its rising defense budget. In light of these tensions, Whiting and Pollack have discussed the implications of Sino-Japanese competition for the future of Asia.[29]

Much more work needs to be done on China's Japan policy. Only Lee has explored in depth the important subject of Sino-Japanese economic relations.[30] The aforementioned issues of domestic-foreign linkages in foreign economic policy, the relationship between strategic and economic factors in China's negotiating strategy, and China's use of its market to promote exports are all central to Sino-Japanese relations. Research in this area would provide a foundation for understanding China's Japan policy after the Cold War.

China's involvement in the international economy of Asia will also be influential in determining China's political and strategic role in the region. Although China has developed significant economic relations with South Korea, Japan, and Taiwan, it has not become a major actor in the economies of the Southeast Asian countries. Moreover, its economy remains significantly less developed than those of the Asian countries that have employed export-led development strategies. An important issue is the impact of China's lower level of economic development on its ability to influence regional economic diplomacy. Will China have the economic authority necessary to be included in multilateral negotiations creating a regional economic order? If so, what role can it play? If not, how will it respond to the resulting economic isolation?

PRC Use of Force

The PLA may have only a peripheral role in the formulation of Chinese policy concerning the superpowers, regional affairs, and PRC trade issues, but in China's use of force and in the making of defense policy, the PLA is a key actor, with a direct voice in the making of policy and in policy outcome. Thus scholars have concerned themselves with not only the international aspects of Chinese decision-making regarding use of force and defense policy, but also the importance of domestic politics and the role of the military leadership.

Cases of Chinese use of force have attracted great attention from scholars. Intrigued with understanding China's perceptions of the risks of war in the nuclear era, scholars have sought to explain China's behavior during crises and its motives for going to war. Through the writings of such scholars as Melvin Gurtov, Byong-Moo Huang, Thomas Robinson, Thomas Stolper, and Whiting, a consensus has emerged concerning PRC behavior.[31] We have learned that in crises China has sought to avoid war, signaled, with varying degrees of success, its adversary of its intention to use force, and, with the exception of the Korean War, has used its military in such a manner so as to be able to avoid rapid escalation and to be able to defuse the crisis quickly. When Beijing has gone to war, it has done so in response to perceived challenges to its security, which have often been accentuated by perceptions of domestic weakness.

As for the influence of domestic politics, judicious scholarship has suggested hypotheses but has concluded that there is, at best, only minimal evidence that Chinese leaders have used force to promote their parochial domestic political interests or that the outcome of factional disputes has determined China's decision to go to war.[32]

The development of this consensus is important, yet it appears to have stifled research into other aspects of PRC crisis behavior. There has been some discussion, however, over China's 1979 invasion of Vietnam. Whereas Ross posits that the invasion reflects the trends in PRC behavior established in the earlier writings on Chinese use of force, others have written that China's invasion was primarily an emotional, vindictive response to its perception of Vietnamese impudent defiance of Chinese demands, which Chinese leaders believed they had the historical and geopolitical right to make.[33] Research should explore this argument, as well as the important and more general issue of nonrational-actor elements in Chinese behavior in any or all of the cases of PRC use of force. Not only is the role of historical attitudes an important subject, but so too are the roles of miscalculations, misperceptions, and accidents in PRC behavior, all of which can lead to inadvertent crisis escalation and, thus, war. In this regard, it is worthwhile to recall Whiting's discussion of "Rationality in PRC Foreign Policy," which analyzes the problem of rationality in crisis situations.[34]

An equally interesting yet murky subject concerns the role of the military in PRC decisions to use force. Although American scholars have gone a long way in establishing linkages with the PLA and, in the abstract, such linkages should vastly improve our understanding of the broader issues of defense and national security policies, we are still at a very early stage in this new relationship and the results are more properly called "insights" rather than a systematic integration of Chinese and American paradigms. Individual American scholars have found the relationship valuable, but there is no sense in which the ability to exchange views with our Chinese counterparts regularly has had a major impact on the American study of the role of the military in Chinese decision-making. Our research remains based primarily on library resources, illuminated by personal contacts with Chinese scholars, soldiers, and officials.

In part this is because security issues remain very sensitive in China; there is no counterpart to the American community of "defense intellectuals" who devote their academic skills to systematic exposition and evaluation of defense issues. The Beijing International Institute for Strategic Studies (BIISS) and the Academy of Military Sciences may well be the closest approximation to this community, but they are both attached to the military hierarchy. Although personal discussions can lead to frank exchanges, the typical meeting consists of an elaboration of official views. Furthermore, there is a mutual weakness in that most of the time neither group of scholars engaged in the meetings has had continuous access to the same set of materials relating to the problem under discussion.

Thus discussions with members of the Chinese defense community remain relatively abstract or speculative, that is, discussions can be held on such topics as the global "balance of power" between the United States and the former Soviet Union or on potential future balances and the possible influence of such changes on the dynamics of global or regional international politics. But attempting to narrow the analysis to potential Chinese military behavior in these same scenarios, or what these changes may mean for Chinese defense policy and military strategy, draws out only constrained commentary. Discussions at this level permit judgments between and among individual scholars, and to some extent institutions, that allow subjective assessments about "hard-line" and "moderate" positions being held on a number of issues or even about specific cases. BIISS, for example, may well see China's future security environment as more threatening than do scholars at the Chinese Academy of Social Science's Institute of American Studies. Nevertheless, these distinctions are crude and do not permit an evaluation of the methodology that led to these divisions.[35]

Up to now, then, contacts with Chinese security specialists have not permitted us to make inroads into one of the central questions in the study of military affairs: the role of the military in the formulation of national security strategy. Indeed, regarding use of force, we have not progressed any further than Whiting's now classic 1975 study of China's deterrence strategies.[36] Future research should include not only the role of force, but also that of the military leadership in defining national security objectives and policies. In a similar vein, the role of the military leadership in crisis situations is also of importance. Areas of collaboration could include those times when the United States and China were in opposition, especially now that U.S. documents are being declassified and both we and our Chinese colleagues can explore the substance and process of American crisis decisions in tandem with Chinese perceptions and decisions.[37] Although it is unlikely that we will initially gain access to Chinese documents to the extent that we can those of the United States, over time this may change. Paralleling research on U.S.-China diplomatic interactions, studies of PRC crisis behavior could examine U.S.-China interactions during the Korean War, the Taiwan crises, and the war in Indochina. It would also be useful to explore the value of "oral history," perhaps following the pattern of memoirs now being published in China.

Chinese Defense Policy

It is in this realm that the increased flow of information from China has been of the greatest benefit in the development of Chinese military studies. The work of William Whitson,[38] Harvey Nelsen,[39] and Harlan Jencks[40] provided the foundation that prepared the field for the more open environment that has emerged in China. Candid discussions of the long- and short-term military "threats" faced by

China and their implications for defense modernization have filled the pages of China's journals and press for more than a decade. Analyses of strategies and procedures for weapons and equipment acquisitions, modernization of the defense industrial base, military strategy and operations, and the nature of modern war both now and in the future have enabled us to gain far greater insight into Chinese conceptualization of defense policies and military strategy than was possible in the 1960s and early to mid-1970s. Those of us who spent days and weeks speculating on the often abstruse implications of allegorical articles in the Chinese press remember those times too well.

One of the most important aspects of the increased flow of information is that we can now more directly observe the continuing progress of a debate from a variety of sources. From the perspective of military studies, the simple fact that *Jiefangjun Bao* (Liberation Daily) is no longer *neibu* (for internal circulation only) enables us to have continuing access to the principal newspaper devoted to military issues. In addition, we have had access to many journals devoted to international politics, which have become increasingly less concerned with ideological issues and more focused on the "realities" of international politics and defense issues than was the case in the past. This concentration has remained despite the obligatory references to "peaceful evolution" as the principal strategy of the West to undermine Chinese "socialism" since the crushing of the demonstrations in Tiananmen Square.

As a consequence of more open Chinese analyses of these issues, the field of defense studies has been able to describe and evaluate not only China's approach to defense modernization, but also the discrete components of what is a very complex process. We can link changes in military doctrine, strategy, operations, and force structure with threat perception and the levels of modernization within the Chinese armed forces. This same open discussion in the Chinese press and specialized journals has permitted investigation of the PLA's reforms in professional military education and training, and the selection and promotion of officers.[41]

The ability to delve deeply into Chinese discussions of their defense modernization needs and programs has enabled us to obtain a better grasp of China's defense strategies.[42] Although there is some debate over the meaning of the ubiquitous term "people's war under modern conditions," used by Chinese commentators and senior military officials to describe virtually every strategy under discussion, there is consensus that China has no intention of conducting war in the future as it did in the 1930s and early 1940s. Whatever debate remains, it is rapidly being settled by the Chinese themselves as they have become more open and sophisticated in their analyses of nuclear war and strategy, and in their own debates over the role of protracted conventional war in the modern era, and the demands of short-duration, high-intensity limited war.

Almost all of these analyses, which have consumed so much of our recent publication on China's defense policy, have been undertaken as library research. To some extent, however, visits to Chinese research institutes and ad hoc discussions with senior Chinese officers and military researchers have afforded us useful insights in interpreting the results of our library research. More recently, visits to PLA centers of professional military education have also allowed us to gain insights into the military's approach to revising its education and training for future senior officers. The results of these visits have shown up in the research of American scholars, but the desire to maintain the confidentiality of face-to-face discussions has not permitted, as yet, any direct evaluation of Chinese views in these matters. In future years, these continuing contacts with the Chinese military should bear greater fruit.

Nevertheless, the research agenda was guided by and has kept pace with China's changing role in the Cold War competition and conflict between the West and the Soviet Union. Thus in analyzing such topics as the move away from people's war strategy, the expansion of China's military academies, and the changing education level in the PLA officer corps, scholars continued to tread proven paths of research. Greater emphasis is now required on the international implications of China's changing defense strategy and capabilities. Specialists in Chinese security policy need to develop the expertise to assess the importance of China's increasing nuclear and conventional capabilities on Asian security.

Although China's nuclear deterrence strategy is well understood, we have far less confidence in our understanding of PRC attitudes toward such concepts as stable regional deterrence. Research on the Soviet Union reveals that it took many years before Soviet leaders began to consider seriously the notion of crisis stability, with critical implications for the U.S.-Soviet arms control process. What are Chinese attitudes toward crisis stability and the importance of particular nuclear force structures in promoting stability? Do Chinese analysts understand the role of arms control in maximizing stability, as well as in minimizing the quantity of weapons? The pioneering work of Morton Halperin and Alastair Johnston[43] needs to be followed by interviews with Chinese arms control specialists in order to seek answers to these questions.

Until very recently, China's nuclear forces were seen as supplemental to their conventional forces in deterring the Soviet Union.[44] Now, with the disintegration of the Soviet Union, Beijing's conservative defense analysts may well see China's strategic forces as a deterrent against any potential transition toward an aggressive security policy by Russia. Nonetheless, the role of China's nuclear capabilities in a post–Cold War Asia raises new questions.

If Chinese analyses of their own concepts of strategy and operations are any evidence, Chinese military planners believe that preparing and training for war is a major contribution to a deterrence strategy. Since 1985, Chinese defense policy has been based on preparing not for a major nuclear and conventional war with what was the Soviet Union, but for wars with limited political and military objectives that occur as a function of unanticipated conflict around China's periphery.[45] This new national military strategy and associated changes in Chinese armed forces' concepts of operations and military force structure have led to an emphasis on force projection and quick, lethal reaction combined with armed forces capable of achieving military victory in the opening phase of a war. By deemphasizing preparation for a major conventional and nuclear war and stressing the need for well prepared forces capable of immediate military action, China's defense posture is now vastly different from what it was in 1985. This change in China's national military strategy raises the issue of offensive versus defensive approaches in PRC strategy and the implications for regional stability and deterrence. Of particular interest and concern for security analysts should be the development of a nuclear-armed China preparing for limited but high-intensity warfare on its periphery.

We also need to understand the implications for post–Cold War arms control in Asia of China's emphasis on developing submarine-launched cruise and ballistic missiles (SLBM) and the continuing modernization of its land-based nuclear forces. Scholars are well aware of the complications that West European defense systems lent to U.S.-Soviet arms control negotiations. As China deploys its own SLBM force and modernizes its land-based systems, how will this affect Russian security considerations and its readiness to undertake multilateral arms control and confidence-building measures in Northeast Asia? Force reduction and confidence-building measures undertaken by the Soviet Union and China along their mutual borders and in Mongolia since 1991 may ease the transition to multilateral agreements. With Chinese policymakers stating six years before the disintegration of the Soviet Union that a major war with the country was extremely unlikely and would no longer be the primary focus of China's defense policy, will the collapse of the Soviet Union make Beijing more amenable to regional arms control agreements in Northeast and South Asia?

Related to China's contribution to crisis stability is its weapons procurement process—a crucial direction for research if we expect to understand China's impact on global stability. John Lewis and Xue Litai's research on Chinese construction of the atomic bomb reflects the new possibilities in studies on Chinese military affairs, taking advantage of the rich new data now available to scholars.[46] Along similar lines, analysis of the contemporary modernization process should also be undertaken. Work on the Soviet Union often underscored the extent to which weapons procurement decisions were made within the military rather than in the civilian hierarchy. Although current budgetary restraints seem to have led to joint civil-military decisions on the procurement of China's major weapon systems, in a richer budget environment with a smaller, more professional military elite will this constraint continue? To the extent that China's military hierarchy becomes independent in weapons procurement, Beijing's ability to develop a defense posture promoting both PRC security and stable mutual deterrence among the regional powers is reduced. Though this is clearly a difficult subject to research, interviews with PRC defense analysts may well prove insightful.

The need to focus on China's role as a regional power becomes ever more critical as the U.S. military presence in East Asia and the Indian Ocean area is reduced. The future defense policies of Japan and India are of great concern to China, as is the potential for a non–Marxist-Leninist, unified Korea. The policies of these states will reflect the absence of a strong U.S. military presence following the demise of the Soviet Union as a threat to American military security in the region. The future direction of regional states' defense policies as they react to the American force reduction is very uncertain, and China's contribution to an Asian security regime is far from clear. The ongoing modernization and expansion of Chinese naval forces are especially important. Moreover, the crumbling of Marxism-Leninism in the Soviet Union and Eastern Europe, and the ascension of pluralistic democracy and market capitalism as the dominant model of political and economic development, represent a challenge to China's security as much as future military threats. For China's security analysts, the future contains very indeterminate military and ideological trends. The combination of military uncertainty and ideological paranoia that now pervades Beijing underscores the need for new perspectives on Chinese security policy.

Conclusion

The security studies field has made major strides over the years and developed important findings concerning critical aspects of PRC behavior. But what is the likelihood that any of these suggestions for new research directions will be taken up by the field? Unfortunately, it is probable that most of the issues will remain unexplored. This is not necessarily because these problems are not interesting or important, but because the China field is not preparing a sufficient number of specialists to take on all the questions that remain unanswered. Indeed, it appears that fewer security specialists are entering the field today than in the past. For a long time the field's concentration on domestic politics was understandable. China's impact on global affairs and its military capabilities were relatively slight, despite U.S. obsession with monolithic communism, while Maoist China was at the forefront of Communist countries attempting social transformation. Domestic politics and comparative communism were pressing issues that demanded scholars' attention.

Today, however, China has begun to expand both its power and its reach beyond its borders. Its military modernization program is steadily progressing and will undoubtedly develop faster as China develops the economic, scientific, and technological bases of military power. To the extent that Beijing's power in the 1950s and 1960s was sufficient to embroil the United States in dangerous crises throughout Asia, in the 1990s and certainly the twenty-first century its power and influence will be even greater, without any guarantee that Asia will be stable or peaceful. On the contrary, the erosion of bipolarity and the growing strength of China, India, and Japan suggest that the future of Asia could be turbulent and unpredictable.

China's role in international economic affairs is also growing, with a predictable corresponding increase in the importance of economic matters in China's political relations with a wide range of countries and in China's influence on international economic stability. This is not to say that the "China market" will become a major factor significantly affecting the economic stability of many countries, but that Chinese cooperation, even should the open door begin to close, will simply be an increasingly important factor in maintaining international economic and political stability.

Under these new and still evolving strategic and economic circumstances, it is all the more important that the China field broaden its focus on Chinese security studies and tackle new agendas, however chaotic and disorganized the initial results might be. China is clearly changing—this makes it imperative that Chinese studies fulfill its responsibility by explaining the importance of a changing China to world affairs.

Notes

The views of Paul H.B. Godwin are his own and are not to be construed as presenting those of the National War College, National Defense University, Department of Defense, or any other agency of the U.S. government.

1. A. Doak Barnett, *Communist China in Asia: Challenge to American Policy* (New York: Random House, 1960); Allen S. Whiting, *China Crosses the Yalu: The Decision to Enter the Korean War* (Palo Alto, Calif.: Stanford University Press, 1960).

2. Melvin Gurtov and Harry Harding, *The Purge of Lo Jui-Ch'ing: The Politics of Chinese Strategic Planning,* R–548—PR (Santa Monica, Calif.: Rand Corporation, 1971); Uri Ra'anan, "Peking's Foreign Policy 'Debate,' 1965–1966," in *China in Crisis, vol. 2: China's Policies in Asia and America's Alternatives,* ed. Tang Tsou (Chicago: University of Chicago Press, 1968); Donald S. Zagoria, *Vietnam Triangle: Moscow/Peking/Hanoi* (New York: Pegasus, 1967). See also the contribution to this debate by Michael Yahuda, "Kremlinology and the Chinese Strategic Debate, 1965–1966," *China Quarterly,* no. 49 (January–March 1972).

3. John Garver, *China's Decision for Rapprochement with the United States, 1968–1971* (Boulder, Colo.: Westview Press, 1982); Thomas M. Gottlieb, *Chinese Foreign Policy Factionalism and the Origins of the Strategic Triangle,* R-1902-NA (Santa Monica, Calif.: Rand Corporation, 1977).

4. John Garver, "Chinese Foreign Policy in 1970: The Tilt towards the Soviet Union," *China Quarterly,* no. 82 (June 1980).

5. Kenneth Lieberthal, *Sino-Soviet Conflict in the 1970s: Its Evolution and Implications for the Strategic Triangle,* R-2342-NA (Santa Monica, Calif.: Rand Corporation, 1978); Kenneth Lieberthal, "The Foreign Policy Debate in Peking as Seen Through Allegorical Articles, 1973–1976," *China Quarterly,* no. 71 (September 1977); Harry Harding, "The Domestic Politics of China's Global Posture, 1973–1978, in *China's Quest for Independence: Policy Evolution in the 1970s,* ed. Thomas Fingar et al. (Boulder, Colo.: Westview Press, 1980), 93–146.

6. Carol Hamrin, "Competing 'Policy Packages' in Post-Mao China," *Asian Survey* 4 (May 1984). See also Carol Hamrin, "China Reassesses the Superpowers," *Pacific Affairs* 56 (Summer 1983).

7. Thomas Fingar, "Domestic Policy and the Quest for Independence," in Fingar et al., eds., *China's Quest for Independence,* 25–92.

8. Robert S. Ross, "From Lin Biao to Deng Xiaoping: Elite Instability and China's U.S. Policy," *China Quarterly*, no. 188 (June 1989): 265–99.

9. Allen S. Whiting, *Chinese Domestic Politics and Foreign Policy in the 1970s*, Michigan Papers in Chinese Studies, 36 (Ann Arbor: Center for Chinese Studies, University of Michigan, 1979).

10. Paul Godwin, "Soldiers and Statesmen in Conflict," in *China and the World: Chinese Foreign Policy in the Post-Mao Era*, ed. Samuel Kim (Boulder, Colo.: Westview Press, 1984), 215–34; Jonathan Pollack, *The Sino-Soviet Rivalry and the Chinese Security Debate* (Santa Monica, Calif.: Rand Corporation, 1982).

11. Michel Oksenberg and Steven Goldstein, "The Chinese Political Spectrum," *Problems of Communism* 2 (March–April 1974).

12. Ann Fenwick, "Chinese Foreign Trade Policy and the Campaign Against Deng Xiaoping," in Fingar et al., eds., *China's Quest for Independence*, 199–224.

13. Kenneth Lieberthal, "Domestic Politics and Foreign Policy," in *China's Foreign Relations in the 1980s*, ed. Harry Harding (New Haven: Yale University Press, 1984); Susan Shirk, "The Domestic Political Dimensions of China's Foreign Economic Relations," in Kim, ed., *China and the World*, 57–81.

14. David L. Shambaugh, "China's National Security Research Bureaucracy," *China Quarterly*, no. 110 (June 1987): 276–304; idem, *Beautiful Imperialist: China Perceives America, 1972–1990* (Princeton: Princeton University Press, 1991).

15. Gerald Segal, "The PLA and Chinese Foreign Policy Decision-Making," *International Affairs* (Summer 1981): 449–66.

16. First steps in this direction include Richard H. Solomon, *Chinese Political Negotiating Behavior*, R-3295 (Santa Monica, Calif.: Rand Corporation, 1985); Lucian Pye, *Chinese Commercial Negotiating Style*, R-2837-AF (Santa Monica, Calif.: Rand Corporation, 1982).

17. Robert Sutter, *Chinese Foreign Policy: Developments After Mao* (New York: Praeger, 1986). See also Sutter's work on Sino-American relations that employ this perspective, including *China Watch: Toward Sino-American Reconciliation* (Baltimore: Johns Hopkins University Press, 1978).

18. Michael Ng-Quinn, "The Analytic Study of Chinese Foreign Policy," *International Studies Quarterly* 27 (June 1983); Michael Ng-Quinn, "International Systemic Constraints on Chinese Foreign Policy," in Kim, ed., *China and the World*, 82–110.

19. Lowell Dittmer, "The Strategic Triangle: An Elementary Game-Theoretical Analysis," *World Politics* 33 (July 1981); Banning Garrett and Bonnie Glaser, *War and Peace: The Views for Moscow and Beijing* (Berkeley: Institute of International Studies, University of California, 1984); Jonathan Pollack, *The Lessons of Coalition Politics: Sino-American Security Relations*, R-3133-AF (Santa Monica, Calif.: Rand Corporation, 1984); Robert S. Ross, "International Bargaining and Domestic Politics: Conflict in U.S.-China Relations Since 1972," *World Politics* 38 (January 1986); idem, "China Learns to Compromise: Change in U.S.-China Relations, 1982–1984," *China Quarterly*, no. 128 (December 1991); Franz Schurmann, *The Logic of World Power* (New York: Pantheon Books, 1974).

20. For a discussion of this, see Steven Goldstein, in *Patterns of Cooperation in the Foreign Relations of Modern China*, ed. Harry Harding (forthcoming).

21. Su Chi, "China and the Soviet Union: 'Principled, Salutary, and Tempered' Management of Conflict," in Kim, ed., *China and the World*, 135–60; Chae Jin-Lee, *Japan Faces China: Political and Economic Relations in the Postwar Era* (Baltimore: Johns Hopkins University Press, 1976); idem, *China and Japan: New Economic Diplomacy* (Palo Alto, Calif.: Stanford University Press, 1984); Robert S. Ross, *Managing U.S.-China Cooperation: Negotiation and Compromise During the Cold War* (forthcoming).

22. Some American scholars are beginning to use these Chinese materials to reassess China's involvement in the Korean War. See, for example, Thomas Christensen, "Threats, Assurances, and the Last Chance for Peace: The Lessons of Mao's Korean War Telegrams," *International Security* 17 (Summer 1992): 122–54; Jonathan D. Pollack, "The Korean War and Sino-American Relations," in *Sino-American Relations, 1945–1954*, ed. Harry Harding and Yuan Ming (Wilmington: Scholarly Resources, 1989), 213–37. The Harding and Yuan volume also represents an early and significant collaboration. For an excellent history of U.S. policy toward China using recently declassified U.S. documents, see Gordon Chang, *Friends and Enemies: The United States, China, and the Soviet Union, 1948–1972* (Palo Alto, Calif.: Stanford University Press, 1990).

23. Samuel S. Kim, *China, the United Nations, and World Order* (Princeton: Princeton University Press, 1979); Harold K. Jacobson and Michel Oksenberg, *China's Participation in the IMF, the World Bank, and GATT: Toward a Global Economic Order* (Ann Arbor: University of Michigan Press, 1990).

24. Peter Van Ness, *Revolution and Chinese Foreign Policy: Peking's Support for Wars of National Liberation* (Berkeley: University of California Press, 1970).

25. Melvin Gurtov, *China and Southeast Asia—The Politics of Survival* (Baltimore: Johns Hopkins University Press, 1971); David Mozingo and Thomas Robinson, *Lin Biao on People's War: China Takes a Second Look at Vietnam*, RM-4814-PR (Santa Monica, Calif.: Rand Corporation, 1965); Jay Taylor, *China and Southeast Asia: Peking's Relations with Revolutionary Movements*, 2d ed., rev. (New York: Praeger, 1976).

26. Eugene Lawson, *The Sino-Vietnamese Conflict* (New York: Praeger, 1984); Steven I. Levine, "China in Asia: The PRC as a Regional Power," in Harding, ed., *China's Foreign Relations in the 1980s*, 107–45; Robert S. Ross, *The Indochina Tangle, China's Vietnam Policy, 1975–1979* (New York: Columbia University Press, 1988).

27. David Mozingo, *Chinese Policy toward Indonesia, 1949–1967* (Ithaca: Cornell University Press, 1976). On Sino-Indian relations, see John Garver's work, including "The Indian Factor in Sino-Soviet Relations," *China Quarterly*, no. 125 (March 1991): 55–85. While not American, Vertzberger is the most informed scholar on Sino-Pakistani relations. See, for example, "The Political Economy of Sino-Pakistani Relations: Trade and Aid, 1963–1982," *Asian Survey* (May 1983).

28. John Lewis, Hua Di, and Xue Litai, "Beijing's Defense Establishment: Solving the Arms-Export Enigma," *International Security* 15 (Spring 1991).

29. Allen S. Whiting, *China Eyes Japan* (Berkeley: University of California Press, 1989); Jonathan Pollack, "The Sino-Japanese Relationship and East Asian Security: Patterns and Implications," *China Quarterly*, no. 124 (December 1990).

30. Lee, *Japan Faces China;* idem, *China and Japan.*

31. Melvin Gurtov and Byong-Moo Hwang, *China under Threat: The Politics of Strategy and Diplomacy* (Baltimore: Johns Hopkins University Press, 1980); Thomas Robinson, "The Sino-Soviet Border Dispute: Background, Development, and the March 1969 Clashes," *American Political Science Review* 66 (1972): 1175–1202; Thomas Stolper, *China, Taiwan, and the Offshore Islands* (Armonk, N.Y.: M.E. Sharpe, 1985); Allen S. Whiting, *The Chinese Calculus of Deterrence: India and Indochina* (Ann Arbor: University of Michigan Press, 1975).

32. For suggestions concerning the domestic politics of Chinese use of force in the 1969 Sino-Soviet border clashes, see Thomas Gottlieb, *Chinese Foreign Policy Factionalism and the Origins of the Strategic Triangle*, R-1902-NA (Santa Monica, Calif.: Rand Corporation, 1977).

33. Ross, *The Indochina Tangle.* See also Levine, "China in Asia."

34. Whiting, *The Chinese Calculus*, 226–33.

35. Bonnie Glaser and Banning H. Garrett, *Chinese Estimates of the U.S.-Soviet Bal-*

ance of Power, Occasional Paper 33 (Washington, D.C.: Asia Program, Woodrow Wilson International Center for Scholars, 1988).

36. Whiting, *The Chinese Calculus.*

37. See, for example, the essays by Gordon H. Chang and H.W. Brands using recently declassified documents to reanalyze the 1954–55 Taiwan Strait crisis, *International Security* 12 (Spring 1988).

38. William W. Whitson, ed., *The Military and Political Power in China in the 1970s* (New York: Praeger, 1972).

39. Harvey W. Nelsen, *The Chinese Military System* (Boulder, Colo.: Westview Press, 1977).

40. Harlan Jencks, *From Muskets to Missiles: Politics and Professionalism in the Chinese Army, 1945–1981* (Boulder, Colo.: Westview Press, 1982).

41. Ellis Joffe is not American but his *Chinese Army after Mao* (Cambridge, Mass.: Harvard University Press, 1987) contains the most comprehensive and recent analysis of the reforms within the Chinese defense establishment.

42. See, for example, Gerald Segal and William T. Tow, eds., *Chinese Defense Policy* (London: Macmillan Press, 1984); Charles D. Lovejoy, Jr., and Bruce W. Watson, eds., *China's Military Reforms: International and Domestic Implications* (Boulder, Colo.: Westview Press, 1986); Gerald Segal, *Defending China* (London: Oxford University Press, 1987); and Paul H.B. Godwin, "Chinese Military Strategy Revised: Local and Limited War," in *China's Foreign Relations,* ed. Allen S. Whiting (Newbury Park, Calif.: The Annals of the American Academy of Political and Social Science, January 1992), 191–201.

43. Morton Halperin, "Chinese Attitudes towards the Use and Control of Nuclear Weapons," in Tsou, ed., *China in Crisis,* vol. 2; and Alastair I. Johnston, *China and Arms Control: Emerging Issues and Interests,* Aurora Papers 3 (Ottawa: Canadian Centre for Arms Control and Disarmament, 1986).

44. These issues are discussed in Jonathan D. Pollack, "China as a Nuclear Power," in *Asia's Nuclear Future,* ed. William Overholt (Boulder, Colo.: Westview Press, 1977), 35–65; Paul H.B. Godwin, "Mao Zedong Revised: Deterrence and Defense in the 1980s," in *The Chinese Defense Establishment: Continuity and Change in the 1980s,* ed. Godwin (Boulder, Colo.: Westview Press, 1983), 21–40, and "Changing Concepts of Doctrine, Strategy and Operations in the Chinese People's Liberation Army, 1978–1987," *China Quarterly,* no. 112 (December 1987): 57–90; and Chong-pin Lin, *China's Nuclear Weapons Strategy: Traditions Within Evolution* (Lexington, Mass.: Lexington Books, 1988).

45. See Godwin, "Chinese Military Strategy Revised."

46. John Lewis and Xue Litai, *China Builds the Bomb* (Palo Alto, Calif.: Stanford University Press, 1988). For some early writings on the Chinese defense industry, see Harlan Jencks, "The Chinese Military Industrial Complex and Defense Modernization," *Asian Survey* (October 1980); and David L. Shambaugh, "China's Defense Industries: Indigenous and Foreign Procurement," in Godwin, ed., *The Chinese Defense Establishment,* 43–86.

Part III
The American China Studies Community

8

The Academic China Specialists

Richard Madsen

Since the end of World War II, academic China scholars in the United States have spent more than their share of time at the center of public controversies. First, there were the accusations of disloyalty leveled from the right wing during the McCarthy era against China scholars who had supposedly helped cause the United States to "lose" China. Then there were criticisms hurled from the Left during the 1960s against China scholars (some of the same ones in fact who had been attacked from the Right a decade earlier) who had supposedly aided and abetted American imperialism in Asia. Finally, in the wake of the 1989 Tiananmen massacre, there have been bitter complaints directed from both the Left and the Right against China scholars who during the 1980s had supposedly encouraged the American public to look favorably on a Chinese regime that had flagrantly abused human rights.

In the heat of these controversies, the entire profession of academic China scholarship was sometimes tarred rhetorically with a polemical brush. Not just a few aberrant individual scholars, but the most respected and influential members of the profession stood accused of political disloyalty, moral insensitivity, and intellectual malfeasance. For example, as Miriam London put it in an article written after the Tiananmen massacre, "an influential group of Sinologists and their disciples in leading American universities" who had "become known respectfully as 'China experts,'" especially to television interviewers, who appealed to them periodically as unravelers of Oriental mysteries and readers of green tea leaves" had created for the American public "a fictional land" that had served to justify a policy of amoral realpolitik toward China. According to London, the perpetration of this fiction was motivated as much by moral failure as by intellectual incompetence.

> For all their bristling academic credentials, the fact is that the China experts did not wish to know—but to believe. Like some Soviet experts before them, on whom they cast no backward glance, they were practitioners of the intellectual pseudo-faith of the century, dreaming up the City of Perfect Justice on earth. The bamboo

163

curtain was indeed essential to the believing Sinologists, freeing them to elaborate their fantasies (in their esoteric way, with footnotes) unconcerned by the intrusion of messy reality or the possibility of verification on the scene.[1]

Like almost all the learned professions, academic China scholarship is rent with controversies often rooted in power struggles between an older establishment and younger generations of scholars. When the public gaze is turned on China scholarship as a result of the academy's inevitable failures to provide a fully adequate understanding of China, the public witnesses some of this unedifying academic politics. Meanwhile, marginalized members of the profession are tempted to address their professional grievances by calling on public support. Miriam London is an example of a (senior) scholar whose very critical writings on contemporary China were never widely accepted by the leaders of the China studies profession. Now, in the wake of the failure of the profession's leaders to predict the 1989 democracy movement and its tragic suppression, she and others like her are gaining public approval by saying "I told you so" to those very leaders. In the process, however, she is contributing to public skepticism about the credibility, efficacy, and moral integrity of the profession as a whole.

It is hard to believe that the leaders of China studies are any more guilty of moral turpitude and intellectual incompetence than the leaders of any other profession. The reason why in the past several generations they seem to have come in for more than their share of criticism has less to do with them personally or with the particular structure of their profession than with the object of their study—with China and its place in the world system. For Americans, China—to twist a famous phrase from the anthropologist Claude Lévi-Strauss—has been bad to think with. China keeps on acting in ways that defy the assumptions of American social science and frustrate the aspirations of many Americans. The consequent lack of ability to understand adequately such a large and strategically important country arouses widespread anxiety in the United States and makes the normal tensions within the profession the object of public scrutiny.

This chapter discusses why China is so "bad to think with" for American academics and shows the problems this has caused for American academics and the American public. But it also explores how the China studies profession can and often has transcended its inevitable limitations. Like all modern learned professions, China studies is vulnerable to criticism precisely because it embodies important ideals and holds out high hopes for world peace and justice grounded in reciprocity and mutual understanding. It is important to know not only how it has not fulfilled its ideas, but how its ideals have continually impelled it to reform itself.

China and the Frustrations of Western Progressivism

Like the other scholarly professions in the United States, China studies had its origins in religious institutions. As Michael Hunt has put it, modern American educators are "the legatees of the missionary impulse."[2] In the writings of early

Protestant missionaries to China we can see a framework of assumptions about how to understand and what to do about China that still forms much of the intellectual and moral foundation of modern, secular China studies.

Consider for instance, the following passage, an account of village ferry-boat operations, from the Reverend Arthur H. Smith's *Village Life in China,* published in 1899. The village ferry, wrote Smith, is "one of the most characteristic specimens of the national genius with which we are acquainted."

> At a low stage of water, the ferry-boat is at the base of a sloping bank, down which in a diagonal line runs the track, never wide enough for two carts to pass each other. To get one of these large carts down this steep and shelving incline requires considerable engineering skill, and here accidents are not infrequent. . . . The more crooked these planks the better, for a reason which the traveller is not long in discovering. The object is by no means to get the cart and animals on with the minimum of trouble, but with the maximum of difficulty, for this is the way by which hoards of impecunious rascals get such an exiguous living as they have . . . .
>
> It is not unnatural for the Occidental, whose head is always full of ideas as to how things *ought* to be done in the East, to devise a plan by which all this wild welter would be reduced to order. He would, to begin with, have a fixed tariff, and he would have a wide and gently sloping path to the water's edge. He would have a broad and smooth gang-plank, over which both animals and carts could pass with no delay and no inconvenience. He would have a separate place for human passengers and for beasts, and in general shorten the time, diminish the discomforts and occidentalize the whole proceedings.[3]

Alas, the Reverend Smith recognizes, there is no short-term prospect that any of these reforms will take place. Making ferry travel more efficient would conflict with the economic interests of all those whose jobs depend on the present system. Moreover, the development of a more rational transportation system would require a broader understanding of the public good than is present in Chinese culture. "No Chinese can for a moment comprehend such a conception as is embodied in the phrase *Pro bono publico*. He never heard of such a thing, and what is more he never wants to hear it."

"We have wasted an undue amount of time in crossing a Chinese river," Smith concludes, "for it is a typical instance of flagrant abuses which the Chinese themselves do not mind, which would drive Occidentals to the verge of insanity—if not over the brink—and which it seems easy, but is really impossible to remedy. *Mutatis mutandis,* these things are a parable of the empire. The reform must come. It must be done from within. But the impulse can only come from without."[4] At the end of his book, Smith argues that the transformation of values necessary to support such reforms can come only from Christianity.

A century after Smith made his observations, most American China scholars would no longer believe that China needs to accept Christianity in order to modernize. They would consider his views ethnocentric, patronizing, and excessively moralistic. But their heads are still "full of ideas about how things ought to be done in the East," and those ideas bear remarkable similarity to those cited by Smith. China's economy, they would say, needs to become more efficient; it needs to conform to universal principles of economic rationality that were first articulated by Westerners; in this sense it needs to "occidentalize."

A core assumption of most modern Western social science is that there are universal laws of economic rationality, knowable through scientific investigation. Another assumption is that economic and social progress will follow if social institutions are ordered so as to conform to these laws. Most academic China scholars have based their studies of China on such universalistic, progressivist assumptions. But the realities of China are frustrating for people who hold such assumptions. China is too big, too populous, too diverse, and too poor to make the path to economic rationalization anything but obscure. As with the ferry crossing during Smith's time, there are too many people whose interests are tied up with maintaining inefficient systems to make it easy to carry out reforms. And Chinese cultural understandings about the relationship between the individual and the community and between public and private do not make it easy to accept certain kinds of economic and political reforms whose value seems self-evident to most Westerners. And the magnitude of China's problems almost guarantees that hopes for progress will be periodically thwarted by tragedy. So China is bad for Americans to think with. It does not develop in the ways we think it should.

Elitism and Populism

When Chinese society does not develop in ways that China scholars think it will or should, sometimes bitter debate arises within the profession of China studies. There has been a remarkable continuity in the terms of this debate, a reflection of basic fault lines that run through the American professions. On the one side are elitists, on the other, populists.

The elitists hold that one can best understand China from the point of view of and with the cooperation of its leaders. The populists insist that China be understood from the point of view of its common people. The way the debate between elitists and populists has been carried out, however, tells us more about the nature of American culture than about the realities of China.[5]

Central to the self-understanding of American professionals is the idea that they constitute an elite. Yet they are elitists with an uneasy conscience, because they also believe in (and often write books about the importance of) the democratic principle, with its insistence on the dignity and worth of each individual and its celebration of the sovereignty of the people.

Although one can identify individual professionals who have maintained a consistent populist or elitist stance—think of the difference in public philosophy between John Dewey, who believed throughout his life in the democratic capabilities of the ordinary citizen, and Walter Lippmann, who was more impressed by the ignorance and apathy of ordinary citizens and believed that the affairs of government should be handled by professionally educated elites—the tension between populist and elitist dimensions is so central to professional self-understanding in American culture that most American professionals ambivalently embrace both. Often, however, they lean toward one or the other at different phases in their careers.

This fluid interplay between elitism and populism within professional life owes as much to American culture as to the internal dynamics of the profession. European professionals—and, certainly, Chinese professionals—tend to express a much less ambivalent, much less apologetic, elitism than their American counterparts. The United States is different because of its culture and social structure.

American culture is distinctive for its individualism, encouraged by the opportunities that American society offers for individual mobility and grounded in a dominant Protestant tradition that stresses the direct relation of each individual to God. Individualism leads to a stress on the value and the potential of each person, no matter how humble—and an aversion to hierarchy. But the need to produce an efficiently organized society gives an ambivalent legitimacy to the role of experts who claim to know how to produce such order.[6] When American scholars with a populist bent looked at China, they saw the immense potential of its vast population, empathized with the terrible suffering of its common people, and often sympathized with the revolutionary struggle of its masses. When elitist scholars looked at China, they saw the potential for enlightened leadership from among those elites, a leadership that, given the proper education and proper expert advice, could bring about the necessary social changes in an orderly fashion. But populists had a difficult time understanding—and an even more difficult time communicating to an American public—the potential violence and brutality of the masses, and elitists had similar difficulties in understanding and communicating the cynicism and corruption of the ruling elites. In the course of its tortured twentieth-century history, China was bound to disappoint both elitists and populists.

Thus in the 1930s and 1940s, as the Chiang Kai-shek government stumbled toward its demise in spite of having been the recipient of large amounts of U.S. aid and professional advice, an upstart younger generation of journalists like Edgar Snow and scholars with at least a moderately populist bent, like John Fairbank, saw in the Communists an authentic, nationalistic voice of the Chinese people, in opposition to the arrogant, decadent elites whom the U.S. foreign policy establishment had supported. When the Communists took power and promptly started to execute landlords, imprison and torture missionaries, lean to the side of the Soviet Union, and take up arms against U.S. troops in Korea, the China experts who, out of a populist perspective, had said even reservedly sympathetic things about the Communists now came under attack by a new breed of American populists, the McCarthyites, who portrayed the China experts as an arrogant, unpatriotic elite ensconced in ivory towers.

The attack of the McCarthyites was directed mostly by people outside the universities against some prominent members of a very small China studies community. But a decade and a half later, when China studies had grown to be a large, important part of the American academic scene, the stage was set for full-scale struggles between elitists and populists within the profession itself. Because of the extent to which this conflict pitted China scholars against each other, and because of the articulateness with which some of the antagonists argued their case, the discussion below focuses more on it than on earlier debates among populists and elitists over China. In the late 1960s, as the United States found itself stalemated in Vietnam and as China erupted into a Cultural Revolution that no American experts had predicted, academic populists, organized this time as the Committee of Concerned Asian Scholars (CCAS), attacked their mentors for having misunderstood China by failing to hear the voice of the authentic Chinese people. The most articulate of such critiques came from James Peck, a graduate student of John Fairbank at Harvard. In "The Roots of Rhetoric: The Professional Ideology of America's China Watchers," an essay written for the CCAS *Bulletin* in 1969, Peck argued that the leaders of the China studies profession had helped to justify American imperialism in Asia.[7] "Assuredly, few American China specialists saw themselves as instruments or official ideologues of the American government. But if few were involved in the actual decision-making process within the government—if, indeed, many were criticized and persecuted during the McCarthy period—nonetheless, by the work they did not do, they upheld significant portions of the official definition of reality and, by the work they did, even elaborated upon it."[8]

China scholars did this, according to Peck, by organizing their studies around the conventional social scientific wisdom of the time, especially around that set of ideas called "modernization theory." According to that theory, "moderniza-tion" was equivalent to what Max Weber had called "rationalization," a process of systemically organizing all social relations so as to make them the most efficient possible means of maximizing wealth and power. Though it had its origins in the West, modernization was based on universal principles and was fated to spread over the whole world. Some non-Western societies, like Japan, had cultures that enabled them to adapt to the requirements of modernization relatively smoothly. Other societies, like China, found modernization a traumatic process. In China, this trauma had engendered irrational, revolutionary upheav-als, which, in the view of these modernization theorists, had led to the tragic mistake of accepting a Marxist-Leninist-Maoist rather than American model of economic and political development. To have avoided such upheavals, West-erners should have done a better job of educating modernizing elites in the proper respect for efficiency, the proper acceptance of orderly change, and proper kinds of public-spirited civic consciousness. To cure China of its revolu-tionary irrationality, Westerners should continue to find ways to impart to the Chinese, especially to Chinese elites, this education in modern liberal values.

Peck argued that this view of China as a culturally backward country, in need of Western tutelage to modernize, was a justification for American imperialism against China and those parts of Asia supposedly under China's influence, just as analogous views of China, propagated by missionaries, had helped to justify Western imperialism during the last century. What the United States should do, and what a new generation of China scholars should help it do, he argued, was to appreciate the universal value of the "revolutionary Marxism" being espoused by the Maoists during the Cultural Revolution.

Peck's essay prompted a sharp rebuttal from his teacher, John Fairbank.[9] Fairbank's position was that Peck had oversimplified the views of American China scholars. These scholars had often disagreed vigorously among themselves, and many had been critics rather than supporters of U.S. policy. Peck replied that Fairbank's response illustrated rather than refuted his argument. Beneath all the disagreements among China scholars and between China scholars and U.S. government policymakers, there had been some common perspectives on China's modernization: China had made a big mistake in accepting communism, and the United States should save it from its mistakes. Liberal and conservative scholars disagreed on how that salvation should be effected. But according to Peck even liberals —and it was the scholarship of liberals like Fairbank that Peck was primarily interested in analyzing, precisely because it was more subtle and therefore more persuasive to intellectuals than that of conservatives—agreed that American models of nation-building were better than those the Chinese had adopted.

The debate between Fairbank and his CCAS critics continued along these lines in the CCAS *Bulletin* intermittently for about four years, from 1969 to 1973.[10] Since the debate centered on broad questions of values rather than on narrow matters of fact, neither side could clearly win the argument. What is important for our purposes is that, at the time, Peck's views were plausible to many younger China scholars.

As junior members of the profession, many of these young scholars chafed under the hierarchical domination of their elders. In 1971 a report collectively authored by the Columbia University CCAS purported to expose this domination.[11] According to the report, and complementary essays by Moss Roberts and David Horowitz, the "China studies establishment" maintained its power by the centralized way in which contemporary China studies was organized.[12] There was a single channel for research funding: the Joint Committee on Contemporary China (JCCC) of the Social Science Research Council and the American Council of Learned Societies. A small circle of senior scholars—most of them graduates of elite research universities, most of them male, most of them white rather than Asian, none of them sympathetic to Marxist revolutions—dominated this committee, and thus set the standards for research in the profession. Only if the power of this establishment were broken and the procedures for allocating research money and rewarding professional achievement decentralized and made more democratic could the profession become an inclusive institution that could support those who wished, as James Peck had put it, "to commit their intellectual work to the oppressed."[13]

As vulnerable graduate students (in some danger, some of them imagined, not just of having their careers terminated by powerful mentors but of being shipped off to be cannon fodder in Vietnam), many CCAS members identified themselves with the oppressed and saw the Cultural Revolution as a populist revolution expressing the aspirations of people like themselves. Mao's China was a "redeemer revolution" that, precisely because it contradicted the assumptions of liberal economic theory, revealed universal truths about how the sovereignty of the people might be achieved everywhere, including the United States.

Of course, as eventually became clear to all, the Cultural Revolution did not represent any democratic liberation of the Chinese people. If that cataclysmic event in Chinese history could not be adequately explained by the social scientific theories of the "China studies establishment" neither did it conform to the populist hopes of that establishment's American critics. In retrospect it appears that neither the establishment nor its critics understood China, and their misunderstanding set off a debate that revealed more about the internal tensions within the China studies profession that about events within China.

The diplomatic breakthrough with China begun by Richard Nixon and Henry Kissinger in 1971 and ended with the normalization of U.S.-China relations in 1979 rendered irrelevant the debates of the late 1960s and early 1970s. Chinese propagandists gradually stopped speaking of the United States as an imperialist country, robbing the populist China scholars of a rationale for attacking their mentors for complicity in imperialism. The horrors of the Cultural Revolution eventually became visible to all, destroying populist illusions about a redeemer revolution. With the passage of time, many once vulnerable junior members of the China studies profession were granted tenure. Others dropped out of the profession and stopped participating in debates about the nature of China studies. Opportunities to travel to China raised hopes that some of the earlier passionate debates might be resolved through new information to be gained by direct research.

In the 1980s, however, China continued to be "bad to think with"; it continued to defy social scientific predictions and continued to frustrate the reformist hopes of American scholars. Once again, the profession was wracked with debate between elitists and populists. But the specific content of the debate was different from before. Now the populists were often people with a right-wing bent like the anthropologist Steven Mosher who outraged Chinese officials and threatened the exchange programs that gave American scholars research access to China. Expelled from graduate school, Mosher claimed that the China studies establishment was unwilling to criticize China for human rights abuses because it was afraid of losing its research access. Mosher claimed that he had been expelled from graduate school because he had written about how, in an effort to enforce a rigorous family planning policy, Chinese officials had forced women as much as eight months pregnant to have abortions. Leaders of the China studies community claimed that Mosher had acted irresponsibly and unethically and that, even if his reports of forced abortions were true, they needed to be understood within the context of a steadily improving Chinese society.[14] (See also David Shambaugh's discussion of the Mosher case in Chapter 1.)

Other China scholars antagonized their official hosts—and often disturbed their academic mentors—by cultivating friendships with dissidents who attacked the legitimacy of the Chinese regime and threatened the stability of the society. With the Tiananmen massacre the views of such populists seem to have been vindicated. But their claims to understand the "real China" may not stand the test of time. Many of the dissidents whom they see as representing the real voice of the oppressed Chinese people are themselves factionalized, elitist intellectuals who do not necessarily have much of a vision for creating an authentically democratic China. Undoubtedly, China will continue to change in ways that will surprise and dismay both elitist and populist China scholars alike.

The Rationalization of China Studies

Up to this point the emphasis has been on continuity in the basic assumptions underlying the academic study of China in the United States. There are, however, important discontinuities. The most important trajectory of change has consisted in what might be called the rationalization of China studies: its organization into ever more clearly defined specialities, in the name of achieving ever higher degrees of theoretical refinement.

This tendency is part of a century-long trend in American academic life. Before the rise of the modern research university in the late nineteenth century, higher education was aimed mainly at providing a general cultivation of mind and character for persons preparing for public service. As late as 1869, Harvard University had only twenty-three faculty members, who taught mostly classical languages and mathematics, and were not divided into departments. The research universities established in the last decades of the nineteenth century were based on a scientific model of knowledge. They aspired to separate the teaching of facts from values, and in so doing they hoped to avoid just the kind of moralism and ethnocentrism that characterized the world view of missionaries like Arthur Smith. In their pursuit of progress, educational reformers divided their expanding faculties into departments that became the centers of increasingly specialized disciplines and subdisciplines, each walled off from the other and from the general public by its distinctive jargon.[15]

China studies lagged behind the general movement toward specialization in the name of scientific rigor, because it did not develop into a substantial part of academia until after World War II. Before the war, there were only a handful of professors teaching about China at American universities (in his memoirs, Fairbank names about twelve).[16] Many of them had first learned about China through having been missionaries or children of missionaries there. In their teaching, they were of necessity generalists; their ties to the missionary movement instilled more of a moral tone into their writing and research, perhaps, than was the norm for scholars claiming to be dispassionately scientific. As the need for more knowledge about East Asia became obvious during and after the war, the government and the "great founda-tions" funded a rapid buildup of the profession. The buildup was led by senior scholars who, out of necessity as much as anything else, had worked as humanis-tically oriented generalists rather than scientific specialists. They instilled some of this orientation into their first students. But as the China studies field grew to maturity by the early 1970s, it embraced the same canons of specialization and scientific expertise as the mainstream social sciences. Leading the move toward this rationalization was that younger generation of scholars, some of whom had taken the populist side of the debates in the late 1960s.

Throughout the last two decades, as several chapters in this volume illustrate, the tendency in China studies has continued to be toward a tightening of boundaries between specialized subdisciplines and larger communities of discourse. In the so-cial sciences, this has led to increasing calls for making theoretical elegance, such as that achieved in mathematical economics, the criterion for good work, the standard for publication and promotion. A consequence of this emphasis on theoretical ele-gance has been a tendency to avoid research into questions that were contaminated with the complexity of the real world. Sometimes advocates of this purist form of professionalism have become curiously apolitical, eschewing the political concerns of their mentors, not because they thought those concerns were morally wrong, but because they distracted the scholar from developing the proper theoretical rigor.

There has been an ironic interplay between this rationalization of China stud-ies and the perennial tension between elitists and populists in the profession. It has been successive younger generations of scholars who, partly in the name of a revolt against the establishment dominated by their elders, have pushed for in-creased specialization and rigor. But the specialization creates in turn its own elitism, which leaves the new elite vulnerable to further waves of populism, especially when the elite's theories fail to match reality. Part of the charge against the China scholars who ignored human rights violations in the 1980s was that they were too preoccupied with their narrow specialties to see the larger picture and too concerned with being scientifically dispassionate to notice or to care about the moral issues at stake in the Chinese government's policies. In so doing, their critics say, they did not escape from the ethnocentrism of the early generation of missionaries but carried it on in a new guise.

The Future of Academic China Studies

Countermovements have recently begun against the fragmentation and special-ization of academic life and professional research, and to the extent that these calls for a new integrative vision of the university are successful, they will certainly influence China studies. But developments peculiar to China studies may have their own independent influence on the larger academic scene. One of the most important of these developments is the interaction between American China scholars and their Chinese colleagues.

At the beginning of the scholarly exchanges made possible by the normalization of U.S.-China relations in 1979, the net effect of these exchanges was to increase the elitist tendencies in the profession. It suddenly became extremely important to have opportunities to do field work in China. The acquisition of these opportunities required the cooperation of official gatekeepers in China, which pressured leaders of the profession to tailor their research in ways that would respect the sensitivities of Chinese elites. At the same time, the increasing theoretical sophistication of China scholarship made it difficult for American scholars to treat Chinese colleagues, who had not been able to acquire such sophistication, as professional equals.

But by the end of the 1980s, the exchanges started to give more support to the populist tendencies. Somewhat to the surprise of scholars like Michel Oksenberg, who had helped to negotiate the initial exchanges, the exchange process rapidly became decentralized.[17] By mid-decade hundreds of universities had relationships with counterparts in China, and dozens of foundations offered funding for exchange programs. This multiplicity of paths to relationships with Chinese colleagues partially lessened the importance of sensitivity to the perspectives of Chinese officialdom. It exposed American scholars to a wide variety of voices of Chinese critical not only of their government but of their traditional culture and their current social structure.

Meanwhile, increasing numbers of Chinese scholars were coming to American graduate schools and developing theoretical and methodological skills equal if not superior to most of the previous generation of American China scholars. Especially after the Tiananmen massacre, many of these Chinese graduate students have determined to pursue academic careers in the United States rather than in China. Undoubtedly, some of them will become new leaders of the China studies profession, and their perspectives will have an important influence on it.

Some of these new, immigrant members of the American academic community may lose their feel for their native culture as they preoccupy themselves with the ideas of American social science. But others, especially in the humanities and some branches of sociology and anthropology, may be encouraged to develop distinctively Chinese voices that are rooted in the particularities of Chinese culture and the uniqueness of Chinese history. Thus an American scholar can relate respectfully to an academic exile like Liu Binyan not on the basis of whether Liu's reportage corresponds to the formal standards of American journalism, but whether Liu's literary voice is courageous and honest. Through exchanges with professional colleagues, the profession of China studies has helped to create new international moral solidarities that allow colleagues with different voices to converse, sometimes contentiously, across international boundaries about concerns, like human rights, that are common to all humanity.

Such conversations are never perfect. Modern critical theory shows us how they are always being shaped by economic interests, distorted by the will to power, contaminated by prejudices, and/or constrained by the limitations of language itself. Yet aspirations for such genuine conversations have driven many generations of our professional ancestors, and to the extent that those aspirations were even imperfectly realized, their work survives as a legacy to us. For all his prejudices, Arthur Smith, for example, was motivated to get close enough to his subjects to write finely observed, socially empathetic passages that still meet the standards of good ethnography. The Fairbank generation of China scholars did much more than provide advice on how to contain Chinese communism—these scholars offered to the American public a deep appreciation of the power and the legitimacy of Chinese nationalism. The CCAS founders did more than accuse their elders of imperialism and romanticize "revolutionary Marxism"—they helped to turn China studies toward a deeper understanding of people at the grass-roots levels in China. In our efforts to reform China studies as well as the other professions in modern society, we should critically build on all that was good in the intellectual and moral aspirations of such legacies.

By and large, the problems of China studies are the problems of all the academic professions in the United States. But China studies may have resources to overcome those problems that many other learned professions lack. From the point of view of some academic professionals, these resources may look like liabilities. To do our research we have to get out of our American academic routines; we have to struggle to communicate with Chinese colleagues who differ from us in outlook, economic resources, academic training. We inevitably have to undergo the humbling experience of being able to fathom only a small fraction of the complexity of a vast and rapidly changing country. All this can help to push us out of the isolation that grips many of the learned professions.

To play such a leadership role in the reformation of modern professions, however, China scholars need to have more confidence in the value of China studies as a professional enterprise with its own requirements, its own historical legacy (including a legacy of mistakes from which much can be learned), and its own approach to scholarship distinctive from the other social scientific disciplines. It can be good for China studies that China is "bad to think with." The study of China encourages us to have a healthy skepticism about the pretensions of universalistic theories. It forces the field to be modest about its ambitions to show the world the way to constant progress. Such prudential skepticism and modesty are good for our colleagues in other disciplines to learn. And they are important in this fin de siècle world for the American public to learn.[18] At this point, however, it is uncertain whether China studies as a profession will gain the self-confidence that would enable it to acquire the humane virtues of skepticism and modesty from the exhilarating frustrations of its study of China.

Notes

Many of the ideas in this paper come from about seventy-five interviews I have conducted with people who have played leading roles in the development of U.S.-China relations over the past two decades. Funding was provided by the Social Science Research Council's Foreign Policy Studies Program.

1. Miriam London, "The Romance of Realpolitik," in *The Broken Mirror: China after Tiananmen,* ed. George Hicks (Chicago and London: St. James Press, 1990), 247–48. For a book-length critique similar to that of London, see Steven W. Mosher, *China Misperceived: American Illusions and Chinese Reality* (New York: Basic Books, 1990).

2. Michael H. Hunt, *The Making of a Special Relationship: The United States and China to 1914* (New York: Columbia University Press, 1983), 312. For an intellectual history of American social science, see Dorothy Ross, *The Origins of American Social Science* (New York: Cambridge University Press, 1991).

3. Arthur H. Smith, *Village Life in China* (1899; reprint, Boston: Little, Brown, 1970), 25–26.

4. Ibid., 27.

5. For a social history of the conflict between elitists and populists in the United States, see Christopher Lasch, *The True and Only Heaven: Progress and Its Critics* (New York: Norton, 1990).

6. For an analysis and critique of American individualism, see Robert N. Bellah, Richard Madsen, William M. Sullivan, Ann Swidler, and Steven M. Tipton, *Habits of the Heart: Individualism and Commitment in American Life* (Berkeley: University of California Press, 1985).

7. James Peck, "The Roots of Rhetoric: The Professional Ideology of America's China Watchers," *Bulletin of Concerned Asian Scholars* 2 (October 1969): 59–69. Peck elaborated his argument more fully in his "Revolution versus Modernization and Revisionism: A Two-Front Struggle," in *China's Uninterrupted Revolution,* ed. Victor Nee and James Peck (New York: Pantheon, 1973), 57–217.

8. Peck, "The Roots of Rhetoric," 63.

9. John K. Fairbank and Jim Peck, "An Exchange," *Bulletin of Concerned Asian Scholars* 2 (April–July 1970): 51–54.

10. *Bulletin of Concerned Asian Scholars* 2 (April–July 1970); 3 (Summer–Fall 1971); 5 (September 1973).

11. Columbia CCAS, "The American Asian Studies Establishment," *Bulletin of Concerned Asian Scholars* 3 (Summer–Fall 1971): 92–103.

12. Moss Roberts, "The Structure and Direction of Contemporary China Studies," *Bulletin of Concerned Asian Scholars* 3 (Summer–Fall 1971): 113–37; and David Horowitz, "Politics and Knowledge: An Unorthodox History of Modern China Studies," *Bulletin of Concerned Asian Scholars* 3 (Summer–Fall 1971): 139–62.

13. Fairbank and Peck, "An Exchange," 67.

14. For a summary and analysis of this case, see Richard Madsen, "Institutional Dynamics of Cross-Cultural Communication: U.S.-China Exchanges in the Humanities and Social Sciences," in *Educational Exchanges: Essays on the Sino-American Experience,* ed. Joyce K. Kallgren and Denis Fred Simon (Berkeley: Institute of East Asian Studies, 1987), 202–6.

15. Robert N. Bellah, Richard Madsen, William M. Sullivan, Ann Swidler, and Steven M. Tipton, *The Good Society* (New York: Alfred A. Knopf, 1991), ch. 7. See also *The Culture of Professionalism: The Middle Class and the Development of Higher Education in America* (New York: W.W. Norton, 1976); and Thomas L. Haskell, *The Emergence of Professional Social Science: The American Social Science Association and the Nineteenth-Century Crisis of Authority* (Urbana: University of Illinois Press, 1977).

16. John King Fairbank, *Chinabound: A Fifty-Year Memoir* (New York: Harper and Row, 1982), 133–35.

17. Interview with the author, Ann Arbor, 1988.

18. For a discussion of the importance of such virtues for "postmodern" scholarship, see Stephen Toulmin, *Cosmopolis: The Hidden Agenda of Modernity* (New York: Free Press, 1990).

9

Government China Specialists: Scholar Officials and Official Scholars

Thomas Fingar

Washington, D.C., is home to the largest and most diverse assemblage of China analysts in the United States, and several agencies of the U.S. government have far more specialists on China than does any university.[1] Indeed, precisely because the government's China studies community is so large, diverse, and distributed among so many agencies with such different missions, any effort to describe in general terms the approach, ambience, and assessments of "government" China specialists is certain to be oversimplified and somewhat misleading. Thus, for example, the mission, methodologies, and analytical products of the Bureau of the Census and the Congressional Research Service are very different from those of the Central Intelligence Agency or the Department of Defense. Partly as a function of where they work, some analysts publish extensively and interact regularly with the academic community; others seldom do either. Some agencies and individual analysts are interested primarily in "understanding China"; others seek only to locate and fit together tiny pieces of a narrowly defined analytical puzzle.

The pitfalls of broad generalization are even greater in attempts to compare work on contemporary China by analysts in government and academe.[2] Although they focus on some of the same topics, ask some of the same questions, and use many of the same sources of information, differences are frequently more significant than similarities. Differences in approach and analytic product are a function of role, resources, and responsibilities. Whereas university-based researchers generally pursue long-term studies designed to explain past developments and/or integrate the findings of other scholars, government analysts typically work with short deadlines on projects intended to be predictive or prescriptive. The work of the latter sometimes has an important impact on policy decision; that of the former almost never does. Government analysts, of necessity, are frequently at the cutting edge of analysis of contemporary events; they are highly unlikely, in their official capacities, to develop bold reinterpretations of the past. These points are obvious—and overstated—but they are also important.

Even though the worlds and work of government and academic China specialists differ, often substantially, neither is inherently or consistently superior. Moreover, the differences between academe and government are—or should be—complementary. Government-based analysts are heavily, and inevitably, dependent on their academic colleagues for microlevel case studies, detailed longitudinal studies, broad theoretical interpretations, and coverage of a wide range of topics tangential to the needs of policymakers. Conversely, academy-based scholars who work on foreign or military policy, technology-transfer issues, and numerous other subjects central to U.S. government assessments could, and really must, draw on the insights and information of their colleagues in government.

World and Work of Government
China Specialists

The scope and diversity of China-related work in agencies of the U.S. government make it impossible to describe a generic "government China specialist." Some government analysts have extremely narrow portfolios (e.g., grain production, the activities of Politburo members, or naval doctrine); others have much broader accounts (e.g., economic policy, relations with the Third World, or domestic politics). At certain stages of their careers (e.g., when assigned to posts in China), some specialists function primarily as data collectors and/or messengers conveying information between officials in Washington and counterparts in Beijing. At other times, those same specialists may help formulate trade policy or explain administration positions to Congress and/or the American public. Some government specialists work entirely in the public domain, using sources available to any student of China; others rely on intelligence reports and write only classified assessments. Drawing broad generalizations about the work of government China specialists is both difficult and almost certain to be misleading. One of the few generalizations that can be made with confidence is that most government China specialists work primarily on contemporary affairs. Since it would be neither practical nor possible to present an agency-by-agency or account-by-account description of the world and work of government China specialists, the government China-studies community is divided below into four function-based categories: policymakers, intelligence analysts, public servants, and database builders. This typology is not used in the government, and others may not fully agree with the way functions have been grouped or characterized here. Despite inherent ambiguities and limitations, the function-based categories used are preferable to agency-based distinctions because some agencies (e.g., the State and Defense departments) utilize China specialists in all four of these functional roles. Moreover, many government China specialists perform two or more of these roles concurrently or at different stages in their careers.

Policymakers and Policy Implementers

As used here, the label "policymakers" subsumes both senior decisionmakers (such as assistant secretaries and deputy assistant secretaries) with China-related responsibilities and country desk–level professionals in agencies as diverse as the National Security Council and the departments of Defense, Commerce, and State.[3] Some of the senior officials in this category have extensive China expertise and qualify as specialists in every sense of the word (recent examples include Douglas Paal, James Lilley, and Richard Solomon), but when serving in top-level positions, their responsibilities neither require nor allow for much independent analysis. Many have served in China (numerous times if one includes postings in Hong Kong and Taiwan), and most have worked previously in jobs requiring detailed analysis of contemporary developments. Some have had formal academic training on China; others have not. Some, such as J. Stapleton Roy and Morton Abramowitz, have spent most of their careers in government service and bring to bear experience and insights obtained working on/in countries besides China. Others, such as Gaston Sigur and Mel Searls, entered government with skills and approaches acquired in academe or business. As a group, the senior people in this category are consumers rather than providers of analytic assessments.

Senior officials often influence what is produced by other government specialists, however, by requesting or demanding studies of specific issues. At times, both the questions they ask and the way new information is received are shaped by insights and methodologies acquired earlier in their careers. The best of the group are receptive to—even fully conversant with—new approaches and interpretations; others sometimes evince "old thinking" and a penchant for frameworks and models no longer deemed useful by most working analysts. Sometimes this means that insights and interpretations derived from "new" approaches do not receive adequate consideration by senior officials. It can, and occasionally does, cause higher level managers to block or change the assessments of subordinates. Most of the time, however, the clash of old thinking and new approaches results in a constructive tension that forces the analyst to sharpen arguments and consider alternative explanations and implications in ways that frequently persuade the policymaker to alter his or her own approach or conclusions.

Officials at the country desk level, such as the China Desk in the State Department, handle the day-to-day requirements of policy implementation— interacting with Chinese officials, answering questions from Congress, the public, and other parts of the executive branch, working technology transfer and human rights issues and myriad other problems—and, less frequently, help to formulate new policies. Some of these officers have spent two or more years working in China; others have no China background at all. Some have excellent Chinese language skills; others have none. A growing number have excellent formal training—Ph.D. degrees as well as one to two years of field work in China —before entering the Foreign Service (or comparable career tracks in other agencies).

Desk officers interact more frequently with the general public than do other government specialists because they tend to be the ones tapped to respond to requests for speakers. The nature of the audiences involved, knowledge that they will be seen as "speaking for the U.S. government," and the fact that they do little detailed research or analysis during their normal workdays sometimes make such speeches appear fluffy, nonspecific, defensive of U.S. policies, and in other ways viewed with derision by China scholars working in academe. It is a mistake to judge the messenger's abilities on the basis of such a message.

The insights and experience of desk-level officers are more apparent when they function as public servants or intelligence analysts, but they are also critical to the performance of other policy-making/policy-implementing responsibilities. For example, when an economic officer meets with Chinese officials to gain enhanced understanding of PRC trade regulations or to represent the interests of American business, that officer must possess (and will acquire even deeper) knowledge of Chinese practices and procedures, individual and institutional players, and PRC (or Taiwan) perceptions of U.S. government policies and corporate demands.

Regular contacts with business executives and corporate representatives who work extensively with the Chinese provide another valuable avenue for learning about China and for sharing information and ideas with important segments of the public. Few university-based researchers will ever have this kind of sustained direct and indirect access to Chinese officials or similar experience working with—or against—the Chinese bureaucracy. Reporting cables on specific encounters and experiences constitute one of the most important resources available to government analysts. However, because they often contain sensitive diplomatic exchanges or proprietary information, few such exchanges are available to China specialists working outside the government.

Another illustration of the ways policy implementers help government analysts to understand and interpret development in China is their ability, and responsibility, to obtain clarification of and contextual background information on a wide range of official statements, published commentaries, and individually authored articles. Background information on the drafting of legislation or official reports, debates among advisers, and myriad other subjects is routinely and openly collected by our diplomatic representatives around the world. Direct observation of individual Chinese leaders, private explanations and assurances from authoritative officials, and the response to direct queries constitute another important source of data available to government analysts.

Intelligence Analysts

Intelligence analysts form the largest and most varied category of government China specialists.[4] With few exceptions, intelligence analysts are largely invisible both to the public and to much of the academic China studies community. The reason, in part, is that they are the opposite of desk officers in many important respects. For example, whereas much of what a desk officer writes or says is for the public record, virtually nothing done by intelligence analysts is intended for external consumption. The desk officer speaks for the U.S. government, and what he or she says or writes is carefully tailored with that in mind. In order to minimize the danger that analysts will shade their assessments in a similar way, and to enhance the likelihood of obtaining "objective" analyses uncolored by "clientitis" or deference to administration policy, intelligence analysts work with the expectation that their assessments will not be released to the public.[5]

Desire for candor is reinforced by the need to protect intelligence sources and methods. As a result, virtually everything this type of analyst produces carries some sort of security classification, at least initially. In theory, this safeguards the integrity of the analyst and the analysis. It also protects the U.S. government; without such an arrangement—and the necessity for review and approval to add appropriate disclaimers—sensitive, speculative, or contradictory assessments could be interpreted, as are the words of public speakers, as official statements of policy. I, for one, would not want my candid assessments of certain Chinese leaders or policies to be disseminated as the "view of the United States." These safeguards complicate, but do not necessarily preclude, publication of research findings if the analyst elects to go through the requisite procedures.

Many intelligence analysts have Ph.D.'s and have spent years, even decades, working on contemporary China. Specialists in this group are in many ways similar to a professor on sabbatical; they can devote virtually their entire day to research and writing on the subjects for which they are responsible. Unlike their colleagues in academe, however, intelligence analysts (as well as some that I have put in the category of "public servant") are regularly challenged to interpret rapidly unfolding events and new information for which existing paradigms and analytic frameworks are inadequate.

Whereas the university-based scholar has the luxury of reviewing events after (often long after) they have occurred, intelligence analysts must interpret developments almost as they are unfolding (or in some cases even before they have occurred). At such times, conventional wisdom—or even the latest interpretive frameworks devised in academe—may be of little help, forcing the government analyst to devise new approaches and methods of analysis. The resultant approaches may later be refined into "analytic paradigms" or "models of Chinese politics," and others may develop more elaborate explanations to account for observed developments, but government analysts are frequently at the cutting edge. Necessity truly is the mother of invention, and government analysts have often been forced by the requirements of their formal roles to break new ground for their academic colleagues. The list of examples in which this was the case includes the origins of the Sino-Soviet split, the beginnings of the Cultural Revolution, the Lin Biao affair, domestic political maneuver in advance of the opening to the United States, Chinese activities in the Middle East, and most recently, developments before and since Tiananmen.

Working in the intelligence community (i.e., in agencies with representation on the National Foreign Intelligence Board) not only forces this group of government China specialists to stay on top of developments in the PRC and Taiwan, it also provides access to information unavailable to university-based researchers (and to some of their government colleagues). Intelligence reports are of many kinds, come from a variety of sources, and run the gamut from rumors to documentary evidence. Learning to use this material requires training and experience because the value and implications of individual reports are seldom self-evident; interpreting fragmentary and at times contradictory evidence is no less a challenge for the intelligence analyst than for the academic researcher. Indeed, the task is made far more daunting by the demand for timely assessments, the possibility—even likelihood—that judgments will shape U.S. policy, and the frequently much larger quantities of information that must be considered.

Interpreting intelligence materials is more art than science. It helps to know what to look for, but looking too hard for evidence of a particular action or relationship can cause analysts to see things that are not really there. It also helps to remind oneself that information is not necessarily better or more accurate because it carries a higher security classification. Materials are classified primarily to protect sources and methods, not to indicate reliability, and a high level of classification is no substitute for skillful analysis.

Public Servants

As used here, the term "public servant" includes those analysts throughout the government whose work is primarily directed not to in-house policymakers, but to particular public constituencies or the public at large.[6] Examples include specialists in the Department of Agriculture who assess China's grain production, fertilizer requirements, and a host of similar matters; demographers in the Bureau of the Census; and trade specialists in the Department of Commerce. Unlike the intelligence analysts, who seldom interact with the public and whose work is often highly classified, public servants are in almost continuous contact with their counterparts and consumers in academe and the private sector.

The China specialists in this category are not mere collectors and disseminators of data; on the contrary, many are skilled analysts whose work is highly regarded in the academic world. Generally speaking, they focus narrowly on specific facets of China and tend not to write about broad questions of system performance or regime stability.[7] As individuals, many are capable of working more broadly, but their official responsibilities require a substantially narrower concentration.

Though frequently narrower in scope and dealing with different issues than the work of intelligence analysts and policymakers, the assessments of those here called public servants can be just as influential and important to the formulation of U.S. policy. Findings of demographers in the Bureau of the Census figure prominently in debates about whether the United States should contribute funds to the United Nations Fund for Population Activities or withhold funding to protest PRC birth control measures. Analyses from the Department of Agriculture help determine China's eligibility to purchase U.S. grain at subsidized prices. Specialists in the government analyze and report on subjects ranging from Chinese labor policies to compliance with international fishing agreements. What they determine may trigger Congressionally mandated actions, prompt formal complaints to the Chinese, or suggest a basis for collaboration with PRC counterparts. In addition, public reports prepared by executive branch analysts, as well as by China specialists working in Congressional agencies (such as the Congressional Research Service, the Library of Congress, and on the staffs of committees or individual members), play an important role in the tug-of-war between Congress and the administration that helps shape U.S. policy toward China.

Database Builders

The term "database builders"—often known affectionately or derisively as "bean counters"—refers to the large and very important group of analysts throughout the government who collect and interpret data on subjects ranging from biographic materials to military order of battle to production of specific commodities.[8] Much of the time, the work of these analysts involves primarily developing and upgrading knowledge of somewhat esoteric subjects to ensure that when it is important to have information about any one of literally hundreds of subjects, that information—and the capacity to analyze and interpret new data—will be available. Thus, for example, there is little demand for frequent assessments of China's capacity to manufacture computers or digital switching equipment, or of the status of military forces in the Chengdu military region, but when needed, the capacity to answer questions must be available to decisionmakers. Events in the international system, statements by domestic or foreign political leaders, the outbreak of hostilities, discovery of new information on PRC interaction with a particular country, and myriad other developments can and do galvanize the attention of senior policymakers and entire bureaucracies. When this happens, the demand for information and interpretation is instantaneous and insatiable.

Working in Government and Academe

China specialists working in the U.S. government have a number of advantages not shared by colleagues in academe. One, clearly, is the superior access to certain kinds of resources. Granted, the ability to tap into the financial, data, and human resources of the government depends, in part, on one's position in the system, but it is only a slight exaggeration to say that any analyst has at his or her disposal virtually the entire China-studies capacity of the United States. Whereas most scholars in the academic community must engage in a more or less perpetual quest for funding to support research on their chosen topic and are often subject to the vicissitudes of funding agencies and competing proposals, the government analyst can command resources simply—or sometimes not quite so simply—by explaining why they are necessary to perform assigned tasks.

A brief description of the way information came to me when I was chief of the China Division in the State Department's Bureau of Intelligence and Research illustrates some of the possibilities and problems confronting government analysts. The flood of information pouring into my in-box on a daily basis was daunting.[9] Counting Foreign Broadcast Information Service (FBIS) *Daily Report* and Joint Publications Research Service (JPRS) translations, as well as wire services, press clippings, State Department cables, and intelligence reports, I received approximately three hundred single-spaced pages per day. This information came to my desk; I did not have to go to the library, make photocopies, or scurry around wondering whether I had missed anything. If the information was available anywhere in the U.S. government, it did, or could have, come to me. Even the narrowest of specialists can receive as much of this flood as he or she wishes (assuming that person has the requisite security clearances), and many at least skim a large portion of what is available.

Even though many government specialists are responsible for narrow and somewhat esoteric portfolios, it is easier, and probably more imperative, for them to remain generally informed about an extremely wide range of developments in China—from technical to cultural, political to demographic, economic to ideological, arms sales to participation in international financial organizations—than it is for university-based scholars. Not all take advantage of this capability, but many do. They might not write on broad subjects, but their analyses are informed by knowledge of the big picture.

If this flood of information does not contain data needed by analysts in the executive branch, they can task our representatives in China to ask specific questions, collect materials, and contact Chinese researchers. I do not mean to suggest that embassy and consulate officials function as glorified research assistants; that decidedly is not the case. But if a subject is of interest to senior officials or Washington-based analysts, it is likely to be of interest to reporting officers in the field as well. Indeed, political, economic, and other reporting officers welcome guidance because that helps ensure that their work is relevant to the policy-making process.

Another advantage of more senior analysts in the government is that we constitute a larger critical mass than is found on any campus. Because our primary responsibility is to analyze developments in contemporary China, it is relatively easy to bring together specialists from different agencies for informal discussions of unfolding events, to obtain prompt feedback—often the same day—on draft papers, and to engage in collaborative projects that tap the expertise of persons with complementary specialties. If we want to discuss unfolding events—such as the ouster of Hu Yaobang, increased tensions on the Sino-Indian border, or Tiananmen-related developments—there is no need to juggle teaching schedules, work around other commitments, or write proposals to convene a workshop or conference. We just do it. We can, and frequently do, convene brainstorming sessions on both fast-breaking events and trends that seem to be emerging over a period of months or years. Such sessions often involve fifteen or more highly capable China specialists. The composition of any particular gathering depends on the topic being discussed; semistructured sessions convene roughly every two weeks; informal discussions occur daily. It is unnecessary, and almost impossible, to work in isolation from colleagues, no matter how narrow one's specialty and formal responsibilities.

Another advantage, particularly for analysts working in the departments of State, Commerce, and Defense, is the ease of interaction with both career officers specializing on China and analysts and career officers experienced in other areas of the world. As used here, the term "career officer" refers to Foreign Service Officers (FSOs) in the Department of State; members of the Foreign Commercial Service (FCS) at Commerce; Foreign Area Officers (FAOs), and Defense Attachés in the Defense Department; and counterparts in other agencies (such as Agriculture Attachés in the Department of Agriculture and Public Affairs Officers in the U.S. Information Agency). Officers with years of experience living and working in China, and accustomed to negotiating, collaborating, or sparring with Chinese officials, are an exceedingly valuable resource. At a minimum, they provide a kind of reality check on speculation and tendencies to overanalyze particular events or individuals.

Similarly, the perspective of persons who see China as "just another country" is a useful corrective to the China as sui generis approach of many China specialists. Moreover, as noted above, career officers serve in countries other than China, and civil servants often have worked on numerous countries or functional issues besides China. This produces a degree of cross-fertilization and vitality seldom found in university-based programs. There is also great advantage in being easily able to tap into the pool of expertise on every other country and region of the world. Thus, for example, if I want to ascertain the accuracy of a Chinese statement on the origins and impact of a particular Hungarian reform or Iranian policy, I—and any other government analyst—can easily check with persons likely to know the answer.

At the risk of appearing to oversell the virtues of life as a government analyst, I wish to note one final advantage, namely, the frequency and inevitability of having one's assessments and predictions subjected to the test of reality. An exciting consequence of working on current events is that the feedback loop is very short. When asked to explain what happened yesterday and to predict what will happen tomorrow, the government analyst knows that two consequences are likely. One is that the United States may do or refrain from doing something on the basis of that assessment; the other is that the accuracy of predictions will be confirmed or disproved almost immediately. Thus, for example, decisions to evacuate Americans from Beijing and to urge PRC officials to eschew the use of force during the Tiananmen crisis reflected judgment calls predicting that troops would be ordered to move against the students and that the People's Liberation Army would carry out those orders. Similarly, U.S. actions following Iraq's invasion of Kuwait in August 1990 were based, in part, on judgments about what China would do, including how it would vote on specific United Nations Security Council resolutions.

When interpretations seem to be confirmed by subsequent information, and predictions are borne out by events, it enhances confidence about one's understanding of how China works. Similarly, when the prediction is wrong or later information casts doubt on the accuracy of interpretations, it is possible—even imperative—to adjust assumptions and modify implicit and explicit "models" of China. Both the nature of what government analysts do and the fact that we frequently have access to information unavailable to academic researchers make it possible to check the accuracy (or at least the viability) of our assessments more easily and more promptly than can be done by outside scholars. In addition, both individually and collectively, we make a lot more calls on a far wider range of questions than do our colleagues in academe. This gives us a larger data set for evaluating our own performance and refining our implicit and explicit assumptions. Moreover, since most of our judgments are conveyed, in writing or orally, to colleagues and senior officials, there is no escaping the need to admit and account for our mistakes. Happily, our overall batting average is quite good.

Life in the bureaucracy is not nirvana, however; there are also disadvantages to working on China within the structure and culture of the U.S. government. Perhaps the most significant drawback is implicit in the fact that I have been asked to comment at length on the subject: most analysts are invisible to the rest of the China field and, frequently, to the officials they serve. While there are tremendous, possibly unequaled, opportunities to interact within the critical mass of government experts, for most government analysts opportunities to attend conferences, collaborate with colleagues in academe, and shape the field by service on such bodies as the Social Science Research Council, the Committee on Advanced Study in China, or the editorial boards of scholarly publications are extraordinarily few.

To reiterate a point, many analysts are invisible because most of their work is classified. But that is not the only reason. For most, there are few incentives and many disincentives for attempting to be active and visible in the field. Whereas university-based scholars are expected to publish and perform other forms of "service to the profession," and are rewarded for doing so, that is not the case with most government China specialists. On the contrary, they are expected to work full time on their government assignments; even those who are very good are hard pressed to meet the requirements of their jobs within the limits of an eight-to-ten-hour workday. If they choose to write additional articles for scholarly publication or to sanitize classified materials for wider distribution, they are frequently expected to do so on their own time. Although at least some agencies formally welcome participation in scholarly activities, regulations and reality (e.g., limited funding and excessive demands) discourage most analysts from doing so. Those I have classified as "public servants" are notable exceptions to this generalization; they can and must publish widely and are often very active in the field.

All government analysts can, of course, write for publication and for conferences on their own time, but they generally cannot accept honoraria for doing so. In some instances, that is a trivial consideration; in others, it is a real hardship. It takes a special commitment to the field, interest in the subject, and perhaps even a martyr complex to play by rules that require government specialists to decline compensation for performing the same speaking or writing assignments as their counterparts from academe. Moreover, while such "extra" efforts are directly relevant to the academician's professional advancement, they are largely irrelevant to the in-government career of the government specialists.

A somewhat different kind of disincentive results from the fact that government analysts devote virtually their entire working day to the study of China. The focus on China is not broken by teaching courses in comparative politics or methodology, attending faculty meetings, or in other ways participating in the life of the university. Some people are willing and able to dedicate all their waking hours to the Middle Kingdom; most want to do something else on their off-hours.

Finally, some government analysts eschew publication and other forms of interchange with their counterparts in academe because of diffidence or disdain. A few government analysts accept, and thus perpetuate, the myth that university-based scholars are superior to and produce more "significant" work than do specialists who work in government. As a result, some persons do not attempt to publish in scholarly journals or to interact with others in the field because they lack confidence in the quality of their own work. Others, perhaps more, subscribe to a different myth, namely, that what government analysts do is the only really relevant and important work on China; everything else is just ivory-tower scholasticism with more fluff than substance. Since government studies are presumed by such persons to have far more "impact" on policy decisions than can ever be true of an academic article, there is little motivation to make the extra effort needed to reach a broader audience.

An oft-encountered—and, I would argue, erroneous—conception is that the study of contemporary China is inherently more vibrant and innovative on campuses than in government bureaucracies. Although it is certainly true that bright graduate students who delight in challenging conventional wisdom invigorate the China field by forcing us to consider new insights and ideas drawn from beyond a single discipline or regional focus, much the same result is achieved in government through the interaction of China specialists and a broader array of regional and functional specialists than is found on any campus. Policy generalists, whose backgrounds may be in African studies, international economics, or weapons procurement, ask the same kinds of irreverent, off-the-wall, and challenging questions as do good graduate students. Moreover, because of their own different experiences and unfamiliarity with conventions and canards in the China field, they are even more likely to question fundamental assumptions and accepted wisdom about contemporary China than are students new to, but already part of, "the field."

At the risk of overstating the vitality and receptivity to new ideas of China studies in the U.S. government, I want to underscore the point made previously about necessity forcing government analysts to come up with novel interpretations. Despite the persistence of old thinking on the part of some government China specialists who have not recently been exposed to the rigors of analysis and the latest insights of academic or government analysts, the purpose and the process of China study within the government precludes stagnation. Whereas the value of academic work on China is judged ultimately by those in the field—and secondarily by specialists who assess the work's contribution to the specific discipline—government analyses are evaluated primarily on their utility in meeting the needs of decisionmakers. As a result, evaluations of individual and collective assessments are based less on their elegance, inventiveness, or enhancement of knowledge than on their ability to explain contemporary developments and facilitate policy decisions. Little value is attached to new approaches or insights unless they prove better than older ones in achieving those objectives; innovation per se has less value than in academe, but conventional wisdom is far more likely to be "overtaken by events" in government than on campus.

Incentives to reexamine assumptions, approaches, and assessments inherent in the more-or-less continuous need to explain and respond to new developments and the ever-present demand for "useful" analysis are sometimes diluted by the obligation to provide assessments and advice in a timely fashion. At times, the demand for answers "now" reinforces propensities to cling to or repackage old ideas and old analyses whenever possible. Whereas university-based scholars have weeks or months to plan and conduct research on some aspect of the changes unfolding in China, the government analyst—except for those whose specialties are not hot at the moment—typically works under deadlines measured in hours rather than days. Since one of the reasons for maintaining analytical capabilities inside the government is to be able to alert policymakers to impending change so that they can decide what to do about it, the demand for information, analysis, and guidance is immediate. A few days—let alone weeks—later, such assessments are absolutely irrelevant, no matter how interesting, accurate, or pathbreaking they might be.

A few examples will illustrate this point. Whenever developments occur that might entail significant consequences for the United States, senior officials want immediate assessments of their genesis, implications, and susceptibility to U.S. influence. Time is of the essence, both to formulate and implement appropriate responses, and to assure that decisionmakers can demonstrate that they are on top of the situation when responding to questions from the press, Congress, or other parts of the government. For these and other reasons, government analysts were expected to—and did—produce "instant" analyses of indications of Chinese sales of intermediate-range missiles to Saudi Arabia, the sharp increase in tension along the Sino-Indian border in 1986, the declaration of martial law in Beijing in May 1989, and many other potentially portentous developments. In each case, the initial assessments were presented to senior officials within a matter of hours, and "definitive" studies were completed in two or three days.

Timeliness is imperative even for less portentous events because the attention span of busy decisionmakers is extremely limited. If China specialists have something to say about events they consider important, they must do so quickly. Thus, for example, knowing that the buildup to the thirteenth party congress had increased high-level interest in Chinese Communist Party General Secretary Zhao Ziyang's report, and cognizant of how short-lived that interest would be, we produced our initial assessment of his speech—fifteen pages with the mandatory one-page summary—less than twelve hours after he stopped talking. We completed our "detailed" analysis of the personnel and policy changes at the congress within a week.

By the time the first scholarly interpretations began to appear several weeks later, senior government officials had long since lost interest and gone on to other matters. However, and this point should be emphasized, those "quickie" assessments and hundreds of similar ones stand up remarkably well in light of subsequent information and more painstaking analyses by university-based specialists or different government analysts. In the case just cited, at least three longer, more detailed, and more fully considered assessments were prepared by other government agencies, but even these studies were completed within two months of the congress. One reason they hold up well is that, despite tight deadlines, every piece is subjected to extensive and mandatory review by other specialists. This is more than the functional equivalent of peer review because it requires examination by specialists in every relevant subfield. Thus, for example, a paper on the politics of economic reform and its impact on PRC arms sales would be reviewed by at least one specialist on China's economy, someone who follows PRC arms sales, and by two to three specialists on Chinese politics. It is not unusual for even a short paper to be reviewed and revised by four to five specialists; longer studies may be vetted by more than twenty peers. Still, because of time pressures, the resultant assessments evince gaps and mistakes. But the errors are almost always at the margins and seldom affect the key judgments or policy implications. When the process functions properly, it strengthens both the quality of the analysis and the confidence policymakers have in the final product. When it breaks down (because of irreconcilable differences among analysts or agencies, intransigence on the part of senior participants, inadequate specification of the questions to be addressed, or some other reason), the result can be a "lowest common denominator" paper of little utility to anyone.

Working under the kind of time pressure that is common in the government has both advantages and disadvantages. One clear advantage, from my perspective, is that really good analysts produce a lot more ideas and insights than they would if working in the differently structured world of academe. In the time it takes colleagues in academe to collect and shift data and weigh alternatives to improve an assessment from being 85 to 90 percent correct (which I think any good China specialist should be capable of achieving in a very short time) to being 90 to 95 percent correct (my sense of the best we can do), the best government analysts have worked six to ten additional problems. In making this point, I do not mean to denigrate the need for careful scholarly studies; I regard them as absolutely essential for purposes of field development, training, and to serve as a check on the accuracy of the "quickie" assessments done in the government. Perhaps their greatest contribution is to illuminate cases in which government analysts may have reached the "right" conclusion despite faulty assumptions and incorrect inferences. Without such correctives, government specialists would have unwarranted confidence in frameworks, methodologies, or instincts underlying judgments that turn out "right" more by accident than by accuracy.

Notable exceptions to the "quickie" assessment approach that illustrate what government analysts can do if given the right incentives can be found in the triennial volumes on China prepared for the Joint Economic Committee of Congress. Many of the papers in these compendia have been written by current or past government analysts. The overall outstanding quality of these volumes illustrates well what can be achieved through careful efforts to capitalize on the complementary strengths of government and nongovernment specialists.

Different Roles, Different Strengths, Different Requirements

Implicit in much of what has been said above is the obvious but important fact that government analysts work in a different culture and serve different constituencies than do our colleagues in academe. To thrive in each culture requires different skills. To succeed in both is rare, but the contributions to the field of scholar-officials such as Allen Whiting, Michel Oksenberg, Richard Solomon, and others demonstrate what can be achieved by moving back and forth between the two worlds.[10] It also argues for greater effort to transcend barriers and take advantage of complementarities than now occurs. Toward that end, this section examines some significant differences between the two worlds.

As noted above, brevity and timeliness are imperative in the realm of the government analyst. In a world of fast-moving events and limited attention spans, tardiness and verbosity are almost certain to render even the best analysis irrelevant. Sadly, these two fundamental requirements of government analysis cause some of those few papers that are disseminated to the academic community to be viewed with a measure of scorn by scholars who deride the absence of historical background, cultural context, and extensive footnotes. Such an attitude is unwarranted, but my goal here is to explain rather than scold.

Having worked in both worlds, I find a number of differences quite ironic. For example, scholarly books and articles on contemporary China are written for an audience consisting almost entirely of fellow China specialists. Members of this community certainly have more than a passing familiarity with China's history, culture, economic performance, and other factors deemed essential to understanding the central argument or finding of any particular research product. Despite this fact, much scholarly writing contains considerable—under the circumstances probably unnecessary—contextual and background material. More than that, the structure of the piece and the extensive documentation of sources characteristic of scholarly writing often seem intended, at least in part, to establish the bona fides of the author. It is almost as if academic analysts feel compelled to prove themselves over and over, and as if the rest of us would consider pulling their credentials if they did otherwise. This is an exaggeration to be sure, and there are, of course, other reasons for careful documentation. My point is not to criticize this tendency, but to call attention to the different conventions of papers prepared for government use.

Unlike the scholarly world, where even the most distinguished members of the profession seemingly must reestablish their competence repeatedly, in government, expertise and meticulous adherence to the rules of evidence and inference are simply assumed. The audience for whom the government China specialist writes takes for granted that the analyst knows what he or she is talking about, and/or that the rigorous review process and collective nature of research and writing in the government have eliminated mistakes. Since expertise is a given, it does not have to be reproved with each piece. Similarly, whereas the audience for scholarly writing on China has extensive knowledge about the Middle Kingdom, the target audience of the government analyst often has only rudimentary knowledge about the subject. But members of that audience have neither the need nor the time to correct that deficiency; they want to know what they need to know in order to make the next decision, prepare for the next event, or, more rarely, to consider longer term options. They do not want or need a weighty scholarly tome, and they will not—cannot—wade through the long studies sometimes produced even by government analysts.

As a result, government analyses have less fact-mongering, fewer caveats, and greater focus on implications than do academic studies. They also tend to have a somewhat greater focus on personalities than does most scholarly writing. The reason for the latter, I think, is that senior U.S. officials have met or expect to meet their counterparts in China and tend to think in somewhat more personal terms (e.g., what Prime Minister Li Peng thinks rather than what other factors will shape Politburo decisions) than do scholars. Analysts cater to the desire for personality-centered assessments, but they also tend to pay more attention to individual leaders than do their academic colleagues because of the nature of the information available to them. This does not necessarily make the analysis better, indeed, much of the time I think it makes it worse, but it does make it different.

It is not much of an exaggeration to say that most of my time and attention since moving to the government have been focused on aspects of China that were of only secondary or even tertiary concern during my graduate study and the ten years of university-based research that followed. This doubtless says something about my own training and experience, but it also says something more important about the differences between work on China in academe and government and the need to rethink the way we prepare China specialists for careers outside the university.

A few examples illustrate the differences. Academic work on China focuses overwhelmingly on internal developments; but U.S. government officials are far more concerned about PRC foreign policy and external activities than about the dynamics of Chinese politics and society. China's view of and policy toward the Middle East is of much greater interest to the policymaker than is the struggle between "conservatives" and "reformers" for control of the party propaganda department. PRC relations with India and Pakistan are more "important" than implementation of the contract responsibility system in Chinese factories. Implications for U.S. investment and exports of technology are of more immediate concern to the policymaker than the details of China's coastal development strategy. Scholars want to know the origin of specific economic reform proposals; policymakers want to know the credibility of Beijing's assurances.

Listing the examples in this way is not intended to slight the importance of domestic developments. Government analysts follow those developments as closely as—probably more so than—most of their counterparts in academe, but the emphasis is on anticipating problems and opportunities for the United States rather than on enhancing understanding for its own sake. Government and academic specialists both ask, "What is happening, why is it happening, and what does it mean for China?" The government analyst also asks, "What does it mean for the United States?"

The net result of these differences in focus and target audience is that government analysts generally pay relatively little attention to such areas as contemporary Chinese culture (literature, art, music, philosophy, religion), education (except as it relates to exchanges), and ideology, and almost no attention to history (history, by definition, has been "overtaken by events"). In contrast, the government devotes substantial analytical resources to virtually all other aspects of contemporary China, including organizational change, biographical information, economic policy and performance, science and technology, political-military relations, arms sales, foreign policy, and PRC relations with Taiwan.

These lists indicate considerable overlap with the principal foci of university-based research as well as a number of significant differences. The differences need to be addressed in the training of new specialists; the complementarities point to considerable untapped potential to strengthen the field as a whole.

Concluding Observations

Although most of them are invisible to the rest of the China studies field, the best government-based analysts are every bit as good as their counterparts in academe. (The opposite is also true.) For reasons noted above, however, the work of government analysts generally does not fit the normal conventions of academic writing, and there are significant obstacles to repackaging assessments to make them available—and acceptable—to university-based scholars. Nevertheless, the relative isolation from the rest of the field of most government China specialists is a loss to both academe and government.

In both worlds, there are more journeyman analysts than outstanding scholars, but the worker bees of our profession play invaluable roles. Unfortunately, we do not utilize or assist them nearly so effectively as we should. True within the government, this deficiency is even more pronounced and more costly when it comes to collaboration across the government-academy divide. Although specialists in both worlds have different roles and responsibilities and inevitably contribute to our overall understanding of China in different ways, interaction tends to be more serendipitous than synergistic. This was not always the case; at times consultation and collaboration were far more common and productive than is generally true today. Diminished interaction results partly from the explosive growth of our field over the past two decades—neither government nor academe "needs" the participation of specialists from the other world to cover "all" aspects of a research project or conference agenda because so many excellent scholars are readily available within each community of specialists. It is also a function of laziness on the part of both academic and government entrepreneurs, tighter restrictions on access to government-produced studies, and the legacy of Vietnam War–era tension between the two worlds. Whatever the precise causes, we all pay a price for the failure to take full advantage of complementary strengths. A single example is sufficient to illustrate this point.

Government-based work on Chinese foreign policy, the interplay of domestic politics and foreign policy, and the entire array of military and security issues is, in my judgment, far superior to most analyses on these subjects in the scholarly literature.[11] The reasons are obvious; the government analyst has access to data that the scholar will not see for many years, if at all, and the priority attached to these issues is much higher inside than outside the government. As China becomes ever more engaged in the international system and its domestic policies are increasingly and necessarily tailored to articulate with foreign policies (and vice-versa), the need for the field to bolster its foreign policy competence is self-evident. Tapping government-based expertise will help in the short run; better training of new analysts for both worlds is a longer term challenge.

In our field, whether in government or academy, the sine qua non for success is competence as a China specialist. I will eschew precise definition of what constitutes a competent specialist because among the hundreds of persons working on China in the government and, I suspect, the hundreds more in academe who consider themselves China specialists, too few have an adequate mix of formal training and exposure to life in the PRC and/or Taiwan. Moreover, too few have the breadth of training needed to overcome the field's unquestionable disintegration into numerous subfields unable to communicate with one another. Over the past two decades, we have emphasized specialization and "depth" within the China field to the detriment of breadth and integration of the knowledge developed in each of the specialties. Inside and outside the government, we probably have too many narrow specialists and too few outstanding generalists.

However one defines minimum requirements for competence as a China specialist, the government-based analyst needs more than knowledge of China. Indeed, my experience suggests that although specialists in both worlds have been trained in essentially the same way, the government analyst often draws more heavily on the disciplinary than the area studies components of his or her academic training. Proper training as a China specialist is required for success in either world, but to succeed in academe requires cultivation of different skills and, perhaps, a different personality type than is required for success as a government China specialist. There are other reasons to be sure, but these differences probably help explain why so few people have gained distinction in both worlds. At present, especially in the case of analysts who wish to work in government, "extraordinary" knowledge of China is no substitute for inadequate analytical training. To work on Chinese politics does not require a Ph.D. in political science, but it does require more than passing familiarity with social science methodologies and the workings of political and economic systems anywhere.

When facing the choice between an additional course on China and something else, more students—including doctoral candidates—should be encouraged to take courses in comparative politics, international economics, and international security. Now that China has joined the rest of the world, the China studies field must stop treating the country we study as if it were completely unique. To understand the forces shaping developments in China today, it is essential to know more about the workings of the international system as a whole and the experiences of other counties than was true even a decade ago. It is also more important to understand non–China-specific subjects than it is to have mastered Mao Zedong Thought, Ming history, and many other subjects we once considered absolutely essential for understanding contemporary China. If we continue to focus on the unique to the detriment of what China has in common with other countries struggling to modernize in the late twentieth century, we are more likely to be led astray than if we do the opposite. Both are obviously important, and the center of gravity of campus-based China studies almost inevitably will continue to be closer to the latter than the former for the foreseeable future, but it must be nudged toward the other end of the spectrum. Especially in the case of would-be government analysts, appreciation of the broader forces shaping developments and the ability to interpret and explain developments in China in terms familiar to officials who are not themselves China specialists are imperative. For scholars in the academic world, such a step would help close the gulf between China studies and "mainstream" work in the disciplines.

Looking toward the year 2000, it will be even more important than it is today to spend time in China—as a student, researcher, government official, or in some other capacity. The perspective of each group is important, and each is different from the others. We have a great many China specialists, but we do not have enough "China hands" with both the in-depth knowledge of specific places, bureaucracies, and individuals, and the ability of a Doak Barnett or a Lucian Pye to move beyond the minutia and microcosm of "my village" or "my bureaucracy" to make sensible statements about "China." Of course we need to recognize the vast and significant differences that exist in China, but we also need to remember that we are dealing with a single country that is attempting to manage this diversity. Returning again to the perspective of a government official, the level of analysis is not the village, the coast, or a particular sector or group—it is China. The subject is enormous, exciting, and imperfectly understood. Government-based analysts can and do make unique contributions to our knowledge and interpretation of contemporary China. Increased and intensified interchange with our colleagues in academe would benefit both worlds.

Notes

1. The author is director of the Office of Analysis for East Asia and the Pacific in the State Department's Bureau of Intelligence and Research. All opinions expressed in this paper are those of the author and do not necessarily represent the views of the Department of State or any agency of the U.S. government.

Several colleagues commented extensively on earlier drafts of this paper, and I wish to acknowledge their assistance and absolve them of responsibility for any remaining errors or subjective judgments with which they disagree. The suggestions of Judith Banister, Frederick Crook, Christopher Clarke, William Drake, Joseph Fewsmith, Carol Lee Hamrin, Jeffrey Lee, William Mills, Ronald Montaperto, J. Stapleton Roy, Robert Suettinger, Robert Sutter, and Harold Wilcox were particularly helpful.

2. Comparisons are based on the author's experience and observations as a graduate student (1968–75) and research associate (1975–85) at Stanford University, and as chief of the China Division (1986–89) and director of the Office of Analysis for East Asia and the Pacific (since 1989) in the Bureau of Intelligence and Research.

3. Whether one serves primarily as policymaker or policy implementer is largely a function of where one serves in the hierarchy of officialdom. Although it is generally true that senior officials decide and subordinates implement, policy options are usually formulated by "working-level" personnel. The ambassador and others serving overseas also play important roles in the elaboration and evolution of U.S. policy.

It would be impractical to present an extensive list of positions and persons currently or previously engaged in the formulation of U.S. policy toward China, but it may be helpful to list a few illustrative examples. Some of the names will be familiar to many readers; others are included precisely because they are less well-known outside of the government. Any such list is certain to omit "key" persons and others would doubtless offer a different set of examples. My list includes Morton Abramowitz, Donald Anderson, David Brown, Arthur Hummel, James Lilley, Douglas Paal, Edward Ross, J. Stapleton Roy, Melvin Searles, Richard Solomon, Roger Sullivan, Kent Wiedemann, and Richard Williams.

4. This category includes more than just those China specialists who work for the Central Intelligence Agency, the Defense Intelligence Agency, the National Security Agency, the intelligence arms of the four military services, the Bureau of Intelligence and Research, and other parts of the "intelligence community." It also includes some who work primarily as policymakers or public servants but who also prepare assessments for internal use. For example, assessments prepared as background for a senior official or in support of a particular policy option are not released to the public even though they may be based entirely on open-source materials. The individual China specialist may not think of himself or herself as an intelligence analyst, but when preparing assessments for internal use, the role is akin to that of analysts in the intelligence community.

Representative analysts who now or previously fit in this category include Christopher Clarke, Robert Michael Field, Carol Lee Hamrin, Ronald Montaperto, Robert Suettinger, Eden Woon, and many of the contributors to the volumes on China's economy prepared for the Joint Economic Committee of the U.S. Congress.

5. Virtually all assessments, whether based on intelligence information or not, are considered to be predecisional studies and, as such, are not released by executive branch agencies.

6. For obvious reasons, persons who function as "public servants" are more visible in the China studies field than are their colleagues in other government roles. Persons currently or recently serving as public servants include Judith Banister, Nai-Ruenn Chen, Frederick Crook, Kerry Dumbaugh, Leo Orleans, Robert Sutter, and Jeffrey Taylor.

7. The work of Congressional Research Service analysts such as Robert Sutter is an obvious and important exception to this generalization.

8. Database builders are least visible to scholars working outside the government, and they are often invisible even to their colleagues in the government. Some willingly spend years working on narrow, but often extremely important, accounts; others serve in this capacity only temporarily before moving to other positions.

9. For most government analysts, the term "in-box" is more figurative than literal. Most information is received electronically rather than in hard-copy form.

10. Others who have worked successfully in both worlds, albeit in positions with less visibility, include Joseph Fewsmith, Lyman Miller, Denis Fred Simon, and Donald Zagoria.

11. This obviously sweeping generalization requires immediate qualification. The work of Harry Harding, Jonathan Pollack, and Robert Ross, among others, demonstrates that high-quality analyses of foreign and security policy issues can be done by specialists working outside the government. However, these individuals and their work underscore the general point I am trying to make, namely, that much can be learned from talking to and/or working with China specialists in the U.S. government.

10

The Private Sector China Specialists

Thomas W. Robinson

Most private sector Americans dealing with China are not "students" of that country in that they do not devote most of their lives to understanding Chinese culture, society, economy, or polity in the fullest professional sense.[1] Most are interested in China for practical reasons—making money, fulfilling a contract, or seeing to some broader interest. They tend to enter the China field quickly and often exit it as rapidly, and for the most part do not possess the quality of training of China-related individuals in the other fields considered in this volume. But most Americans involved in the China field at any given time probably fall into this category. Moreover, the "private sector" includes a wide variety of China-related activities and organizations, including research institutions and independent consultants; businesses and banks; consulting, accounting, and law firms; foundations; nonacademic training institutes; interest groups of various kinds; travel organizations, hotel-keepers, and guidebook writers; and international institutions with a high American personnel quotient or underpinning. Most day-to-day American activity regarding China and with China probably occurs in this sphere. Because they are in close contact with other aspects of the American study of, and relations with, China (and frequently come from and move back to these other arenas), such individuals and institutions form one of the vital centers of this endeavor.

To estimate accurately the number of individuals in this general category is impossible, given the rapid expansion of Sino-American relations in the 1980s and the relative contraction after 1989. But the figures appear surprisingly high. For instance, the number of American businesspeople in China (before the spring 1989 turmoil) was about 1,050,[2] with about 3,000[3] in Hong Kong, and these were supported by perhaps half that number at headquarters in the United States.[4] Think tank and independent consultant personnel working on China amounted in 1991 to perhaps 150;[5] law firms, management consulting organizations, and accounting firms employed about 150 such people;[6] foundations approximately 15;[7]

training institutes 50;[8] interest groups another 60;[9] the travel industry about 300;[10] and international institutions another 75.[11] The total is thus about 5,300, more than all other categories of Americans studying or working in regard to China. Perhaps a third of these people are not in the China field permanently and will have gone on to other duties and interests within about two years. But while it is unlikely that numbers will increase greatly, if at all, during the next several years (and have undoubtedly fallen as a consequence of the Tiananmen incident), those working in such areas in the early 1990s were many times the number engaged in China-related activities in the early 1970s, when perhaps 1,500 people were involved, mostly businesspeople dealing with Hong Kong.

The training background of private sector China specialists varies considerably. Most have a training base ranging from one or two weeks of lectures and a reading base of perhaps ten articles and one book, to master's degree–level study or even a doctorate. The weighted average is toward the low end, however, which is very little considering the importance of this group to Sino-American relations. This results in a great deal of on-the-job training and many errors, false hopes, cultural clashes, and other potentially avoidable problems, given more in-depth training and cultural sensitivity. If it were somehow possible to calculate the expertise involved in this professional sphere, however it would be considerable indeed. Experience and self-study make up for many initial inadequacies. A person who has worked in the China area for three years probably has more than made up for training deficiencies. Many businesspeople are obviously in this category; indeed, some of America's best China "specialists" have attained their positions of authority by virtue of experience rather than training. Even given the language barrier, many Americans in these areas have lived in China long enough to have acquired adequate language skills. Americans of Chinese descent often—but not always—possess linguistic and cultural advantages that facilitate their work in China, which other Americans lack. Of course, many people sent to China on short-term assignments have no real need for more than a minimum of training. The oil company employee on contract to explore for petroleum does not really need to learn about Chinese history or culture to do the job well. Indeed, given the numbers involved and the rapidity with which they increased after 1978, reports are minimal of the "ugly" American who, unprepared for what he or she must face in China, never recovers from the initial cultural shock and must be sent home.

This chapter does not, however, focus alone on cataloguing, quantifying, or evaluating the adequacy of preparation of the private sector China specialist. Rather, we are interested in how such individuals go about their business in terms of their analytic approach to China: what are their sources, assumptions, and prejudices; how do their employers or customers shape their agendas and findings; how do they go about their work, particularly in producing research products; and what similarities and differences are there between China specialists in this sector and those in the academy, the government, and the media?

With such a wide variety of occupations comprising this sector, it is natural to expect an equal diversity along each of these dimensions. That makes summation and comparison difficult. But some surprising uniformity emerges, as the following exposition attempts to demonstrate.

Research Institutions and Independent Consultants

Research institutions and independent consultants form a vast industry. They are principally of three types: nonprofit, not-for-profit, and for-profit.[12] For our purposes, the first two can be considered together.

An extensive network of such organizations exists, exemplified by the not-for-profit Rand Corporation and the nonprofit Brookings Institution. Since its inception in the late 1940s as America's first—and perhaps still foremost—think tank, Rand (which stands for "Research and Development") has consistently maintained a strong China expertise. Formerly it included only one or two persons with doctoral training in the field, but its staff until the early 1990s comprised several people with advanced degrees. Although Rand's funding for China studies stems almost exclusively from the U.S. government, primarily the Air Force and the Defense Department, its output is not always geared to military or even current policy questions. Rather, there is an attempt to be comprehensive by supplying as much background relevant to contemporary policy issues as possible. Often that leads to the production of long books, documented with original Chinese sources, historically informed, and with no major intent other than to enrich the general knowledge of the field. The difference between this kind of study and purely academic work is almost nil. Rand can produce work of no immediate and direct policy relevance to its sponsor because of the unique nature of its contractual relationship with the government. The government provides Rand with a certain sum, and directs the corporation to research whatever areas it thinks are in the U.S. national and the security interest and to communicate the results within government and in the public domain. The government also seeks a more direct return on its investment through more relevant research products. Rand China specialists are thus under some pressure to write about current trends and developments in the Chinese military, foreign policy, politics, and economics.[13] But even here, the tendency is to do longer work, of high academic quality, suitable for eventual open publication. Rand cannot wander too far from contemporary China matters for too long, but it is surprising how much of the "permanent" literature of the field (that which has proven academically acceptable and has stood the test of time) has been produced by this quasi-governmental institution and others like it.

Indeed, the think tank as an American social invention has demonstrated its efficacy in the China field for several reasons. First, the contract between institution and government must be reasonably general in scope, not require immediate performance on narrow customer-supplied issues, and surely avoid any hint of arriving at government-preordained conclusions. Second, the research product must be well reviewed and edited internally before it is sent to the sponsor, and this requirement—seminaring, reviewing, forcing the author to respond to all critical comments, and very careful editing—normally guarantees a high quality of product. Third, a Rand China researcher can generally find intramurally the answer to many questions in whatever field, because other researchers are literally "down the hall." They make themselves available as a matter of course and are intrinsically interested in doing collaborative research. In addition, high-quality research assistance is immediately available, and the funds to procure research material—in terms of research trips as well as quick placement of written sources on one's desk—are available with a minimum of delay. It is impossible to duplicate these working conditions in the government, academia, or journalism, and this is the "secret" of Rand's (and other Rand-like institutions') success. Interestingly, the availability to Rand China researchers of classified government data is not, in this writer's opinion, a major advantage. The sources for classified China-related research generally vary little from those in the academic and journalistic spheres. (See Chapter 9 in this volume by Thomas Fingar in this regard.)

What America knows about contemporary China can be traced in no small measure to the China-study efforts of Rand-type researchers, including a long list of consultants who have produced studies on subcontract.[14] This is the case not only in the areas of reporting and analysis, but also cross-disciplinary studies, interview studies, and work supplying the conceptual framework for thinking usefully about the subject. It helps, of course, to be paid a decent salary for the sole purpose of thinking and writing about the subject, with little interference in that process. But the major reason for the success of this kind of work is its contractual freedom and internal research style. A propensity does exist, however, to produce more work in certain areas than others. For example, there is a greater bias toward explaining Chinese politics and foreign policy in terms of factions within the Chinese Communist Party than is the case in the academic world. Another characteristic is that a research product derives directly from such primary data sources as radio broadcasts, the print media, and interviews. This leads to a pronounced bias against theoretical frameworks and existing secondary literature. Rand-type institutions therefore tend to be heavily inductive, empirical, and nontheoretical. A third tendency is to explain contemporary Chinese developments and policy in historical terms rather than more conceptually complicated or mixed variables. That is perhaps surprising, given the inventiveness of such institutions in new areas of thinking (game theory, information sciences, deterrence theory, and so forth). The reasons for these tendencies lie in the data-rich, highly intensive support environment in these institutions as well as a self-generated and -supported mystique concerning the uniqueness and quality of their work. Detailed research files can be compiled with comparative ease on any subject of interest and, together with the Rand assumption that no previous work of consequence exists, thinking is done, as it were, from scratch.

Lastly, there is a tendency toward prolixity. If one has free, high-quality, personalized, and near-instantaneous research backup, more as well as better and more intensely researched work will emerge.

Notable differences exist between Rand-style research on China and that produced by nonprofit research institutions, best illustrated by the Brookings Institution. Brookings studies tend to be somewhat more scholarly (in the sense of having somewhat less immediate and obvious policy relevance), are produced for immediate public sale rather than transmission first to a governmental sponsor, are financed largely by nongovernmental sources, are entirely unclassified (perhaps 40 percent of Rand's China output remains classified), tend toward books rather than a combination of reports, papers, and books only later, and are almost always single-authored. Otherwise, there is comparatively little difference. Quality is high in both institutions' products; the tendency toward policy-relevant studies is also present at Brookings and other such institutions, given their charters, and the antitheoretical bias is also evident.[15]

Lack of direct and immediate access to government-supplied data, especially classified material, could result in different orientations and perhaps even lesser quality of output at nongovernmental research institutes. The difference, if any, is in fact minimal for two reasons. One is that access to classified information is not so helpful as might be presumed. Analysis of details on Chinese military production and deployment might critically depend on such data, but the vast majority of research does not. In the China area, most of what is available is already public in the form of Chinese newspapers, journals, translations of radio broadcasts, and, since the 1980s, Chinese books. Classified material sometimes confirms what is apparent from the public media, but only occasionally—and mostly for only a short time—goes beyond what normal research (heavily supported by research assistance to be sure) can produce. The other reason is that use of classified research material guarantees classification of the product, restricted circulation, and consequently lack of the generally productive scholarly critique and cross-fertilization of product characteristic of open publication.

Research institutes in the third think tank category, for-profit organizations, share many characteristics of the first two in their China-related work, but differences are greater than between nonprofit and not-for-profit institutions. For one, classified information is almost a sine qua non of their work, which tends to be almost exclusively for the Defense Department or the intelligence community. The assumption is that the sponsor is more likely to read the product if it has a red cover (i.e., that it is classified). Allied with this is the tendency to stress topics with immediate policy implications. Detailed analytical and historical studies are therefore generally avoided. Some methodologies crowd out others: the political-military exercise is the favorite, with a generalized, nontheoretical, military strategy-oriented, straight-from-the-facts analysis a close second. Statistical or other quantitative approaches—especially those associated with some theoretical orientation—are almost never used for fear of putting off the reader.

Great effort is put into writing a summary because the busy policymaker will probably not have time to wade through lengthy studies, and much attention is paid to presenting a finely honed oral briefing. The written report is often an afterthought, since its distribution is often small, controlled by the sponsor, and for government eyes only. One consequence is redundancy and a lack of cross-fertilization of work. Another is frustration for the researcher in trying to obtain clearance for open publication. This results in significant delays, the necessity to rewrite (or to play the game of finding unclassified sources for what the author knows to be true from classified data), and permanent classification of a large portion of the work of these institutions.

For-profit organizations vary greatly in size, from small partnerships to huge organizations with annual budgets of more than a billion dollars and staff of thousands. China-related work is usually a very small portion of the whole, however, and this author knows of none with a staff of more than two. Given the resources involved, that is a pity. Generally, when a contract is obtained, most funds are spent on consultants for written portions of a study or for participating in a simulation. Often, China work derives from some larger contract on a non-China related study (usually technical in nature) and the China specialists then become essentially internal consultants. Like internally produced Defense Department/intelligence community work on China, the quantity of work is large. Its quality varies considerably, however, and in any case its staying power is small since it is designed to answer contemporary policy questions quickly. However, because of the often tempting honoraria and the chance to rub shoulders with a combination of other China specialists and government policy analysts, these organizations have considerable power to marshal China expertise. Specialists can thus be drawn together on short notice and tend to put other work aside temporarily in favor of quick policy input. While that function tends to be denigrated in the academic arena, its utility is sometimes high in terms of production of ideas and access to otherwise fenced-off data.[16]

Independent consultants are few in number because most are soon absorbed into other organizations analyzed in this chapter, especially business and consulting firms. Nonetheless, at any given time, enough people—perhaps 50—are in this category to warrant inclusion. Most work as external experts to for-profit think tanks, the government, and various businesses. Some academicians—often the best known—must be included in this category, engaging in China-related moonlighting activities that take up much of their time but supplement their academic incomes. Many ex-government officials, usually retired but not always of retirement age, also fall into this category. Some influential reports on China and American-Chinese relations have been produced, or greatly influenced by, independent consultants.[17] Consultants perform another valuable function: they carry ideas and experience from one arena to another, thus permitting personnel from often closed communities—intelligence organizations and banks, for instance—to communicate with each other. Moreover, in the case of academic-government relations, a professor who consults to a government institution profits in terms of gaining knowledge not otherwise available. This is especially the case where classified material is involved: consultancy conveys an advantage in terms of data and prestige, and is often useful in terms of access to high Chinese officials.

The Business Community

Business organizations employ the largest number of China-related private sector Americans. By 1990, over three hundred large corporations and perhaps three thousand total American concerns were doing business in or with China.[18] The saga of Sino-American business relations is the subject of an increasingly voluminous and enlightening literature.[19] Our interest is how American business studies China, that is, how firms decide to move (or not) into the China market, how they prepare their China-related employees, and how they evaluate their China experience. In theory, that process is not different in the China case, except in degree, from the manner in which American corporations approach business activity with any other country. Initial analysis is performed on a product and industry basis, since corporations are always eager to find new markets for their products and cheaper and more effective ways to find raw materials and employ factors of production.

In practice, however, from the beginning of the American Republic, American business has exhibited a well-known propensity to sell to, and to a lesser extent to buy in, the China market despite the many innate difficulties of conducting business there. And since the reopening of the China market in the 1970s, a rush took place—receding, however temporarily, after the Tiananmen incident—to try to position one's firm favorably for the presumed large orders for American products by Chinese state and private trading corporations eager to modernize their country rapidly. American businesses thus went to great lengths, much beyond what they would do to try to break into other markets, first on assumption that China's immense consumer potential would eventually return very high profits on investment and second out of fear that, if one did not become established in China, the regime would choose one's competitor. This included entering into agreements largely on Chinese terms, often vague, arrived at only after much negotiation, and often subject to unilateral revision by the Chinese side; investment in regions and industries where the promise of return, while possibly high, would come much later if at all; putting up with all manner of inconvenience and discomfort while in China; and spending much money on a Beijing office and constant trips to the country.

This willingness to go many extra miles in quest of the China market reflects not only an American cultural bias in favor of doing business with that country despite great obstacles but also a level of knowledge of Chinese realities that is sometimes quite low. That in turn cannot be traced to the lack of information on

China, especially since many years have passed since the reopening in the early 1970s. As noted below, the readily available information base for American firms is diverse, helpful, and sophisticated. Rather, it points to the unwillingness of many American businesses to do their homework on China: to employ trained people, to listen to those inside the corporation who have the requisite knowledge and experience, to research the market properly, to find out how the Chinese negotiate a contract and what kind of business conditions actually exist in the country, and what the future portends. This charge is often leveled against American business in general but appears to be all the more applicable in the Chinese case. While many American businesspeople are experienced in the China trade, preparation is still poor: most are sent out suddenly, with one or two weeks' crash training, no language background or the chance to acquire any, and with the knowledge that they will not be responsible for this portion of their company's efforts for more than several years at most. There is also the propensity to presume that corporate officers a priori possess the necessary knowledge about China and therefore can make decisions without a great deal of analysis and background information.[20]

The quality of market research available to American business is more difficult to judge. The U.S.-China Business Council (formerly the National Council on U.S.-China Trade) performs general surveys for its member organizations and its journal, The China Business Review, has many excellent articles on market conditions in the country. The council's standards and staff quality are high, and if the information it provides to its corporate members comes into the hands of the top decisionmakers on a regular basis, American business should have no difficulty in adopting prudent investment and trade strategies in China. In 1991, however, it suffered a severe budgetary and staff reduction, the product partly of the relatively poorer business climate after Tiananmen. The council is a semiofficial, Washington, D.C.–based organization established by Congress expressly to assist American business in China, but is funded by its members. It has some three hundred member firms, conducts a variety of research on Chinese economic conditions, holds seminars and larger meetings on a particular market or topic for corporate clients, maintains a small library for its members (and others on request), sends library materials to its members, and provides detailed advice and counsel, also on member request. The council president has had personal access to the top Chinese leadership, an important asset. The organization also conveys its assessments, positive and negative, to members at an annual meeting.[21]

Several competent market survey and business consultant organizations specialize on China, as noted below. Conferences abound on establishing one's company in China.[22] Yet American companies constantly express surprise and dismay about China, and that can only indicate a propensity to make decisions in haste and on the basis of highly inadequate information. A reasonably highly developed network of law firms and others specializing in contract negotiation has also emerged, as noted later in this chapter. But stories continue to emerge of

American companies that went to China unprepared for the Chinese negotiating style (which has long been well understood), agreeing to contracts that contain many dubious provisions, and expressing resentment when post-negotiating developments deviate substantially from what they had been led to believe.[23] Most serious of all, perhaps, is an unwillingness to inform themselves about Chinese culture and history. That is not unusual in a people with a short history and a rapidly changing culture and is an attitude to be found in American dealings with other countries as well. With China, however, it appears to have been taken to extremes and is largely responsible for the American inability to look into the Chinese future with any degree of comprehension.

Mention should also be made of the USA-ROC Economic Council, an organization similar in intent to the U.S.-China Business Council but whose purpose is furthering commercial ties with Taiwan. It is a large private organization of businesses, with a board of directors drawn entirely from that sector, headquartered as of 1991 in Washington, D.C., and possessing close ties with not only the Taiwanese business community and political leadership but also trade development and promotion offices in most American states. Its sister organization is the ROC-USA Economic Council in Taiwan, also a large organization. The principal function of both councils is an annual joint business conference, alternating between the United States and Taiwan, which normally attracts over a thousand registrants and top officials from both countries. It maintains close contact with the American Institute on Taiwan and the Coordination Council for North American Affairs, the unofficial but government-appointed offices charged with conducting relations between the United States and Taiwan. It publishes a useful quarterly newsletter, *Taiwan Economic News,* which analyzes economic and political conditions relating to U.S.-Taiwan trade.[24]

Other consultant organizations provide similar services, on a smaller scale, to private clients, which often include the best-known American business concerns. Some of these have been on the scene long enough to have established excellent access to the Chinese leadership and a proven track record. This is true, for instance, of Kamsky Associates in New York and Kissinger Associates in New York, WJS Asia Limited in Hong Kong, and China-America Business Consultants in Washington, D.C., to name but four. Their reports are not publicly available. In some cases, namely Kissinger Associates, they take on quasi-official functions by serving as consultants to the Chinese government, providing a back channel for diplomatic contacts when it serves state interests, and drawing together influential China-related *cognoscenti.*[25] Since their written output is almost never made public, objective review of their activities is impossible. The suspicion is natural, therefore, that they may on occasion tell clients what they want to hear. And since some do not reveal their list of clients (and, even in the case of Kissinger Associates, deny representing the Chinese government itself, contrary to much evidence), a further suspicion arises that some are not above taking money from opposing sources. Nonetheless, their staffs are regarded as competent and experienced, and take advantage of the vast amount of material generally available on China. Original research is not undertaken, and their direct contact with the scholarly world is limited to a small number of consultants.

Several state-level associations also serve their membership in a manner similar to that of the U.S.-China Business Council. The most well-known of these is the Washington [State] China Relations Council, which has been active in promoting trade since the mid-1970s and has become a model of its kind. The states of Ohio, Michigan, New Jersey, and Illinois have similar councils for promoting China trade, and the governors of these states have had special staff assistants for China trade. A number of organizations and individuals publish newsletters or periodic reports, of which the *International Contract Advisor* and *East Asian Executive Reports,* both published in Washington, D.C., are two examples. Some of the major accounting firms have developed expertise on China business conditions, maintain offices in China, publish sometimes extensive reports and handbooks, and provide proprietary consulting services to their clients. One such is Price Waterhouse, which publishes a useful information guide on doing business in China. Another is Coudert Brothers, whose Washington, D.C., office is well staffed with experienced businesspeople.[26]

If one totals the number of professionally trained, experienced, or involved people in the consultant and adviser category, probably more than a hundred Americans, and perhaps a similar number of noncitizens in the United States and abroad, owe their livelihood to this branch of China-related work.

Finally in this category are the risk analysts. Business International, which publishes *Business Asia* in Hong Kong, is perhaps the largest and best-known such firm. It not only conducts forecasts of business (and hence political and general economic) conditions in and with regard to China but will also do contract research on particular subjects for specific clients. Other risk analysis firms include China in their purview, a good example being Political Risk Services (PRS). Until 1988, this organization was a branch of Frost and Sullivan, an American risk analysis and market research organization. Now a division of International Business Communications/USA, PRS publishes annual fifty-page reports on some eighty-five countries, including China. These are written in a standard format for comparative purposes and include a number of five-year moving time-line quantitative indicators. These are made to fit into a political risk forecasting model developed by Syracuse University professors Michael O'Leary and William Coplin, and are revised annually to fit into a semiannual book-length publication comparing all eighty-five countries. A team of four American China experts writes the original report, which is then put into the O'Leary-Coplin framework. The general idea is to look for "leading indicators" of political and economic change that can be expressed numerically and hence compared across time and political boundaries. Qualitative variables, such as personality, political culture, and factional divisions, are not excluded. The forecasting model that results is not unreasonable for medium-term (two–five-year) futures. This approach has not found resonance in the American academic world or the government but has been useful to the business community, which continues to pay the high fees charged. One reason for the continued success (that is, survival) of this kind of operation is that it tailors its research and writing style to the desires of American business, while neither academic nor government China analysts take much interest in developing such contacts, much less trying to service their needs.[27]

An interesting example of a mixture of academic analysis and policy forecasting for corporate readers is *Global Assessment*.[28] This biannual journal comprises high-quality articles on major countries, including China, assessing the previous half-year's events and forecasting the next six months' developments. Similar to the annual summaries available in the *Far Eastern Economic Review, Current History,* and *Asian Survey,* they provide an efficient way to keep abreast of developments in China, sensitize the reader to the likelihood of change or constancy concerning Chinese conditions, and compare the Chinese business climate with that in other nations. If corporations were to avail themselves of these kinds of resources, digest them properly, and place the product in the hands of their leaderships, there would be little need to worry about their decision-making competence. Unfortunately, that is not always the case.

The Banking Community

Banks deserve special mention because of their centrality to the American business approach to China. Most large New York banks and several large regional banks have China departments that provide information and services to their clients. Thus, Citibank, Manufacturer's Hanover, Chase Manhattan, Barclay's, First National City Bank in New York, First National Bank in Chicago, and Bank of America in San Francisco, to name some of the principals, all maintain departments or staff specializing in China business and trade matters. However, most of these intramural operations are decentralized and modest, depend mostly on the activities and expertise of branch offices in China and Hong Kong, and do only trade financing. Little if anything is published externally and the outsider often has difficulty finding China-related departments (if not experts) at headquarters. Most activity and specialized personnel are located in branch offices, and they are often given wide latitude to conduct business operations. Many banks have branches in Beijing as well as in Hong Kong, and it is their on-the-scene expertise that the main office generally depends on, the specialists in headquarters being more organizers and passers-through of field data than independent analysts.

As in the case of American manufacturers or importers, many banks consider a China presence desirable not because of imminent prospect for profits but because the competition is there and out of the assumption that, "someday," China will become an important market. It may be surprising that such a seemingly unprofessional attitude pervades American banking circles. But that merely reflects the nature of American banking, which has always been short on solid research and planning in general and long on wishful thinking regarding China in particular. That is not to say that banks do not avail themselves of the available external research resources or that their in-house analysts are not first-rate in many cases. Some banks—Chase Manhattan and Bank of America, for instance —do maintain good, if still small, numbers of country risk experts focused on China. They depend on the standard daily and weekly publicly available written materials—the Foreign Broadcast Information Service's *Daily Report, China,* the *Far Eastern Economic Review,* and World Bank reports being the most widely used—as well as reports from the field. Their products do for the most part adequately sum up the state of play at any given moment regarding investment opportunities and risks in the country. Nonetheless, when one totals the numbers of banking people whose full-time occupation is China (most of whom have acquired "expertise" more through on-the-job training than through the more rigorous route of language, area study, and in-China living experience), the figures are probably no more than several dozen, an insubstantial amount compared with other sectors.[29]

Particular note should be taken of the great international government-controlled banking institutions, principally the International Bank for Reconstruction and Development (the World Bank) and the International Monetary Fund in Washington, D.C.—known as the "Bank" and the "Fund"—and secondarily, the Asian Development Bank in Manila. The World Bank in particular maintains a large research division of economists working on Chinese economic matters and publishes, both for its members and through them for the public, high-quality reports on Chinese economic (and other related) conditions. This publicly available literature is a small fraction of the volume of internally generated research reports.[30] More than fifty staff members are engaged in such research at the headquarters. Many are professionally trained, Chinese language–competent economists. Some are American citizens, and thus warrant inclusion in this survey. The bank also rotates other economists who are not China degree–trained into the China departments for three-to-five-year postings; they acquire their expertise by reading, consulting, and frequent consulting trips to China. Given the World Bank's salary structure, these professionals are, with the exception of lawyers, perhaps the most highly paid research personnel in the American China field. There are five China divisions: Country Operations, Agriculture Operations, Industry and Finance Operations, Transport and Energy Operations, and Population, Human Resources, Urban Development, and Water Supply Operations. These departments produce written reports for, and serve as internal consultants to, other parts of the bank. It must be said, though, that the World Bank is not particularly helpful to the nongovernmental outsider in quest of information or access to personnel pertaining to China. Research personnel rarely appear in public fora, and there is no felt compunction to deal with non-bank requests for literature or information. Indeed, the atmosphere of quasi-secrecy in which the bank operates skews the product, already slanted politically because of the necessity to please sponsoring governments, to say nothing of China itself. The research products consequently sometimes miss the unique opportunity presented, in the form of near-total access in many cases to the best data and the full range of decisionmakers. They often bear the markings of having been watered down, overly optimistic, and apolitical.

Nonetheless, the unique access that the World Bank has in China makes it a major source of economic and statistical information on the country. Moreover, the bank does not limit its investigations to purely economic matters but conducts research on a broad variety of topics that bear on the entire spectrum of issues arising at various stages of economic development. These include population studies, general social and cultural analysis, detailed work on regions and subregions of China, and even analysis of Chinese politics and foreign policy. Aside from publications that are cleared for open publication and available through its Washington and Paris publications offices, the China Country Operations Division produces *China Development News,* an internal photocopied compendium of journal, wire-service, and newspaper articles quite similar, in quantity, quality, frequency, and utility, to the Department of Defense daily *Current News* and similar reproduction journals published by other American government executive departments. The World Bank is like the Rand Corporation in one regard: its combination of official access, wealth of material, salary scale, and care taken to ensure a quality staff guarantees (with the qualifications noted above) a top quality product.

The Legal World

American lawyers concentrating on China can be regarded as a distinct subclass of private sector specialists. Not counting academic legal specialists, they are relatively few in number, totaling perhaps less then sixty. Many of them are highly trained and engage in a wide variety of China-related work not always found in other reaches of the legal profession: researching investment possibilities and pitfalls, finding Chinese partners, conducting feasibility studies and the legal aspects thereof, drafting, negotiating, and supervising the execution of contracts, investigating tax strategies, and the like. Since what law there is in China is essentially administrative law, American lawyers must closely inform themselves of the politics and the party-governmental personages of the country. Because promulgation and interpretation of laws and regulations in China thus varies with person, place, and time, the American lawyer must make him/herself an expert on many aspects of the country outside the strictly legal domain. This combination enables such people not only to see into the inner sanctum of the Chinese system but also in many cases to participate in the making of essentially domestic Chinese decisions concerning a wide variety of economic, political, and social issues. It therefore requires becoming familiar not only with the details of Chinese lawlike practices and their basis in Chinese culture and the Chinese Communist Party's interpretation of Marxism-Leninism but also conducting one's own original research on Chinese law, traditional and contemporary. Many practicing lawyers are thus legal scholars as well as practitioners, while some of America's best China scholars are consequently also intimately involved in practical legal matters.[31]

The practicing lawyer engages in two kinds of legal "traffic": outbound and inbound. Outbound practice is either regulatory or transactional, that is, dealing with those on the Chinese side who have general regulatory—political—power (government and party officials, normally) or with those on the Chinese side who are able to plan or carry out some specific agreement. Inbound practice, much less common, consists of representing the few Chinese firms active in the United States. So far as legal scholarship is concerned, the process is similar to that known to students of China everywhere. There must be thorough background preparation, including intimate understanding of Chinese history, culture, society, economics, and politics. The lawyer must also possess a solid capability in Chinese language. Ideally, there should be experience living in China, including some brush with doing field research and conducting interviews. Familiarization must be obtained with the various sources of Chinese law and how the system operates in practice as opposed to theory. That means familiarization with legal and political documents as well as doing case work.

Because the practicing attorney has a sometimes unique opportunity to penetrate some of the layers of the Chinese political-cultural protective overlay, the way is more open to obtaining a more detailed and realistic understanding of the way the system "works" than is the case with many other China-related professions. The result is that their quality of output is usually as high as is the diversity of input sources uniquely available to them. Some American lawyers therefore achieve deserved scholarly reputations at least as well deserved as the "best" in the university arena. One only need mention Lucille Barale, Jerome Cohen, Charles Conroy, Tim Gelatt, Stanley Lubman, Lester Ross, and Mitchell Silk, who move with equal ease in the practical and the scholarly worlds.[32] Their law offices in fact take on the atmosphere of miniature research corporations. This creative cross-fertilization of scholarship and practice works both ways, of course. The small number of university professors of Chinese law—Hung-dah Chiu, James Feinerman, and Randall Edwards, to name three—are often drawn into practical legal work so that the quality of their work is also enhanced.

The Tourist Industry

Transportation-tourism is one of the most active private sector areas in Sino-American relations, with perhaps several hundred professionally trained Americans working full time, enjoying intimate day-to-day contact with a broad reach of Chinese citizens and institutions throughout the country, and in charge of, or working in, organizations ranging from transportation to hotels to tour operations. They are responsible for bringing by far the largest number of Americans into contact with China—in 1988 approximately 350,000[33] Americans visited the country—and the nature of their work takes them to every corner of China. The frequency and breadth of their contacts thus make them a valuable source of information on the state of overall bilateral relations, provide useful employment for many with training at the entry level and above in various China-related fields, and enable those who choose to write about or otherwise relate their travel experiences an excellent opportunity to bring to China studies in general a wealth of specific, on-the-ground observations. Much of the historic literature on China, from Marco Polo forward, was nothing more than travel literature[34] and that tradition continues in the contemporary era, thereby supplying much of the richness of the field. Since the reopening of China to Americans in the early 1970s, tourism has burgeoned. By the late 1980s, many firms were operating that did not previously exist, air (and, to a lesser extent, sea) transport companies were scheduling over a hundred flights weekly (and several cruise ships monthly) to and from China, and many new hotels (both joint venture and Chinese-owned but often Western-managed) had already changed the face of many Chinese cities.

The official China International Travel Service (CITS) has designated over a hundred American operators, with whom they deal directly, to run tours of China. Some of these, such as Pacific Delight (which sends ten thousand tourists per year) and Pacific Best Tours (which sends five thousand), are so-called wholesalers, large organizations that gather up small numbers of tourists from local travel agencies and divide them into fifteen–twenty-person groups. Others are smaller, such as Academic Travel Abroad, and cater to a more select clientele. Most Americans traveling to China are tourists and are over fifty years of age, though 20 percent of the total are businesspeople, 8 percent are on official passports, and another 20 percent are from the academic world. Three-quarters of Americans traveling to China go as part of a group.[35]

The travel industry employs several hundred China-related professionals on a full-time basis. Their training and experience vary greatly, from those who, like many businesspeople, have become acquainted with China over the years to those who have graduate degrees and language capabilities. Some are non-American, mostly Chinese or Hong Kong citizens. All must maintain strong personal and professional ties with a broad range of Chinese, not only in the CITS headquarters in Beijing but also in its regional branches, the direct booking hotels, the various semiprivate Chinese tour-assisting organizations, and government transportation ministries. That puts them in a position to acquire a depth of contacts and a breadth of travel experience open to few other Americans. Their expertise is therefore a valuable and, for the most part, untapped store of knowledge about China. Sometimes, that can be put to effective research use, for example by

Anne Thurston, who has written some fine studies of Chinese society while the resident Beijing representative of Academic Travel Abroad.[36]

Akin to this group is the China guidebook writer. By the late 1980s, more than fifty such books in English alone had been produced by a group of writer-travelers who, given the very small number of Americans and others previously able to travel to China, did not exist in the professional sense before then. They also represent a valuable resource; the products of their labors are often of high quality and are well-researched.[37] Moreover, there are several hundred employees of American (and other) transportation companies—pilots and flight attendants, sea captains and other ship officers, travel agency specialists, and hotel executives and employees—who, though not normally "experts" on China in the sense of having language and area studies backgrounds, are nonetheless knowledgeable about the country with regard to their own fields of endeavor. In many cases, they are concerned with China on a full-time basis and are as deserving of inclusion in the category of private sector specialists as any of the other groups comprising this chapter. A final group in this category includes the many—by the late 1980s perhaps a thousand—Americans who have served as tour guide leaders to China. Particularly for professors and other teachers, such sponsored and remunerated travel represents one of the best ways to travel to China and view regions and institutions not otherwise accessible. The degree of knowledge thus acquired is also an important source for research and writing about the country. Although there is no single organizational center to this diverse group, the China-Orient Tourism Advisory Committee, located in New York City, attempts to promote tourism to that country and disseminate information about China.

The Foundation World

Foundations exert a major influence on the American study of China. While they do not normally produce their own studies of the country and do not maintain in-house research centers on China, their influence on the field as a whole is enormous, as Chapter 15 in this volume by Terrill E. Lautz demonstrates.

The field has long been dominated by the Ford Foundation, which since the 1960s has funded many of the important departures in the field and kept solvent several of the major activist, exchange, and scholarship institutions of American China studies—one need only list the National Committee on U.S.-China Relations, the Committee on Scholarly Communication with the People's Republic of China (now called the Committee on Scholarly Communication with China, CSCC), the principal university China centers, the Social Science Research Council, the American Council of Learned Societies' Joint Committee on Contemporary China, and the Association for Asian Studies. In recent years, the Ford Foundation has strived to develop direct collaboration between American and Chinese scholars, foster the growth or rebirth of major Chinese programs in the social sciences—particularly economics, sociology, law, and international relations—

and made possible a broad range of exchange activities, including the National Program for Advanced Research and Study in China.

Other foundations have similar programs and have funded major American work on China. These include the Luce, MacArthur, and Rockefeller Foundations, and the Rockefeller Brothers Fund. Each of these major foundations, as well as several smaller ones, has at least one professionally trained China expert, and Ford has maintained a Beijing office since 1988. Mention should also be made of the American government foundations, the National Science Foundation, the National Academy of Sciences, which has no less influence and expertise than the major private foundations mentioned above, and the U.S. Institute for Peace, which entered the field in the late 1980s. Probably about fifty American China specialists are employed in these institutions.[38]

The funding orientation of these foundations deserves some scrutiny, not only because of the disposition they impart to the field but also because a research orientation is made evident thereby. There seems little doubt that the major foundations are pronouncedly "pro-Chinese" in the sense that they consider more American work on China, more exchange with China, and more internationalization of Chinese scholars and decisionmakers innately good. In that sense, they are the contemporary secular successors of the American Christian missionaries of the hundred years ending in 1949. It is unlikely that they have sponsored studies that sought to demonstrate Chinese iniquity in one or another field (such as, say, the familiar one-child birth control policy of the 1980s) or that they took as a working assumption a generally hostile attitude on the part of Chinese decisionmakers or Chinese culture in general toward the United States. While there were charges that, in earlier times, the major foundations held a Cold War attitude toward China, since the restoration of Sino-American contacts in the early 1970s their inclination seems to have been much to the contrary. In recent years, as Harry Harding points out in Chapter 2, these foundations have begun to expend more funds on China and Chinese than on American China scholars and studies. This is an alarming trend.

Funding of American China studies has, in fact, been bifurcated politically, with the most respected studies generally supported by the major foundations with a more or less "liberal" orientation. That has opened up a gap in the field that has been filled to some extent by smaller conservative foundations—Scaife, Coors, and Earhart being three examples—by the private sponsors of conservative research institutions—for instance, the Foreign Policy Research Institute and the Heritage Foundation—and by the Taiwan government. The latter in particular has expended large sums in the United States for China studies and for supporting individuals, groups, universities, and other institutions with a presumably anti-Communist orientation. These include the Hoover Institution, university programs at the University of California at Berkeley, Claremont, Georgetown, Tufts, St. Johns, and Pennsylvania State universities (to mention only a few), research programs at the American Enterprise Institute, the Center for Strategic and International Studies, the Heritage Foundation, the Woodrow Wilson International Center for Scholars, such groups as the American Association for Chinese Studies, and a broad variety of China conferences in the United States and Taiwan.[39] Supported by Taiwan funding these institutions have produced major works on China that in some instances have gained broad respectability and acceptance. But it has often been the case that a scholar or an institution has been labeled "liberal" or "conservative" on China, based as much on funding source as on supposed innate political orientation. Once so branded, it sometimes proves difficult to obtain funding from sources on the other side of the political divide.

Cultural Exchange Organizations and Interest Groups

Interest groups represent an important component of private sector American expertise on China. There are three types of such organizations: groups advocating, and practicing, the improvement of Sino-American relations; those applying a moral test to policy evaluation of Chinese governmental activities within China; and those administering exchange and training of American and Chinese personnel. Functionally, the first and the third overlap considerably. Advocacy groups are headed by the "two committees," the National Committee on U.S.-China Relations and the CSCC.

The National Committee, a member organization (by invitation) founded in 1966, is dedicated to "building constructive and durable ties between the leaders and citizens" of the United States and China. Funded by private, foundation, corporate, and some government contributions, it is governed by a board of directors comprising a mixture of well-known academics, business and banking leaders, and former government officials. Until the establishment of formal diplomatic relations, the National Committee—along with the CSCC and the U.S.-China Business Council—was one of the principal means of contact, official and otherwise, between the two countries. It sponsored many delegations from both sides, held important conferences, and generally served as one of the main conduits and testing grounds for American policy toward China. Since state-to-state ties were reestablished in 1979, the National Committee has concentrated on high-level delegations—particularly on hosting visiting Chinese groups, defining the nature and direction of American-Chinese relations, especially for the New York–based elite—held conferences that brought together in one place leaders in the academy, the marketplace, and the polity, and taken a leading role in introducing Chinese students in the United States to a diverse geographic and cultural group of Americans. In essence, the National Committee has stood at the top and the center of American public-private efforts to improve popular and governmental ties with China. Although its staff and its budget are relatively small, its expertise and its influence have been critical to the smoothness with which relations were restored and broadened during the decade and a half ending in mid-1989 and in attempting to rebuild bilateral relations thereafter.[40]

The CSCC has played a similar function in selecting, sending, and to some extent training American scholars; in establishing close working ties with Chinese academic institutions (the Academy of Sciences, the Academy of Social Sciences, the State Education Commission, and the State Science and Technology Commission); and in describing and assessing the character of the exchange relationship, including the number and status of Chinese students in the United States. A more nearly official organization than the National Committee, its sponsors are the National Academy of Sciences, the American Council of Learned Societies, and the Social Science Research Council. All of these are nongovernmental or quasi-governmental groups, but funding stems mostly from governmental sources, with some additional foundation and private monies (see Chapter 14 by Mary Bullock in this volume). It is not a membership organization; rather, its directors (that is, the committee) are limited to eleven representatives or nominees of its sponsors and funders. The CSCC is a major center for deciding who in the American scholarly community goes to China, under what financial and institutional auspices, and what kind of training is to be made available. It acts as negotiating representative for American scholars under the National Program. Were it not for the committee's effective work, much of the high-quality field research conducted by American scholars since 1979 could not have been done, nor would such solid working relations with Chinese institutions and scholars have been possible. It has also sponsored some of the best evaluative work on exchanges yet produced. Its staff in Washington, D.C., and Beijing (an office was opened there in 1985, closed temporarily in late 1989, and reopened in 1990) is highly knowledgeable, experienced, and well-trained.[41]

The China Institute in New York is similar to the Asia Society in structure and function as regards China-related work. The institute was founded in 1926 by John Dewey to serve as a center for increasing the understanding of Chinese culture and language in the United States. The institute has three major programs: the school of Chinese studies, which offers courses on such topics as language, art, modern politics, history, and cooking; the China House Gallery, which mounts scholarly art-historical exhibitions; and the student service program, which provides social programs for Chinese students studying in the United States. The China Institute has a staff of fourteen but relies primarily on guest faculty and visiting speakers for its scholarly programs. Although its programs obtain occasional grants from, for instance, the New York Council of the Arts, the institute relies primarily on funding from corporations, foundations, and foreign sources. Until the mid-1970s, the institute received considerable funding from Taiwanese sources and was firmly pro-Taiwan, but since that time it has broadened its funding base and shifted its focus to the mainland as well, and attempts to mediate between American groups on both sides of the PRC/ROC divide.[42]

Two other groups have as their goal the improvement of American-Chinese relations. The first is the China Council of the Asia Society. In existence from

1975 to 1989 (when the society disbanded it), the council operated out of the Asia Society headquarters in New York, monitored, knitted together, and provided programs—mostly in the humanities—for its network of twelve Regional China Councils (mostly in university towns) and sponsored occasional conferences. For over a decade it published the valuable annual survey volume *China Briefing* (which continues as an Asian Society publication). The council was not really a "council." Rather, there was a director in New York, an advisory group of twelve leading China specialists appointed by the society, and autonomous groups scattered throughout the country.[43] The society attempted to provide some continuity in terms of programming for the regional councils and drew together the advisory group periodically to suggest how the society might operate its China programs. It also provided the news media with guidance on China matters. By intent, the China Council attempted to access a broader reach of the interested public than the National Committee or the CSCC.

The second is the U.S.-China People's Friendship Association. The association is as close as the United States has to a mass organization cum interest group regarding the People's Republic of China. In 1989 it had about five thousand members in some sixty chapters nationwide, grouped into four regions served by regional councils, with a national office in Washington, D.C. Many of the chapters and regions have their own newsletters, and the association publishes its own quarterly, *U.S.-China Review.* There is an eleven-person national board, some of whom are elected through the regions and others nationally, and a national director. The association holds semiannual conventions of some two hundred representatives elected by weighted vote. Its functions include holding chapter and regional meetings on China-related topics, helping Chinese students in the United States acclimate themselves to their new environment, hosting visiting Chinese friendship groups, and sponsoring member tours of China. Since its inception in 1974, several thousand Americans have traveled to China with such groups. The association is the pro-PRC successor to the pro-Kuomintang Committee of One Million, the only other such mass organization in the country devoted to Chinese affairs. Like that committee, its appeal has been much dependent on the state of relations between the two countries. As relations improved in the 1970s and 1980s, the association grew rapidly in size and the Committee of One Million shrank. Once Sino-American relations "topped out" in the mid-1980s, the association also ceased to grow; after the Tiananmen incident in 1989, the association also experienced a drastic falloff in membership. It nonetheless remains the only outlet for many ordinary Americans of good will to obtain more detailed information on China than is available in their daily newspapers, and as such probably continues to fulfill a need.[44]

Three human rights organizations include China and Taiwan in their work. The first is Amnesty International (AI), which conducts careful, documented (where possible), independent investigations on the state of political liberty in China, issues periodic reports and findings, and attempts through publicity, personal contacts, and pressure on governments to expose shortcomings and improve the welfare of Chinese citizens. Because of the care with which its research is done, its reputation is high throughout the world. Its China reports in recent years have concentrated on the situation in Tibet, the Tiananmen repression, and the status of political prisoners in China. It has many personal contacts in China and its staff, in New York and London, is in a position to detail human rights infringements in China.[45]

The second is Asia Watch. Similar to Amnesty International, it concentrates on Asia, as the name implies, including China. It is an American organization (AI is multinational) and maintains offices in New York and Washington, D.C. It publishes frequent reports on political conditions in China and lobbies the American government for policy changes and legislation concerning that country. (For instance, after the Tiananmen incident, it strongly supported the imposition of sanctions against China and, in 1990 and 1991, nonrenewal—or conditional renewal—of most-favored-nation treatment for China.) In this regard, it differs from AI, which generally confines itself to publishing and publicizing its research, and is similar (where human rights are concerned) to the lobbying efforts of the Heritage Foundation. Like AI, Asia Watch employs a staff with China expertise and maintains person-to-person contact with Chinese citizens.[46]

Finally, there is Freedom House. This research organization publishes the annual authoritative *Freedom Survey*, which rates the degree to which a given nation is "free," "partly free," or "not free." Reasonably sophisticated, partly objective criteria are used. Since its inception, China has always been "not free," though Taiwan has mostly been considered "partly free" ("mostly," because of its nonsocialist economy and, after 1988, its democratizing polity). It depends largely on secondary sources for its evaluations.[47] AI and Asia Watch are, generally speaking, liberal organizations, while Freedom House is conservative. All three come to similar conclusions concerning the state of political liberty in China. Perhaps no more than ten China specialists (not including a larger number of part-time unpaid academics) work in this area.

Private interest groups concerned with China also include three organizations that operate a diversity of programs on, in, and together with China. The first is the Institute of International Education. Based in New York, it operates many exchange programs with China (including Taiwan) and 153 other countries. It has an office in Hong Kong, is governed by a board of trustees composed of corporate, academic, media, and individual members, and has a budget of over $200 million, comprising contributions or gifts from the American government, corporations, foundations, and individuals. It also has regional offices throughout the United States. Its activities regarding China include hosting Chinese delegations and other visitors, previously housing the Committee on International Relations with the People's Republic of China, and arranging research and training programs in the United States for Chinese academic and research institute scholars. It also assists private American corporations in training Chinese personnel in a wide variety of businesses, offers orientation for Chinese and Hong Kong students coming to the United States (and publishes in China the Chinese-language *IIE/Guangdong American Study Newsletter),* and provides a variety of services (administration, consulting, research, publishing, testing, etc.) to agricultural, arts, business, linguistic, and multisector organizations in China.[48]

The second is the Council on International Educational Exchange (CIEE). Also based in New York, it acts on behalf of a large number of American universities that comprise its membership and that elect a board of directors, almost all of whose members are academics. It is nonetheless a private organization. In contrast to the Institute of International Education, the CIEE derives most of its income from fees for services, only a small percentage from foundation and government grants and contracts, and almost nothing from private contributions or endowment income. Most of its activities involve arranging student travel and exchange between the United States and other countries in the traditional disciplines. It does some research, conferences, and publishing of its own. Its China-related work is at a comparatively early stage and was set back by the Tiananmen repression of mid-1989. Since the early 1980s, the council has nonetheless established ongoing language and study programs at Beijing, Nanjing, and Fudan universities, a business program at the University of International Business and Economics in Beijing, arranged for several teaching and delegations exchanges with American universities, sent a few high school students to China, and helped many students with travel plans to visit the country. China has not yet participated in the council's student work exchange and workcamp programs, its contractual training of foreign professionals in the United States, and its high school exchange program and other services offered to foreign students. The CIEE plans to open a Beijing office and has already provided some services for Chinese students hoping to study in the United States.[49]

The final such organization is the Asia Foundation. Headquartered in San Francisco with offices in Washington, D.C., and throughout Asia (including Taiwan and Hong Kong, but not Beijing), the Asia Foundation is more a research, training, and exchange organization than a traditional foundation (in fact, by law it is not a private foundation). Importantly, most of its operating income comes by annual appropriation from the American government, through the State Department and the Agency for International Development, and matching Asian funding. Most of the rest of its revenues of over $50 million per annum are represented by the value of books contributed by commercial and university publishers, bookstores, and libraries. Its board of trustees is composed of academics and businesspeople. It has long had close ties with Taiwan and continues to maintain an office in Taipei. Generally, its Taiwan activities focus on funding visits to the United States of various governmental organizations and conducting seminars, studies, and conferences in Taiwan on topics related to the political and social modernization of the island. The foundation has also moved to conduct activities in, and with regard to, China. Most of its work there has concerned funding Chinese academic training in the United States, mostly in law, international affairs, and business. In both Chinese entities, the Asia Foundation distributes a large number of books and journals, which account for most of the approximately $700,000 spent annually on China-related work, not an insignificant amount.[50] The foundation's Center for Asian Pacific Affairs also devotes attention to China.

Conclusion

It is difficult to sum up the activities of such a diverse group of private sector institutions and individuals relating to China. Perhaps, however, a few generalizations can be ventured.

First, a broad spectrum of interest, institutions, and persons comprise this group of American China specialists. Part of this reflects its catch-all nature, but it also permits the observer to appreciate the diversity of the field as a whole, which, when this category is included, expands considerably beyond its traditional academic-governmental limits.

Second, if importance is measured, among other things, by numbers, this sector is central to the field merely by being the largest. In addition, some of the institutions described and analyzed above stand at the very center of the field by setting or heavily influencing American China policy and activity as a whole. Third, there is, likewise, a spectrum within this sector ranging from relative isolation from the other sectors, on one extreme, to full day-to-day contact with leading figures in the other sectors. If a rough weighted average of this sector were to be taken (by somehow combining numbers and influence) probably the outcome would show a greater tendency toward isolation than contact.

The consequence, fourthly, is a somewhat distinct approach to China by people in this sector (again, with the exception of those policy-setting institutions such as the "two committees" and certain foundation officials). That is a tendency to figure out China from one's own parochial perspective without heavy reliance on background studies, government advice, or "expertise" in general. From this arises a habit of deriving one's attitudes and policies toward China from mostly firsthand, personal experience, and basing one's attitudes directly on hands-on, knowledge-based field reports. What was described initially as a research propensity of Rand-type think tanks is in fact characteristic of this sector as a whole (with certain obvious exceptions). Last, in terms of contacts with Chinese and Americans interested in China, this sector has exceptionally broad reach. Businesspeople, interest groups, and travel personnel, for instance, manage to reach farther into the two societies, in terms of geography and personal contact, than the other sectors. Yet much of that contact is superficial and temporary, and can thus be lost in terms of its additive effect unless remedial measures are taken (which, mostly, they are not). The problem is that (again, with the exception of the "two committees," think tanks, and the like) most of those in this sector are sojourners only and thus have no permanent, personal commitment to the study of China.

It is therefore difficult to draw a descriptive bottom line for this sector. If a reduction to a few words were required, however, it would be: private sector Americans comprise the quantitative center of the American study of China, penetrate most extensively into China, and represent American attitudes (for better or worse) toward that country most accurately, but are also less enamored of China, less well informed about that country, less fully committed to furthering Sino-American relations for their own sake, and less likely to spend their careers on the subject. They are an important, very active, but sometimes neglected portion of the whole.

Notes

1. The author is grateful to Audrey Weg, Jennifer Arnold, Robert Boardman, and Donna Schaller for timely and effective research assistance, and to David Shambaugh for helping to shape substance and detail.

2. Information from Allen de Harrport of the U.S.-China Business Council.

3. Author's conversations in Hong Kong with representatives of the American Chamber of Commerce.

4. Author's estimate, based on conversations with bankers, aerospace executives, business consultants, and others.

5. Author's estimate, arrived at as follows: nonprofit research institutions, thirty; not-for-profit research institutions, thirty; for-profit institutions, thirty; and consultants, sixty.

6. Author's estimate, from conversations with individuals in each of the following types of organizations: law firms, 50; management consulting organizations, 30; and accounting firms, 50.

7. Conversations with China specialists at the Ford Foundation, the MacArthur Foundation, the Asia Foundation, and others.

8. Mostly language teachers, but also including the full-time equivalent of part-time lecturers and organizers of China-related courses.

9. Author's conversations with individuals at each of the interest groups referenced in the relevant section below.

10. Conversation with Frederic Kaplan, vice president, China/Orient Tourism Advisory Committee.

11. Mostly World Bank specialists (fifty).

12. A not-for-profit organization is one that can accept fees above cost for services, whereas a nonprofit research organization cannot accept such fees. "Fees" are not "profit" because they are not distributed to employees or owners of the organization but rather, are plowed back into funding and research.

13. Author's survey of Rand publications on China from 1950 to 1985 reveals that approximately two-thirds of these studies, in terms of total pagination, were directly on policy questions, whereas the remaining third were of the academic background variety.

14. Perhaps one-third of all Rand China-related publications come from this source. Such well-known academic China specialists as Richard Baum, Harry Harding, Harold Hinton, Kenneth Lieberthal, Michel Oksenberg, Robert Scalapino, Richard Solomon, and Allen Whiting have produced books and articles under Rand sponsorship.

15. For example, the Brookings Institution's *Annual Reports* for selective years during the 1970s and 1980s, as well as the author's survey of Brookings's China publications, especially those of A. Doak Barnett, Ralph Clough, and Harry Harding.

16. Author's conversations with Robin Laird and Susan Clark at the Institute for Defense Analyses, William Bader at Stanford Research Institute, and Wendy Frieman at Science Applications International Corporation.

17. To cite two: Richard Moorsteen and Morton Abromowitz, *Remaking China Policy* (Cambridge, Mass.: Harvard University Press, 1971), and the Atlantic Council, *China Policy for the Next Decade* (Cambridge, Mass.: Oelgeschlager, Gunn, and Hain, 1984).

18. Author's conversation with Sharon Ruwart, current editor, and Madeline Ross, immediate past-editor, *China Business Review.* In 1990 the number of American business projects in China actually rose 29 percent, although their average value fell by 45 percent. Of the total 21,767 foreign investment projects during 1979–89, 952 were from the United States. Of the 7,276 in 1990, 357 were American.

19. The U.S.-China Business Council annually publishes a series of bibliographies on China, Sino-American relations, business conditions in China, etc., as well as reviews of recently published material in the *China Business Review.* The most authoritative information in book form are two reports also issued by the U.S.-China Business Council: *U.S. Joint Ventures in China: A Progress Report* (1987) and *A Special Report: U.S. Investment in China* (1990). There are also statistical compilations and handbooks available, exemplified by *China Statistics Monthly* (Chicago: China Statistics Archives) and Arne J. de Keijzer, *The China Business Handbook,* 3d ed. (Elmsford, N.Y.: Pergamon Press, 1989).

20. These judgments are the product of the author's experience over the past decade consulting for several American business corporations and training businesspeople at the Business Council for International Understanding.

21. *Annual Reports,* U.S.-China Business Council, 1980–90.

22. For instance, the annual "Doing Business with China, Japan, Korea, and Taiwan" conference sponsored by the Pacific Rim Management Programs of the University of Southern California; the corporate conference, "The Future of Asia/Pacific Relations" sponsored by the *Asian Wall Street Journal,* the Hong Kong Trade Development Council, and the Asia Society; and the SAT International Conference Center in New York, "China Business for the 1990s: Challenges and Opportunities."

23. See, for instance, Lucian Pye, *Chinese Commercial Negotiating Style* (Cambridge, Mass.: Oelgeschlager, Gunn, and Hain, 1982); and Jim Mann, *Beijing Jeep: The Short, Unhappy Romance of American Business in China* (New York: Simon and Schuster, 1989).

24. USA-ROC Economic Council, *Progress Report,* 1987–.

25. See "Kissinger, Commentator on China, Has Business Ties with Beijing," *Asian Wall Street Journal Weekly,* September 18, 1989, 3ff.

26. Price Waterhouse, *Doing Business in the PRC* (1988). *East Asian Executive Reports* is edited by John Boatman and *International Contract Advisor* is written by Martin Klingenberg. See also Lucille Barale, *Courdert Brothers: China Practice,* July 1991. The latter is a law firm, not an accounting concern, but its publications and practice often spill over to not strictly legal matters. Note should also be taken of the engagement by the Chinese embassy in July 1991 of the Arthur Anderson Company to assist in its efforts to convince the U.S. Congress to pass unconditional extension of most-favored-nation treatment for China.

27. Author's conversation with Mary Lou Walsh of Political Risk Services, Syracuse, New York.

28. *Global Assessment,* produced at Bankers Trust Company in New York, is edited by Sally Shelton-Colby and Jay Woodworth.

29. Author's conversations with Wilfred Koplowitz, Citibank; Robert Grealy, Chase Manhattan Bank; Paul Spooner, Barclay's Bank; Elizabeth Cleary, Chemical Bank; and Anne LeBourgeois, Manufacturers Hanover Trust, all in New York.

30. The researcher does have access to *The World Bank Research Program* (annual),

Abstract of Current Studies, and *The World Bank Information Guide,* which at least provide some information on publicly available materials. But see also World Bank Staff, *China: Long Term Development Issues and Options* (Baltimore: Johns Hopkins University Press, 1985), as well as the following examples of high-quality reports for public sale: *China: Macroeconomic Stability and Industrial Growth Under Decentralized Socialism* (1990), *China: Revenue Mobilization and Tax Policy* (1990), *China: Between Plan and Market* (1990), *China: Financial Sector Policy and Institutional Development* (1991), and *China: Options for Reform* (1991). An example of the bank's internal reports is: *(China) A Country Economic Memorandum* (June 1989).

31. These two paragraphs derive from the author's conversations with Mitchell Silk of Hughes, Hubbard, and Reed in New York.

32. Author's conversations with Charles Conroy at Baker and McKenzie in New York, Stanley Lubman formerly of Thelen, Marrin, Johnson, and Bridges in San Francisco, and various of their writings, together with those of the other four mentioned herein.

33. Conversations with Patricia Dooley, formerly of Academic Travel Abroad, Kate Simpson, of Academic Travel Abroad, the China National Tourist Office in New York, Frederic Kaplan of the China/Orient Tourism Advisory Committee, New Jersey, Peter Yeung, Pacific Best Tours, and Chang Huei-ning, formerly of the China International Travel Service, in Nebraska.

In the first six months of 1989, 128,300 Americans visited China, and in the second half of the year that figure was 54,200, 167,500 less than the 1988 total *(New York Times,* January 14, 1990, travel section, p. 3). Travel tilted slowly upward in 1990 and 1991, but probably did not recover to pre-Tiananmen levels (conversation with Patrick Freeman, Department of State, August 1991).

34. See, for example, Fernao M. Pinto, ed., and Rebecca D. Catz, trans., *The Travels of Mendes Pinto* (Chicago: University of Chicago Press, 1989); Edward W. Marsden, *Travels of Marco Polo* (New York: Hippocrene Books, 1987); Aurel Stein, *On Ancient Central-Asian Tracks: Brief Narrative of Three Expeditions in Innermost Asia and North Western China* (Pasadena, Calif.: Oriental Book Store, 1982 reproduction of 1933 ed.); Paul Theroux, *Riding the Iron Rooster: By Train Through China* (New York: Ivy Books, 1989); Pico Iyer, *Video Nights in Kathmandu; And Other Reports from the Not-So-Far East* (New York: Knopf, 1989); Fergus M. Bordewish, *Cathay: A Journey in Search of Old China* (Englewood Cliffs, N.J.: Prentice-Hall, 1991); and Colin Thubron, *A Journey Through China* (New York: Harper and Row, 1989).

35. A very useful survey of Chinese tourism is Linda K. Richter, *The Politics of Tourism in Asia* (Honolulu: University of Hawaii Press, 1989), especially chap. 2, "About Face: The Political Evolution of Chinese Tourism Policy," and the many references cited therein.

36. Anne Thurston, *Enemies of the People: The Ordeals of the Intellectuals in China's Great Cultural Revolution* (Cambridge, Mass.: Harvard University Press, 1988). Thurston combined her presence in Beijing with a foundation grant and residence at Harvard University, as well as half-time employment at the National Committee on U.S.-China Relations in New York, to produce this volume, a good example of how private sector and university-centered activity are sometimes combined.

37. See, for example, Frederic Kaplan, Julian Sobin, and Arne de Keijzer, *China Guidebook,* 11th ed. (Teaneck, N.J.: Eurasia Press, 1990); Ruth L. Malloy, *Fieldings Travel Books* (New York: Fielding Press, 1989); and *Fodor's 1989 People's Republic of China* (New York: McKay, 1988).

Mention should also be made of *Travel Weekly,* which has many articles on tourism in China, and the subcommittee on Chinese tourism at the U.S.-China Business Council.

38. This section draws on the annual reports of all the foundations mentioned, the

three government organizations noted, and the author's conversations with Halsey L. Beemer, Jr., at the National Academy of Sciences, Ruth Adams at the MacArthur Foundation, Peter Geithner of the Ford Foundation, Terrill E. Lautz of the Luce Foundation, Ken Jensen at the U.S. Institute for Peace, and Alice Hogan at the National Science Foundation.

39. Author's conversations with Roger Brooks of the Heritage Foundation, Cecilia Chang of St. John's, Gerritt Gong of the Center for Strategic and International Studies, Ying-mao Kao of the American Association for Chinese Studies, Ramon Myers at the Hoover Institution, Steven Mosher at Claremont College, Jan Prybyla of Pennsylvania State University, James Reardon-Anderson of Georgetown University, Robert A. Scalapino of the University of California, and Denis Simon at Tufts University.

Mention should be made in particular of latter-day Taiwan foundations, governmental and nongovernmental: the Twenty-first Century Foundation, the Chiang Ching-kuo Foundation, the Vanguard Foundation, and the Institute for National Policy Research. Since the emergence of democratization on Taiwan, there has been a proliferation of nongovernmental foundations, which for the American study of China (including Taiwan) has significant potential for broadening funding sources and deepening understanding.

40. National Committee on U.S.-China Relations, *Annual Reports*, 1980–90, and conversations with David M. Lampton and Jan Carol Berris.

41. *China Exchange News* for the 1980s and conversations with Mary Brown Bullock, Robert Geyer, and Kathlin Smith. The committee's work was severely affected by the aftermath of the Tiananmen incident. The National Academy of Sciences, a government organization, suspended exchange ties with China and did not fully restore them until late 1991. Moreover, several post-Tiananmen incidents over the joint American-Chinese conduct of survey research in China led to a further difficulty between the National Academy of Sciences and its Chinese counterparts.

42. China Institute, *Annual Report*, 1987–90, and accompanying materials as well as author's conversation with Michael Bless of the China Institute.

43. Asia Society, *Annual Report*, 1987–1990, and information on the China Council provided by its director through 1990, Anthony J. Kane.

44. Author's conversation with staff personnel of the Washington, D.C., national office of the association.

45. Material provided to the author by Amnesty International, in particular, the series of publications surrounding the Tiananmen incident. These include "Violations of Human Rights," "Trials and Punishments Since 1989," "The Massacre of June 1989 and Its Aftermath," "Prisoner Concerns Compilation Document," "Torture and Mistreatment of Prisoners," and the yearly *Amnesty International Report*.

46. Asia Watch material on China, 1989–91, and author's conversations with Sidney R. Jones, executive director.

47. Author's conversation with Raymond Gastil, former editor of *Freedom Survey*. Note should also be taken of several U.S.-based Chinese human rights organizations established during the 1980s or after the Tiananmen incident. These include the Chinese Democratic Solidarity Alliance (which publishes *China Spring* monthly), the China Democratic Solidarity Front, and the Chinese Student Autonomous Federation.

48. Institute of International Education, *Annual Reports*, 1988–90, and author's conversation with Peggy Blumenthal, vice president.

49. *Annual Reports*, 1988–90, Council on International Educational Exchange and conversations with Sidney L. Greenblatt of Syracuse University.

50. Asia Foundation, *Annual Reports*, 1988–90, and coversation with Cinnamon Dornsife, former Washington representative.

11

The Journalist China Specialists

Jay Mathews and Linda Mathews

Even today, when journalism demands more depth and detail than ever before, specialists have to watch their backs. They still incite suspicion and unease in many newsrooms. Editors wonder whether they have the common touch, the ability to look up from their books and charts and seminar invitations and find a story that might interest the typical reader of the morning newspaper.

Fellow reporters, the majority of whom still work on what is called "general assignment," often see specializing journalists as college professors in disguise. They might know something about their specialty, the old police reporter announces over his beer at happy hour, but they would be lost if told to cover a fire on the next block.

That goes double for China specialists. The difficulty of the language, the exotic flavor of the country, and the complexity of Chinese history and politics and its distance from ordinary American life severely limit the number of American journalists specializing in China and increase doubts about their usefulness to their news organization over the long run.

American newspaper and magazine readers have been absorbing the work of journalistic China specialists since the early part of this century, when Edgar Snow and his wife, Helen Foster Snow, Harold Isaacs, and a few other correspondents took root there. Theodore H. White, one of the first to have some academic training in the field before reaching China, set a high standard for thoroughness and breadth, even if his employer, *Time* magazine, did not always print his stories as he wrote them.

American reporters operated on the fringes of China in the 1950s and 1960s, with Edgar Snow the only professional American reporter able to do useful work inside the country. The barriers began to crumble with the Kissinger and Nixon trips of the 1970s. In 1979 the Chinese government let several U.S. wire services, newspapers, and magazines establish bureaus in Beijing. But access to China and closer relations between Washington and Beijing did not necessarily make the China reporter's job any easier, or more acceptable back in the newsroom.

In the late 1960s, when newspapers were beginning to cultivate some expertise in Chinese affairs, the *Washington Post* hired a young man who had prepared for an academic career in East Asian studies at an important Eastern university. While in graduate school, he found his interest in his thesis topic waning and tried his hand working for a local wire service. That led to a job on the *Post*'s local reporting staff in Washington, D.C., mostly covering police headquarters. It was with a measure of mixed awe and discomfort in the newsroom that the most popular story circulating about this young reporter concerned the day he asked the city editor, a gruff character right out of *The Front Page,* whether he could have a Friday off. "Hmmph," the editor said. "What for?"

"Well," the reporter said timidly, "there's a graduation ceremony, and I'm going to get my Ph.D."

That this sparse tale brought loud laughter is a measure of how removed journalists consider themselves from academic life. Many of them felt somehow vindicated when the young reporter tired of covering murders and drug deals and waiting for a Hong Kong assignment, and went back to teaching and research.

Within this story lies one important, but rarely mentioned reason why reporters trained as China specialists were so pleased when Beijing bureaus for Americans began to open in 1979. We lusted, of course, for the chance to absorb the sights and scents and sounds of the country twenty-four hours a day. We wanted the chance to build long relationships with China and give our stories the depth and vividness that could come only from living there.

But there was something else: an assignment in Beijing also freed us from a great many distracting duties that had demanded hours of our time when we were based in Hong Kong, Japan, or the United States.

Hong Kong correspondents were regularly dispatched to cover stories in the Philippines, Thailand, Vietnam, Indonesia, Singapore, Malaysia, and anywhere else the territory's excellent air connections could take a traveler within a day. Journalistic China specialists in the United States rarely had China as their principal beat. They were assigned as diplomatic, political, or local government reporters and were discouraged from spending too much time on events eleven thousand miles away.

Once in China, air travel to other countries became difficult (though Beijing's increasing international status has brought some changes). A Beijing correspondent could also argue with some effect, when asked to cover riots in Seoul, that such a trip would force cancellation of an interview with a Politburo member or a trip to a little-visited province that had taken weeks to arrange. Beijing bureau expenses were so high that few editors had the courage to interfere with the chance to show that the money was well spent.

The result of all this was that reporters in China were much more often left alone, a relief to them and a stimulant to much better stories and analysis.

Journalists in Relation to Academic and
Government Analysts

A few reporters in China came to journalism from academia. Far more slipped into China-watching after their reporting careers had begun. In either case, their work pulled them somewhat outside the network of researchers and policy analysts who see each other regularly at conferences, read each other's papers in draft form, and jointly nurture the careers of younger scholars and analysts on their way up.

Many journalists feel a part of that network, or at least would like to join in it more than they do. But the demands on their time and the nature of their work are so different that they cannot realistically share in the day-to-day contact that determines who is a member of that network and who is not. And most journalists would be somewhat uncomfortable with such regular contact, for independence is prized much more highly among reporters than it is among government analysts. China-watching journalists have a sense that careers go sour for those perceived as getting too close to their sources, unwilling to stand back and take a contrary view.

In part, the professional advantages of remaining an outsider have kept journalistic China specialists from being as well trained as they might be. Young scholars who have spent three or four years in graduate school and abroad developing their linguistic skills, absorbing the history and culture, and researching a detailed thesis do not look forward to putting all that aside for a few years of police or school board reporting—usually the minimum prerequisite for anyone who wishes to become a Beijing correspondent. Reporters who already have journalistic skills and want to acquire real expertise in China cannot easily take off three or four years to acquire it, unless they are independently wealthy. The most generous midcareer study programs for journalists—the Nieman fellowships at Harvard and the Knight fellowships at Stanford—are for only a year. That is long enough to gain only a tenuous grasp of the Chinese language and not nearly enough to absorb all the historical and cultural background.

Only a handful of American reporters in China ever come close to having the academic preparation of a freshly minted Ph.D. looking for an assistant professorship at some small college. The reporters will often be making a good deal more money than the young academic, and their reports will have much wider circulation, but they will be working with significantly fewer intellectual tools.

Government China specialists, in general, do not appear to have as much academic preparation as college professors dealing in the same subjects, but by virtue of their daily work in the China area, they are usually well ahead of the average journalist. And since their linguistic skills are so important—perhaps even more useful to them than to a young academic—they have received far better training for a longer period than all but a tiny minority of the journalists calling them for tips and analyses.

Given that they remain outside the inner circle of China experts and usually must make do with less training, journalists' analysis of Chinese affairs is fated to lack the depth and range of their government and academic counterparts. They will not be able to recognize names as readily. They will need more help deciphering interesting posters on university walls. They will not as readily discern historical allusions in *People's Daily* editorials.

By and large, journalists do not consider this something to worry much about. Their function as reporters, whether covering Beijing or the budget or the Chicago Bears, is to gather information from knowledgeable sources, the more the better, and pass on this wisdom to the reader. Unfortunately, in a subject as complex and difficult as China, asking the right question requires more background than usual, and the undertrained reporter (which is still the norm) will be less likely to detect the subtle but important areas he ought to explore.

Journalists covering China are aware of this, and most of them conscientiously spend much of their spare time reading and practicing their language skills in order to extend their range. That is all to the good, but the depth and sophistication of their analyses are unlikely to approach those of academic analysts so long as one crucial difference remains between them: the nature of their audience.

Journalists write to inform ordinary Americans, for whom China is usually a subject of only passing interest. The ordinary Americans who are the most important members of this audience are their editors, who may include a wide range of people with differing interests and biases. The kind of organization a journalist works for will often dictate what his or her editor does or does not want. A *Washington Post* or *New York Times* reporter can usually write longer and somewhat more complex stories than a wire-service reporter. A newsmagazine reporter will be required to write reams of material, but only a small part of this will ever be published.

The critical point, repeated in a thousand introductory journalism classes every year, is that the typical reader will not read a twenty-five-page monograph on price control policy under Chinese Premier Li Peng. Therefore, no editor of any mass circulation news organization—the only kind that can afford Beijing bureaus—will print such a report. A reporter with the skills and background expertise to write such an analysis will do well in journalism, provided he can write other kinds of things as well, but he will never have a chance to display such depth, and thus few if any will try to cultivate it.

Many journalists covering China write much less than they know—that is why a fair number of them, largely out of frustration, go on to write books about their experiences. Little is required to fill an average American news story, about a thousand words, or four double-spaced, typewritten pages. Most reporters can, if pressed, turn out such an article in little more than an hour. It is the exceptional reporter who bothers to gather significantly more information than is required.

What Journalists Have in Common
with Other Analysts

Whatever journalistic analysis of China lacks in length, depth, and subtle insight, it more than makes up for in impact. Reporters who spend most of their time writing about China are very few and work only for publications with large circulations. (This also holds true for television and radio journalists, but with a few exceptions, such as the Voice of America, electronic reporters are given so little air time that their impact on the nature of American opinion about China is probably much less. We are considering only the impact of their personal analysis here. As we saw in the work of the Cable News Network and other television organizations covering the demonstrations and deaths in central Beijing in 1989, the *pictures* and *sound* they transmit have enormous influence, at an emotional rather than intellectual level.)

Journalists share with academics and government analysts an urge to inform, which in most cases is part of an urge to *re*form. We are all missionaries, to a certain extent, as concerned with the way Americans look at China and the way American leaders treat China as the first few Presbyterian preachers were solicitous about the future of Chinese souls.

That means that our analyses share a common interest in testing popular American notions of China: Are Chinese so used to emperors that Communist totalitarianism seems natural to them? Do Chinese worry continually about "face" (appearances and mutual respect)? Are Chinese crowding themselves into economic and political collapse? Will Chinese students and intellectuals have the courage to rise again against the government that crushed them in 1989?

We all address those questions because they are important to U.S. policy toward the country. Few of us in journalism, academia, or government are nearly so interested in Chinese fashions in flower arrangement, or the route of trade through the Gobi desert, or the debate over romanization. As with academic and government analysts the ultimate consumers of journalistic analysis decisively shape the product.

Journalists realize that their words reach a wide variety of people. Physics professors are as likely as taxicab drivers to buy a newspaper or scan network news. But to reach so many different audiences requires some common denominator.

Reportage must be short, simple, and, most important of all, *vivid.* Foreign editors of major American newspapers look most closely for this last quality in the clipping files of the people they are considering sending abroad. This is particularly true of China coverage, since it is very easy to sit in Beijing reporting the latest economic debate and bore readers to distraction. The vivid events of 1989 were an aberration in many ways, not least of which was that they provided much more drama than Beijing correspondents will encounter during 99 percent of their time in China.

The China reporters and analysts most praised by other journalists, such as John Burns of the *New York Times* and John Fraser of the Toronto *Globe and Mail,* had the ability to paint multicolored pictures of the often seemingly drab situations they were reporting and to make comprehension much easier than it might have been in other hands.

The strength of such vividness is that it catches readers' attention and thus can stimulate thought and understanding, the ultimate goal of any China analysis. The weakness is that such vividness usually requires a certain narrowness. A reporter will begin his analysis with a description of a very specific time and place: a peasant caught drowning his baby daughter, a student returned from the United States arrested for prodemocracy demonstrations, a factory clerk wasting his afternoons on number puzzles. Such opening stories compel the reader to go further, yet they color understanding of the rest of the report. The broad, more measured analytical point—that infanticide is restricted to certain areas, that free speech behind closed doors has revived, that sloth is being punished—is often eclipsed by the power of the opening anecdote.

When considering the similarities of journalistic, academic, and government analysis, one should also recall that most reportorial opinion is deeply influenced by—and often borrowed wholesale from—academic and government research. This is less so with the arrival of American reporters in Beijing, where they can occasionally interview Chinese sources firsthand, and with the modest increase in the number of journalists with some academic preparation in China studies. But no good reporter will write a story of any significance without first checking his conclusions with researchers in the government or academia. The few instances in which journalists have gone out on limbs alone have been almost universally disastrous, saved only by the perishability of newspaper, magazine, and television analysis, and the reluctance of journalists to hold fellow reporters up to public ridicule.

Why Journalistic Analysts Make Mistakes

Reporters also commit errors, even when they carefully check with all their best sources. Mistakes are good measures of the sharpness of their analytical tools. A look at a few press mishaps, without naming too many names, will shed light on what forces drive journalistic analysis, and what pitfalls are most likely to materialize.

Some examples:

• In mid-1976 the *Washington Post* reported that the influence of the People's Liberation Army was declining rapidly in China. A few months later, the Chinese military proved instrumental in the downfall of the Gang of Four, and several military commanders were rewarded with jobs as party secretaries in key provinces.
• In December 1978, on the day President Jimmy Carter and Chairman Hua Guofeng announced the normalization of Sino-American relations, the *Los Angeles Times* reported that China and the United States had decided to ignore their differences over Taiwan. The two countries had "agreed to disagree" and no more would likely be heard from Beijing about U.S. arms sales to the Nationalists on Taiwan, the newspaper said. Within a few months, the issue was once again very much alive and continued to be a major irritant in relations between the two countries through the Carter administration and into the early years of

the Reagan administration.

• During the summer of 1976 the *Far Eastern Economic Review* concluded that Deng Xiaoping, then in disgrace, had no chance of ever recovering his political influence and that after Mao Zedong died, the new leader of the Chinese Communist Party would almost certainly be Zhang Chunqiao, then head of the Shanghai Revolutionary Committee. Before the year was out, Zhang was in prison and Deng's friends and allies were beginning a process that would eventually give Deng more power and influence than he had ever had in his life.

• In mid-1976 the *New York Times* reported on its front page that then Chinese Defense Minister Ye Jianying had been dismissed and had probably also lost his position on the Politburo. Instead, the aged leader would continue in office for several more years.

• During the week after the massacre of hundreds of Chinese civilians by Chinese troops on June 3 and 4, 1989, several major American and other foreign news organizations reported that Chinese military units seemed to be maneuvering in opposition to each other and that a civil war appeared imminent. Instead, the crackdown on dissidents continued and the hard-line leadership in Beijing carried on with no discernible opposition within the army.

Why have so many good reporters been so wrong so often about China? The reasons are complicated, but mistakes of fact and interpretation appear to stem from peculiarities of the news business not shared by academia and government and from the Chinese preference for secrecy, a curse to all analysts.

By its nature, journalism exaggerates. An ambitious reporter who loves his beat and wants to please his editors can be tempted to reach for the lead that will land him on page one. A carefully qualified story, one that points out all the subtleties in a government announcement or mentions everything that could go wrong with a new program, may talk itself off the front page. Managing editors love novelty, radical departures, and dramatic reversals of policy. They are often bored, and they think readers are bored, by inch-by-inch progress reports.

When the press's tendency toward exaggeration is applied in China, the result is reams of distorted copy. The facts are not wrong; no one is purposely misleading readers. But those of us who reported from China in the 1970s and the 1980s are at least partly to blame for many popular misconceptions about that country.

From the beginning, we exaggerated the pace of China's modernization. In a cover story on China's oil resources, *Newsweek* once called China the new Saudi Arabia and suggested that its oil reserves might equal those of the North Sea and Alaska's North Slope combined. *Time* made Deng Xiaoping its Man of the Year in 1979 and depicted him as a colossus, single-handedly lifting the world's most populous country out of poverty.

The newsmagazines were not the only offenders, of course; we newspaper reporters did our part. When the Four Modernizations were first announced, we reported, with little criticism, that China intended to build ten major new oilfields and to double the country's steel production. Within two years, the Chinese had admitted that those goals were woefully unrealistic and had embarked on a period of retrenchment. But this shift never quite got the same play in the United States as did the original modernization program.

The American press also has tended to overwrite the story of China's opening to the West and to hype Beijing's willingness to do business abroad. Many of the big business deals we wrote about—U.S. Steel's iron ore project, Intercontinental's hotel chain, Fluor's copper refinery—either did not come to pass at all or fell far short of the magnitude we reported. If all the aborted projects were ever pulled together they would provide the industrial base of a medium-size U.S. city. And the innovations that did get off the ground—joint ventures and Special Economic Zones—approached expectations very slowly.

To some extent, we also misled our readers about the social changes that are taking place in China. The Associated Press reported in 1985 from Beijing that China was moving to resurrect its legal system. Reading that in California, we were overcome with a sense of déjà vu. We had written that same story five years before, when several Chinese lawyers and law professors sat down with American reporters and described China's program to revive its judicial system.

Was the story any truer now? Maybe. Are the Chinese readier now than they were in 1980 to follow the rule of law? Probably. They are training more lawyers and have drafted many new legal codes. Are there more trials and court proceedings now than before? Perhaps, but trials are still the exception rather than the rule. It is still difficult to find anything resembling a court proceeding in Beijing.

The reporting of the events in and around Tiananmen Square in 1989, though often exceptional in its range and clarity, provided a final example of the journalistic weakness for exaggeration. The first reports of casualties after the army crackdown said there had been thousands of deaths, which later reporting indicated was well above the mark. Editors could not resist printing the highest figure they saw in the frantic early hours of the attack on central Beijing.

Journalists are also to blame for the legend of the massacre in Tiananmen Square. In the first day or two, unconfirmed accounts of students being lined up and shot in the square appeared in several major publications. Even two years later, most Americans we have encountered still think that such an event actually occurred. Editors printed the false accounts because they were too vivid and too dramatic to resist. The correcting work of several fine Beijing reporters—Pulitzer Prize–winners Nicholas Kristof and Sheryl NuDunn of the *New York Times* was particularly valiant in debunking other newspaper errors.

Searching for a Common Ground: The United States as a Distorting Mirror

One of the greatest sources of errant analysis among American journalists is the persistent search for signs that China is remaking itself in our own country's image. Some of this obsession can be blamed on the unusual demands of reaching our audience. American readers and American editors are far more likely to pay attention to a story that suggests some link, artificial or otherwise, between China and the United States.

In the early 1980s, for instance, the idea took root in the United States that China had gone capitalist. When President Ronald Reagan set out for China in 1984, he talked about the "so-called Communists" who ruled that country. The conservative organization Accuracy in Media declared that China's turn away from Marxism was the most significant story of the quarter-century.

Such impressions had a factual basis. Stories of economic experiments filled the Chinese press. Collectivized agriculture was revamped with the introduction of the "responsibility" system and the return to family farming. The communes were formally abolished, and rural China reorganized into townships. Rural factories appeared to proliferate. Free markets grew and thrived. Peasant incomes rose and the countryside seemed more prosperous than it had been in thirty years.

Cities also saw changes, with entrepreneurial efforts welcomed and tailors, seamstresses, barbers, chefs, photographers, and innkeepers doing well with private businesses. Zhao Ziyang, then premier and later party general secretary, was quoted as saying that China's commercial system would become competitive, with state-owned, cooperative, and private enterprises vying for customers.

All this reached a peak with a December 7, 1984, front-page commentary in the *People's Daily* entitled "Theory and Practice." It declared that the writings of Marx and Lenin could not be used to solve all the country's problems. Marxist ideas had to be interpreted in a way that took account of modern conditions in China.

The more careful American correspondents in Beijing, those with a great deal of experience in such pronouncements, wrote up the commentary as an interesting and new ideological justification for the wave of reform, but not a fundamental change of direction. The article was aimed at party officials who opposed the economic reforms and used quotations from Marx to fuel a counterattack.

Unfortunately, such widespread, measured analysis can easily be drowned out by a quick, short boom of hyperbole. In this case, the Associated Press provided the disruptive ingredient with a story, marked "URGENT," that reported that China had abandoned Marxism. The *People's Daily,* AP said, had made it official.

That was the story that caught the attention of editors throughout the world and forced many other reporters who had ignored or missed the commentary to write about it. Some repeated the gist of the AP lead. Some contradicted it. But the commentary assumed far more importance than it should have, particularly because it came during a holiday season in the United States, when other news was in short supply.

In the *New York Times,* columnist William Safire declared that China's rejection of Marxism and embrace of capitalism was the big event of 1984. The *Asian Wall Street Journal* ran a headline that said simply, "MARX IS DEAD."

Time has shown, as many analysts knew from the beginning, that such a comment was based on false premises. The reluctance of the Chinese leadership in 1988 to dip a toe into price reform and the violent reaction in 1989 to organized anti-Marxism in Tiananmen Square proved that. The entire Marx-is-dead episode demonstrated in vivid fashion how susceptible American reporters are to any story that suggests the Chinese are becoming more like us. That, of course, is a misperception that leads not only to erroneous copy but to a smug, ethnocentric view of the world that insults the people we write about.

The Burden of Preconception:
Riding the Rollercoaster

Even journalists with an advanced degree or two in China studies are not immune to giving events they see an inappropriate hue, like the photographers in Tiananmen Square who used to tint our red-headed son's hair light brown before mailing us the proofs.

On our first Sunday in Beijing as resident correspondents, we wandered up and down the streets north of the Beijing Hotel in search of clues to our new neighborhood. In one alley we came upon a crowd of teenagers and young adults, shouting at one another, breaking into little groups, caucusing, and then assuming some new arrangement.

What was this? We had spent much of the previous three years in Hong Kong reading *People's Daily* editorials and other political tracts. We still saw China as a very political country, an abstraction, rather than the real thing. So we guessed that this was a meeting of wallposter writers, or perhaps a black market or some other controversial activity. The truth was somewhat disappointing and revealing: we were watching stamp collectors.

That little incident reminded us that while Communist Party directives and *People's Daily* editorials may explain why some things happen in China, they don't explain everything. Our reporting and analysis from Hong Kong had been colored by the persistent notion that the Chinese were the most regimented people in the world, a billion souls marching in lock-stop, dressed identically in their Mao jackets. What we discovered when we finally had a chance to live in China, and what we were able to convey to the world after that, was that Chinese society was every bit as complex and vital as our own.

But when forced to write about the still inaccessible political debates in the government compound of Zhongnanhai and the offices in the Great Hall of the People, we tend to fall back into this black-or-white mode. This may account for the sudden and rather dramatic shifts we have seen in journalistic coverage and analysis of China over the past twenty years.

If one could graph American press treatment of China according to whether it was favorable or unfavorable toward Beijing, the result would resemble a rollercoaster. It would start in a trough, in the 1960s, when China was in the throes of the Cultural Revolution. Americans who thought about China at all believed that the Chinese were on a self-destructive rampage. The line on the graph would start to rise in about 1971, when China and the United States welcomed each other's table-tennis teams and Henry Kissinger made his secret visit to Beijing.

A peak would come sometime in 1972 or 1973, after President Richard Nixon's precedent-setting trip and the signing of the Shanghai Communiqué. The American press, euphoric over the breakthrough, enchanted with everything Chinese, was full of stories that depicted China as a classless, egalitarian society of hard-working, selfless peasants and workers, poor but noble.

Then the line on our graph would dip in the mid-1970s, as the press became impatient with waiting for normalization. The line would go lower and lower, jump up for normalization in December 1978 and January 1979, a time of gushing pro-American wallposters in Beijing, then descend again as the Chinese democracy movement was suppressed. By mid-1979 several American journalists had been permitted to move their bureaus from Hong Kong to Beijing, and many of them decided that the society they were seeing, close up for the first time, did not meet their expectations. News coverage in this period was very harsh and did not swing up again until President Reagan's 1984 trip to China and the rash of Marx-is-dead stories.

The line swung down in the winter of 1986–87 when student demonstrators were arrested, the country's three leading intellectual critics ejected from the Communist Party, and reformist General Secretary Hu Yaobang demoted. It swung up with the initial, moderate response to the demonstrations in Tiananmen Square in 1989 and then plunged to a record low for the post-Mao period when the Chinese army crunched into Beijing in June 1989 and killed hundreds of innocent civilians.

There are certain to be more rollercoaster rides in the future, with stories that will consequently fall short of the truth. The problem is emphasis and space. A journalistic analyst rarely has enough words allotted to him to provide shades of meaning, and he must be emphatic enough on some point to catch his editor's and readers' attention. That explains in part the stories that came out of China after Nixon's 1972 visit, painting the country as a socialist paradise. The American press indicated that China had reduced differences between rich and poor; individuals had put aside selfish desires to serve the people. There was no unemployment, no crime.

A favorite report of ours came from an otherwise clear-thinking journalist who has since written several distinguished books about China. He suggested in print that the Chinese had eradicated tooth decay. He asked several Chinese to open their mouths. He looked around, saw no cavities, and on the basis of his small sample concluded that the Chinese did not have to bother with dentists.

The folly of such sweeping analysis, if not clear on its face, becomes evident in the light of what the Chinese themselves have reported in the years since Mao's death. At the time American reporters were filing their wide-eyed copy during the Nixon visit, Chinese factories were still suffering from chaotic management and low worker morale. Peasants wrestled with work-point systems. Private plots were limited. Farm earnings were small. Doctors and dentists who had trained during the Cultural Revolution were avoided by all but the most foolhardy patients. It was hardly a socialist paradise.

The journalistic failings of the 1970s aggravated the backlash when reporters put down roots in Beijing in the 1980s. We set out to show the world that we were not fools; we were not going to write the limp, apologetic stories that travel editors and food critics turned out during two-week tours of five cities.

The result was what we sometimes called the malady-a-week syndrome. Every week we found something new that was wrong with China, some truism that we could disprove. We demonstrated that China suffered from unemployment, waste, corruption, injustice, pollution, and most other twentieth-century ills. Many of those stories were easy to write at the time because the Chinese themselves were openly admitting many of their shortcomings. And most had the virtue of being true.

But the impression, once again, was distorted. We painted China often as a dungeon, a picture oversimplified and out of date. Often we retold tales of the Cultural Revolution without making it clear that that period of turmoil was over. The rollercoaster was rolling to the bottom of the grade, and more positive stories were lost in the downward trend.

Likewise, our euphoria during the height of the Tiananmen Square demonstrations —when it seemed like the country might actually achieve some kind of democratic reform—left us severely unbalanced when the troops arrived. A more even-handed report on the flag-waving and speech-making in the square might have better prepared our readers, and ourselves, for what came next.

The Search for Balance: A Back Alley View

The relative balance and coherence of journalistic China analysis in slow periods, when CNN cameras are nowhere to be found, may stem from more than just tepid interest on part of editors. When the home office is not demanding a certain story, reporters enjoy more latitude to expand the range of their coverage. But the growing experience of American reporters living in Beijing may have also added a balancing element.

March 1993 marked the fourteenth anniversary of American news bureaus in Beijing. During that period, many individual reporters have come and gone, and sometimes succeeding generations of correspondents have not communicated well with each other. But there has emerged, bit by bit, a fund of experience that can be shared. Institutional memories do survive, to an extent. We know now that the Chinese media can make mistakes through pure incompetence, not political design. We know that some underground relationships can be maintained, with care, and that others are bound to result in surveillance and pain for the Chinese involved no matter what we do.

American journalistic analysts have acquired a very strong anchor they did not have before—a firsthand grasp of Chinese daily life, with all its mysteries and banality and poetry and lovely inconsistencies.

Whenever we see the next *People's Daily* commentary, or Great Hall of the People press conference, we are not likely to jump so quickly to conclusions that clash with what our own Chinese friends are saying and what our eyes see each day. There is some advantage in that, if we measure it all carefully and are as careful as always to poke in odd corners and to share whatever we find with our analyst comrades at the embassies and the academic enclave at the Friendship Hotel. We are all working the same territory, with the same goal—to understand something too big for any of us to understand alone.

Part IV
Infrastructure

12

Chinese Language Training for New Sinologists

Timothy Light

This chapter, in three parts, attempts to outline the current state of Chinese language training with regard to its role in preparing people for work in sinology. The first part gives a fairly brief account of the current scene in Chinese language teaching and learning in the United States and summarizes the major approaches to this subject, the results of our teaching as seen in the performance of graduates of our Chinese language, the roles of planning, and various changes that are taking place in the field. The second concentrates on certain features of the current situation that are of particular importance and need greater explication. While both parts include the predictable references to textbooks, teaching methods, numbers of students, and so on, the dynamics of the field and how they affect language teaching are also discussed. The third offers some concrete recommendations for the future.

The Current Scene in Chinese Language Teaching:
A Brief Summary

Numbers

About sixteen thousand students currently study Chinese in American colleges and universities. During most of the 1970s, the maximum number was usually around ten thousand, with a rise to twelve thousand only at the end of the decade. The 1980s, therefore, witnessed a noticeable increase in the number of students. While there are no comparable figures for the number of students studying at each level of instruction across the country, such figures are available from a subset of institutions teaching Chinese. As of 1984, with an estimated one-third of the approximately two hundred colleges and universities that teach Chinese reporting, the enrollments for first-year Chinese were around 4,500; for second-year, under 3,800; for third-year, around 2,800; and for fourth-year, approximately 800. Because it is likely that the schools responding to the survey represent the more committed institutions and have the more developed programs, the proportion of those in the third or fourth year of instruction is probably smaller nationally than these numbers would suggest. These figures indicate that about one-sixth of those who begin Chinese continue through the fourth year. If that ratio were extrapolated to the total number now studying Chinese, the figures would be: first year, 7,000–7,500; fourth year, 1,200–1,250. On the basis of experience, I would suggest that such figures should be considered high and that most or all of the institutions that actually offer more than two years of instruction in Chinese were probably included in the responding group, so the fraction of students who carry on through the fourth year is likely to be less than one-tenth instead of the one-sixth suggested by the figures.

From these statistics, it is clear that there is some good news: The number of students studying Chinese is generally increasing, though there have been dips in the overall rising curve over the past two decades. Intriguingly, during the 1970s, Chinese language enrollments in the United States rose dramatically when President Richard Nixon and his successors traveled to China, and fell dramatically after the undoubtedly unjustified euphoria that accompanied the public actions vis-à-vis China was dampened by a shot of reality. Also good news was the rapid increase in the number of high schools across the United States teaching Chinese, led by the Geraldine R. Dodge Foundation in New Jersey and the nearly sixty schools sponsored by that institution. Salutary as well is the fact that substantial numbers of American students are spending time in a Chinese-speaking environment, either on the Chinese mainland or in Taiwan. But the dramatic falloffs that occur in the enrollments between the first year and the third or fourth year are sobering. It is generally assumed in the field that at least three years of language study in the United States followed by an intensive year in a Chinese-speaking environment are necessary to reach a reasonably modest level of fluency in all four skills (speaking, listening, reading, and writing). Obviously, studying in the United States for a fourth year before going abroad produces even better results. The enrollments in advanced-level Chinese are tiny compared to the overall enrollments, and one of the clear problems of the field is the fact that the vast majority of the students who are studying Chinese in this country complete at most two years, which does not give them a sufficient basis for any later use of the language. Also sobering is the fact, which does not emerge in any statistics, that most American students who study in China are not there for a very long period. The majority go for either a summer or one term—the minimum needed to establish a foundation for later fluency, a full year, is undertaken by only a minority of students.

Teacher Training

A variety of teacher-training facilities in Chinese is available, though most teachers in the field have had little or no training. The only degree course in teaching

Chinese as a foreign language is that offered at the master's degree level at the University of Hawaii. However, several universities have recently begun to make language-teacher training a part of the graduate program in foreign language and literature departments, and Chinese has benefited from this trend. Notable means to provide such training include both a preterm workshop for those who are going to be teaching assistants and then continued instruction during the academic year, with close supervision of the teaching as the term goes on. In addition, several universities have introduced courses in language pedagogy directed toward Chinese or Chinese and Japanese combined. Moreover, in recent years there have been workshops and pedagogically oriented conferences for in-service training held at various venues around the country. The famous Middlebury Summer School figures prominently in this effort, which was begun with high school teachers in mind, but which now offers training for tertiary-level instructors as well. The American Council on the Teaching of Foreign Languages (ACTFL) provides training in the "Proficiency Testing Model" (see below), and workshops sponsored by the United States Department of Education through ACTFL are available at various places throughout the year. As recently as ten years ago, it could be confidently said that almost all those who had been in the profession for some time and most of those who were coming into the profession through graduate school teaching had had little if any training in language teaching and were generally innocent of movements, improvements, and technique development in foreign language teaching in general. Now, many institutions are making sure that their graduate students in Chinese language, literature, and linguistics have at least rudimentary training in basic language-teaching approaches, and supervised experience as teaching assistants, so they are able to begin several steps ahead when seeking a job in language teaching.

Teaching Materials

During the past decade, materials available for first- and second-year instruction have multiplied in variety. Up to the 1980s, the most widely used textbooks in American Chinese courses were the famous Yale series (by which is meant either *Speak Chinese* or *Speak Mandarin*) or the equally famous DeFrancis series. While some schools were using textbooks produced in the PRC, and while a few were using basic textbooks produced in Taiwan, the overwhelming choice was one of these two. The textbook that had really initiated systematic and effective teaching of oral Chinese, Yuen-ren Chao's *Mandarin Primer*, had already faded from use in all but a small number of institutions. In recent years, a flood of textbooks has come from the PRC, mostly from various units of the Beijing Language Institute. In addition the well received Tung and Pollard text *Colloquial Chinese* has become widely available in this country, and the text produced by T.T. Ch'en and others, *Chinese Primer*, has been widely adopted (discussed in greater detail below).

Beginning Chinese and early intermediate Chinese classes have also been supported by the production of nontext materials (see below). Several computer programs for learning characters and grammar that have been produced are the focus of increasing marketing from their publishers. At least two well-acted video dramatizations of the lessons in textbooks have been produced, and the contextualization of material in those books is thereby ensured to a degree that has hitherto been impossible. Moreover, in recent years, the vast amount of supplementary materials that almost all teachers have been preparing and keeping quiet about has begun to see the light of day and to be shared. In short, at this point the field does not lack for beginning-level materials.

At the intermediate and advanced levels (roughly latter second-year and all third- and fourth-year), the situation is quite different. The classic problem in Chinese language teaching has been the sudden and traumatic jump that students must take between the second and third years of instruction. First- and second-year instruction has typically relied on material that was written specifically for foreigners, which therefore has complete vocabulary and syntactic control. Third-year Chinese has been confined almost entirely to read; it has been the course where students got their first crack at "real" Chinese, that is, Chinese written for educated native speakers. The gap between the student's earlier experience and the attempt to tackle Chinese written for native speakers has been huge, leading students to become discouraged and drop out. Lacking suitable textbooks, teachers have been unable to do much to solve the pedagogical problems presented by this gap. A few schools have tried to address this problem with in-house materials written for the intermediate level, while most third-year and fourth-year instructors have compiled their own lists of reading materials and indeed have provided glossed essays, stories, and poems for reading.

Models of Organized Courses

The models of teaching, textbooks used, the approaches taken to those textbooks and to the subject in general, and the output results in terms of students' ability to function in Chinese in all four skills vary considerably across the nation. Indeed, one could say (not surprisingly) that the variation in our national attainment in Chinese parallels that of higher education in the country generally. There are three basic models of language teacher. That which has the longest tradition grew out of the "linguist-cum-native-speaking informant" pattern used in World War II, which became directly transported to several Ivy League universities and to a few prestigious public universities. This model presumes a fairly strictly defined division of labor wherein the "linguist" serves as the explainer of grammar and other aspects of the language, is the only one designated to use English in the classroom, and carries all authority for designing the course, while the native-speaking instructors are, in effect, drill instructors and are generally discouraged from teaching about the language, particularly in English. In this model, those who actually do most of the language instruction are, of course, the drill instructors, who carry various made-up titles of low status such as "preceptor," "lector," or "lecturer," and who have no hope of promotion to the professorial ranks. The "linguist" is often not a linguist, but a specialist in literature; in any case, whether linguist or literatus, that individual holds a professorial appointment and is designated as director of the language program because of his or her academic specialty, not because of any credentials or even demonstrated prowess in language teaching.

A further definitional note on the "linguist" in the linguist-cum-native-speaking-informant model is in order here. In this model, the term "linguist" really refers to a fluent speaker of the *students'* native language who is sophisticated enough to explain those items in the target language that cause conscious intellectual difficulty for adult learners. For a brief period that ended as long as thirty years ago at most universities, training in the discipline of linguistics included a modicum of attention to some fundamentals of the explication of target-language grammar. Linguists so trained in a graduate linguistics program were indeed better prepared than their literary colleagues to give systematic explanations of language material. Nowadays, the training received in a Ph.D. course in a linguistics department may be no more relevant preparation for the task of explaining a specific language than the training received in a literature department. In some programs, pure linguistics training is demonstrably less appropriate for the task of teaching language than the training received by literature specialists in those language and literature departments that now require all doctoral candidates to take courses in language pedagogy and undertake genuinely supportive and supervised teaching.

The second model is that of "alternate team teaching," which is practiced at several larger public universities that have substantial graduate programs. In this model, the teaching staff have more equal duties. Jobs are defined in terms of relatively equal numbers of contact hours (in the linguist-cum-native-speaking-informant model the native-speaking language teachers carry very heavy loads, and the professional director generally carries a load as light as that of his or her peers among the academic non–language teaching faculty in the same department). Whether native or nonnative speakers, the teachers alternate so that on Monday, for example, one of the two instructors assigned to a course will meet all sections of that course and on Tuesday, the other one will meet all sections. In several institutions, it has become a matter of principle to try to pair native and nonnative speakers in order to give students both a model of complete language fluency and a role model of someone like themselves who has had to learn this language as a foreigner. However, this difference in language background does not result in a hierarchical ordering of the tasks of the individuals. Frequently in this model, professorial staff and teaching assistants share the duties. The professorial partner in this model has a Ph.D. in a relevant subject, and he or she is expected to participate in the same type of training as the teaching assistant so that he or she will "be up to speed" in terms of pedagogical sensitivity, materials, and so forth.

The third teaching model is that which is necessarily found in most small schools where there is a single Chinese teacher who must carry the whole burden alone. In this model, the teacher—whether native or nonnative—is both role model and language model. This last model has become increasingly prevalent since, as relationships with the PRC have grown, schools could hire assistants from mainland China who would increase students' exposure to the language, thus allowing more sections and hours to be taught.

Students

The students who comprise the Chinese classes in the United States have also changed in character over the past three decades.

A colleague in Japanese language teaching remarked a few years ago that before the early 1980s his students all had a historical reason for studying Japanese, while those of the 1980s had a future reason for studying Japanese. His earlier students had had some family connection with Japan (parents had been missionaries or businesspeople in Japan), or there was a courtship arrangement already initiated before the student entered the class, or some deep friendship had occurred before electing to take Japanese. While some of his current students continued to study for those reasons, they generally reflected much more a career hope in business, government, or teaching. The same comment could be made about many students in Chinese classes across the country, but with two differences. Two or three decades ago, it was not uncommon for between a quarter and half of a beginning Chinese class to be composed of newly enrolled graduate students who were just beginning their study of the Chinese language on an odyssey that would eventually take them seven or eight years before they would complete a Ph.D. in some field of China studies. There are still some graduate students in Chinese classes, but they do not form so significant a proportion as before, and very often they are those for whom the use of the language will never be a particularly crucial matter. Nowadays, the study of Chinese among undergraduates is sufficiently common that most students who have some sense of wanting to go into China studies pursue the language before graduation. In addition, depending on the region of the country, the ethnic mix in Chinese classes can be a significant factor in the dynamics of the class and in the curriculum planning undertaken by the instructor. In areas of the country with large ethnic Chinese populations, a majority of the class might well be ethnically Chinese.The ethnic mix represents a substantial pedagogical problem because some of those who are ethnically Chinese already have some passive command of a Chinese dialect; this inevitably puts them ahead of their classmates, who have not had any previous exposure.

An interesting subset of the student population that has appeared in recent years merits mention at this point. A few established sinologists have returned to the classroom to "retrieve" (or perhaps initially acquire) missing skills that are found to be needed in mid-career. The Inter-University Program in Taipei (the so-called Stanford Center) has provided a much needed resource for this kind of training through a small postdoctoral research and language fellowship program that has attracted individuals in their thirties and forties back for refresher and advanced language training. Less programmatic (and without special fellowships), the New Asia–Yale-in-China Chinese Language Center and some PRC centers have offered the same opportunity to those willing to undergo the work and role-reversal that a return to language study entails. It is hard to estimate the anxiety and disorientation that a decade of access to China has brought to scholars trained with the implicit assumption that they could never work in China and would therefore have to do research entirely through others. This assumption has been a crucial factor in limiting the aspirations of the field as a whole regarding language teaching. In light of that anxiety, it is a credit to the field that some have taken the risk of refurbishing skills and that the field has been modestly supportive of such scholars.

The changed characteristics of Chinese class populations—the dramatic increase in the number of students who have a career reason for studying the language and the dramatic reduction in the number of graduate students in the early years of Chinese instruction—have accompanied a change in the goals of the average student. A generation ago, when graduate students were prominent in first- and second-year Chinese classes, the goal of instruction was adequately expressed in the frequently used explanation, "I am studying Chinese in order to learn to read materials in my field with the aid of a dictionary." There was little interest in obtaining great facility in the active skills (writing and speaking), and there was an explicit or implicit signal given by the teacher that command of the active skills was, in any case, impossible for nonnatives ever to attain. For students who intend to do business in China or hope to work in the government or to be involved in other work in China, a command of the active skills as well as the passive skills is crucial; they come to the course with the same expectations as do students who take the European languages, that is, they expect at the end of a given period of time to be able to read, write, speak, and understand Chinese.

Standards

The variety of students, of programs, of teaching preparation, and of American institutions of higher education has led to wildly different standards among the schools that teach Chinese. Studying Chinese at an American college or university for only one year does not necessarily reflect anything in terms of skill that is uniformly measurable. The ranges run from one end of the spectrum, where the classroom attention is almost entirely on aural-oral work and where the acquisition of the writing system is minimal, to classes where the focus is on the mastery of reading, in which students are required to learn up to a thousand characters within a year and where oral drilling is done only to prepare students for reading. Even though most courses fall in between these two eccentric extremes, even in the mid-range there are considerable differences in attainment from one program to another. For students who transfer from one university to another, placement in a Chinese course must be based far more on placement evaluation than on the credits provided by the registrar's office. When students are sent abroad, the receiving institutions are now well aware that American students' background cannot be predicted on the number of years of study. For many years the test given for entrance to the Inter-University Program in Taipei was the only national measure for evaluating students and programs. In recent years, the Chinese Language Proficiency Test developed by the Center for Applied Linguistics has become available, though the results of using that test are rather mixed. In addition, the aforementioned ACTFL workshops in proficiency-based testing and instruction are designed to license some teachers as proficiency testers on the Foreign Service Institute model. Further, the Beijing Language Institute has prepared a proficiency test that seems promising for students going to Beijing to study, so in the future it may be possible to evaluate American students' Chinese proficiency on a somewhat more uniform basis.

Areas of Special Concern

In 1983–84 I had the opportunity to visit six institutions in China that teach Chinese to foreigners. While I would not call those visits "surveys" or "formal investigations," the major lessons that I learned at those institutions accord with observations made during many subsequent visits to China (including participation in several conferences held in China on Chinese language teaching) and Taiwan, and based on my experience living in Hong Kong in the 1960s and 1970s. These observations point up what we do and do not do. Three areas of concern emerged as the most saliently reiterated items from those visits.

The teachers with whom I spoke at all the institutions uniformly characterized arriving American students who had had two or more years of Chinese before arriving as overall the best-prepared group in terms of oral skills of any group of foreign students. The Americans' command of the basic patterns of Chinese, control of the phonology, and ability and willingness to express their basic needs and wants clearly outstripped those of any other country's students who had come to the PRC with prior training. At the same time, the Americans' aural comprehension was not seen as outstanding, and the Americans' ability in reading and writing was clearly regarded as well below that of a number of other groups. Though the teachers were generally reluctant to say this unless directly asked and prompted, the Americans' ability to continue to make progress in any of the four skills over the long run while studying in China was thought to be considerably below that of students from many other countries that sent substantial numbers of students to continue studying in the PRC. The one group of teachers that I got to know best and that therefore felt comfortable with more frankness once spent well over an hour discussing with tremendous emotion and anger the now fabled unwillingness and inability of the average American student to do the kind of memory work that is necessary to master any foreign language and particularly one with a very difficult writing system. The Americans, then, were seen by their teachers in China as initially very well prepared in one skill but not well prepared in the other skills and overall far from the top in long-term progress.

By observing Americans in action for a long period of time at the Beijing Language Institute and for shorter periods of time at several other places, and by listening to their own testimony, American students appeared far from the best-assimilated foreign students in Chinese society. The American students as a group seemed to be the least ready and able to engage in any lengthy and wide-ranging conversations in Chinese with a mixture of students that I happened to be with in any number of settings. Obviously, the major (or only totally available) lingua franca among the foreign students from the hundred or so countries who are studying in China is, of course, Mandarin. I did not find this an impediment to communication with students from several African countries, Eastern or Western European countries, or other parts of Asia, but I repeatedly noticed that Americans who were among such mixed groups generally stayed silent or tried to approach me on the side in English without participating in the group discussion in Chinese. Further, attitudinally the Americans that I have run into have been most characterized by the extent of their complaints against individual Chinese, Chinese institutions, or Chinese politics and government, which they assert are the reasons that they are not able to assimilate into Chinese society, make Chinese friends, or become part of anything going on around them. The same complaints when repeated to students from other countries do not receive complete credence. Even among sinologists working in China, Americans evince a remarkably high level of complaint and a rather low tolerance level for adapting one's strategies and behavior to the normal expectations of a Chinese society. Students from all countries in China have certain complaints regarding assimilation, freedom of movement, and so on. Relatively speaking, however, the students from most other countries find ways to get around the barriers and end up with a happier experience. Some American sinologists have a remarkable ability to adapt to Chinese society, but as a group, we appear to be lacking. (The high level of complaint and remoteness from Chinese society also characterized most of the Americans I knew in the 1960s and 1970s in Hong Kong; therefore, I do not believe that the political and social structure of the PRC is the dominant problem.)

So far as I could tell, for most of the teachers with whom I had lengthy conversations regarding their experiences teaching American students, this was the first time that an American Chinese language teacher had visited their institution and sat down and talked with them regarding their teaching, their students, and their perceptions. This is not to say that none of the teachers that I met had spoken with American counterparts. Some had at that point, and many more have done so subsequently, owing to the international conferences that have been run by the Chinese Language Teachers Association of China. Also, American institutions that have programs located at a Chinese school send American representatives and/or visitors to meet with the teachers regarding students of their own institution. But wide-ranging evaluative discussions and programmatic discussions seemed to have been a rarity involving both American and Chinese language professionals, and there was a certain sense that such discussions were normally carried out between administrators or are a specialists, who obviously would not have had access to the kinds of information that I have just indicated as most salient.

My visits lead me to articulate four areas of particular concern for people involved in planning for the future of American sinology:

1. the goals of our Chinese language teaching and how we should evaluate and attempt to reach them;
2. the teaching methods and materials that we should use in order to reach our goals;
3. cultural preparation for assimilation to a Chinese society;
4. the dynamics of the field of sinology itself.

Language Teaching Goals and Ways to Define and Achieve Them

The first day of my first-year Chinese class in the United States began with the teacher explaining to us that our goal was to learn to read with the aid of a dictionary. Politely, but with no room for doubt, she also explained that we Americans would never be capable of speaking Chinese fluently, understanding adult Chinese when it was spoken at a normal pace, or writing anything worth reading in Chinese. Not surprisingly, the strictures of that teacher and scores like her proved eminently successful predictions. It is a truism in any kind of teaching that students will learn only what they are expected to. What was equally true, though not evident from what the teacher said on that day and certainly not desired by her or any others (one presumes), was that very few students actually learned to *read*. The activity that they eventually learned to perform was more like decoding, that is, painfully slow, character-by-character puzzling out of the meanings of texts confined largely to the subfield in a discipline that an area specialist had chosen as his or her topic of research. Only very few Chinese language students ever seemed to have learned to read in the normal sense of being able to pick up reading matter and read it and/or skim it for content; even fewer have learned to read it for pleasure. In contrast, the programs for foreign students in institutions located in Taiwan and on the Chinese mainland have assumed that the best students will reach a level of attainment in all four skills, which is not too dissimilar from the level reached by Chinese students studying English in the United States for similar periods of time. Not surprisingly, when teachers in institutions hold this up as a goal and when teachers teach in expectation of achieving that goal, many foreign students do indeed reach it.

The personal anecdote and the contrast between the American condition in foreign language teaching and learning (certainly as it was and as it may remain) are apt thumbnail descriptions of the source of a national problem—that in the United States we do not train sufficient numbers of people to an adequate standard in *any* language, and we are particular ineffective in training people in languages that are not cognate to English. The national scope of the problem has been outlined in many reports, most graphically in *Strength through Wisdom,* the report of the President's Commission on the Foreign Language and International Studies, which was issued in 1979. This section begins with a reference to that national problem only to set the present discussion in its proper context. There are many aspects of language instruction for which we have not achieved notable success in Chinese. In general, those failures are the same for Chinese as they are for most other languages as taught in the United States.

Simply put, our failure is that we are not in the habit of establishing performance goals in the target languages that we teach. Neither are we in the habit of evaluating our students and ourselves by the achievement of those goals. In the section above I briefly described the widely varying standards among programs across the country. It is not only that a given period of time in different institutions may mean radically different things in terms of Chinese language proficiency but that many programs are not designed with a clear idea of what those students should be able to *do* in Chinese once they have finished a given period of time studying the language. Rather than defining our goals in terms of abilities to use the language under given circumstances, we typically define the goals in terms of mastery of certain amounts of textual material. Thus at teachers' meetings, one may hear conversations on how many chapters (or, in extreme cases, how many volumes) of the DeFrancis or Yale or a given PRC text teachers have been able to rush their students through in a semester or a year. One will also hear extensive claims of how many characters students have been required to master in a given period of time. While reference to amounts of textbooks that have supposedly been digested is somewhat indicative of the material to which students have been *exposed,* such indications may have very little to do with students' actual mastery. Such indications also have very little to do with the actual sequence of learnability of various linguistic items, and in general such indications tell us little about what students can and should be able to achieve over the course of a given period of instruction.

Current language teaching jargon assigns the terms "achievement," "achievement orientation," and "achievement tests" to goal setting and evaluation of students according to the amount of material that has been covered. It is understood that from the teacher's point of view a certain amount of achievement orientation is necessary and in the short term (daily quizzes, weekly tests, and even semester tests) achievement evaluation is terribly important for ascertaining how much of what the teacher has presented has been absorbed. The terms "proficiency," "proficiency orientation," "proficiency evaluation," and "proficiency testing" are reserved for a focus on what students are actually able to do in the target language and for evaluative measures that give a fairly objective account of how well students function in the language.

Following is an example of a proficiency orientation; several students sign up for a Chinese course so that they will be able to go to China as English teachers. They need to have extensive oral-aural fluency, be able to take care of all their daily needs in Chinese and read the major signs, such as signs for bathrooms, directions to places, store signs, and so forth, but they will not need to read extensive discourse. A proficiency-based course for such students would break down into units those things that are prerequisites to taking care of one's daily needs in China and would then evaluate the students on the ability to handle those tasks. Correspondingly, the course syllabus would be designed in sequence to introduce the vocabulary, the structures, and the social customs necessary for that purpose.

The same precision in identifying the language needs of the students and attempting to meet them specifically would obtain in applying proficiency criteria to a normal college-level course in Chinese. Typically, students in any college foreign language course hope to be able to get around the target country by using the target language, read road signs, directions, the newspaper, and so on, and communicate to friends in writing at least through notes. Because of the particular demands of its newspaper language, Chinese instruction would probably require at least three years to achieve these goals, and that fact should be clearly stated at the outset, but a two-year course could make headway on the other goals, and a detailed analysis of what specific skills are needed and an equally specific set of pedagogical steps would yield rather accountable results.

The impetus for the distinction between proficiency and achievement as defined above comes largely from the experience of the U.S. State Department and other government agencies. Several decades ago, the government discovered that normal language teaching practices were not producing Foreign Service officers who were able to function in the target language, and proficiency measures were then established in order to have practical benchmarks against which to measure government courses and the products thereof. The famous (or infamous) FSI ratings from 0 to 5 resulted from this concern. An FSI rating of 0 is exactly what it sounds like, no command whatsoever of the language. A rating of 1 indicates a rudimentary acquaintance with the language, but no effective control over anything except rote phrases. A rating of 2 is an indication that the individual can take care of all daily needs in the language. A rating of 3 is an indication that the individual can carry out his or her work in the language. A rating of 4 is equivalent to a foreigner who has attended college in the target language, and a rating of 5 is equivalent to a college graduate who is a native speaker of the target language.

Beginning about a decade ago, leaders in academic language training began to acknowledge widely that our performance in training students in colleges and universities and high schools was not successful in producing people who could use the target languages being taught. The American Council of Teachers of Foreign Languages (ACTFL) began to develop a set of guidelines for evaluation based on the Foreign Service Institute guidelines, but stretched out at the lower levels in recognition of the fact that no known academic program would ever train people beyond the 3 level, and very few would even reach that, so the academic goal would be approximately at the 2 level. With government sponsorship, ACTFL has supported the development of evaluative measures in all the major languages taught in the United States.

Because there is a certain amount of controversy over the notion of proficiency and a good deal of misunderstanding of what those who advocate the use of proficiency criteria aim to accomplish, following are some objections that have been raised to the FSI approach. The FSI approach has been charged with being only oral. It is true that the earliest models of the FSI evaluative measure were an oral guideline to evaluation, but that was about three decades ago, and the current use of the model involves not only the four skill areas but some evaluation of cultural sensitivity as well. In some circles the FSI model has been accused of being anticlassical and antiliterary. Quite the contrary; the goals of a particular language course can be defined in classical and literary terms, (and that fits entirely within the thrust of the FSI/ACTFL approach. Finally this approach has been called mechanical and less demanding than focusing on reading with a dictionary and conducting classes in English for the purpose of translating and illustrating major grammar points through English. Again, the opposite is true. Because the Foreign Service approach requires that students reach certain explicit, agreed-on standards, it is, of course, much more demanding.

The principal benefits of the use of the proficiency model can be summed up in one word: accountability. The use of the proficiency guidelines for Chinese provided by ACTFL gives teachers and students a set of fairly clear measures for charting the progress of the student and the effectiveness of the course. In addition, the use of these guidelines gives teachers very specific tasks as objectives, so material writing, syllabus planning, and indeed daily lesson plans can be structured, not according to the teacher's guess as to what the textbook writer meant, but according to the sets of goals outlined by the teacher herself or himself at the beginning of the course. The problem with the entirely achievement-oriented model is that it effectively throws at the students all the language material that can be crammed into a given period of time in the hope that the students will absorb the right things in something close enough to the right order that they are able to perform normal tasks in the language. Because we have built-in language learning mechanisms in our cognitive makeup, most of us do indeed learn a good deal even from the most awkward teaching, but it is not an efficient way to learn. The advantage of the proficiency model is that it breaks down the task according to the specific goals set out in advance and gives students direct paths to the reaching of those goals and then tests them to be sure that those goals have been reached. The ACTFL initiative has received a somewhat mixed reception from the Chinese language teaching profession. However, government pressure and increasingly effective propaganda and workshop instruction by ACTFL itself have led an increasing number of teachers to take the training necessary to use the ACTFL guidelines effectively and objectively. As many readers of this volume will have already discovered through experience, the Department of Education has tied continued funding under the National Resource Center program of Title VI to demonstrated use of proficiency criteria in the establishment of language programs. This one step has probably had as much beneficial effect on long-term preparation of area specialists in all fields as anything the government has done in education since the launching of *Sputnik*.

The implementation of a proficiency-based model is somewhat thorny, and a couple of cautionary descriptive comments are in order at this point. A careful study of the guidelines produced by ACTFL will convince the attentive reader that some or many items in the Chinese guidelines are inappropriately included, possibly incorrect, or simply put in the wrong place. Indeed, almost any reader who knows some Chinese could change them around to suit himself or herself. This also is true in most other languages. Initially, too much insistence on the details of the staging from level to level caused a good deal of justified resistance on the part of teachers who did indeed know better. In recent years, a more reasonable approach has evolved, essentially asking teachers to replicate for their own courses proficiency-based models that move from level to level, with the levels being largely defined in the same way as they are in the ACTFL guidelines, but with the details probably varying widely. A corollary to this revised approach is the understanding that each program, rather than slavishly following the guidelines as a cookbook recipe for a syllabus, should design its own syllabus with a proficiency orientation. This involves having to set out in precise detail how many hours of instruction one has, how much homework one can expect of one's students, and so forth, and then coming to a common agreement among the teachers as to which of the goals can be achieved within a given span of time. Working this way eliminates the problem of a year of Chinese not being equivalent across the country. Using proficiency guidelines, a student's degree of mastery is no longer indicated by the number of years of instruction, but instead by the level of skill reached according to ACTFL guidelines, an indication that tells all experienced teachers roughly where that student belongs.

The majority of the Chinese programs in the United States still do not teach with stated expectations of what their students should be able to do in the four skills upon completion of their stated course of instruction. In other words, the majority of Chinese courses in this country are not accountable by any recognized common standards of performance. Nevertheless, a growing number of schools are adopting this approach. An even larger number of schools, though not formally adopting anything similar, are working under this influence, and the notion of accountability (however it is defined) is becoming increasingly closer to being a norm.

Methods and Materials

The proficiency-based approach is *not* a method. Rather, it is simply an *approach,* a way of evaluating methods, a way of integrating methods, and most of all a way of making ourselves accountable and thereby raising our standards. American foreign language teaching has been characterized over the past thirty or forty years by the introduction every few years of a new method that is supposed to have miraculous results. The method that is most familiar to most American students of languages and on which all the American-produced Chinese language texts and most of the PRC-produced Chinese language texts are based is called the Audio-Lingual method. This method relies extensively on oral drills of a fairly formal nature and concentrates on the acquisition of formal language matter (phonology, morphology, and syntax) with the idea that the student who masters the formal aspects of the language will be able to manipulate them successfully in any kind of communicative environment. It is this method and the materials based on it that have given American students going to China such a headstart in oral skills. It is also the nearly exclusive attention to the rather mechanical set of concerns making up this method that leaves the students relatively less able to advance beyond their beginning stage once they get to China. Methods of language teaching about which one may hear less in the United States, but which have gotten attention in recent years among language teaching professionals, have such labels as the "notional-functional" method, the "situational" method, the "silent way," the "counseling-learning" method, and "total physical response." This chapter does not aim to tout any one of these. On the contrary, an experienced, clear-headed approach to foreign language teaching will suggest that each of these methods arises from a particular set of concerns and, used in the context from which each one comes, each has considerable validity. What is required, then, is teachers who have the sense of eclecticism to make use of methods and materials at the appropriate time and for the appropriate purpose.

The accountability that is the keystone of using proficiency-based criteria on which to base a course also makes the evaluation and selection of methods and materials appropriate to the tasks at hand much easier and indeed necessary. The teacher who plans out a course for two or three years of instruction would naturally begin in the typical American fashion with an Audio-Lingual approach, wanting to achieve a minimal oral/aural mastery right off. However, that same teacher would recognize, after a few months of instruction, that a great deal of attention will have to be given to the types of language appropriate to different situations, to vocabulary acquisition, and, of course, not only to reading but to very extensive writing practice. Later on, that same teacher will understand that whenever the immediate task at hand results in utterances extending in length beyond four or five syllables that the student will revert to beginning habits and that the Audio-Lingual method and its drills and attention to details of structure are again called for. Certainly, the demands on the teacher, as well as on the student, are much heavier than they are under an achievement-based model. However, the results are demonstrably more satisfying, as both teacher and student begin to notice the explicit progress made from day to day and week to week and month to month— progress that was defined ahead of time by realistic goals, considering the students, the time at hand, and the materials being used. (See Light 1987, ch. 2, for a full discussion of the staging of proficiency levels in Chinese.)

In general, the most successful language courses aim for proficiencies in all four skills. As indicated above, this goes counter to the tradition in Chinese language teaching, where the training of sinologists has often focused almost entirely on the single skill of reading after a beginning introduction to the patterns of Chinese grammar. While there are many reasons for urging a four-skill approach, only two are particularly relevant here. First, work in each of the skills in fact greatly reinforces all the others. A major reason (probably the most important one) that those who were trained only in the reading skill never learned to become good readers in Chinese is because the language never became a *language* to them, but only a set of codes. One does not genuinely *read* a language that one cannot speak, write, or understand when spoken. Second, the demands made of sinologists in Chinese-speaking communities today are very similar to those that we make of Chinese students of English in an American community. That is, it is expected in China that specialists who study the country will be able to give papers in Chinese, write articles in Chinese, engage in intelligent conversation in Chinese, understand lectures given in Chinese, and do such modest things in Chinese as complete forms and write notes to their friend. The unhappy day when one could be a sinologist and not get along in Chinese in a Chinese society is fortunately over. Nevertheless, this does not mean that at some points the explicit measures by which given courses are to be planned and judged should not concentrate *at times* very heavily on a single skill, most probably reading. This certainly is necessary for the purpose of moving graduate study more rapidly than it otherwise would be able to go. But even such a concentration must be undertaken in a context of openly recognizing and dealing with the needs of all good students to attain a sufficient proficiency in all four skills.

While there is nothing like a sufficiency of materials dealing with all the problems that Americans face in trying to reach an FSI level 2 in all four skills (that is, the ability to handle oneself in daily life in the target culture), the situation has greatly improved over a decade ago. There is an increasing choice of textbooks from the PRC, and each new textbook is less political and more sophisticated in the variety of methodologies used to achieve explicit goals. Indeed, there has been such a flowering of materials production in the PRC in recent years that it is impossible even to list all the items available. (At the first International Conference on Teaching Chinese as a Foreign Language held in Beijing in 1986 190 separate volumes of materials were on display at the bookfair, and that number has been greatly added to since then.) In the United States there has been also a modest growth of materials. Most of these have been targeted toward very specific purposes and, with one exception, there is much less attention than used to be the case given to the production of all-encompassing texts. Computer programs for instruction in Chinese writing are increasingly being developed; at least two excellent videotapes for beginning instruction have been produced; a much needed and highly imaginative book of games to use in Chinese classrooms has recently appeared; there are now available at least three manuals to teach foreigners how to write letters in Chinese; and there are now early-level textbooks to instruct students in the writing of connected discourse so that, by the time they reach an intermediate or advanced state, they will have few difficulties in composing letters, papers, reports, and notes in Chinese. Despite the trend, there is one exceptional, new, all-encompassing text: *Chinese Primer* by Ta-tuan Ch'en and others at Princeton and the Middlebury Summer School. This text deserves particular mention because it is the explicit and direct heir to Chao's *Mandarin Primer,* because it has been developed over three decades at the unparalleled program at Princeton and Middlebury, and because it represents an eclectic and interesting approach to the Chinese language that has been missing in many other texts. My purpose in so positively reporting on this text is not to laud that book over others, but to note that the best experience in the field is beginning to bear fruit in terms of materials that can be used widely beyond the campuses where the authors work.

The most serious gap relates to the post-beginning stage. We have a certain number of materials, mostly in photocopied form prepared by individual teachers for their own students, for what is generally considered second-, third-, and fourth-year Chinese. As one advances toward the fourth year, the focus becomes increasingly heavy on reading, and the materials most teachers use are largely glossed texts. A few programs have begun to produce materials that are oriented toward the active skills as well as the single passive skill of reading, but we lack a great deal in this area, and the letter-writing manuals referred to above are a notable exception to the general absence of intermediate and advanced materials.

Cultural Matters

The cultural ignorance and the inappropriate behavior even on the part of trained American sinologists working in China alluded to above are the results of at least two factors in our Chinese language teaching habits. First, it is notable that the majority of the most widely used texts give very little attention to daily cultural habits in common social intercourse in a Chinese society. While it is not quite true that the DeFrancis and Yale texts could be translated into French or German with little loss of cultural specificity, it is certainly true that these texts could not be used as guides to how the Chinese see social relations and how they expect foreigners to behave, nor to how the Chinese use their language in social situations. Ironically, the same can be said very largely for most of the texts produced in the PRC itself.

The second factor, which leads to the first, is that there have been to date insufficient studies regarding the actual use of language in society in China to inform textbook writers, so texts are written at a level of artificial formality reflecting neither how Chinese speak with each other nor how foreigners are expected to speak once they arrive in China. For example, while foreigners are taught that there is a greeting such as "Chifanle meiyou?," they are not generally told that there are other greetings such as "Shang nar?," "Qu nar?," "Ni laide zhenme zao!" (All of these phrases are functionally only greetings and could be supplanted in English with "How are you?" Literally, they mean respectively, "Have you eaten yet?" "Where are you going?" "Where are you going?" and "You have come so early.") Further, most young Americans do not know that concern about how much one is wearing on a cold day is in fact just concern and not an attempt to control the young American's (especially male) life, that the teacher's concern for the student's progress is not an indication of disdain for the student but particular regard for the student, and so on. Moreover, the actual registers of language that are used by shopkeepers, people from whom one asks directions, bus conductors, and others are far from the registers of language encased in most textbooks.

There is, in short, both a great need for greater personal sensitivity and sophistication on the part of textbook writers and a tremendous need for basic sociolinguistic studies in China so that we will have a database on which to found dialogues that actually reflect the language as it is used.

There is no question that instruction in the United States cannot fully prepare Americans for living in any other culture. Nevertheless, there are plenty of examples in our teaching of European languages—and also in our teaching of Japanese—that indicate that it is possible to improve our preparation of young Americans for the types of things they will meet and to focus their minds on the kinds of adaptation and growth that they will have to undergo when they arrive in China. The frequency of misunderstanding and miscommunication on small matters—and occasionally on very big ones—is astonishingly high, and anyone who takes the time to travel around and listen and watch Americans interacting and not interacting in China might well be amazed by the number of times that even another American could pick out miscues and miscommunications in situations where the American interlocutor had no idea that anything had gone wrong.

The Dynamics of the Field

As suggested above, the greatest inhibiting factor to progress is the dynamics of the field; I shall now try to explain briefly what that means and why it is so. The compensation level, the rankings, the general level of prestige, and the overall treatment within universities of those who spend most or all of their time teaching foreign languages are probably the lowest among the teaching staffs in American institutions of higher education. (That may not be entirely true. There is a certain amount of debate as to whether those who actually do the teaching of English composition or basic mathematics are treated worse.) Young postdoctoral scholars who have both developing scholarly interests and a genuine interest and talent in language teaching quickly understand upon getting employment that when they are judged very little weight will be given to their language-teaching expertise. The disincentives for people of any genuine scholarly bent and ambition to engage much of their energies in language teaching are so strong that it is the exception rather than the rule to find well-trained individuals in an academic subject putting much time into the teaching of language, and where language teaching is an important part of a scholar's teaching load, that language teaching is generally confined to the reading of texts (usually topic-specific texts) in a class conducted in English for the purpose of reading and translation. The management of area studies in the United States reflects this prestige hierarchy. Those who are called on to make the plans, set the trends and priorities, and represent the field to the sources of funding and to those who will generally establish the patterns in universities and colleges are social scientists who have an area interest. In the Chinese field, planning meetings and funding organizations are generally structured just as the meeting that produced this volume was, either with a single language person in the midst of a great many others, or more often, none at all.

To be sure, this situation is not inherently inimical to the progress of the field. In few organizations is the work distributed evenly, and so long as a given field is able to find people who are willing to work longer hours at less pay and with little participation in management, there will be more resources to spread elsewhere. The problem, however, is that this division of labor and authority is also reflected in both the attitudes toward language teaching and in the actual practice of training area specialists. At Chinese language teachers' meetings, once the injustice of their own treatment has been thoroughly aired, the next largest source of dissatisfaction among the hardest-working teachers is the lack of genuine interest in language learning evinced by their area colleagues. While most reputable graduate programs and even a few undergraduate programs have stated numbers of years of language training that individuals must undergo in order to be certified for an area, the experience of the language teacher is generally that the language training is undertaken as a burden of secondary or tertiary value and that in any conflict of time, language is always considered to be the most dispensable subject. It is typical for language teachers to be berated by their area specialist colleagues for not providing sufficient training for their graduate students and yet hear from those same colleagues that those same graduate students do not have time to attend the courses prepared for them. Very often these interesting contradictions will occur within the same week—often the week of registration for a given term.

It is not only the relegation of language study to the category of the unimportant when there are time conflicts that hinders the field but also the definition of what language study should involve. The unhappy definition of language training as training merely to learn to puzzle out a written text, character by character with the aid of the dictionary, referred to above, is the result not only of a misunderstanding of what is possible and what is necessary but also of an unfortunate symbiotic relationship between area studies and those language teachers who genuinely do not believe (or do not want to believe) that their students could do anything better. It is ironic that students in China from some of the most impoverished Third World countries achieve levels of proficiency in all four skills in Chinese that seem almost miraculous to their American counterparts, who have had the benefit of the most lavish educational system in the word.

In discussions on what kinds of language preparation are needed for scholarly work in sinology, suggestions to employ proficiency criteria and criticism of teaching laborious decoding under the name of "reading" are frequently rebutted by charges of a lack of seriousness and a disrespect for the past. Literati and historians have been known to state that such concerns inevitably run counter to their need to have students prepared for scholarship. The implication is that the only training for the use of difficult scholarly tools is an initial or very early exclusive devotion to the decoding of those tools or of texts of a similar time depth. Modern language pedagogy (as well as simple common sense) tells us that at least some knowledge of the language is required before one can begin to read that language. That basic knowledge is attained through acquisition of all the skills of language at the beginning. Further, once the basic language foundation has been laid, development of the reading skill is attained by *reading*. "Reading" here means just that: that is, spending enough time actually reading anything in Chinese that one can relatively easily understand so that one begins to move one's eyes relatively rapidly across the page and actually gain new information through that process. It is only for already formed readers that training in scholarly tools and methods makes any sense. No Latin teacher would think of attempting to teach this classical language to illiterates who do not know the Roman alphabet. Nor, indeed, would such teachers consider teaching Latin to those who know only the alphabet and can puzzle out road signs and menus syllable by syllable.

Specific training for scholarship on Chinese depends primarily on the development of effective and efficient reading skills in modern Chinese (since that is the only kind of Chinese that foreign students will be able to read reasonably well). For students with a particular interest in the grand tradition of China, similar skills need to be developed in basic classical Chinese after a sufficient base has been laid down in modern Chinese. After students have developed those skills, they will more easily learn the particular vocabularies of various fields in modern Chinese and the special syntax and vocabularies of various periods of the long history of writing in Chinese. For modern specialties—such as sociology, linguistics, philosophy, politics, or economics—the vocabulary that is actually special to the discipline is no greater in Chinese than it would be in English, and acquisition of the principal vocabulary items and guideposts to discovering the less frequent ones when they occur should not take longer than a semester or (at the outside) a year. Indeed, specialized academic vocabulary is among the easiest things to acquire in studying a foreign language so long as one knows that vocabulary in one's native language first. There is frequently considerable misguidance on this point. The difficulties that most sinologists have in reading materials in their particular subfield are basic reading difficulties and have little to do with the technical vocabulary that crosses linguistic boundaries more easily than any other semantic field because there is a much greater one-to-one correspondence between precisely defined terms in academically technical areas than in any other sphere.

The task is more difficult for the classical sinologist than it is for the modernist, and the special training must correspondingly be more elaborate. This is just as true in Latin, classical Hebrew, and classical Greek as it is in Chinese. The areas of difficulty that the student encounters are of three major kinds. The first is that by definition a "classical language" *qua* classical language has substantially different structures and vocabulary uses than does any of its modern counterparts. The basic classical language course aims to introduce the majority of those differences and provide guideposts to the acquisition of less frequent ones when those are encountered. The second difficulty is that all "classical" periods cover tremendous time depths. The time covered by the use of Latin as an actual tool of written communication exceeds two millennia. The time depth of the works collected in the Hebrew Bible alone covers over a millennium. And, of course, the time depth of written Chinese covers something around three and a half millennia, with the most important works being committed to writing beginning no later than twenty-five hundred years ago. Languages constantly change, and one adept at the language of one period is not necessarily fluent in reading the language of another period. Native speakers of either standard British or standard American English cannot read the Shakespeare of four hundred years ago without extensive footnotes, and the Chaucer of six hundred years ago is virtually a foreign language. If we have such difficulty with these relatively brief time periods in our native language, it is easily comprehensible why we need special instruction for different periods of Chinese.

The third difficulty has to do with the conventions and tools of scholarship that different time periods have imposed on the most treasured works of their tradition. In classical Hebrew the anachronistic insertion of vowels into sacred texts many hundreds of years after they were originally committed to writing has all by itself provided a livelihood for many generations of scholars because the presumed language that those vowel "points" were intended to reflect may or may not have ever existed, since the redactors were speculating centuries afterward on received pronunciations of written words whose spoken counterparts had already drastically changed. Similarly in Chinese, the pronunciation dictionaries (rhyme books and rhyme tables), the handbooks to Regulated Verse, the commentaries of various generations on the Classics and on other major works, the *congshu* (compendia of older or ancient books) and other collections, and the vast (but highly varied) practice of reproducing the works of the past with contemporary annotations not only on the revered text itself, but on one or more sets of annotations as well—all of this scholarly apparatus requires time and effort to master because it involves understanding not only the tool that each scholar devised but the contemporary audience that he was attempting to address and their language. The "research tools and methods" course that our more established graduate programs offer is designed to deal with this problem, which is not unique in nature to Chinese, but whose variegated complexity and volume probably is found only in this tradition.

Although there is often much talk about specialty training among graduate students (and far too frequently among their discipline-based mentors), the truth of the matter is that the specialty training—whether modernist or classical—is largely self-contained, readily defined, and generally easier to acquire than is the basic skill of reading. In short, we as a field already do pretty well in specialty training. Our problem is that we too often pretend it can be provided to people who have not yet become readers.

One further dimension of the unhappy tension between the discipline-based specialist and the language teacher has to do with the use of time spent abroad. Problems in training our specialists to assimilate into Chinese culture and in our basic language training are discussed above. Whether in Hong Kong, Taiwan, or the PRC, the area specialist who is already in the professoriat or who is in training to become a professor is likely to be living and interacting at the remotest possible distance from Chinese counterparts. The approach to China from a remote distance becomes symbiotic with a habit maintained by some (but not all) Chinese. Through its long history, China has developed a set of social functions and functionaries to deal with foreigners who could not handle the Chinese language and who did not want to make the adjustments necessary to become a full guest in that society. The much maligned (and very often justly maligned) *waiban* (external affairs office) system is simply the latest iteration of that cultural pattern. The crucial thing about that system—and the aspect that is most quickly misunderstood, even by China specialists—is that the *waiban* is merely the entry point for acquaintance with Chinese society; it is not intended to be the ending point. Much too often it is the ending point; where that is the case, there is a very clear signal of a lack of adaptability on one side or both.

In sum, the structure of our field speaks volumes about how language learning and actual interaction with the culture are matters to be picked up with the pursuit of the Ph.D. in a given discipline or subdiscipline (but are not to interfere with that more important task), and the time spent abroad is to be spent in specific research and in acquiring the tools for that specific research, and not first in learning to act properly as a foreigner in Chinese society. This structure and the attitudes that produced it and that are produced by it are the real sources of definition of language learning and teaching for sinologists. We have inadequate training in most of the language skills and in most of the cultural skills because in effect that is what the field truly wanted. The proficiency movement in foreign language teaching is directly aimed to combat that academic subcultural ethos, and the new requirements for the continuation of Title VI National Resource Centers were deliberately designed to decouple language training from the agenda that has certainly been reflected by the major trends in area studies since the end of World War II. As indicated above, so far it appears that the proficiency movement and the government's insistence on it have been the most favorable things for Chinese language teaching in several decades. The ultimate test, however, will come if and when the field as a whole decides that certification within the field depends on a stated level of language proficiency. For example, would the field tolerate and support a university that insisted that its graduate students in any discipline of China studies must reach a Foreign Service level 3 before being awarded the Ph.D.? Would the field tolerate and support a graduate program that even required a level 2? Ultimately, the seriousness with which language teaching is taken will be determined by such questions. In general, they have not even yet been engaged by the field as a whole, so the ultimate future of the role of language teaching and cultural preparation in the training of sinologists is still very much in doubt.

Recommendations

Based on the account above of Chinese language teaching, its problems, and its needs, I recommend the following as minimal steps for improvement:

• That the field suggest a minimum proficiency standard as measured on the FSI scale to be attained before obtaining a Ph.D. in any field of China studies. Level 2 (being able to conduct one's daily life in the target language) should be the goal in all four skills, and in those skills relevant to the individual's particular discipline and research interests level 3 (ability to conduct one's occupation in the target language) should be required. If there were a common understanding that this was an expectation of the Ph.D., the resources and moral support necessary in order to achieve these goals would be forthcoming. Also, a much better understanding of what it will take to reach these goals would develop than most of the field appears to have at this point.

• The undergraduate years are, of course, the crucial ones so far as language training is concerned, and greater emphasis should be placed on undergraduate language training, so that students are better prepared once they get to the Ph.D. level. Specifically to be recommended are the attainment of stated proficiency levels, preferably level 2, for both undergraduate majors in Chinese and for those who intend to specialize in China studies in a given discipline after graduation. Further, study abroad for at least a term in a course designed to provide maximal language enhancement should be an *expected* part of the undergraduate major in any China field. (Note that this definition of study abroad excludes anything of a junket nature, and it presumes that there will be much more coordination between language teaching in the United States and language teaching abroad, without the unfortunate consequences of having to set up our own language centers abroad and have them run by Americans.)

- Ph.D. programs in Chinese language, literature, and linguistics should require training in language teaching. The field should expect that those appointed to positions in language and literature departments will have substantial language teaching duties, and the practicing scholar in literature and linguistics shall have as part of his or her job definition active participation in language teaching and should expect to be rewarded for excellence in language teaching.

- The highest priority should be placed on relieving the terrible shortage of usable materials at the intermediate and advanced levels for training students in all four skills. Governmental and nongovernmental funding agencies should be made aware of this gap and of the need to provide continuous funding for the development of not only reading materials beyond the beginning level, but also materials for instruction in speaking, listening comprehension, and writing.

- Funding should be obtained for those practical sociolinguistic and cultural studies that will lead to a better and more systematic understanding of the ways in which the Chinese language is used in ordinary discourse, so that we can begin to instruct our students at a much earlier level in how to behave in a Chinese society and how to understand cultural cues.

- While the ACTFL effort in training teachers and oral proficiency testers appears to be achieving some success, we still lack an effective instrument with which to evaluate proficiency levels in the other skills that is sufficiently discrete at the lower levels of proficiency. The development of such an instrument should be a national priority.

Note

Portions of this chapter have been given as talks presented at the University of Oregon, the University of California at Berkeley, and the University of Arizona. I wish to thank those responsible for making these opportunities possible and the participants in the meetings where the talks were given for stimulating discussions.

References

Ch'en, Ta-tuan (T.T.), Perry Link, Yih-jian Tai, and Hai-tao Tang. 1989. *Chinese Primer.* Cambridge: Harvard University Press.

Li Peiyuan et al. 1981. *Modern Chinese Reader.* Shanghai: Commercial Press.

Li Tianmu (T. Light). 1987. *Xiandai Waiju Jiaoxuefa: shijian yu lilun* (Modern Foreign Language Teaching Methods: Theory and Practice). Beijing: Beijing Language Institute Press.

Light, Timothy, and Tao-Chung Yao. 1985. *The Character Book*. New Haven: Yale Far Eastern Publications.

Liu Xun and Yenling Li. Forthcoming. *Letter Writing Manual in Chinese*.

Liu Xun et al. 1988. *Practical Chinese Reader*. Beijing: Commercial Press.

Perkins, James, et al. 1979. *Strength through Wisdom*. Washington, D.C.: U.S. Government Printing Office.

Tung, P.C., and D.E. Pollard. 1982. *Colloquial Chinese*. London: Routledge and Kegan Paul.

Yao, T.C., and Scott McGinnis. 1989. *Let's Play Games in Chinese*. Lincolnwood, Ill.: National Textbook Company.

13

Library Resources for Contemporary China Studies

Eugene W. Wu

For more than four decades since the end of World War II, major American libraries have been diligent in their efforts to develop and maintain an essential corpus of research materials on contemporary China, including the history of the Chinese Communist movement.[1] Today, the combined strength of such resources in the United States is undoubtedly the greatest and the most comprehensive in the Western world. This chapter attempts to survey the past achievements, the present status, and the future prospects of the development of research resources on contemporary China in American libraries, and offers some recommendations.

Systematic collecting of primary sources for the study of the Chinese Communist movement by American libraries began in the late 1940s with the establishment of the Chinese Collection at the Hoover Institution and the appointment of the late Mary Clabaugh Wright as its curator. Having just been released from the Japanese internment camp at Weixian in Shandong province, Professor Wright traveled to all major cities in China in search of publications important to the study of twentieth-century China for the Hoover Institution. Her acquisitions in Yan'an yielded many rare contemporary Chinese Communist publications, the best known of which was probably a nearly complete set of *Jiefang ribao* (Liberation daily), 1941–47, the organ of the Chinese Communist Party. Later on, in the United States, she acquired the Harold Isaacs Collection and the Nym Wales Collection. The former consists mostly of underground Chinese Communist pamphlets and journals published (many were mimeographed) from the late 1920s to the early 1930s, and the latter includes a number of original Chinese Communist documents of the mid-1930s. The Hoover Institution's collection of Chinese Communist documentation was further enriched in 1960 when the present author, then curator of its East Asian Collection, arranged for and supervised the microfilming in Taiwan of the Chen Cheng Collection, consisting of some fifteen hundred Chinese Communist documents relating exclusively to the Jiangxi Soviet period just before the Long March.[2] These three collections and other related materials, especially those published during the Anti-Japanese War of Resistance (1937–45), which had also been collected by other American libraries, constituted the first body of primary sources for the study of the Chinese Communist movement in its early phase to become available in the United States.

The 1945–49 period saw the publication of many books, journals, and newspapers under the direct sponsorship of either the Chinese Communist Party or its front organizations. While the coverage of these publications by American libraries is by no means comprehensive, many of the more important sources, including those published in the Communist-controlled "border areas," are readily available. To these acquisitions have been added during the 1980s microfilms of some of the Chinese Communist journals and newspapers published in the 1930s and 1940s as well as many documentary compilations on the history of the CCP published for the first time in the PRC. American scholars have also had access since the early 1960s to several repositories of Chinese Communist documentation on Taiwan, the most important of which is the one-hundred-thousand-volume collection at the Library of the Bureau of Investigation of the Ministry of Justice, mostly dating from before 1949.

Since 1949, American libraries have maintained a rigorous acquisitions program of PRC publications on contemporary China. For purposes of discussion, this can be divided into the pre–Cultural Revolution and the post–Cultural Revolution phases.

During the first phase, from late 1949 to the late 1970s, it was not possible to purchase books directly from the PRC; instead orders had to be placed with dealers elsewhere, principally in Hong Kong and Tokyo. Local newspapers were not available by subscription to foreign libraries, and exchange was limited to the National Library of Beijing (since renamed the National Library of China). Although indirect buying was a nuisance at best, the dealers did offer all that was allowed for export. The problem was that many of the local publications were published in small print runs, and even when cleared for export, they were often difficult to obtain; and those having a *neibu* (internal) classification were not available at all, at least not officially. Furthermore, since commercial dealers depended on Chinese publishers for supply, the vicissitudes experienced by the Chinese publishing industry in those years naturally limited what and how much the dealers had to offer. For example, during the 1950s, when the Chinese publishing industry enjoyed a period of rapid expansion, the supply was plentiful in both volume and variety. However, when book production declined, because of either a shortage of material resources such as occurred throughout China in the early 1960s or political upheavals such as took place during the Cultural Revolution, the selection became first smaller and less diverse, and then practically nonexistent.[3] Exchange with the National Library alone proved unsatisfactory, since the items it provided were also easily available from book dealers, and its offering to American libraries never compared in either volume or variety with what it sent to libraries in the Soviet Union and Eastern Europe when China's relations with those areas were still friendly. These problems notwithstanding, during this period American libraries managed to build up impressive collections of research materials on the PRC. The listings in *Contemporary China: A Research Guide,* by Peter Berton and Eugene Wu (Stanford: Hoover Institution, 1967), attest to this achievement. In this effort American libraries benefited from the release of a number of PRC publications and documents in Hong Kong, Taiwan, and the United States. The Union Research Institute in Hong Kong maintained an excellent file of Chinese newspaper and journal clippings, which contained materials not then available in American libraries. From time to time the URI also made available PRC documents that had come into its possession. In Taiwan, the government released over a long period of time a large number of important CCP documents it had acquired. Among these releases, the many Central Committee directives, the "Lien-chiang Documents," the famous "571 Engineering Manual" (Lin Biao's crude plan for an armed uprising against Mao), and the *Mao Zedong sixiang wansui!* (Long live Mao Zedong thought!) volumes are probably the best known. Early in 1960, the U.S. government released its holdings of some twelve hundred pre-1960 Chinese local newspapers, many of them county- and subcounty-level publications, to the Library of Congress. While the great majority of these newspapers were incomplete and many were fragmentary (some containing just a few issues), the significance of this release cannot be overemphasized, since none of the publications were available for foreign subscription at the time, and they still are not today. In 1963, the State Department made another release to the Library of Congress, this one a set of Chinese military papers that *The China Quarterly* described as "the most illuminating first-hand material that scholars have had on the Chinese Communists since the Hoover Institution acquired the Yan'an Documents in the mid-forties."[4] The papers consisted of twenty-nine issues of the secret military journal *Gongzuo tongxun* (Bulletin of activities), covering the period from January 1 to August 26, 1961. Edited and published by the General Political Department of the People's Liberation Army, the bulletin was distributed to officers at the regimental level or above, with the top-secret issues distributed only to divisional commanders.[5]

The severe disruption of the publishing industry brought about by the Cultural Revolution has been noted above. The almost complete halt in the publication of scholarly and research works during those years forced American libraries to place a high premium on the collecting of all kinds of Red Guard publications. Although some of these materials are highly polemical, most contain a great deal of valuable information not available elsewhere at the time. For example, there are directives from all levels of the party and speeches by party leaders, including a good many by Mao Zedong, all from this period; "negative materials" on those being purged; documents on party history; and "news flashes" on people and current events. Initially, libraries competed with each other in the acquisition of the limited amount of such material available in Hong Kong, and prices soared. At the request of China scholars, the State Department agreed to release its collection of Red guard materials to the academic community. The releases were first made through the Harvard-Yenching Library, and then made to the Center for Chinese Research Materials (CCRM) after its establishment in 1968. In 1975, the CCRM reproduced these releases, along with some additional materials acquired from other sources, under the title *Red Guard Publications* in nineteen volumes for general distribution; in 1979 a general table of contents to the nineteen volumes was also issued. Another eight volumes were published as a supplement the following year. Together they represent the single largest collection of Red Guard publications available in the Western world. A modest amount of additional Red Guard publications has become available during the last few years. They, too, will be reproduced by CCRM for distribution.

Since the late 1970s, Chinese publishing has undergone a remarkable quantitative and qualitative transformation. In this post–Cultural Revolution period, the Chinese publishing industry not only regained its vitality but also began to publish more objective and scholarly research.[6] Documentary compilations, memoirs of party leaders, new journals, specialty newspapers, and scholarly works that for one reason or another could not be published in the past have all appeared in quantity, and the quality of many of the research publications has shown a remarkable improvement in depth of treatment and diversity of approach. New types of publications such as yearbooks, statistics, and legal materials also have proliferated.[7] One serial publication that merits special mention is the *Fuyin baokan ziliao* (Reprints of newspaper and periodical articles) issued by the Chinese People's University. This series began publication in the 1950s for internal use and was made available for foreign subscription in 1978. These facsimile reprints, originally covering only twenty-two topics, have been expanded to cover over a hundred, with articles selected from two thousand newspapers and periodicals published in the PRC. While articles on all aspects of contemporary Chinese affairs are included, those concerning military affairs were omitted from the public offering until 1989. Most volumes in the series are monthly publications, and each issue carries its own index. There is also a cumulative annual index. The importance of this publication lies in its wide coverage, which includes articles selected from *neibu* newspapers and periodicals that are not available for foreign subscription. It is also extremely convenient for users, since articles on a given subject, published in a variety of sources, are grouped together in handy volumes. However, the selection process is subject to the prevailing political climate at any given time. For example, before the 1989 prodemocracy movement, articles selected for the volumes on *Zhongguo zhengzhi* (Chinese politics) included those by people like Yan Jiaqi and Su Shaozhi on political reform, but, during and since the movement, the selection has been limited to those supporting the party and the government.

On the acquisitions side, since the late 1970s direct purchases from China have become routine; Chinese libraries are now permitted and are eager to enter into exchange arrangements with foreign libraries; some local newspapers, mostly on the provincial level, are available for foreign subscription for the first time; Chinese book fairs have been held in China and abroad; visitors are free to purchase publications in state-run stores as well as at privately managed book stalls that are set up on sidewalks in many major cities; and most visiting scholars are accorded the privilege of photocopying at their host institutions.

Yet, against this encouraging background of vast improvement, certain old problems in procurement linger and some new ones have surfaced. The old problems concern *neibu* materials, local publications, and local newspapers. The wide and continuing use of the *neibu* classification on many publications means that once a book is so classified, it does not get listed in dealers' catalogues; and even when sent on exchange by a Chinese library, it is invariably stopped by customs and returned to its sender. The trouble with local publications seems to be that none of the local publishing houses is either equipped to sell directly overseas or is permitted to do so by the Chinese government because of regulations governing foreign-exchange transactions. Foreign libraries have to depend on the few national book-export corporations for supply. Since local publications are usually issued in small editions, even when they are listed in the catalogues, supply is not always guaranteed. A further complication here is that a publisher is free to withdraw a book from publication after announcement, if advance sales are insufficient to guarantee a profit. As for local newspapers, while almost all provincial dailies are now available, the ban against the export of subprovincial-level publications remains; and not all city newspapers are available for foreign subscription.[8]

Chief among the new problems are the quality of service provided by the book-export corporations in China, the problems arising from exchanges, and the difficulty of acquiring out-of-print publications. In our dealings with the export corporations, it is not uncommon to place an order only to learn six to twelve months later, if ever, that the order cannot be filled. In the meantime, one often misses the opportunity to obtain a copy from another source while it is still available. This is a particularly serious problem with regard to local publications in limited supply. The problem with exchange is that the price differential between American and Chinese publications is such that no Chinese library would agree to any exchange based on equal value. For the same reason, American libraries are unwilling to enter into any agreement that is purely on a volume-for-volume basis. Consequently, exchanges are conducted on a "gentlemen's agreement" basis, with each side exercising its own discretion as to what constitutes a fair trade. While some Chinese libraries do oblige requests for publications issued in their respective localities, the standard exchange offerings, more often than not, consist of publications from national publishing houses that are easily available from commercial sources. Last, while it was always difficult to search for out-of-print publications in China, the situation has not improved now that we are able to deal directly with the export companies. Given the problems just described, American libraries have supplemented the usual and more formal channels of acquisition by relying heavily on the assistance of individuals who travel to China and on personal relationships formed with Chinese colleagues. These private contacts have been very productive, and will certainly continue to be a significant factor in the further development of research resources for the study of contemporary China in the years to come.

At present, there are some sixty libraries in the United States that are collecting Chinese-language publications from the PRC, Taiwan, and other Chinese-speaking areas. But not all maintain the same degree of comprehensiveness in coverage or the same collecting intensity. The larger and better-funded libraries naturally achieve a wider coverage and acquire more materials than the others. Generally speaking, all libraries, regardless of size, concentrate on publications in the social sciences and the humanities; natural science and technical materials are not collected except reference tools, principally dictionaries, and those publications, mostly journals, that are received as gifts or on exchange.

Are we keeping up with the current output of publications from the PRC? The answer is a qualified yes, if we consider only those publications on the contemporary period that are allowed for export. According to official statistics for 1989, the latest year for which detailed figures are available, the total number of publications in China that year was 74,973 titles (including 55,476 new publications and 19,498 reprints) under the following categories: books, 57,476 titles (45,432 new, 12,042 reprints); textbooks, 11,706 titles (4,721 new, 6,985 reprints); and pictorial materials, 5,791 titles (5,320 new, 471 reprints).[9] In addition, 6,078 periodicals and 1,576 newspapers were published. Table 13.1 shows their coverage by subject.

How do we measure up, in view of these figures? On the basis of information from nine Chinese collections in the United States (Harvard, Columbia, Yale, Princeton, Chicago, Michigan, University of California at Berkeley, Hoover Institution, and University of Washington), the average number of books acquired from the PRC in 1989 was around 5,300 titles (from a low of 2,400 to a high of 8,000, with most clustering around 5,000 to 6,000); the average number of periodicals was 942 (from 496 to 1,279, including four subscribing to over 1,000, and two, 900); and the average number of newspapers was 42 (from 10 to 123).[10] As already mentioned, East Asian libraries usually do not collect in the natural sciences and technology, or textbooks; pictorial materials are collected only highly selectively. Excluding these categories, the number of books (new titles and reprints) in the social sciences and humanities published in 1989 would have been 51,856, and of periodicals, 2,674. Using these adjusted figures for a comparison, we find that these nine libraries were collecting from 4.63 percent to 15.48 percent of the 51,856 books; from 18.54 percent to 47.83 percent of the 2,674 periodicals; and from 0.63 percent to 7.80 percent of the 1,576 newspapers.

Table 13.1

Publications, 1989

	Number of Titles
Books, by Subject	
Philosophy and Social Sciences	12,426
Culture and Education	25,541
Literature and Arts	13,889
Natural Science and Technology	14,977
Pictorial Materials	5,791
General	2,349
Total	74,973
Periodicals, by Subject	
Philosophy and Social Sciences	1,359
Culture and Education	653
Literature and Arts	662
Natural Science and Technology	3,019
Juvenalia	83
Pictorial Materials	81
General	221
Total	6,078
Newspapers, by Type	
Central (National)	138
Provincial and Municipal	714
County and Specialty	724
Total	1,576

However, the following should be kept in mind while looking at these comparisons: (1) the publications figures include works on both the contemporary and the earlier periods; (2) not all books published are allowed for export; (3) American libraries collect only selectively in popular contemporary fiction and translations of foreign literature, both of which have proliferated since the Cultural Revolution (the Library of Congress, as a matter of policy, does not collect any translations at all); and (4) among the large number of reprints that were issued, it is very likely that many were already collected by American libraries at the time of their first publication. What all this means is that, as far as books on the contemporary period are concerned, our coverage is definitely far better than the percentage figures here would indicate. But there remains the question of *neibu* material and local publications, to which we shall return shortly.

As far as periodicals are concerned, our coverage is excellent. While more than 6,000 titles were published in 1989, less than half were made available for foreign subscription. The 1989 catalog of the China National Publishing Industry Trading Corporation (CNPITC) offered only 2,501 titles for this purpose, with about 41 percent in the natural sciences and technology. Since few or none of the scientific and technological periodicals were subscribed to by any of the nine libraries surveyed, their average receipt of 942 titles, the vast majority being in the social sciences and humanities, is a worthy record indeed.

As for newspapers, the record is not nearly so good. The 1989 CNPITC catalog lists 136 newspapers for which they will accept foreign orders, including the once-classified *Jiefangjun bao* (Liberation Army news).[11] About half the titles offered were national, provincial, and city newspapers, and the other half specialty newspapers, each devoted to a single subject such as marketing, advertising, broadcasting, health, shipping, textiles, laws, women, or athletics. County newspapers were not, and still are not, offered at all. The 136 titles represent 8.63 percent of the 1,576 newspapers published in 1989. Compared to this, the nine libraries' average receipt of 42 titles can only be considered fairly satisfactory.

In conclusion, it may be said that while there is much more that can be accomplished, American libraries collectively have done a remarkable job in the development of research resources on contemporary China, given the constraints imposed by the availability of materials and ever-shrinking acquisitions budgets. The following examines the areas in which action could be taken to improve and ensure the continuing health of our collection development programs in support of contemporary China studies.

Coverage

Our coverage of PRC publications on the contemporary period could and should be widened. Even though our basic source of supply will continue to be the export corporations, there are several other ways that we can achieve a wider coverage. Libraries with existing exchange relationships with Chinese libraries should insist that their exchange partners send only local publications from their respective regions, including those published by their own university presses, if such exist. Libraries not engaged in exchanges may wish to do so as a means to increase their acquisition of local publications. Chinese bibliographers or acquisitions libraries of large Chinese collections should be able to make frequent trips to China, not only to search out publications but also to develop personal contacts with publishers, book corporations, and Chinese scholars and librarians. Experience indicates that books that are hard to get from dealers can often be obtained from local bookstores or street vendors. Negotiations conducted in person are always more effective than correspondence. Research and editorial offices as well as university libraries also have proved a rich source for out-of-print book and journals. Many are reluctant or not equipped to send such materials to a foreign library, but most are willing to accommodate personal requests made in situ in return for some form of exchange arrangements.

Libraries that are not already doing so will find it useful to search out and acquire documentary collections and monographs on contemporary China from other countries, especially Japan and Taiwan. (It is assumed that American libraries' coverage of Western-language publications on contemporary China is adequate.) Some important journals and monographs published in Japan on contemporary China may be missed by Chinese collections, since very few Chinese bibliographers look at Japanese catalogues and Japanese bibliographers usually pay attention only to materials related to Japan. While the volume of PRC documentation through Taiwan has been reduced in recent years, some very significant materials continue to be available. For example, a large number of unofficial magazines and wall posters of the late 1970s and early 1980s have been reproduced in Taipei under the title *Ta-lu ti-hsia k'an-wu hui-pian* (A collection of Chinese mainland underground publications), of which twenty volumes have so far been published. Acquisitions of this type should certainly enhance our research capabilities on contemporary China.

Other types of research sources that we have traditionally ignored are audiovisual materials and ephemeral publications. While different in form, these materials are no less important than printed books and are sometimes even more valuable to a research scholar. Photographs, video and audio tapes, mimeographed handbills, appeals, and pamphlets of the 1989 prodemocracy movement in the PRC are good examples. These materials lend a sense of immediacy that cannot be easily conveyed by the printed text. The East Asian libraries at Harvard, Columbia, Chicago, UCLA, Yale, and the New York Public Library have each established a "Tiananmen Archives" containing such materials. If the collecting can be extended backward in time to cover other major political movements in the PRC since 1949, such as the Cultural Revolution and the Anti-Rightist Campaign, we will have greatly enriched our library collections for contemporary China studies.

"Neibu" Materials

Neibu is a generic term used for publications not meant for public distribution, but not all *neibu* publications are "secret" or "classified" in the Western security sense. Many scholarly publications, translations, and even reference works, the publication of which has circumvented the official channels, bear the *neibu* designation.[12] Some university presses in China have further complicated the situation. In an effort to keep some of their publications away from central distribution abroad by the government-designated export corporations, they have resorted to using the *neibu* label to gain control over their own distribution overseas.

Generally speaking, there are two basic categories on the *neibu* classification: *neibu faxing* (internal distribution) and *xian guonei faxing* (for domestic distribution only). Under the first are also subcategories such as *neibu wenjian* (internal documents), *neibu ziliao* (internal material), *neibu cankao* (internal reference), *neibu duwu* (internal reading material), *neibu kongzhi faxing* (controlled internal distribution), and *dangxiao xitong neibu faxing* (internal distribution within the party school system), but in most cases, only the generic term *"neibu faxing"* is used. Preliminary drafts of books marked as *zhengqiu yijian kao* (drafts for the solicitation of comments) also fall under the *neibu* category, as do other *shiyongben* (trial editions) of publications. While all *neibu* publications are issued in short press runs and are not officially available, some of them, as has been mentioned, do find their way to the outside world. Reprint publishers in Hong Kong offer them for sale from time to time (at a not insignificant price) and increasingly more have been available from private sources in the United States and other countries as well. The problem so far has been one of knowing what has been acquired, and of making the materials more readily available to the scholarly community at large. The Center for Chinese Research Materials (CCRM) in Virginia (formerly in Washington, D.C.), a not-for-profit organization, has already reproduced some two hundred titles of *neibu* publications.[13] But at present the CCRM does not have sufficient manpower to search out the many others that are scattered in various places.

Therefore, there is an urgent need to establish some sort of clearinghouse of information so that the existence of materials may be made known to scholars and the materials made available for reproduction. The recently launched *CCP Research Newsletter* (editor, Timothy Cheek) serves this purpose admirably. The *Newsletter* is designed to disseminate research information and critical notes on sources, primarily *neibu* publications, and their interpretation among scholars doing research on the pre-1949 Chinese Communist movement, the PRC party/state, and the post-Mao reform of socialism.[14] Arrangements have been made with the CCRM to reproduce publications mentioned in the *Newsletter*. Individual scholars and libraries, having come upon any *neibu* publications, are encouraged to transmit that information to the *Newsletter* for publication and to lend the materials to the CCRM for reproduction and wider distribution. The *CCP Research Newsletter* and the CCRM provide the best vehicle available to us for sharing our collection of *neibu* publications.

Resource Sharing

The publishing explosion, the devaluation of the American dollar, and the spiraling costs of maintaining research collections have made self-sufficiency of research libraries a thing of the past. Resource sharing has now become the cardinal principle in collection development. The introduction of automation in libraries and the creation of library networks have further hastened and facilitated this concept of mutual dependence. The experience of East Asian libraries indicates that, while a national cooperative program in acquisitions may not be practical, a great deal can be achieved on a regional basis. The example of the University of California at Berkeley and Stanford is a good case in point. The East Asian Library at Berkeley and the East Asian Collection of the Hoover

Institution at Stanford have instituted cooperative acquisitions programs for Chinese newspapers and local histories, and they consult each other when considering purchases of expensive materials. A similar program is now in effect among the six East Asian libraries on the East Coast, Columbia, Cornell, Harvard, Princeton, Yale, and the New York Public Library. Under this program, each takes primary responsibility for collecting available periodicals and newspapers as well as other publications of a local nature that fall into the respective areas of their collecting responsibility. These cases illustrate the advantage of a realistic and practical regional approach to collection building that will provide more in-depth collecting with little or no increase in budget. Resource sharing calls for better communication and coordination among libraries. Fortunately, automation has made possible the instantaneous transmission of information on access through library networks.

Library Automation

There are now two national networks that are capable of processing Chinese-, Japanese-, and Korean-language (CJK) materials: the Research Libraries Information Network (RLIN) and the Online Computer Library Center (OCLC). The RLIN CJK system, introduced by the Research Libraries Group (RLG) in 1983, now has more than one million CJK records in its database (all with vernacular scripts), of which more than four hundred thousand are unique Chinese titles. There are currently thirty-three East Asian libraries using the RLIN CJK system, including three in Canada and one in Germany. OCLC has more than 680,000 unique records in its CJK database, of which more than 328,000 are Chinese titles. Of this total, more than 235,000 records contain Chinese characters, and more than 92,000 in romanization only. There are thirty-four East Asian libraries using the OCLC CJK system, including one each in Hong Kong and Taiwan, and two in Australia. In both databases, records for Chinese books published in the 1980s account for 53 percent and 55 percent respectively of the RLIN CJK and OCLC CJK totals. The Library of Congress catalogues its East Asian materials into the RLIN CJK database and a tape is available to OCLC for the latter's use. RLIN and OCLC exchange their CJK records directly.

The two available systems provide excellent bibliographical control over current imprints, but they do not cover retrospective publications. In other words, the vast majority of American East Asian libraries' holdings remain outside automated control, and researchers by necessity must continue to consult the manual catalogues. Now that the technology is in place, a national effort should be mounted to seek funding for a retrospective conversion project to convert the manual records into machine-readable form.

As mentioned above, bibliographical data of current imprints can now be easily retrieved from the databases. What we might also consider as a further step is "full-text processing" by which entire books are made computer-accessible, which would permit the texts to be searched. Many Western-language publications are now available on CD-ROMs (Compact Disk–Read-Only Memory), especially reference works and indexes. In Chinese, there is the outstanding example of the Twenty-Five Dynastic Histories Database jointly developed by the Institute of History and Philology of Academia Sinica in Taipei and the academy's Computer Center. This full-text database, consisting of some sixty million Chinese characters, which make up the entire text of the twenty-five dynastic histories, can be searched for personal names, place names, phrases, and so on. The time and effort it will save future generations of scholars is certainly immeasurable. This database has been installed at the East Asian Library at the University of Washington and at the Harvard-Yenching Library at Harvard University. Of course, it would be impossible and unnecessary to computerize everything with "full-text processing," but the technology can be employed to process selective types of materials important to contemporary China research.

Research Tools

While computerized databases can provide valuable information on holdings and print out lists of publications by subject, the importance of carefully compiled research tools such as annotated subject bibliographies, research guides, indexes, and the like will not diminish. For example, Peter Berton and Eugene Wu's *Contemporary China: A Research Guide* should be updated—its coverage ends with 1964, and a supplement should be compiled to cover the later periods, perhaps in two parts, one on the Cultural Revolution years, and another on the post-Mao period. The twenty-volume collection of *Red Guard Publications* and its eight-volume supplement, both reproduced by CCRM, will require a subject index more detailed than the guide to selected contents compiled by Hong Yung Lee published by M.E. Sharpe. Union lists of PRC periodicals and newspapers likewise should be published, preferably with detailed holdings information. Other annotated subject bibliographies should be considered, as should checklists of special types of publications such as yearbooks, laws and statutes, demographic compilations, and the like.[15]

In conclusion, it may be said that American libraries have accomplished much during the last four decades in building up an impressive amount of research materials for contemporary China studies. Looking to the future, it seems that they should do at least as well, as China continues to publish more and American libraries move forward to further strengthen their collections. It is true that, since the prodemocracy movement, there has been a decrease in the kind of research and publication that we witnessed during the 1980s. But unless the present strict enforcement of ideological control over scholarship and publication becomes permanent policy, it is reasonable to assume, judging from the history of publishing in the PRC, that once that control is relaxed, we will once again witness the appearance of a variety of new and exciting research sources. When that happens, and when more Chinese scholars again venture into the more controversial areas of research, such as those related to the history of the Chinese Communist Party, the assessment of Mao's leadership in the Chinese Revolution, the debates on reforms and so forth, new documentary evidence and other primary sources are bound to be introduced and new publications to appear. During the 1980s, we saw a large group of such materials being published, including new sources on the Zunyi Conference, documentary histories of the Communist movement in various provinces, biographies of party leaders, eyewitness accounts of important historical events such as Li Rui's *Lushan huiyi shilu* (A veritable record of the Lushan conference), and new texts of Mao's writings and speeches. It seems likely that the cycle will repeat itself when more favorable conditions obtain. Of course, it will remain unrealistic to expect, for instance, that the Central Party Archive would be open at any time in the future, but there is also no reason to believe that the practice of releasing historical documentation to justify policy will become a thing of the past.[16]

What is the implication of all this for American scholarship? For one thing, information we already have from such sources made available in the 1980s will be helpful in bridging the gaps in our knowledge and understanding of people and events in the People's Republic. Such information will create a new context in which to reassess our past findings. Surmises may now be confirmed or rejected in some cases, and once unreliable data corrected in others. Research on topics heretofore impossible to undertake for lack of sources may now be attempted. But there is the problem of an embarrassment of riches. When researchers find themselves faced with a huge harvest of new materials, more care will have to be exercised to separate the wheat from the chaff, a task that will take more time and research. For example, the biographical literature of party leaders enables us to gain much insight into the personalities and styles of the people under study, and adds considerable detail to our knowledge of the events in which they had personal involvement. But the inherent bias of this genre of writing requires one to cross-check certain information found in these publications with other sources. While the Chinese newspaper and periodical press of the 1980s became much more open and no longer published just articles publicizing current policies, but also made room for some debates on alternatives, it is important to know the editorial policy of the sponsoring bodies of these publications. Generally speaking, publications sponsored by academic research institutes during this period tended to be more analytical and independent in their approach to public policy questions than publications sponsored by the party or government ministries or agencies. The latter tended to view problems more from ideological or organizational perspectives and parochial interests.

As an aid to the use of newspapers and periodicals, publications such as the *Zhongguo baokan daquan* (Directory of Chinese newspapers and periodicals) (Beijing: Renmin youdian chubanshe, 1987) are very useful. This two-volume publication lists sixteen hundred newspapers and fifty-three hundred periodicals published in China in 1987, complete with bibliographical information for each entry, including the name of the sponsoring organization, a brief account of the history of the publication and its scope, and whether it is a *neibu* publication.

Also, among the large amount of statistical data that has been made available, census reports and other demographic data are found to be most reliable. Economic statistics, however, pose certain problems of interpretation, as economists have discovered that the sources that provide such data do not make explicit such information as the definition of categories, procedures used in data collecting, or the purpose for which the data were collected. In some cases, the rich descriptive materials in the various provincial and local yearbooks can be of help in this respect. Other documentary collections of laws and regulations, and handbooks regarding foreign trade, private enterprises, factory management, and other areas, are very informative on economic reform of the 1980s, but most suffer from the ephemeral nature of their contents, since the laws and regulations and such are subject to frequent change from time to time, and from place to place. Thus, the time- and locale-specific nature of these publications is a very important consideration in their use. The above are merely a few examples of the weaknesses of some of the large outpouring of research materials we have from China during the 1980s. While the documentary basis of contemporary China studies will continue to be the norm, it must be supplemented by empirical data gathered from on-site field investigations. Questions such as the degree to which central government directives are implemented at the local level, the interaction between the masses and party cadres, and the social behavior of small groups or whole communities all have to be studied in situ and cannot be adequately understood merely through documents.

The challenge for American libraries is how to further strengthen their collections on contemporary China—not only on the so-called reform decade of the 1980s, but on the entire period of the People's Republic since its founding in 1949—and how to make them more easily accessible to support contemporary China studies.

The following highlights some of the ways in which this can be accomplished, most of which have been briefly mentioned earlier in this essay:

Acquisitions. In order to increase the breadth and depth of our collections, there should be more regional cooperative acquisitions programs for the purpose of resource sharing. The programs that have already been developed between the University of California and the Hoover Institution and among Harvard, Columbia, Yale, Princeton, Cornell, and the New York Public Library can serve as models. The collecting of ephemeral and audiovisual materials should be improved. Individual scholars and libraries should be willing to lend hard-to-get publications, including *neibu* materials, to the Center for Chinese Research Materials for reproduction and distribution. Chinese studies librarians should be encouraged to develop professional contacts in and to make periodic acquisitions trips to China in order to acquire materials that cannot be obtained otherwise.

Access. National library networks now provide easy intellectual access to library collections. However, currently available databases of Chinese-language materials include only publications catalogued since 1984, at the earliest, and the vast majority of East Asian libraries' collections remain outside automated control. Since this is a massive undertaking requiring substantial funding, and libraries do not have the means to do it, a national retrospective conversion program should be mounted for this purpose with government and foundation support. Technology should also be employed to speed up interlibrary loans and to facilitate document delivery such as facsimile transmission of journal articles.

The ultimate in access for American scholars and libraries would, of course, be the ability to find out what is available in libraries in the PRC, and to have physical access to their collections. For this purpose, it is to be hoped that some cooperative arrangements can be worked out between Chinese and American libraries to produce machine-readable records of the Chinese libraries' holdings that can then be added to American databases such as RLIN and OCLC. The agreement between the National Library of China and OCLC to have the former's 130,000-title collection of books published during the Republican period (1911–49) catalogued into the OCLC database shows how this can be accomplished.

Bibliographical Research. A systematic bibliographical research program should be initiated, preferably under the guidance of a national committee, to produce research tools on contemporary China studies such as annotated subject bibliographies, union lists of newspapers and periodicals, indexes, and other reference aids.

American libraries have come a long way in developing research resources for the study of contemporary China since the Hoover Institution pioneered the way in the late 1940s. What we have accomplished did not come easily or by accident. It is the result of careful planning backed up by a firm commitment by university administrations with generous financial support. The future success of the American study of contemporary China will require, as part of the centerpiece, the continuing and expanded development of library resources. That is the heart of the matter.

Notes

1. Parts of this essay are based on the author's chapter, "Contemporary China Studies: The Question of Sources," in *The Secret Speeches of Chairman Mao, From the Hundred Flowers to the Great Leap Forward,* ed. Roderick MacFarquhar, Timothy Cheek, and Eugene Wu (Cambridge: Harvard Council on East Asian Studies, 1989), 59–73.
2. All items in the Harold Isaacs Collection and those in the Nym Wales Collection are listed in Chün-tu Hsüeh, *The Chinese Communist Movement, 1921–1937, An Annotated Bibliography of Selected Materials in the Chinese Collection of the Hoover Institution on War, Revolution, and Peace* (Palo Alto, Calif.: Hoover Institution, 1960), and its

sequel, *The Chinese Communist Movement, 1937–1949, An Annotated Bibliography of Selected Materials in the Chinese Collection of the Hoover Institution on War, Revolution, and Peace* (Palo Alto, Calif.: Hoover Institution, 1962).

For a bibliography and complete checklist of all the documents in the Chen Cheng Collection, see Tien-wei Wu, *The Kiangsi Soviet Republic, 1931–1934, A Selected and Annotated Bibliography of the Chen Cheng Collection* (Cambridge: Harvard-Yenching Library, 1981).

3. The fluctuations in publishing activities in the PRC are shown by the following statistics (book figures include both new and reprint editions): in 1958, a total of 45,495 books, 822 periodicals, and 491 newspapers were published; in 1961, the numbers were reduced to 13,529 books, 410 periodicals, and 260 newspapers, down by 70.26 percent, 50.12 percent, and 47.04 percent respectively; in 1967, one year after the start of the Cultural Revolution, production dropped precipitously to 2,925 books, 27 periodicals, and 43 newspapers (excluding Red Guard tabloids), representing a further reduction of 78.37 percent, 93.41 percent, and 83.46 percent against the 1961 figures. See *Zhongguo chuban nianjian 1985* (China publishing yearbook 1985) (Beijing: Shangwu yinshuguan, 1986), 744, 750.

4. *China Quarterly*, no. 18 (April–June 1964): 67.

5. For an English translation of the papers, see J. Chester Cheng, ed., *The Politics of the Chinese Red Army: A Translation of the Bulletin of Activities of the People's Liberation Army* (Stanford: Hoover Institution, 1966). For analyses of the documents, see John Wilson Lewis, "China's Secret Military Papers: 'Continuities' and 'Revelations,'" *China Quarterly*, no. 18 (April–June 1964): 68–78; Alice Langley Hsieh, "China's Secret Military Papers: Military Doctrines and Strategy," ibid., 79–99; and J. Chester Cheng, "Problems of Chinese Military Leadership as Seen in the Secret Military Papers," *Asian Survey* (June 1964): 861–72.

6. Book production increased from 17,212 titles in 1979 to 45,603 titles in 1985, periodicals from 1,470 to 4,705, and newspapers from 69 to 698 for the same period. See Zhongguo guojia tongji ju, comp., *Zhongguo tongji nianjian 1986* (China statistical yearbook 1986) (Beijing: Zhongguo tongji chuban she, 1986), 781–82.

7. See, for instance, Barry Naughton, "The Chinese Economy: New Sources and Data"; William R. Lavely, "Chinese Demographic Data: A Guide to Major Sources"; and Tao-tai Hsia and Wendy Zeldin, "Legislation and Legal Publications in the PRC," *China Exchange News* 15 (September–December 1987): 8–16.

8. The Universities Service Centre (USC) in Hong Kong, now a part of the Chinese University of Hong Kong, managed to acquire in 1987 from China complete sets of 39 Chinese national, provincial, and municipal newspapers published from 1950 to 1987 (some date from 1949). This is now the largest and most complete collection of Chinese local newspapers available anywhere outside of China. USC has begun microfilming this newspaper collection for general distribution. Inquiries may be sent directly to the Universities Services Centre, Chinese University of Hong Kong, Shatin, N.T., Hong Kong.

9. Information by courtesy of the China National Publishing Industry Trading Corporation (CNPITC). The latest available edition of *Zhongguo chuban nianjian* (China publishing yearbook) was published in 1991, containing information only for 1988. Figures include both new publications and reprints. Separate figures are not available.

10. The Library of Congress is excluded from this count because LC figures, if included, would skew the picture and make the tabulation less meaningful. Official LC statistics show that in fiscal year 1990 the LC received a total of 15,070 titles of books from the PRC (9,554 by exchange or gift and 5,516 by purchase). The receipts were in all categories, including a large number of scientific and technical publications, textbooks, minority-language materials, "how-to" types of publications, etc. Since it is not possible

to separate these from the social science and humanities publications the LC does keep, and because of the considerable number of duplicates involved, it is wise not to include LC figures in the count here. The LC currently has subscriptions to 1,835 periodicals from the PRC, plus some additional titles which it received with varying degrees of regularity as gifts or on exchange. The LC also receives 30 newspapers from the PRC.

11. The *Liberation Army News* was first offered in 1987, and American libraries' holdings date from that time. The University of Heidelberg, Germany, recently acquired a complete set of this newspaper from China, and the Australian National University also has acquired a set covering the period from 1977 to 1986.

12. See Li Paoguang and Zhao Huachun, comps., *Quanguo neibu faxing tushu zongmu, 1949–1986* (National bibliography of internally distributed works, 1949–1986) (Beijing: Zhonghua shuju, 1988). The bibliography covers 17,754 first editions and 547 revised editions. For a review of this publication, see Flemming Christiansen, "The *Neibu* Bibliography: A Review Article," *CCP Research Newsletter* 4 (Fall–Winter 1989–90):13–19. See also Liu Changyun, "A Preliminary Analysis of the Characteristics of *Neibu* Materials in the Social Sciences," ibid., 20–21. This is a translation of "Shehui kexue neibu ziliao tetian shixi," *Qingbao ziliao gongzuo* (Information and materials work) (March 1985), 18–19.

13. Inquiries concerning these reproductions may be sent to the Center for Chinese Research Materials, P.O. Box 3090, Oakton, VA, 22124.

14. Published by the Chinese Communism Research Group, Colorado College, 14 E. Cache La Poudre, Colorado Springs, CO, 80903.

15. *Current Yearbooks Published in the People's Republic of China*, including holdings of East Asian libraries at Berkeley, the Hoover Institution, Harvard, Columbia, Cornell, Yale, the New York Pubic Library, and the Universities Service Centre at the Chinese University of Hong Kong, was published by the Center for Chinese Studies Library of the University of California, Berkeley, in 1991. An updated edition is in preparation.

16. The Standing Committee of the Sixth National People's Congress passed an archives law at its 22d meeting, August 28–September 5, 1987, which provides that "state archives will generally be open to the public after 30 years." The law, which became effective on January 1, 1988, also stipulates, inter alia, that "archives related to state security or other major national interests, as well as those unsuitable for the public, can remain confidential after 30 years" (see *Beijing Review* 30 [September 21, 1987]: 6). According to another report, "China has already opened to the public more than 3,000 of its archives recording events before Liberation in 1949" (see *Ta Kung Pao English Weekly*, December 24, 1987).

14

Scholarly Exchange and American China Studies

Mary Brown Bullock

One of the surprises of the late twentieth century is the extraordinary renewal and resilience of intellectual ties between the United States and the People's Republic of China. On the eve of China's Tiananmen tragedy, more than forty thousand Chinese students and scholars were studying in the United States, more than two hundred American universities enjoyed reciprocal agreements with Chinese institutions, and genuinely collaborative research in the social and natural sciences was beginning to flourish. In less than two decades, American scholarly exchange with China had evolved from an abstract dream to an accelerating reality. The events of 1989 initially halted this momentum. Yet, despite continuing ideological constraints and some restrictions on American research in China, scholarly relations between the United States and the People's Republic of China were flourishing in 1993 (Bullock 1991; Strevy 1990). By some estimates nearly eighty thousand Chinese students and visiting scholars now reside in the United States.

During the twenty-year period since the 1972 Shanghai Communiqué "facilitated academic relationships," the premises, issues, and underlying institutional structure of scholarly exchange with China have dramatically changed. The tightly monitored delegation visits of the early 1970s grew into a normalized pattern of highly differentiated individual and institutional relationships. Early models of academic exchange were modified as China's political and intellectual circles behaved pluralistically and became more supportive of an American research presence in China. This transition away from "scholarly tourism" paralleled the reemergence of a vibrant and needy Chinese intellectual community that urged that "exchange" also include rebuilding an institutional infrastructure decimated by the Cultural Revolution. Today "scholarly exchanges" encompass everything from short-term undergraduate language training to complex collaborative research to large-scale educational assistance programs.

Within this broad panoply, the American China studies community has been primarily concerned with graduate and faculty research and language training, though China specialists have been involved in all aspects of educational relations. Denied access to China for a quarter of a century, the China studies community was initially concerned with the need to gain access to the "real China." (For scholarly issues during this earlier period, see Cohen 1987.) Theories about China developed from a distance—Hong Kong, Taiwan, Japan, and the United States—needed to be tested by the realities of China itself. Earlier chapters in this volume attest to the degree to which access to the mainland now informs the American study of contemporary China. From a research agenda dictated from the periphery is emerging a China-centered field. "Exchanges" too have moved from the institutional margins to become an integrated part of most university and China center programs.

Exchange Models

Several models of intercultural relations significantly influenced U.S.-China intellectual relations, including American experiences with the Soviet Union, Taiwan, and Hong Kong, though it has been the underlying, uniquely Sino-American historical legacy that has ultimately prevailed.

A full range of American intellectual interests in China was demonstrated in the 1971–73 period as Chinese-American scientists, American physicians, the Committee of Concerned Asian Scholars, and the American Federation of Scientists were instrumental in the initial opening to China. While the number of Americans traveling to China in this period was small, it was clear that the American university community enthusiastically envisioned a comprehensive program of educational programs with China. Predictive of the pluralistic patterns that emerged in the late 1970s and 1980s, this first wave of scholarly exchange did not last long; from 1973–78 it was regulated and almost curtailed by Chinese authorities. A more sober, hardheaded model prevailed during most of this decade.

A narrowly reciprocal, centralized U.S.-Soviet model of academic exchange was dominant in most academic organizations and the U.S. government, and was especially prevalent in the China studies community throughout most of the 1970s. In an almost forgotten 1972 article titled "When the Academic Door to Peking Opens," Sovietologist Robert Byrnes urged China specialists to recognize that China would seek American science and technology, and that China studies should marry itself with the natural sciences in order to create "linkage" and obtain access to China (Byrnes 1972). Almost a decade earlier, in 1964, several China specialists, including John Lindbeck, A. Doak Barnett, Alexander Eckstein, and William Skinner, had come to the same conclusion. They hoped to avoid the fragmentation between the social scientists and natural scientists that had developed in exchanges with the Soviet Union, and to create a strong, national, multidisciplinary exchange organization.

The alliance they formed between the American Council of Learned Societies

(ACLS), the Social Science Research Council (SSRC), and the National Academy of Sciences—which became the Committee on Scholarly Communication with the People's Republic of China (CSCPRC)—was designed to provide an administrative vehicle for ensuring that American academic interests, not just Chinese technological needs, would be served "when the door to Peking opened." Those involved were not unsympathetic to a broader cosmopolitan discourse between Chinese and American intellectuals, as Lindbeck's writings make abundantly clear: "The Committee was convinced that the intellectual values underlying American, as well as all scholarly and scientific endeavors, required the elimination of barriers to open intellectual discourse" (Lindbeck 1970). But China's rigid autarky and centralized control of access reinforced initial tendencies to emphasize American interests and centralized reciprocity in the management of exchanges with a Communist country.

The Soviet exchange model affected the China field in other ways. A single institution, the International Research and Exchange Board (IREX), coupled exchange with the Soviet Union with financing American-based research and training. Some believed that preoccupation with Soviet exchanges resulted in the dilution and politicization of domestic-based Russian and Soviet studies. The ACLS and SSRC, sponsors of both IREX and the Joint Committee on Contemporary China and the Committee on Studies of Chinese Civilization, decided that IREX's China exchange counterpart (the CSCPRC) should not usurp the domestic research and training agenda functions of these preexisting ACLS/SSRC China committees. Throughout the 1970s and 1980s this division of labor continued, with the CSCPRC responsible for managing and funding research and training programs *in* China, and the joint committees (later combined to become a single entity, the Joint Committee on Chinese Studies) responsible for research and training outside mainland China, but including the United States, Hong Kong, and Taiwan. This division had several consequences. The CSCPRC accessed new funding from the U.S. government (most notably from the U.S. Information Agency [USIA], the National Endowment for the Humanities [NEH], the National Science Foundation [NSF], and the Department of Education) for scholarly exchanges, while the ACLS/SSRC China committees continued to fund domestic-based research. More important, the overall intellectual agenda of the China field was insulated somewhat from the allure and the vagaries of new access to China.

Institutional exchange models did not come just from the Soviet Union. For the China studies community, the Taiwan and Hong Kong experiences were close at hand: the consortial Inter-University Program (IUP) for language training managed by Stanford University in Taipei and the Universities Services Centre for research in Hong Kong. Leaders in the China field worked hard to guarantee that the romance of China did not result in the closure of these two independent institutions. And when the opening to China proved slow and problematic both institutions proved of continuing importance, if institutionally nontransferable. Language training programs in China were slow to develop the pedagogical sophistication and individual tutoring of IUP, while social science interviewing of various population groups in urban and rural China was affected by an informal "moratorium" until the mid-1980s.

The early academic exchange structure was thus influenced by the Soviet model, but was never as tightly centralized. Earlier institutional structures coexisted with new ones. While this resulted in a proliferation of "China committees," it did mitigate against the prevalence of a single institutional or intellectual approach to mainland China.

Reciprocity

During the 1970s, concern over reciprocity dominated the lexicon of this quasi-centralized exchange community. Deriving from the Soviet experience this concern had two dimensions: that access to America for Chinese scientists and engineers should provide reciprocal access to China for American social scientists and humanists, and that exchanges should be balanced numerically.

In 1973 the first American exchange agreement achieved some balance in fields and numbers. For example, the Chinese agreed to accept delegations in rural small-scale industry, art history, and early childhood education in exchange for Chinese delegations in medicine, solid state physics, and computer science. Through most of the 1970s, however, even this relative balance between American social science interests and Chinese technological needs proved politically elusive. Frank Press, chairman of the CSCPRC, assessed the constraints in 1977:

> Efforts to provide a balanced program representing American interests have not been particularly successful, as the People's Republic of China is highly selective as to whom they admit. For example, it has been difficult to arrange programs on contemporary Chinese society. Admitting social scientists and China specialists is probably not considered to be useful and, in fact, may be perceived as potentially dangerous by the Chinese. (Press 1977, 40)

Balancing numbers was initially easier than balancing fields of interests. Numerical reciprocity governed American exchanges with the Soviet Union and Eastern Europe. In the early years of China exchanges, a similar quantitative reciprocity of sorts prevailed. Both the National Committee for U.S.-China Relations and the CSCPRC annually negotiated a formula for groups in each direction. The understanding was that numbers would be roughly equivalent. The same formula applied to the several professional associations and universities that arranged programs in the mid-1970s.

It was widely believed that after China opened its door more widely and student exchanges materialized, these two aspects of reciprocity would continue to define the exchange structure. In return for Chinese students in the sciences and technology, Americans expected to send social scientists and humanists to China's universities. European and Canadian student exchange programs with China in the 1970s were carefully balanced in this way. In 1975 and 1977 the CSCPRC provided Secretary of State Henry Kissinger and National Security Adviser Zbigniew Brzezinski, respectively, proposals for Sino-American student exchanges—ten in each direction.

No one anticipated Deng Xiaoping's 1978 decision to send five hundred students and scholars to the United States. This announcement provoked a quick reassessment of the concept and implementation of reciprocity in cultural exchange with China. The unprecedented decision of a Communist country to train its successor generation in the United States ended, for all practical purposes, the viability of the concept of formal reciprocity, especially quantitative reciprocity. Americans had no need to train thousands of students in China. Fully aware of the tens of thousands of foreign students studying in the United States, Deng's decision also pointed up the "open-door educational policy" of the United States itself.

The appropriate response to Deng's initiative caused considerable debate. By 1978, scores of American universities had hosted visiting Chinese delegations, and hundreds of American scholars had visited China. An informal pluralistic pattern of direct exchanges between Chinese and American institutions was evolving, albeit modest and generally limited to short-term delegations. Given this experience, American universities signaled to both the U.S. and Chinese governments a preference for a decentralized educational relationship with China, more like the one with Taiwan and India than that with the Soviet Union. In contrast, the U.S. government (the Department of State, the National Security Council, and the NSF) generally preferred a Soviet-style, centrally managed educational program. This was in keeping with overall U.S. policy toward China during the normalization period in which technological and trade restrictions against China as a Communist country were continued. The policy question was resolved by the Chinese negotiators who insisted on a bilateral educational agreement sanctioning direct university-to-university agreements, individual access to American universities and American university funding, and the absence of a centralized exchange organization (Bullock 1987).

The China studies community viewed the abandonment of formal reciprocity with concern. Many believed that the decentralization of student exchanges would dilute American leverage in obtaining access for American students and scholars in China. Accordingly, during 1978 American China specialists led by the CSCPRC lobbied hard for U.S. government support of an American training and research program in China. Thus was born the concept of the "National Program" for Advanced Study and Research in China, a U.S. government-funded program for support of American research and training in China that would parallel, if not intersect, the Chinese "national" program for sending hundreds to the United States each year. In constituting this program, the U.S. government agreed to provide annual funding for fifty American students and scholars to go to China. This American "National Program" was an effort to retain some semblance of reciprocity for the hundreds of Chinese students about to come to the United States. Documents outlining its goals of advanced graduate training, research, library, and archival access, and the special importance of fieldwork in the social and natural sciences were incorporated into the final official "Understanding on the Exchange of Students and Scholars."

The CSCPRC, which had been instrumental in its creation, was asked to assume responsibility for this federally funded National Program. The first group of American students and scholars sent to China in January 1979 was deliberately chosen to reflect the broad range of American scholarly interests in China: sociology, anthropology, seismology, art history, paleoanthropology, history, and literature. They were to establish a beachhead for American research access in China. Since then the CSCPRC has sent more than five hundred graduate students and scholars to China for extended periods of study and research. Most of the contributors to this book and many of the publications they evaluate were funded with grants from the CSCPRC. Even though the federal funding has declined, supporting approximately thirty-five students and scholars a year, this program remains one of the major venues for American research in China.

The publications that resulted from National Program grants over a decade clearly demonstrate the effectiveness of the program (CSCPRC, 1990). When it began, however, the National Program had little authority: it was not established as a two-way reciprocal program and had no formal leverage with which to open research doors in China. My own writings at the time reflect a preoccupation with new definitions of reciprocity—"reciprocal," "symmetrical," or maybe "reasonable." These tried to reconcile a concept of reciprocity that would permit quantitative imbalance but somehow maintain a qualitative balance:

> The problem of obtaining reciprocity with China is complicated by asymmetry, in both numbers and educational systems. One will not be able to balance numbers and categories of Chinese students against numbers and categories of American students.... This is related to the U.S.'s decision to accept large numbers of Chinese students at their own expense. From the long-range perspective of U.S.-China relations, this is a very encouraging development, but it initially dilutes the leverage which would have accrued from a rigid system of equally balanced man-months (such as with the USSR)....
>
> It should be recognized that equivalent quantitative reciprocity is probably not meaningful at this time, but equivalent qualitative reciprocity is highly desirable. Equivalent qualitative reciprocity includes such basic principles as freedom to talk easily with one's own colleagues and open access to research materials, including libraries, journals, data, and so forth. (Bullock 1978, 9)

What was needed was a new concept of Sino-American educational relations that continued to recognize the legitimate interests of the China studies field, as well as other disciplines, and accommodated growing Chinese educational needs. What emerged in the early 1980s was conceptually incomplete and is perhaps best expressed as symbolic reciprocity or symbolic leverage; it was primarily rhetorical in nature. It is best understood by examining the roles of both the U.S. and Chinese governments, and of American universities.

Symbolic Leverage: The Role of Government and University

In his thoughtful essay "The Trajectory of Cultural Internationalism," Frank Ninkovich observes that "one of the first things that strikes the historian's eye in the new era of cultural interchange with China is the frank acceptance of a political framework which at one time would have been thought intolerable" (Ninkovich 1987). The role of the American government vis-à-vis scholarly exchanges with China during the past two decades has indeed been critical. Since the 1970s opening to China coincided with the political polarization of American academe during the Vietnam era, it is perhaps surprising that this did not become more controversial. A few examples give evidence of the U.S. government's central role: in 1964, the National Academy of Sciences (NAS) sought and received permission from the Department of State and the National Security Council to form what was then called the Committee on Scholarly Communication with Mainland China; during the 1970s the secretary of state routinely discussed scholarly exchanges in high-level governmental meetings; the Chinese decision to send hundreds of students to the United States was conveyed not to a delegation of university presidents, but to an official of the U.S. government; the first negotiations concerning educational relations between China and the United States were managed on the American side by the White House and the National Science Foundation; access issues concerning archives and field research were on the agendas of presidents Jimmy Carter and Ronald Reagan in discussions with Deng Xiaoping and then Chinese Communist Party General Secretary Zhao Ziyang; the placement negotiations for American students and scholars in the CSCPRC's National Program were handled by the U.S. embassy until 1990; and 100 percent of the funding for the National Program came from four government agencies.

What does this mean? At its most insidious, it suggests pervasive government control of academic exchanges. At its most benign, it suggests responsive government support for American academic initiatives. At its most revealing, it illustrates the intersection between academic and political diplomacy.

Establishing an effective, independent exchange program on behalf of the American academic community and in partnership with several agencies of the U.S. government was one of the early tasks of the CSCPRC. Governance by the ACLS, the SSRC, and the NAS, private academic organizations with long traditions of independent inquiry, peer review, and academic management, provided an institutional culture that contributed to the effort. Funding from multiple government agencies (the NSF, the USIA, the NEH, and the Department of

Education) to some extent avoided the problem of a client relationship with a single government agency. The decision as to who should receive grants was left in the hands of rotating panels of scholars appointed by the SSRC, the ACLS, and the NAS. Although the USIA's Board on Foreign Scholarships retains a legal right of review, this has been exercised in only a pro forma fashion.

The American academic community, adamant about the independence of the selection process, has sometimes eagerly sought "symbolic leverage" from the U.S. government in obtaining research access and in placement negotiations. Until research access eased in the mid-1980s, many China scholars believed that the U.S. government should take a more aggressive position in negotiating access by using access to American science laboratories for Chinese students as leverage for U.S. field research in China. Some in the early 1980s urged a tit-for-tat visa policy. But other American scholars simultaneously argued that negotiations and management of research access in China should be independent of the U.S. government.

The model was the Inter-University Program in Taipei, with its tradition of scholar-directors and independent operation in Taiwan. At the request of the CSCPRC, senior U.S. government officials explored this concept with the Chinese government, but were rebuffed. The U.S. government reluctantly settled for a fallback position—an American academic stationed in the U.S. embassy. John Jamieson served as academic adviser within the U.S. embassy from 1979 to 1981, during a critical period of defining American training and research objectives. But the U.S. embassy was never totally comfortable with an "outsider" and ultimately rejected the appointment of Jamieson's successor, Frederic Wakeman.

The CSCPRC was successful in establishing an independent office in Beijing in 1985, but until 1990 the U.S. embassy retained primary responsibility for negotiating placement of American students and scholars in the National Program. Over the years American participants had mixed feelings about their status as "officially sponsored." There is little doubt, however, that in China this identification of the U.S. government with the American research agenda did provide effective symbolic leverage. This is primarily because high-level Chinese government approval was required for most breakthroughs in academic relations.

It is now known, for example, that until his death in 1976, Premier Zhou Enlai was personally consulted on most major issues involving exchanges, including whether or not social science delegations would be included or China scholar escorts permitted in the annual exchange package. After normalization and continuing through the early 1980s, Chinese academic organizations, including libraries, research institutes, and universities, generally looked to central authorities for guidelines on the management of exchanges, especially on critical issues concerning American research access to China.

Prodding by the U.S. government in tandem with direct appeals by representatives of the American academic community was generally required to begin the gradual loosening of restrictions and the more sustained opening of Chinese facilities to American scholars. A few examples are illustrative. On the eve of Deng's 1979 visit to the United States, the first American anthropologists selected for research in China, Jack and Sulamith Potter, were denied placement by Chinese authorities. The issue was added to President Carter's agenda with Deng, who then instructed that American anthropological research be facilitated. During the 1980s other access issues—the opening of the Ming-Qing Archives, advanced graduate student research status, and improved field research access for social scientists—were repeatedly on the agenda of high-level bilateral governmental negotiations.

The involvement of high-level U.S. government officials in negotiations linked the academic agenda with the political agenda. Yet when political relations became strained, both governments generally tried to maintain a reasonable level of academic exchanges as one sign of a continuing relationship.

During the 1980s this close relationship of the U.S. government to exchanges in the China studies field, absolutely central in the early years, generally fragmented. As the normalization of institutional and bureaucratic ties between the two governments proceeded, the concerns of American academe became both more diffuse and less central to the U.S. government policy process. A wide variety of government agencies, including the United States Information Agency and the National Science Foundation, developed direct academic programs with China. While the USIA's Fulbright Program occasionally included China specialists, its primary goal was to develop American studies in China. In contrast, the NSF did include the social sciences in its mandate and increasingly became a significant advocate for improved access by American scholars.

During the 1980s, the role of the American university in exchanges with China also began to change (Clough 1981; Maddox and Thurston 1987). With Deng's "open door," the earlier vision of comprehensive university relationships with China materialized. Describing academic exchanges in the mid-eighties, David M. Lampton observed, "The speed with which Chinese students, scholars, and institutions have adapted to the American university scene since 1978 is one of the most notable features of Sino-American academic exchange" (Lampton 1986). In addition to the tens of thousands of Chinese students coming to American colleges and universities, a host of university-to-university agreements proliferated, numbering more than two hundred by the end of the 1980s. These relations were frequently with provincial universities or research institutes outside the political gaze of Beijing, such as Sichuan University, Tianjin University, and the Shanghai Academy of Social Sciences. As a result, a more flexible and sometimes less bureaucratic intellectual network began to emerge. Since disciplinary development in China was often a goal of these programs, American faculty participants were not limited to China specialists, but included economists, demographers, sociologists, or historians on short-term visits. Whetted by this initial exposure, many began to incorporate the China dimension into their teaching and writing.

Ironically, with these broader institutional interests, American university leaders were less likely to be firm advocates of American China specialist research access than were representatives of the U.S. government. They were generally more concerned with sustaining the ongoing flow of Chinese students and scholars to their respective campuses. For example, when Columbia anthropologist Myron Cohen was denied placement in China in 1981, the university debated, but then rejected, reducing access to Columbia by Chinese students. No American university was prepared to use Chinese access to science laboratories or engineering departments as leverage for reciprocal access for its students and scholars in China. In a more subtle way, however, multiplying pluralistic ties between American universities and a wide variety of Chinese research and academic communities gradually developed traditional Chinese *guanxi* networks. Over time, these also began to provide effective "symbolic leverage" for American research and training in China. Many of the innovative research and training programs of the second half of the 1980s resulted from foundations established through these first American university programs in China.

Access

If reciprocity was the issue of the 1970s, access was the keyword for China specialists during the early and mid-1980s. What American China scholars expected by way of access to the PRC was conditioned by several decades of archival and field access in Taiwan, and by the Hong Kong Universities Services Centre. When the mainland began to open, American anthropologists, sociologists, historians, and even political scientists enjoyed relatively unfettered access to Taiwan's villages, archives, and political institutions. The USC had been in existence for over two decades. There access to documents and refugee interviewing was direct—no living society or bureaucracy intervened.

Thus expectations of access to the mainland called for research opportunities simulating conditions in Taiwan or Hong Kong. Also sought was access that would penetrate China's bureaucratic and political obstacles to the "real China." In this context, access took on the aura of an abstract God-given right. Some American scholars were not prepared, especially in the beginning, to recognize legitimate obstacles to access—the disarray of archives and the political constraints on Chinese scholars. Others were not prepared to recognize that a cumbersome bureaucracy and political constraints were the "real" China and that from this reality a new, and equally legitimate, research agenda would evolve. Lack of access, insufficient access, belated access—these became the key concerns for the China studies field.

Frequently perceived as Chinese government restrictions on foreign scholars, access problems also resulted from the relative weakness of the social sciences and humanities in China. Dormant and oppressed for more than two decades, the indigenous social science and humanities community was just beginning to revitalize itself when foreign students and scholars arrived in significant numbers (Thurston and Parker 1980). Foreign demands for access to libraries and archives sometimes smoothed the way for Chinese scholars as well, but aggressive Western expectations were often resented. Foreign demands for field access caused a different kind of problem. Few, if any, Chinese social scientists had been trained to undertake sophisticated field surveys. Beyond the political sensitivity of many social science inquiries, Chinese scholars themselves were concerned that foreigners, especially Americans, would dominate both the study and interpretation of contemporary Chinese society. What is remarkable, however, is that over the course of a decade, these problems gradually lessened. The improvement in access that occurred throughout the 1980s must be understood in the context of the growing health and self-confidence of China's own academic community as well as to China's growing political and economic openness.

Progress in gaining access to written collections, both archives and documents, continued steadily through the 1980s into the post-Tiananmen period (*China Exchange News* Fall–Winter 1991). Approval from central-level authorities was initially necessary, but over time local mid-level officials assumed greater responsibility for collections under their jurisdiction. Most significant in the early 1980s was the gradual opening of the renowned Ming-Qing Archives in Beijing, China's most important historical archive to which American scholars have regular access today. This was followed by the partial opening of the No. 2 (Nationalist) Archives in Nanjing, as well as the Shanghai Municipal Archives. While these archives were primarily of benefit to historians, they paved the way for the wider opening of more contemporary documentary collections in libraries and archives throughout China. Chinese Communist Party archives remain closed, but a plethora of published memoirs, statistical records, provincial surveys, and institutional and party histories has provided the new database on which the contemporary China field now depends. Major American libraries collect some of this material, but most scholars find that regular and repeated visits to Chinese university and institute libraries, not to mention bookstores, are required to maintain some sort of bibliographic control.

The Chinese system of classifying written materials, historical and contemporary, published and unpublished, has caused many problems. *Neibu* (internal circulation) documents are proscribed for foreigners. Yet they are widely available in bookstores and from Chinese colleagues. For many Chinese scholars the designation *neibu* means something like "draft." It bypasses the final censorship that a completely open publication may demand. In other circumstances, a *neibu* designation is politically designed to "protect state secrets." Foreign scholars continue to struggle, legally and ethically, for the most appropriate way in which to handle *neibu* materials. (For more on *neibu* documents, see Chapter 13 by Eugene Wu in this volume.)

In contrast with documentary and archival access, field research has been more difficult, more mercurial, and more controversial. The initial access to rural counties obtained in the late 1970s through the National Program, a university, and some individual connections gave way to a period in which an informal "moratorium" on social science field research prevailed. This was only partly because of the controversies surrounding the case of Stanford student Steven Mosher. (For details of the Mosher case, see David Shambaugh's Introduction, page 13 n. 4.) For example, in 1980–81, the year after Mosher's research, the CSCPRC was especially successful in placing sociologists and anthropologists in China, including arranging a complex multivillage project for Arthur and Margery Wolf. Announced in January 1981 by the Chinese Academy of Social Science, the "moratorium" was provoked by a number of factors, including the sensitivity of American anthropological research, a tightening ideological climate, tension in U.S.-China political relations (Reagan's new administration was flirting with improving ties to Taiwan), and official Chinese apprehension about foreign access to Chinese society.

When field research access began to improve in the mid-1980s it came about in a rather piecemeal fashion largely because of local, rather than centralized, decision-making. The increasingly decentralized political and economic context, as well as the gradual maturation of a counterpart group of Chinese social scientists, contributed to the changed atmosphere. Central-level units frequently served as useful facilitators, but final decisions concerning access were made by the local unit involved. Here the bilateral university ties that had been nurtured began to show significant results. By the late 1980s access had become highly idiosyncratic and dependent on many factors, including personal and institutional *guanxi*.

Since 1985 social science access to China has been truly extraordinary. The CSCPRC-sponsored multidisciplinary project in Zouping county, Shandong, which began in 1985, was initially designed to break the logjam in social science field research. It was quickly followed by access to multiple rural sites arranged directly by individuals and universities. The Friedman/Pickowicz/Selden village study in Hebei, initiated in 1978, gained momentum. University of Michigan collaborative projects with Sichuan and Beijing universities were approved, as were Columbia University collaborative programs in anthropology. By 1989 sustained access to rural China by anthropologists, political scientists, and sociologists had become the norm, rather than the exception. While minority studies flourished in Inner Mongolia, Yunnan, Sichuan, and even Tibet, the North China Plain with its traditional Han population also became the site of numerous comparative studies. Guangdong province, especially the Pearl River Delta, increasingly became a focus for those interested in comparative Hong Kong/Taiwan/PRC sociological studies. Urban sites also became more accessible for research on topics ranging from demography to religion.

The results of this access-driven research are increasingly becoming available to the China studies field and the public at large. While the quality of American writing on contemporary China has improved dramatically, there has been a cost in bilateral intellectual relations. Few policymakers or China specialists have seriously pondered the longer term implications of this American academic obsession with access during the 1980s. Chinese political reactions have been frequent, but for Chinese scholars as well the issue is just below the surface. In 1988 an internationally experienced senior Chinese scientist raised the problem of academic imperialism. He noted that American preoccupation with Chinese data, Chinese specimens, and Chinese population groups had occasionally clouded the integrity and mutuality of bilateral academic relations in the social and natural sciences.

Fortunately, the growing ease of access gradually reduced the stridency of a somewhat abstract American concept of "access." Most realize that, as Vera Schwarcz put it in an informal report to the CSCPRC, after her first year in China, "Access in China is always contextual." The growing trend toward collaboration that emerged in the 1980s further ameliorated this issue, even though in the post-Tiananmen period it has raised new and equally troubling concerns.

Collaboration

If reciprocity and access were the issues of the 1970s and early 1980s, collaboration emerged as the opportunity of the late 1980s. A decade earlier China specialists had given collaboration short shrift:

> Such [cooperative] research could be carried out in all fields of scholarship, although it is expected that this program would be most suited to work in the natural sciences, medicine, agricultural sciences and engineering. Research in the social sciences and the humanities, because it tends to be carried out in the individual mode, is less applicable. (CSCPRC 1978)

The near-absence of a Chinese community of social scientists and relative unfamiliarity with China's humanists explained American lack of enthusiasm for collaboration. The more individualized tradition of research in the humanities, and to a lesser extent in the social sciences, was another. But at that time it was also feared that, given contrasting research agendas, interpretations, and methodologies, collaboration might compromise the integrity of American research.

Many who have been actively involved in exchanges with China have noted the philosophical differences between the Chinese and American social science and humanities communities. Natural scientists and engineers speak the same language, and usually have common points of departure. Much less frequently have social scientists and humanists shared the same philosophical premises, especially during the early years of exchange. It was not just the residual Marxist canon that enforced orthodoxy. A traditional Chinese emphasis on moral judgment was another significant difference. Qian Zhongshu, a leading Chinese literary comparativist, told the American Social Science and Humanities Commission in 1981: "It may surprise you to learn that the humanities are the most ideological of all disciplines in China." At a 1985 American history conference, Americanists were left speechless when Chinese graduate students and scholars asked: "What is the *true* interpretation of American history?" After visiting American colleagues for three months in 1987, Chinese political scientist Yan Jiaqi complained that American political scientists "did not ask important questions." In Chapter 8 in this volume, Richard Madsen has perceptively analyzed these differences between what he calls "the knowledge communities" of China and the United States.

These differences persist, but the rapid influx of Chinese students and scholars being trained in the United States, coupled with steady improvement in the social sciences in China, has created more common intellectual ground for collaboration. A growing number of American China specialists have extensive collegial and institutional ties in China and are training Chinese graduate students in their departments. This led to numerous small-scale individual collaborative projects that became the key to successful American field research in both rural and urban China. For example, Burt Pasternak and Janet Salaff in Tianjin and Inner Mongolia, Deborah Davis in Shanghai and Wuhan, and Stevan Harrell in Yunnan designed their research to fit into ongoing Chinese research projects, with stunning success.

The scale of collaboration expanded when Chinese social science departments, especially in the fields of economics, sociology, anthropology, and demography, became receptive to proposals for joint social science field surveys. Sociologist Lin Nan's studies of quality of life in Shanghai may be the earliest example of this kind of large-scale collaboration. Major collaborative projects were further encouraged by a Luce Foundation Collaborative Research Program announced in 1987, as well as the continuation of NSF's funding for collaborative research projects in the social sciences. By the time of the Tiananmen incident, these projects had become fairly sophisticated, including training, extensive use of sample interviewing and computerized questionnaires, computerized analysis, and joint authorship of the final product. Institutionally, universities and major China centers took the lead in organizing these programs, which required counterpart agreements and a supporting infrastructure. The topics ranged the gamut of Chinese society, from health to political participation.

Collaborative research did not mean the end of concern over individual access, nor was it a panacea for many of the continuing dichotomies between the two academic communities. New kinds of issues surfaced, including the growing commercialization of research access. But collaboration signaled a new era in the exchange program. For better or worse, it linked American China specialists more closely with the state of scholarship in China.

Educational Assistance

The China studies community has been primarily concerned neither with training Chinese students and scholars nor with upgrading Chinese university and research facilities. In the late 1970s and early 1980s there was fear that meeting Chinese educational needs might jeopardize American scholarly interests. In 1982, the ACLS/SSRC Social Science/Humanities Commission reaffirmed the centrality of American interests in the exchange program:

> In the judgment of the Commission, the program should have as one of its central purposes the long-term research and training interests of American humanists and social scientists. . . . In stating American purposes so bluntly, we do not recommend indifference to the Chinese interests; as the report makes clear, the Commission is genuinely supportive of many of the goals which the Chinese have set for themselves. . . . Throughout the exchange program, however, a clear vision of American scholarly purposes should be maintained. (Prewitt 1982, 5)

By the late 1980s a more inclusive definition of American scholarly interests emerged—a growing American commitment to Chinese academic institutions and disciplines. In the absence of a formal U.S. government technical assistance program for China, American foundations took the lead in allocating resources that would strengthen the social sciences and humanities in China. The Ford Foundation designed special programs in economics, law, and international relations. Other foundations, including the Rockefeller Foundation, the Rockefeller Brothers Fund, the Kellogg Foundation, the United Board for Christian Higher Education, and the MacArthur Foundation followed. Government funding also increasingly moved in this direction. Under the aegis of the United States Information Agency, priority has been given to strengthening American studies in China, through fellowships for Chinese as well as resident American faculty in China. This program decreased support for the CSCPRC National Program, which remains the major source for American graduate training and research in China. As Terrill Lautz argues in Chapter 15 in this volume, these changes in funding patterns are also affecting support for the infrastructure of the China studies field.

The American China studies community may have long-term concerns about the domestic health of the field, but their professional commitments now routinely include activities that directly and indirectly contribute to Chinese academe. By the late 1980s the American China studies community had emerged as an important participant in upgrading the social sciences and humanities in China. China specialists serve on the advisory committees that manage the Ford training programs, serve as consultants for World Bank and other multinational assistance programs, and routinely lecture in Chinese universities and participate in Chinese academic conferences. Perhaps even more important and just as time-consuming, they serve as mentors within their own universities for Chinese students and scholars in a wide range of disciplines. Today, many of these students from China have matured into research collaborators and professional colleagues. They are in an integral part of the American China studies community of the 1990s.

Emerging Issues

By 1989 one could argue that scholarly exchanges with China were fully normalized. A distinctly Sino-American exchange culture had reemerged in which American universities played a central role, providing the premier training site for Chinese students and scholars. As these students matriculated, many were absorbed into teaching roles, particularly in the natural and engineering sciences. The increased participation of Chinese students and scholars in American university life, either in residence or in short-term transit, had also changed the culture of the China studies community. Although concern about the nonreturn of Chinese students and scholars was growing (Orleans 1988), the steady two-way flow of American and Chinese students and scholars had created closely interlinked academic communities.

China's Tiananmen tragedy created a crisis in U.S.-China academic relations. Many China specialists and China centers were especially active in providing assistance to Chinese students and scholars in escaping from China, while many more provided support and encouragement for stranded students and scholars in their own institutions. Most American scholars left China or canceled plans for 1989 summer research. Given their close ties with Chinese intellectuals, in the United States and in China, American China specialists wrestled with the most appropriate response to human rights violations. Concepts of leverage, abandoned in the early 1980s, reemerged. Some advocated curtailing all exchanges, especially those in the natural sciences, in order to send a punitive message to the increasingly ideologically repressive Chinese government. Others advocated maintaining channels of communication with Chinese intellectuals who remained in China. Only when it became clear that Chinese intellectuals encouraged the return of American scholars and that China's intellectual door generally remained open did the flow of scholars gradually resume.

After 1990 American scholars in a number of different fields continued field and archival research, despite continuing ideological constraints on Chinese scholars within China. Historians and humanists enjoyed relatively easy access to libraries, archives, and individual scholars. Somewhat more surprising, Chinese government edicts against foreign participation in archaeological digs were rescinded, laying the foundation for several joint archaeological expeditions. Long-cultivated university efforts (the University of California at Berkeley and Harvard University, for example) finally brought results as bilateral field exploration and technological analysis moved forward in the post-Tiananmen period *(CEN* Summer 1992). In general, professional ties established during the 1980s persisted, signaled by the continuation of individual scholarly visits in both directions (Bullock 1991; *CEN* 1990–91).

Despite these auspicious signs, there was also growing evidence that central-level Chinese authorities sought new restrictions on American scholarly access to China. In December 1990, China's State Education Commission announced a new directive curtailing collaborative research with foreigners (Southerland 1991; WuDunn 1991a). During the course of 1991 and 1992, several previously agreed on collaborative field research projects encountered serious obstacles in data-retrieval and ground to a halt. Some individual scholars encountered new difficulties in conducting interviews in selected cities and counties. But several equally sensitive and ambitious social science surveys continued with reasonable success during the summer of 1991.

The problems that emerged that year were sufficiently serious that the National Science Foundation, the Luce Foundation, and the CSCPRC jointly convened a meeting of selected scholars involved in collaborative social science projects in November. It became evident that no clear pattern of difficulties existed. Projects affiliated with Chinese universities under the jurisdiction of the State Education Commission have been primarily affected by the government edict, but there are exceptions. During 1992, several individual and large-scale collaborative projects continued. Those that have encountered obstacles appear subject as much to local, institutionally idiosyncratic issues as to central-level edicts. In the present climate, however, new collaborative social science projects may be difficult to initiate.

As political constraints continue in China, the American concept of leverage has been revitalized once again. The NSF, which has become one of the most important funders for projects in the natural and social sciences, withheld renewal of its overall Basic Science agreement (which includes the social sciences) pending resolution of problems related to bringing field data out of China.

Problems are not confined to large-scale collaborative social science projects. The persistence of ideological controls in China and the deterioration of political relations between China and the United States have increasingly taken a toll on overall cultural and educational relations (WuDunn 1991b).

The post-Tiananmen period has thus brought a renewed awareness that academic relations with China, especially the study of contemporary China, are subject to the continuing political and ideological vicissitudes of modern China. In this context, it is difficult to assess which of the many emerging issues may be most critical for the future. Some of the more prevalent issues actually predate Tiananmen. These include the growing commercialization of research access, the relationship between exchanges and the U.S. government, and the infrastructure of exchanges within the China studies community.

In the early 1980s, problems of access primarily concerned political and bureaucratic barriers. As these barriers were gradually lowered, cost issues grew. China's preoccupation with economic growth dictates that even academic units should earn their own way, including developing sources for their own foreign currency. Foreign students and scholars are increasingly viewed primarily as revenue opportunities. There are many different examples of escalating and inappropriate costs. Chinese universities have dramatically raised the tuition costs for foreigners to attend Chinese universities, to a scale far beyond what is charged

Chinese students. A number of local counties now welcome foreign scholars for field research—but at outrageous fees for lodging, transportation, and miscellaneous "services." Research institutes have periodically imposed a general "research fee" for scholars who seek affiliation. Housing costs for foreign scholars have been a concern from the early 1980s since many must be housed in hotels at daily tourist rates. The increase in university guesthouses is beginning to ease this problem, but the cost of living in China remains very high for foreigners.

A 1991 survey by the Joint Committee on Chinese Studies revealed that these nagging issues were less severe than anticipated. Based on the responses of 136 persons who had recently conducted field work in China, Deborah Davis concluded, "Costs for field work in China continue to be modest. Daily living expenses average US$30, and most scholars pay few extraneous fees. Not a single scholar provided a vehicle and only one contributed a computer as part of the research fee" (Davis 1991). Nonetheless, as both the Chinese and American academic communities experience reduced funding, problems concerning fiscal arrangements for research and training in China can be expected to continue.

A second issue is the need for a new partnership between the American China studies community and the U.S. government. With today's normalized and decentralized pattern of academic exchanges, scholars and government officials should jointly redefine the role of the government in academic relations with China. The relative largess of the 1970s and early 1980s has been eroded by shrinking budgets and competing priorities. Two key federal agencies (the NSF and the USIA) have reduced their support for research and training in China. The NSF's China-targeted budget has been reduced by half. Within the USIA, priority is increasingly given to funding American training of Chinese through lectureships and seminars in American studies. This change in emphasis now jeopardizes the future of the National Program, which provides support for scores of students and scholars from American colleges and universities.

More important than funding is the nature of the American cultural relationship with China. The direct cultural role of the U.S. government—whether through the Fulbright Program, the visa policy for Chinese students, educational assistance to China, or "Radio Free Asia"—has been little debated. The repoliticization of academic relations with China in the wake of Tiananmen calls out for attention from the China studies community. I share Tom Fingar's call in this volume that there is a need to re-engage the China studies community with the U.S. government community, and to jointly redefine an appropriate educational and cultural agenda for the troubled decade ahead.

A third issue concerns the future structure of the exchange program and China studies community. The collective decision of the Chinese and American governments to permit and encourage decentralized academic exchanges has had a profound effect on the character of scholarly relations. For both Chinese and Americans, it has encouraged the extraordinary flourishing of direct individual and institutional ties. The receptivity of American universities to Chinese students and scholars has ensured the success of this overall relationship. Over time, China centers in the larger universities have played a greater role both within the university, and in organizing ongoing relationships and research opportunities in China. The flow of students and scholars between the two countries for both graduate training and research is now taken for granted.

With this normalization, which has survived Tiananmen, it is time to reexamine the national infrastructure of the China studies field and the role of exchanges within it. Decreased funding and a proliferation of multiple training and research programs have weakened the several China committees and study abroad centers, including the Joint Committee structure, the CSCPRC, the Inter-University Program in Taipei, and the Universities Service Centre in Hong Kong. Within China itself, there are several American-managed institutions concerned with research and training, including the CSCPRC Beijing Office, the Johns Hopkins–Nanjing Center, and a number of university-based programs, all experiencing funding problems.

It is time to look again at this structure and to systematically assess what would be most effective during the rest of the decade. New institutional structures, especially those that are more consortial, are needed; alternatively, older structures might be effectively merged or reinvigorated. A growing consciousness of "Greater China," culturally, historically, and in the future, suggests the need to integrate exchanges related to the mainland into a broader regional approach. The recent decision of the CSCPRC to change its English name to the Committee on Scholarly Communication with China is one step in this direction.

While this new look is needed, the events of Tiananmen and its aftermath have brought a sobering political reality to the China studies field. Not only is it evident that access to China cannot be taken for granted, the political dimensions of that access and its effect on American scholarship are being reassessed by the China studies field as a whole. Thus, as in the early 1970s, the role of "exchange" with China is once again at center stage of the bilateral academic relationship. Far more important than exchange structure, the cultural and intellectual relationship between the two countries is at a turning point. As the 1990s continue, American China specialists, heretofore somewhat preoccupied with their own scholarly interests, are called on to address the broader, historically repetitive, challenge of Sino-American scholarly and cultural relations. In doing so, they will simultaneously be addressing the future of the American study of China.

References

Bullock, Mary. 1978. "American Scholarly Interests in China: Towards a Framework of Reasonable Reciprocity." Unpublished paper.

———. 1987. "American Exchanges with China, Revisited." In *Educational Exchanges: Essays on the Sino-American Experience,* ed. Joyce K. Kallgren and Denis Fred Simon, 23–43. Berkeley: University of California Press.

———. 1991. "The Effects of Tiananmen on China's International Scientific and Educational Cooperation." In *China's Dilemmas in the 1990s: The Problems of Reform, Modernization, and Interdependence,* 611–28. Washington, D.C.: U.S. Congress, Joint Economic Committee.

Byrnes, Robert F. 1970. "When the Academic Door to Peking Opens." Prepared for the Subcommittee on National Security and International Operations, Committee on Government Operations, U.S. Senate. Washington, D.C.: Government Printing Office.

Clough, Ralph N. 1981. "A Review of the U.S.-China Exchange Program." Washington, D.C.: United States Information Agency.

Cohen, Warren I. 1987. "While China Faced East: Chinese-American Cultural Relations, 1949–71." In *Educational Exchanges: Essays on the Sino-American Experience,* ed. Joyce K. Kallgren and Denis Fred Simon, 49–57. Berkeley: University of California Press.

Committee on Scholarly Communication with the People's Republic of China (CSCPRC). 1972–91. *China Exchange News.*

————. 1978. "Proposal for Sending American Students to China." Unpublished paper.

————. 1990. "List of Publications from Grantees in the National Program, 1978–90."

Davis, Deborah. 1991. "Research Costs of Social Scientists: Initial Report." Unpublished paper.

Lampton, David M. 1986. *A Relationship Restored: Trends in U.S.-China Educational Exchanges, 1978–84.* Washington, D.C.: National Academy Press.

Lindbeck, John M.H. 1970. "The Committee on Scholarly Communication with Mainland China." Paper presented at the Association of Asian Studies annual meeting.

Maddox, Patrick G., and Anne Thurston. 1987. "Academic Exchanges: The Goals and Roles of U.S. Universities." In *Educational Exchanges: Essays on the Sino-American Experience,* ed. Joyce K. Kallgren and Denis Fred Simon, 119–48. Berkeley: University of California Press.

Madsen, Richard. 1987. "Institutional Dynamics of Cross-Cultural Communication: U.S.-China Exchanges in the Humanities and Social Sciences." In *Educational Exchanges: Essays on the Sino-American Experience,* ed. Joyce Kallgren and Denis Fred Simon, 191–213. Berkeley: University of California Press.

Ninkovich, Frank. 1987. "The Trajectory of Cultural Internationalism." In *Educational Exchanges: Essays on the Sino-American Experience,* ed. Joyce K. Kallgren and Denis Fred Simon, 8–22. Berkeley: University of California Press.

Orleans, Leo. 1988. *Chinese Students in the United States: Policies, Issues and Numbers.* Washington, D.C.: National Academy Press.

Press, Frank. 1977. "Scholarly Exchanges with the People's Republic of China—Recent Experience." In *Our China Prospects: A Symposium,* ed. John K. Fairbank, 37–43. Philadelphia: American Philosophical Society.

Prewitt, Kenneth. 1982. *Research Opportunities in China for American Humanists and Social Scientists.* New York: Social Science Research Council.

Southerland, Daniel. 1991. "When the Learned Are Feared." *International Herald Tribune,* May 20.

Strevy, Carol. 1990. *The Current Status of Academic and Cultural Exchanges between U.S. and PRC Institutions a Year after Tiananmen.* New York: Institute of International Education.

Thurston, Anne F., and Jason Parker. 1980. *Humanistic and Social Science Research in China: Recent History and Future Prospects.* New York: Social Science Research Council.

WuDunn, Sheryl. 1991a. "Beijing Is Said to Curb Foreigners Gathering Data on Social System." *New York Times,* May 25.

————. 1991b. "Cultural Links with Chinese Are Eroding." *New York Times,* November 6.

15

Financing Contemporary China Studies

Terrill E. Lautz

Before Richard Nixon's historic trip to Beijing in 1972, most Americans viewed China as isolated, mysterious, and threatening.[1] Not surprisingly, the study of China seemed like an exotic and marginal pursuit. In spite of these negative public perceptions, private and government funding sources in the United States invested heavily in the field of contemporary China studies during the 1950s and 1960s. Thus when the door reopened to Americans, a substantial scholarly and institutional base already existed for understanding China.

As U.S.-China relations have matured over the past decade, funding patterns have changed and financing for China studies has become more complicated. As China has opened up to the outside world, the general pattern has been for "external" funding (money coming from outside an institution) to move *away* from support for China studies at American universities and *toward* China itself.

China studies programs have benefited enormously from direct contact with the PRC and the total funding pool for all China-related activities grew substantially through the 1980s. But new American funding has appeared mainly in response to new categories of interest—bilateral exchanges, training programs for PRC citizens, and development and research programs in China—rather than widespread concern for sustaining China studies per se. Funds for activities *in* China both complement and compete with the scholarly study *of* China.

The suppression of the democracy movement in June 1989 did not fundamentally alter this pattern. Almost all the grantmakers involved with China before the crackdown continued their programs, believing that engagement represents the best opportunity for ongoing reform. But almost no new funders have become involved with China or China studies because of China's negative public image. An exception to this generalization has been the emergence of the Taiwan-based Chiang Ching-kuo Foundation, which has quickly become a major new source of funding for China studies in the United States and Europe.

The rapid changes of the past dozen years have redefined China studies, broadening the field, making it far more visible and far less ideological. But paradoxically, American universities, which now have extensive involvement with their counterparts in China, find it increasingly difficult to maintain the expensive infrastructure for China studies on their own campuses. As a consequence, essential but undramatic needs such as library development, language training, faculty development, and student fellowships may be neglected.

There are various explanations for the movement of funding agencies away from direct support to American university area studies programs on China. First, the study of China has now been accepted and integrated into many university structures. Over twenty major centers for China or East Asia have been established, and dozens of programs exist at the undergraduate level. Because universities and colleges themselves now assume most of the ongoing costs for these programs, China studies is no longer perceived by most funders as a subject in need of special nurturance. Having played a key role in helping to establish the field, key funders have moved on to other concerns.

Second, the boundaries of the field have spread out far beyond the universities as new sources of information about contemporary China have become readily available. As the contributors to Part III of this volume amply attest, the scholarly community has lost its near-monopoly on expertise to American journalists, businessmen, diplomats, and think tank analysts. Even foundation officers have spent prolonged periods of time in China. When Americans rediscovered China in the 1970s, China scholars became authorities on virtually every aspect of Chinese society. During the 1980s, knowledge of China became both more common and more specialized. The growth of interest and expertise on China means that colleges and universities must compete with numerous nonprofit organizations seeking funds for China-related activities. What was once a small field with rather narrow parameters is now much larger and less clearly defined.

A third reason relates to tightened federal, state, and university budgets and to new areas of interest for foundations, such as Eastern Europe. Federal funding has become a mainstay for international studies, but it is by no means assured that higher education will receive substantial new funding from Washington. At the same time, many foundations are more concerned with transnational and current policy issues than with the study of language, history, and culture—the traditional core of area studies programs.

As a consequence, less money seems to be available for the humanities and social sciences. Both the American Council of Learned Societies (ACLS) and the Social Science Research Council (SSRC)—national bellwethers for research funding—have curtailed the number and size of their grants for area studies programs. One exception to this trend has been a Ford Foundation program starting in 1990 to provide overseas experience for graduate students in social science disciplines.

A final explanation for declining direct support of China studies programs is related to the American response to China's "open door" policy. The PRC's turn to the outside world for help with its modernization efforts in the late 1970s rekindled a latent American missionary impulse to "change" China. Numerous institutions and funding sources responded and returned to an early twentieth-century movement of working to foster a stable, friendly, and more democratic society in China.

A proliferation of exchange and training programs between the two countries resulted. The sizable flow of Chinese students to American universities and smaller numbers of Americans to China has been well documented,[2] but there has been little systematic study of how China's open door has affected the scholarly base for China studies in the United States. On the positive side, an intricate web of personal relationships has given a new generation of American sinologists a far more tangible and immediate appreciation of Chinese culture and society. Interaction with Chinese scholars is now crucial to the vitality of contemporary China studies. But as academic exchange programs have become a central means for funding research on China, some topics and disciplines are emphasized over others and some funding requirements go largely ignored.

Considerable sums have been allocated to help support the PRC's modernization drive through training and development assistance programs, though the U.S. government still operates no aid programs in China. Almost $1 billion in World Bank loans has been invested in China in the fields of science, engineering, agriculture, and medicine. Various United Nations agencies are heavily involved in training programs for Chinese specialists. The Rockefeller Foundation supports research programs in China and other developing countries in the fields of agriculture, health, population, and the environment. The Ford Foundation has addressed the development of law, sociology, economics, and international relations in China, and is now turning to issues such as rural poverty and women's health. Programs like these have enhanced our understanding of contemporary China, but support for American students and scholars is usually a by-product, not the prime objective, of efforts to assist with China's advancement.

As a result of these factors—the institutionalization of China studies within universities and colleges; a much wider definition of expertise on China; a contraction of external funding for all area studies; and a shift of focus to China itself—the funding picture for China studies has become more complex, and sources more varied, than ever before.

The Impact of China's Opening

The most obvious and important change for China watchers since the 1970s has been the opportunity to have direct contact with citizens of the PRC. The framework of academic exchange programs has provided the means to see China at close quarters, and substantial new funding has materialized to support study and research in China.

The Committee on Scholarly Communication with China (CSCC), based at the National Academy of Sciences, is the largest single source of funding for academic exchange, with a 1991 budget of $3.5 million. Close to $1 million of this amount goes for fellowships that support Americans to study in China. Much of this funding has come from federal sources that would not otherwise be available to China studies, such as the U.S. Information Agency and the National Science Foundation. (As Chapter 14 by Mary Bullock indicates, government support for the CSCC National Program became endangered in 1992.) Additional support for the CSCC has come from the National Endowment for the Humanities and the Ford, Luce, MacArthur, Mellon, Rockefeller, and Starr foundations.

The concept of academic exchange with China has been loosely defined. It encompasses a broad range of activity including research, conferences, and language training, but implies some element of reciprocity and mutual benefit with scholars and institutions in the PRC. Whatever one means by "exchange," it is clear that a complicated, symbiotic relationship has grown up between funding for scholarly exchange programs and funding for China studies.

It is inaccurate to say that scholarly exchange has developed at the expense of China studies; on the contrary, exchange programs have stimulated an impressive new body of publications and have attracted scholars who are not trained as China area specialists but are interested in China as a comparative research topic.

It could be argued, however, that the large infusions of money for exchange activities may produce an uneven or unbalanced base for sinological studies. The majority of fellowships for American scholars now require that the research be conducted in China, but topics are sometimes limited by what is allowed by the authorities or permitted by conditions in the PRC. It has been difficult to conduct fieldwork or carry out surveys at the local level in China and, until recently, access to archaeological sites has been restricted. During the 1980s, there were fewer incentives for Americans to study Taiwan or Hong Kong, and scholarly resources there have been overlooked. With the development of new funding sources in Taiwan, this situation is changing.

As was apparent during the June 1989 crackdown in China, academic exchange programs with the PRC are vulnerable to swings and shifts in Sino-American relations. Even if U.S. relations with China remain on an even keel, future political or economic instability within the PRC might present obstacles to foreign scholars. Because so much funding for the academic study of China is now tied to exchange, the impact on the field would be severe if access to China or government funding for scholarly exchange with China were curtailed.

Have American China scholars become overly dependent on exchange programs as a primary source of support for research and training? Has our national enthrallment with Sino-American exchange led funders to lose sight of basic, long-term needs such as preservation and conservation of library materials, or development of new language training materials (see Chapter 12 by Timothy Light in this volume)? There are no simple answers, but we do know that relatively few American students and scholars are truly fluent in Chinese, partly because of financial constraints and despite their increased contact with China.[3] A closer look at the strengths and weaknesses of the China field and a better understanding of issues motivating funders would be a good starting point. This volume is an unprecedented and important contribution in this regard.

Sources of Funding

Contemporary China studies is a classic example of a concerted effort by philanthropy and government to meet an important need. The case for foreign area studies was made in conjunction with the assumption by the United States of global military responsibilities in the aftermath of World War II. After the 1949 victory by the Communists, China became important as a Cold War enemy, but it was also believed in the United States that a country of China's size could not be ignored; that its long history and culture merited attention; and that China might eventually become a major trading partner. America's long-standing fascination with things Chinese played a part as well. It is nonetheless ironic that large amounts of funding became available for China studies at the height of China's isolation from the rest of the world.

During the "developmental decade," from 1959 to 1970, the Ford Foundation invested $23.8 million, the U.S. government, $15 million, and American universities, another $15 million in China studies. Ford's strategy was to concentrate on a limited number of key university centers. Funds were channeled mainly to nine universities and to national research and fellowship programs administered by the SSRC and the ACLS.[4] Federal monies, available to a wider range of universities, came through the National Defense Education Act (NDEA) of 1958, which identified China as one of six world areas of critical national interest. Chinese language training and fellowship support was provided to nineteen NDEA university centers by 1965 and twenty-eight centers by 1968.

Succeeding the NDEA, the Department of Education's Title VI program, authorized under the Higher Education Act of 1965, has consistently provided direct support to university area studies centers for faculty positions, language instruction, library development, student fellowships, and public education. Twelve university "National Resource Centers" for East Asia (China, Japan, and Korea) received a total of nearly $1.5 million during the 1991–92 academic year.[5] An additional $2.25 million was allocated for 182 student fellowships at twenty-one universities for the same period. Approximately 50 percent of the East Asia funds support China studies.

Until recently, East Asia received more funding than any other world region under Title VI. It is now equaled by support for area programs covering the former Soviet Union and Eastern Europe. After remaining static for a number of years, the money allocated under this legislation has been increased, mainly to support more language fellowships. But the absolute amounts are still modest, and area studies remains a small category in the federal budget approved by Congress. The National Security Education Act, passed by Congress in 1991, does provide an important infusion of funds ($150-million endowment) for area studies at a critical time.

The National Endowment for the Humanities has been another important federal source of support for the China field. It has steadily funded fellowships and research conferences through the Joint Committee on Chinese Studies, the exchange programs of the CSCC, translation projects, summer seminar programs for faculty, films, exhibitions, library preservation, and special projects such as *The Cambridge History of China* and an annotated collection of Mao's writing. The Fulbright program (curtailed after the Tiananmen massacre but now revived on a smaller scale) sends lecturers in American studies to China and supports Chinese visiting scholars at American universities. In sum, government funds have been essential to all aspects of the China field, but recent budgetary changes at the Department of Education and USIA threaten China studies in the 1990s.

Some China scholars have been quite enterprising about raising funds from new sources, but these tend to be sporadic and unpredictable. After diplomatic relations were established with the PRC in 1979, U.S. corporations were briefly seen as a source of potential financial support for China studies. Trade between the two countries has increased steadily but has not been the bonanza that some anticipated, so relatively modest contributions have materialized for American universities. Hong Kong and Taiwan alumni of American universities are approached with occasional success, but most such graduates are in scientific and technical fields and have limited interest in funding China studies programs.

Another potential category for funding is private philanthropy in Asia. China is one of the largest area studies fields in the United States, but Japan is by far the best funded, thanks largely to the initiatives of Japanese government and corporate foundations. Faculty positions, research and exchange programs, Japanese language training and public education about Japan have been well supported on the theory that better American understanding of Japan will help to sustain this vital bilateral relationship. A similar philosophy motivates U.S. government support for American studies in many countries around the world, including China.

The PRC, of course, cannot yet afford to follow Japan's example. One interesting exception has been a major commitment on the part of the Chinese government, through the State Education Commission, to help construct and operate the Johns Hopkins–Nanjing University Center for American and Chinese Studies in Nanjing. (This jointly run program, launched in 1986, offers training for young Americans and Chinese intending to enter various professions concerned with U.S.-China relations.)

There is a well-established tradition of philanthropy and charitable giving in Hong Kong, but up to now it has focused mostly on local needs. Pressures for Hong Kong foundations to support various causes in China will no doubt increase as the economies of the two societies become more closely connected and as the shift to Chinese sovereignty in 1997 approaches. One exception is a research project on South China jointly organized by the Chinese University of Hong Kong and Yale University that will receive several million dollars from private Hong Kong sources.

Although Taiwan has less experience than Hong Kong with organized philanthropy, a variety of foundations has been set up by private companies and families, mostly to support charitable or educational programs. Two recently established think tanks reflect Taiwan's growing political pluralism. The Twenty-first Century Foundation and the Institute for National Policy Research, both funded by corporations, have professional staffs and well-organized research agendas aimed at social, economic, environmental, and political issues. Chapter 10 by Thomas Robinson in this volume discusses other Taiwanese foundations that have joined the China studies funding world.

In the absence of formal diplomatic ties with many countries, Taiwan has substituted economic and cultural diplomacy. Initial efforts to fund China studies programs in the United States met with mixed success because of the conditions that were sometimes attached to grants. Attempts to impose political qualifications for faculty appointments and pressure to shape research agendas in directions favorable to Taiwan caused considerable concern among American scholars. As in many countries, there is a common view in Taiwan that "international affairs belong in the domain of the government rather than the private sector."[6]

The Taiwan government has encouraged foreigners living in Taiwan to pursue China studies. Scholarships to study Chinese language are readily available and the Ministry of Education has established a fund to support research by foreign scholars. The Inter-University Program for Chinese Language Studies (the Stanford Center), an American university consortium that has trained several generations of American scholars, is located on the National Taiwan University campus and receives substantial assistance from Taiwan's Ministry of Education and Committee on Scientific and Scholarly Cooperation.

The first major American university programs for Taiwan studies were established in 1989 at Columbia University and the University of California, Berkeley. These programs support research and teaching, graduate fellowships, library materials, conferences, academic exchange, and publications on the subject of Taiwan and have been administered on the principles of academic openness and scholarly fairness.

Another highly significant development—not only for the study of Taiwan but for the China field in general—is the establishment of the Chiang Ching-kuo (CCK) Foundation for International Cultural Exchange. The CCK Foundation, which has an endowment of about $90 million raised from government and private sources in Taiwan, started to offer substantial support for China studies in the United States and Canada in 1989–90. Considerable emphasis has been placed on creating new teaching positions, especially for Chinese language instruction, at several universities and liberals arts colleges. Another major category of support has been research grants at the dissertation, postdoctoral, and senior scholar levels. Unlike many other Taiwanese funding some Chiang Ching-kuo grants have been offered with no apparent political strings attached.

The Role of Private Foundations

American foundations are best characterized by their independence and diversity. Each pursues its own agenda, guided by concern for a major issue or problem, be it the environment, research on AIDS (Acquired Immune Deficiency Syndrome), or minority education. Corporate foundations have emerged as strong supporters of local community projects, pre-college education, and the arts. Every philanthropy seeks to identify a special or unique interest that will serve to define its goals. No foundation can afford to be all things to all people.

Higher education has been a consistent focus for foundations, even though their contribution accounts for only a modest percentage of the total budget for colleges and universities. The number of foundations involved with international affairs is limited, because most follow the old adage that charity begins at home.

The comparative advantages of foundations are flexibility, the ability to provide a quick response, and a willingness to take risks. American foundations have an admirable record of supporting new initiatives, the strongest of which become self-sustaining. The most obvious disadvantage is that foundations rarely provide ongoing support—hence the term "soft money" to describe foundation grants. Funding typically declines as the newness of a topic wears off, or when a field or an institution is no longer at a critical stage of development.

The Ford Foundation moved away from funding China studies in the United States during the mid-1970s because of budget constraints and changing priorities. It has since developed sizable training and developmental programs in China, and Ford established the first American foundation office in Beijing in 1988. The Chicago-based MacArthur Foundation has provided substantial assistance for international relations and policy studies programs concerned with China, some of which are based at American universities.

The Rockefeller Brothers Fund supports environmental and international relations projects dealing with the PRC and other parts of Asia. The Starr Foundation has funded many excellent China-related projects, including some based at universities (major funding to renovate Columbia University's East Asian Library is one example). The Geraldine R. Dodge Foundation has supported an innovative program to introduce Chinese language instruction at the high-school level for the past several years. The Albert Kunstadter Family Foundation has provided modest but well-chosen assistance to various China projects. During the late 1980s, the Wang Corporation sponsored a postdoctoral fellowship program for American scholars.

The United Board for Christian Higher Education in Asia has supported a large number of Chinese students and visiting scholars at American colleges and universities, drawing on an endowment as well as funds from other sources. The Lingnan Foundation, which also operates from New York, supports programs at Zhongshan University in Guangzhou, the Chinese University of Hong Kong, and Lingnan College in Hong Kong. The Asia Foundation, known as an operating foundation because it makes grants with funds from other sources, has sponsored training programs for Chinese specialists in the fields of law, foreign affairs, and business management. Many of these efforts benefit contemporary China studies in one way or another.

Most philanthropies have little interest in making grants for endowment because foundations function as endowments themselves. Before exiting the field in the mid-1970s, however, the Ford Foundation made major "tie-off" endowment grants for East Asian studies to seven universities: Berkeley, Chicago, Columbia, Cornell, Harvard, Michigan, and Stanford.

The Andrew W. Mellon Foundation also followed a long-term approach with endowment grants to nine universities (the seven above, plus Princeton and Washington) in 1977 and 1986, to provide ongoing support for East Asian studies (China, Japan, and Korea). The Mellon grants, mostly on a three-to-one matching basis, will total $9.25 million with the successful completion of the match. The Mellon Foundation has recently moved away from Asian studies in favor of Middle Eastern, Latin American, and East European studies, based on the judgment that these fields have greater needs. Over the years, both Ford and Mellon have also invested several million dollars in grants for ACLS/SSRC–sponsored China programs.

The Henry Luce Foundation's long-standing interest in China and U.S.-China relations derives from the eponymous Henry R. Luce's birth in Shandong province of missionary parents. The Luce Foundation has worked, primarily through support for research and academic exchange programs at the postdoctoral level, to improve American understanding of China. During the 1980s, Luce funded a program for senior PRC scholars to visit American campuses. A cluster of projects on the history of Christianity in China has been another focal point. More recently, Luce has supported several three-year cooperative research projects between Chinese and American scholars in the humanities and social sciences.

Toward a New Agenda

The period 1979–89 might well be characterized as "the exchange decade" in modern China studies. Direct contact with China brought new vitality to the field, and continued access to China is necessary, but it is not sufficient to sustain the infrastructure for China studies in America.

China studies is by no means in dire straits and is probably better funded than most regional studies programs. Scholarly interest is strong, as evidenced by the fact that 40 percent of the 5,713 Association for Asian Studies members in the

United States listed China as their primary area of concern in 1991. History is the most common discipline for China specialists (776 members), followed by literature (302), political science (231), anthropology (133), art history (106), language (94), religion (77), library science (75), linguistics (72), international studies/affairs (55), economics (53), sociology (49), law (36), philosophy (34), education (34), and geography (24).

The China field does not face a state of crisis, but its parameters and identity are being redefined. As the field expands and achieves a degree of maturity, does the academic pursuit of China still require special attention from funders, or can China specialists now compete with others on an equal basis? What is the appropriate balance between funding for programs in China and funding for China studies in the United States? Will the escalating costs of conducting research in China impose unmanageable financial limitations on American scholars? What effect will China's political uncertainty and uneasy relations with the United States have on the field? A sophisticated statistical survey of the size and financial status of China studies would help establish a baseline to answer such questions. This survey might also serve to create a consensus about critical gaps and long-term priorities for the field as a whole.

Endowed funding for faculty positions, libraries, fellowships, and administration offers an obvious long-term solution for the financial security of China studies. But endow.nents are extremely hard to come by, and usually realize only 5 percent in interest for a program. Various endowed chairs are held by China scholars at major universities, but most are controlled by departments and are not designated in perpetuity for China studies.

It is no longer realistic to look to foundations to provide basic ongoing support for China studies. By and large, this must come from government sources or from colleges and universities themselves. But foundations can provide critical leverage within universities to help maintain high-quality training and research programs.

To be most effective in raising money for China studies, universities should identify critical needs that will promise lasting results. For example, funders should give higher priority to the development of intermediate and advanced Chinese language materials, as compared with a one-day conference on economic reform in China. Umbrella programs that combine the resources of several institutions—such as the eleven-university Consortium for Language Teaching and Learning based at Yale University—are effective vehicles for focusing attention on critical needs. Cooperative agreements among groups of universities for acquiring or conserving library materials is another means to achieve economies of scale by joining forces.

The use of computer technology to catalogue Chinese language library materials promises new efficiencies but involves additional costs. (See Chapter 13 by Eugene Wu in this volume.) One new project, assisted by the Luce Foundation, bears special mention because of its potential to create new scholarly resources as well as contribute to China's modernization efforts. The On-line Computer Library Center (OCLC) is working with the National Library of China in Beijing to catalogue materials on Republican China (1911–49) and make them known to specialists worldwide. This will give scholars unprecedented access to a vast collection on twentieth-century China, while introducing modern library technology to the PRC.

Projects like this one suggest that the time has come to push the concept of "exchange" to a more sophisticated level. One increasingly attractive avenue for this is research projects jointly designed and administered by Chinese and American scholars. The National Science Foundation has supported Sino-American collaborative research in the physical and social sciences over the past few years. The Luce Foundation's "United States–China Cooperative Research Program," which is open to scholars from Taiwan and Hong Kong as well as the PRC, supports three-year projects on topics in the humanities and social sciences. The collaborative approach ensures that both sides have vested interests in seeing results.

Forty years ago, it was necessary for modern China studies to establish an identity separate from the study of early China because sinology had strong traditions of its own. Today, there is much to be gained by seeking the common ground between the traditional and modern branches of the field. The use of 1949 as a demarcation between historians and political scientists is increasingly artificial as Chinese intellectuals look to the past to explain current trends and events. To cite just one example, studies of China's premodern urban development and economic history tell us a great deal about present-day reforms.

There is also a need to bring China more effectively into high-school courses and the undergraduate liberal arts curriculum. Columbia University is working to integrate Asian topics into the academic mainstream through an ambitious project supported by the National Endowment for the Humanities and the Luce Foundation. Related to this effort is an important need to understand China better in the regional context of Asia.

Even after millions of dollars of investment, most of our conclusions about China's modern history and revolution remain quite tentative. This is because China is large and complicated and has changed quickly, at least on the surface. It is also the consequence of forty years of mutual isolation.

Simply put, the case needs to be made for funding sources to support the familiar but essential work of our colleges and universities in training and maintaining scholarly expertise on China for the sake of knowledge as well as national need. Federal agencies, state legislatures, private foundations, university alumni, corporate supporters, and Asian philanthropies should be enlisted in the task.

Notes

1. The author acknowledges, with appreciation, comments on an earlier draft by Mary Bullock, Peter Geithner, Robert Geyer, David Shambaugh, and Frederic Wakeman.

2. See David M. Lampton, *A Relationship Restored: Trends in U.S.-China Educational Exchanges, 1978–1984* (Washington, D.C.: National Academy Press, 1986), and Leo A. Orleans, *Chinese Students in America: Policies, Issues, and Numbers* (Washington, D.C.: National Academy Press, 1988).

3. Lampton, *A Relationship Restored*, 123. Chinese language competence may improve substantially in coming years because students are receiving better preparation at younger ages.

4. John M. H. Lindbeck, *Understanding China: An Assessment of American Scholarly Resources* (New York: Praeger, 1971), 78–82.

5. The National Resource Centers for East Asia currently include five private and eight public institutions (one center is joint): University of California at Berkeley, Columbia, Cornell, Harvard, University of Hawaii, University of Michigan, Ohio State University, University of Pittsburgh (undergraduate center), University of Southern California and UCLA, Stanford, University of Washington, and University of Wisconsin.

6. Barnett F. Baron, "Organized Private Philanthropy in East and Southeast Asia," East Asian Institute, Columbia University, September 1988, unpublished paper, 11.

Part V
Epilogue

16

The American Study of Modern China: Toward the Twenty-first Century

Michel C. Oksenberg

The American study of contemporary China is likely to undergo major changes in the twenty-first century. Opportunities beckon, and issues loom that have made the 1990s a decade of stimulating departures and bold insight. The same factors that contributed to the dynamism of modern Chinese studies during the past thirty years are likely to persist: the borrowing and adaptation of analytical approaches from other fields, the recruitment of bright young people into the field, access to new sources of information, changes in the organization and funding of the field, and, above all, developments within China and changes in Sino-American relations, as well as continued evolution in the intellectual milieu in which Chinese studies in the United States takes place.

Several discernible trends are well under way. Geographically, the previously heavy emphasis on mainland China is likely to broaden to include more attention to greater China—the mainland, Taiwan, Hong Kong, the overseas Chinese, and the interaction among them. Temporally, the distinction between contemporary China—the People's Republic of China since 1949—and modern China—China since the eighteenth century—is likely to fade. That is, the 1949 establishment of the People's Republic will diminish as a significant watershed in Chinese history, and the importance of knowing the deep past for understanding the present will become more pronounced. The focus will also shift from Beijing (the power struggles and policies emanating from the capital) to the local levels, the behavior and beliefs of the populace, and interaction of state and society. And more scholars will place China in a comparative context than will treat it as a unique phenomenon. These trends will expand the disciplinary perspectives that illuminate modern China. No longer will political scientists and economists heavily dominate the effort; historians, anthropologists, sociologists, philosophers, psychologists, demographers, lawyers, and students of literature will become even more central.

As the essays in this volume demonstrate, most of these trends began in the 1980s. They are likely to be even more evident in the 1990s. To understand the reasons for these developments, we begin with a backward glance at the organizational and political factors that shaped contemporary Chinese studies in the United States and China in the 1950s and 1960s. We then identify ten trends that will shape the field in the 1990s. And we then mention some of the research opportunities that will lure the field forward.

The Changing Domain of Contemporary Chinese Studies

In quite different ways, political considerations in the 1950s and 1960s significantly shaped the concepts and organization of Chinese studies in both China and the United States. In both countries, for different political reasons, ideas—some might say ideologies—became embedded in research organizations that affected the study of China for many years. But in both countries, the research structures and their conceptual foundations began to change in the late 1970s and 1980s; these changes both reflected the field and enabled it to move in new directions.

The Chinese Case

Until the 1980s, the leaders in Beijing and their ideologues simply banned the scholarly and objective study of the history of the Chinese Communist movement and forbade scholarly research into the post-1949 era. The leaders structured research institutes and universities to reflect their power needs and Marxist-Leninist ideological preferences, and they granted access to party and government archives only to trusted researchers who wrote in accordance with the shifting orthodoxies stipulated by the leaders. (In fact, some scholars did write works that subtly challenged orthodoxies; their research sometimes led to private conclusions that surfaced after the control apparatus had eroded.)

Until recently, the leaders and their ideologues enforced a rather rigid system for organizing and conceptualizing modern Chinese history. The rulers decided that Chinese history should be divided into two periods: *jindai shi,* or *xiandai shi* (before 1949), and *dangdai shi* (after 1949). Complicating the explication of these terms in English is that the three Chinese terms—*jindai shi, xiandai shi,* and *dangdai shi*—can all be accurately rendered in English as "contemporary history," while both *jindai shi* and *xiandai shi* can also alternatively be translated as "modern history." *Jindai* literally refers to a time that is close at hand or recent, while *xiandai* precisely means the present; *xiandai* is closer to the current moment than *jindai*. As a field of study, *xiandai shi* was well established in China at the time of the Communist revolution. It referred to contemporary history, which meant history of the Republican period (1911–49). The Communist leaders permitted *xiandai shi* to continue, but froze the time span. They precluded it from extending into the Communist era. The official formulation roughly equated *jindai shi* with *xiandai shi*, and restrained scholars of *xiandai shi*—even if the concept accurately means contemporary history—from studying the current period.

In the 1950s, this orthodoxy acquired institutional definition in the mandate of the Modern History Institute of the Division of Social Science and Philosophy (DSSP) under the Chinese Academy of Sciences. This institute, the Jindai Lishi Yanjiusuo, was precluded from studying the pre-1949 history of the Communist revolution or the history of the People's Republic. Research on history of the Chinese Communist Party (CCP) and on post-1949 China was carried out in separate institutes and departments, especially at the People's University and the Central Party School. Though the structures were severely battered during the Cultural Revolution, with the DSSP being abolished during the Cultural Revolution, the conceptual scheme remained in force into the early 1980s. Then, the Chinese Academy of Social Sciences was formed out of the reconstituted DSSP, and the Modern History Institute was placed within it.

In the Deng Xiaoping era, the study of party history and post-1949 China became legitimate domains of scholarly research by modern historians. Deng provided the initial impetus to a somewhat objective assessment of the era with his sponsorship of the reappraisal of Mao Zedong and the reexamination of the history of the party in 1981. In 1984, the thirty-fifth anniversary of the founding of the PRC, many publications examining Chinese history from 1949 appeared. Several research institutes also launched publication series of memoirs, documentary collections, and historical monographs on post-1949 developments. The conservative ideologues Hu Qiaomu and Deng Liqun were particularly energetic in initiating these projects. Since *jindai shi* and *xiandai shi* were still primarily limited to the Republican era, a new term had to be employed to describe post-1949 studies—*dangdai shi*—which mainland translators render in English as "contemporary history." Another popular term for the newly legitimate field of study is *dangdai Zhongguo*, or contemporary or today's China. And as the study of *dangdai Zhongguo* became legitimate, some historians at the Jindai Lishi Yanjiusuo began to study aspects of post-1949 China, especially its diplomatic history. Further, a new Institute of Contemporary History was established in 1991 to study post-1949 history.

Not surprisingly, this orthodoxy has enshrined the 1949 divide between the Nationalist and Communist eras. In fact, until recently, the political leaders on both sides of the Taiwan Strait wished to emphasize the discontinuities and differences between the Nationalist and Communist regimes. Kuomintang (KMT) Nationalist officials sought to portray the Communists as alien to Chinese tradition; they emphasized the Soviet origins of the mainland regime. The Communists, meanwhile, described the country under their regime as New China. Their revolution was a dramatic break from a sordid and sad recent past. They certainly did not wish to acknowledge any possible intellectual debts to the Republican era for their approach to governance. Both the rulers in Beijing and

Taipei and the scholars they patronized therefore emphasized that a chasm divided Republican from Communist China. To both sides in the Chinese civil war, the 1949 Communist ascension to national power was a watershed event.

The Chinese structures and ideologies embedded in them had a considerable impact on the American study of China. Most important, until recently, no indigenous scholars existed on the mainland to serve as colleagues who could freely introduce American academics to their own contemporary history, economy, and society. This is something that American area specialists of Western Europe, Latin America, Japan, and South Asia take for granted. Note, for example, the great influence Latin American social scientists have had on the American study of the region. Further, Chinese scholars on both Taiwan and the mainland were unable to acknowledge or explore the linkages between the Communist regime and its predecessors. As we note in the next section, one reason the 1990s can be expected to be years of innovation in Chinese studies is that these structures and ideologies are now changing. Mainland and Taiwan scholars are beginning to explore the contemporary era with fewer constraints than in the past, and on both sides of the Taiwan Strait political incentives now exist to explore the Chineseness of the mainland regime.

The American Setting

Political considerations also affected the development of China studies in the United States. Since the 1950s, the term "contemporary China" usually has referred to one of three time spans: (1) China from 1949 to the present; (2) this year's or current China; or (3) China during its latest policy phase. According to the last of these interpretations, contemporary China in the mid-1950s meant China of the First Five-Year Plan; in the late 1960s and early 1970s, it meant Cultural Revolution China; in the 1980s, China of the Deng reform era; and the early 1990s, contemporary China has meant the post–June 4 mainland. Geographically, contemporary China has usually been equated with the territory under CCP control before 1949 and mainland China after 1949. In short, the temporal and spatial definition of contemporary China has tended to commit scholars to a post-1949, Beijing-centered view of Chinese affairs.

How did this definition of "contemporary" arise? That, of course, is a complicated matter, but one rooted partly in reality. After all, for much of the Mao era the mainland was under rather centralized rule; in some respects Maoist rule did represent a break from the past; and until the 1970s, developments on Taiwan had little economic or intellectual effect on the mainland. But the temporal and geographic definition of contemporary China also grew out of the political fissures that split the China field in the United States in the early 1950s. The McCarthy era had a pernicious influence on not only the careers of distinguished Foreign Service officers but the academic community. The Institute of Pacific Affairs (IPR), which had been the meetingplace for China specialists in journalism, government, and universities, suffered from the slanderous charges that its officers were disloyal to the United States and that the organization had served as a conduit for passing valuable intelligence to Chinese Communists. Its publications were disrupted. Academics were inescapably drawn into the uproar over the IPR and over the reckless charges against the China hands in the Department of State. Some academic China specialists delivered testimony in Congressional hearings impugning the patriotism and integrity of academics at other universities. The ugly conflict was nurtured by the Taiwan lobby. The government on Taiwan encouraged loyalists to rally to its side, and its supporters directed blame for the Kuomintang's retreat from the mainland on the treachery of American China specialists rather than KMT inadequacies.

The legacy of this period lasted through much of the 1950s. On the whole, the field languished. Some important exceptions existed, such as the project at Harvard University under John Fairbank's sponsorship to understand the history of the Communist revolution and the origins of Mao Zedong's revolutionary doctrine; a project at MIT under the guidance of W.W. Rostow to assess the Chinese economy; a project organized by the Air Force at Lackland Airforce Base; and individual efforts such as those by Richard Walker at Yale and the economist Yuan-li Wu. Animosities and suspicion prevented intellectual exchange among scholars at different China centers. The bitterness between the two communities at Harvard and the University of Washington was particularly noteworthy and debilitating.

Not until the late 1950s was it possible to try to reassemble and reinvigorate the moribund field. And this necessitated developing an acceptable set of terms and concepts that would transcend the political divisions of the day. But how to refer to China? The study of the "People's Republic" was not acceptable to scholars who did not wish to accord the new regime legitimacy. After all, U.S. government policy at the time was premised on the assumption that the mainland regime was a "passing phase," to use Secretary of State John Foster Dulles's description. "Red China"—the term used by many newspapers through the 1950s and 1960s—did not have an acceptable scholarly ring to it. "Communist China" and "mainland China" were definite possibilities, but to those who wished some ambiguity and who thought both the mainland and Taiwan merited study, these two phrases were unacceptable; they excluded the other China. A similar problem existed in the search for an appropriate appellation for that entity located a hundred miles away from the mainland: Formosa, Taiwan, or the Republic of China. Each of these had acquired political overtones in the 1950s. Formosa was the name employed by pro-independence people. The Communists referred to the province of Taiwan; and Chiang K'ai-shek and his supporters preferred the Republic of China. U.S. government jargon referred to the "ChiComs" and the "ChiNats."

No sane American would have considered adopting the Communist-devised, *pinyin* system of romanizing Chinese written characters or referring to the Communist capital as "Beijing." That would have signified a total capitulation to the

Communists. The missionary-devised Wade-Giles system for writing Chinese characters continued to prevail. Even to say "Peking"—meaning "Northern Capital" —placed one in the Communist camp. "Peking" did not pass the lips of an official U.S. government spokesman until 1969. Rather, Americans only gradually ceased to call the northern Chinese city "Peiping" ("Northern Peace"), the pre-1949 appellation still used in Taiwan. Civil wars and cold wars do not provide an easy environment to develop a value-free vocabulary to discuss the object of scholarship.

American scholars who wished to facilitate serious, in-depth study of recent developments in China had to decide how best to organize the effort. One national scholarly organization already existed to foster the study of Chinese history and civilization—the Committee on Chinese Civilization. Housed in the American Council of Learned Societies, it was deeply steeped in the sinological tradition, and the initiators of the effort to encourage research on recent China concluded that their inquiry would best prosper in a separate institution. They wished to distinguish their concerns from research into ancient Chinese philosophy, classical texts, and premodern history.

In the late 1950s, such leading academics as John Fairbank, Robert Scalapino, George Taylor, Doak Barnett, John Lindbeck, and Alexander Eckstein hammered together the organizations. They then selected terms that surmounted the political divisions and enabled interested scholars to get on with the core task at hand, namely to understand the origins, development, consequences, and implications of the Chinese Communist revolution, while also paying some attention to the evolution of Taiwan. Organizationally, in 1959 these visionary and entrepreneurial academics, with generous foundation support, founded the Joint Committee on Contemporary China (JCCS) under the Social Science Research Council (SSRC) and the American Council of Learned Societies. The ideally vague term to describe the object of study was "contemporary China." The formula did not preclude the study of Taiwan or pre-1949 China, but the focus was on the rise of the Communists and their rule on the mainland after 1949. The nesting of the new committee within the SSRC and the composition of the JCCS ensured that the social sciences—especially political science and economics—would receive considerable attention. The creation of a separate area studies committee, rather than one linked to existing Asian, Soviet, or Japanese scholarly associations, circumvented the politically sensitive issue of whether the People's Republic should be academically nested in an Asian or a Communist context. But it also increased the likelihood that China would be studied in a distinctive rather than comparative context.

In the context of the time, these were remarkably visionary and ecumenical decisions. In a related development, the Soviet launching of the *Sputnik* satellite prompted the U.S. government to increase the national capacity to understand all foreign areas, especially those under Communist control. Government funding became available for Chinese studies at the graduate level and for research on the Chinese Communist revolution. The ideas embodied in the establishment of the JCCS were also reflected in the major centers of Chinese studies that grew rapidly in the early 1960s, not only in the United States but with American financial patronage in Britain, Australia, India, and Hong Kong. The temporal and conceptual definition of contemporary China was also embedded in the editorial policy of the influential new journal established in 1960: the *China Quarterly*. All these developments rapidly yielded results. By the mid-1960s, the study of post-1949 mainland China had taken off.

The late 1950s–early 1960s conceptualization of the appropriate temporal and geographic domain of contemporary Chinese studies relaxed somewhat but basically persisted into the 1970s. It became the boundary of core expertise of the many graduate students of contemporary China recruited into the field and trained during the 1960s and of the many major monographs and conference volumes published in that decade and the next.

For a brief interlude, the activities of the Committee on Scholarly Communication with the People's Republic of China (CSCPRC) intensified the focus on post-1949, mainland China. This committee, established in 1966, was at the forefront in reestablishing scholarly contact between the United States and China in the 1970s and early 1980s. The CSCPRC was able to attract considerable government and foundation support to enable American scholars in the natural sciences, social sciences, and humanities to learn about developments in their disciplines on the mainland since 1949 and to establish contacts and exchanges with mainland colleagues. The CSCPRC from an early date sought to nurture exchanges in party history, contemporary literature, archaeology, sociology, and anthropology; but for reasons described above, Chinese authorities were not eager or able to reciprocate overtures in these areas.

Conceptual breakthroughs at one stage of intellectual development, however, become the confining conditions in the next state. Even in the 1960s the initial temporal and territorial definition of contemporary China began to be tested and stretched. The initial definition seemed increasingly inadequate and began to yield to a focus on modern, greater China. Work by people such as Benjamin Schwartz, Joseph Levenson, Albert Feuerwerker, Mary Wright, and G. William Skinner demonstrated the insight that came from placing current developments in historical perspective. They showed that the 1949 divide was less significant than either the Nationalists or the Communists had claimed. Soon after its establishment, the JCCS extended its temporal domain to 1911. But the organizational distinction between traditional and contemporary China persisted until the early 1980s, when the JCCS merged with the descendent body of the Committee on Chinese Civilization to form the Joint Committee on Chinese Studies. The merger terminated the division between the study of contemporary and traditional China, and by physically locating the new committee in the American Council of Learned Societies, the field acknowledged the central role to be played by the humanities in understanding the contemporary period. Also in the late 1970s and early 1980s, the CSCPRC pressured the Chinese government to open the country to study by sociologists and anthropologists, and pioneered conferences on contemporary literature. Many American scholars who availed themselves of opportunities created by the CSCPRC had previously done research in Taiwan or Hong Kong. These researchers discovered a Chinese society with which, in many respects, they were quite familiar. The Communist revolution had not totally transformed the country. In some respects, at least, one could speak about a "Greater China" and its various regional differences.

Ten Likely Trends in the 1990s

As the preceding section indicates, the American study of contemporary China since the 1940s has been greatly influenced by international affairs and domestic developments in both China and the United States. The McCarthy era of the early 1950s, the Sino-Soviet alliance of the 1950s and split of the 1960s, the Vietnam War, the Sino-American rapprochement of the 1970s, Deng's reforms of the 1980s, and the suppression of popular demonstrations in 1989 all significantly affected funding, research opportunities, the research agenda, and recruitment of new people into Chinese studies. During the years of Sino-American hostility, from 1950 to 1971, American students of contemporary China had no opportunity to observe the object of research in situ or to have direct exchanges with scholars in that country. After Henry Kissinger's trip to Beijing in 1971, American contemporary China specialists began to visit the mainland as academic tourists, usually as members of delegations studying specific aspects of China, and they hosted touring mainland Chinese delegations in the United States. The establishment of full diplomatic relations in 1979 permitted American researchers to work in the PRC and engage in field research, while the Chinese mainland scholars who began to spend extended periods of time in the United States influenced American research on China.

What developments are likely to occur in the 1990s that will have a similar impact on the American study of contemporary China? Attempting to answer this question at the end of the Deng Xiaoping era is particularly hazardous, since at this writing China's future is highly uncertain. China's developmental path in the post-Deng era could go in many directions, ranging from a transition to democracy to harsh authoritarianism to fragmentation. Recognizing the many unknowns, ten trends can nonetheless be identified in the 1990s that probably will affect the American study of contemporary China. Five of them involve likely changes within China: (1) changes in relations between state and society; (2) developments between the center and its periphery; (3) the consequences of increasing global interdependence and hence of China's relations with the outside world; (4) the evolution of Chinese intellectual communities; and (5) the persistence or reappearance of certain fundamental problems in the governance of China. Related to these developments are five other likely changes within the field of Chinese studies: (1) the maturation of the study of Chinese history in the United States and the increased emphasis on local social and economic history; (2) the addition of over a thousand émigrés from mainland China to the United States in the 1980s who have become part of the American community of contemporary China specialists; (3) the increasing sophistication of Japanese scholarship on contemporary China and the possibility of increased contact with scholars from the former Soviet Union; (4) the emergence of new sources of information about China; and (5) likely changes in the availability of funding for the China field in the United States.

These ten likely developments will probably nudge the American study of contemporary China in exciting and beneficial directions. The new directions are related to the organizational and conceptual changes described in the preceding section. The temporal and territorial domain of contemporary Chinese studies will be altered: temporally, to reach further back in time and, geographically, to extend outward to the Chinese periphery. That is, the trends will probably encourage many academics to define themselves as students of modern China (meaning China since the decay of the imperial order). Instead of equating China with the mainland core, the study of China is likely to broaden to embrace the periphery, Taiwan, and Hong Kong, and their interaction with the mainland. Significant aspects of the mainland cannot be understood without reference to Hong Kong, Taiwan, and their impact on the mainland. In addition, the worldwide study of modern China will probably not be as dominated by American scholarship as in the past few decades, with the consequent need for American scholars to have competence in the analytical paradigms, research methods, and languages (such as Japanese, Russian, German, or French) of the non-American world. The era of U.S.-centered scholarship, which was never really intellectually justifiable, will simply be unsustainable. Finally, the centrality of academic China specialists in the study of China is likely to continue to diminish. In the 1980s, journalists, businessmen, bankers, foundation executives, and lawyers acquired their own impressions of China through their own personal involvement with the mainland, and their companies developed in-house China expertise. This will continue in the 1990s. In addition, specialists in substantive issues—ranging from demographers to environmentalists, agronomists, and epidemiologists—will increasingly collaborate with colleagues in China, become deeply knowledgeable about specific aspects of the China scene, and compare the Chinese case with other situations. How to incorporate this research into holistic studies of China—the forte and classic responsibility of area specialists—will be an increasing challenge in the coming decade. In this environment, academic China specialists are likely to gravitate toward studies where they enjoy a comparative advantage: placing current developments in an appropriate historical and comparative perspective.

Major Developments Meriting Study

Developments in China cannot help but affect the American study of China, as demonstrated in the chapters in this volume.[1] These developments are fueled by China's rapid economic growth, the expansion of its foreign trade, its transition to a market economy, and its changing demographic profile. China's economic transformation is having a profound effect on the society, culture, and political system. Untangling this process—what has and has not changed, how, and why—has invigorated the American study of China, generating new questions and spawning much debate.

Changing State-Society Relations

A lively debate now exists in the China field over the consequences of the Deng-era economic and political reforms on the capacity and reach of the state. We need not summarize this interesting and important discussion to make two observations. First, while specialists disagree over whether the strength of the state on balance is growing or weakening vis-à-vis the society, no one denies that the nature of the interaction is changing. As China urbanizes, more of the interaction between officials and the populace will take place in cities rather than villages and marketing towns. As the population becomes more literate and mobile, more citizens are likely to address their demands directly to the intermediate and higher levels of the state than to lower levels. As the demographic profile changes, and more of the population is elderly, the goods and services that the people seek from the state will change.

Moreover, while China specialists differ in their assessment of the state's evolving power relative to the populace, they generally agree that the central state apparatus has seen a long-term erosion in its power and authority over provincial and local levels. Some trace the origins of this trend to the Great Leap Forward, while others attribute the trend to the Cultural Revolution and its aftermath (particularly the decentralization measures of 1970); yet others argue that the growth in the power and authority of provincial, municipal, and county units stems from Deng's reforms. No matter what the causes, in the realms of ideology, personnel management, finances, and revenue, Beijing's control over provincial and county governments appears less pervasive than in earlier days of the People's Republic, and several efforts to recover portions of this lost authority—such as over off-budget revenues—have not worked. This trend can be expected to persist and accelerate in the 1990s.

The research on state-society relations is also likely to yield a more complex conceptualization of those two entities. At present, much of the scholarly writing juxtaposes the two: the state versus the society. Growing out of developments in Eastern Europe and what was the Soviet Union, the question of the moment is whether a "civil society" is emerging, particularly in urban China. To some analysts, the massive demonstrations in Beijing in April and May 1989 revealed the existence of—or at least the capacity to form—voluntary associations that are autonomous from the state and infused with values not propagated by the state. Civil society is structured from the bottom up, rather than being formed by the state. Such structures, it can be argued, are essential for democracy and freedom to flourish.

Researchers will watch for additional signs of the emergence of a civil society in China in the 1990s and of the evolving relationship between state and society. But in the course of doing so, they may find that at least in some regions and at some levels of the hierarchy, state and society are commingled and interpenetrated. For example, as was the case in traditional China, many of the popular values and behavioral patterns in society—even when followed autonomously or voluntarily—are congruent with the values of the state. The "little traditions" of peasant and urban society today and in the past partake of the "great" (or elite) traditions. In rural areas, many state cadres at the county and township levels are native to the county in which they serve. Their spouses and children work in local factories. They sweep their ancestors' graves during the Qingming festival. While biking on country roads, they stop to have their fortunes told by soothsayers proficient in Daoist texts. Yet these same officials enforce Beijing's family planning, marriage, and burial regulations, all of which attack rituals that are at the core of the civilization. The boundary and tensions between state and society exist not only in the external world but perhaps, more important, in the minds of individual Chinese.

Research on state-society relations, therefore, is likely to engender even greater attention to analysis of Chinese at the individual level: how different roles are reconciled and integrated; what motivates individuals; and what strategies are quietly pursued to advance private, familial, and group interests.

The Center and the Periphery

Reflective of the weakened central state apparatus and of altered state-society interaction is the greater permeability of China. Partly by design, as a result of the Special Economic Zones, open coastal cities, and the general opening to the outside world, China is more vulnerable to the commercial and intellectual influences of Hong Kong and Taiwan. The links between Hong Kong and Guangdong province and between Taiwan and Fujian province are multiplying very rapidly. Though such things are hard to quantify or prove, one is tempted to say that in many respects the social, economic, and cultural life of Guangzhou is now tied at least as intimately to Hong Kong as to Beijing. South Korea is developing links with Shandong province, while Japan, Russia, and South Korea are resurrecting connections with Manchuria. The gaze of Shanghai entrepreneurs, as during the century from the 1840s to the 1940s, is again directed toward the Pacific as much as toward the interior. Leaders of Sichuan, Yunnan, and Guizhou provinces plan for expanded economic relations with Southeast Asia. The discontent and the greater autonomy of the Muslims in Central Asia—the Uygurs, Uzbeks, Kazakhs, Tajiks, and others—are penetrating into Xinjiang and Qinghai provinces. And one wonders whether the developments in Mongolia, which has moved toward democracy, will soon reverberate among the Mongols in Inner Mongolia and perhaps even intensify Tibetan yearnings for autonomy. (Belief in Tibetan Buddhism is strong among Mongols, and throughout history there have been periods of intense interaction and attraction between the Tibetans and Buddhist Mongols, often to the detriment of Han interests.)

The point here is simple but important. From 1960 to 1976, mainland China had very little interaction with its adjacent areas (except North Korea, Hong Kong, and Indochina), and the center was firmly in control of its periphery. This was a historical anomaly. During imperial times and the Republican era, the boundaries of China were ill-defined and porous, and there was considerable intercourse between the outlying regions of China and the inhabitants just beyond the Chinese realm. Thus the great growth of contemporary Chinese studies in the United States coincided with an unusual era, when it was possible to look on mainland China as a well-defined, distinct, separate entity. That era is probably irretrievably gone. Especially Taiwan and Hong Kong, but also Tibet, Xinjiang, Inner Mongolia, Manchuria, and probably the coastal region from Shandong to Fujian will be locations of increasingly high interaction between mainland and external influences. These are the locales where the Chinese state traditionally competed for influence with non-Chinese entities. In the 1990s the central government, as throughout most of Chinese history, will probably not be totally able to control the flow of goods, ideas, and people across its borders, and the influences that penetrate into its border regions will then seep into the interior of China. And these peripheral regions, in turn, will have a great impact on the Chinese interior, that is, such provinces as Hunan, Hubei, Henan, Shaanxi, Shanxi, and Sichuan.

G. William Skinner's repeated urgings to think of China in terms of macroregions and within macroregions in terms of core and periphery have never been more germane. The foregoing analysis suggests that several of China's macroregions (or more precisely, the core of those macroregions) are being magnetically drawn into the world economic and intellectual systems: the Pearl River Delta, including Hong Kong; Fujian, across from Taiwan; the region stretching from Nanjing to Shanghai along the lower Yangtze River; the Tianjin-Beijing megalopolis on the North China plain; and the Manchurian corridor from Harbin to Dalian. Each of these regions will forge links with different parts of the outside world. But other vast regions—the middle Yangtze, the upper Yangtze, the Yungui plateau, the northwest—will continue to be constrained by transportation and poverty from developing equally extensive linkages to the outside.

Global Interdependence

The changes in state-society interaction and in the center's control over its periphery are largely manifestations of more fundamental global trends: the telecommunications transformation, pressures on the environment, and the emergence of a global economy. All states are finding it increasingly difficult to control the flow of goods, ideas, and people across their boundaries. Further, common problems press increasingly on all countries, including global climatic change, deforestation, desertification, narcotics, control of communicable diseases (especially AIDS), and sustainable agricultural production. The leaders of both mainland China and Taiwan in the past four decades formed their political views early in the twentieth century, during the era of raw imperialism; they matured when China was weak, divided, and a victim of external aggression. Their lifelong nationalistic commitment, understandably, was to remedy these deficiencies, to restore Chinese greatness, and to defend Chinese sovereignty. But the 1990s are likely to demonstrate to the successor generation of leaders that their pursuit of national sovereignty must be tempered by an acknowledgment of the interdependence of countries. Even the more conservative members among China's next generation of leaders, many of whom received a technological education, appear to recognize that many of China's problems cannot be alleviated by China alone.

Similarly, despite the efforts by the industrial democracies to impose economic sanctions on the Chinese government after its June 4, 1989, crackdown and subsequent campaigns of repression, worldwide leaders have not rushed to isolate China's rulers. On the contrary, a general recognition exists in the West and Japan that humankind cannot surmount its common challenges in the decades ahead without the active involvement of one-fourth of the world's population and its government. China, for example, will be the largest new net contributor of carbon dioxide emissions in the coming decade, and its participation will be crucial in any effort to reduce the greenhouse effect. Because of the rapid expansion of refrigeration on the mainland, China's use of chlorofluorocarbons (CFCs)—a major chemical contribution to the depletion of the ozone layer—is rising rapidly. AIDS (Acquired Immune Deficiency Syndrome) and drug addiction have begun to appear in southwest China.

Most of the problems of interdependence have technical dimensions, and the solutions to them frequently involve the natural sciences, engineering, and such professions as law, medicine, economics, and business. Knowing how global trends affect China, understanding the effect of China's behavior on global trends, and shaping the Chinese response to these trends will require cooperation among knowledgeable Chinese and foreign social scientists and natural scientists. As a result, Chinese professionals in such diverse fields as arms control, family planning, international finance, administration of textile quotas, and coal benefication are becoming members of their international professional communities. Further, Chinese involvement in such international organizations as the World Bank, the International Monetary Fund (IMF), and the General Agreement on Tariffs and Trade (GATT) has created strong bonds between these keystone international economic organizations and mainland China.

These developments, which are likely to accelerate in the 1990s, open myriad research topics concerning China's economic, political, and scientific interaction with the outside world. Political economists, in particular, will find grist for their mills as they track the integration of China's economy into the productive and commercial processes of the Asia-Pacific region.

A Worldwide Chinese Intellectual Community

A decade ago, intellectual communities on the China mainland were isolated from communities using the Chinese language as their medium of discourse in Hong Kong, Taiwan, Southeast Asia, and North America. As a result of the changes noted above, however, that is no longer the case. Mainland intellectuals read the leading fiction writers on Taiwan, while intellectuals on Taiwan are familiar with the new wave of poets and short story writers on the mainland. Such writers as Liu Binyan (a mainland essayist now resident in the United States), Bei Tao (a mainland poet), Bo Yang (a Taiwanese satirist), and Chen Jo-hsi (a U.S.-based writer who has lived in both Taiwan and the mainland) are among writers whose publications reach a global Chinese audience.

The political leaders of China can no longer halt the circulation of an idea by incarcerating its exponents. For example, the 1987 withdrawal of party membership from Fang Lizhi, Wang Ruoshui, and Liu Binyan, and the criticism of them in the mainland media, did not halt the dissemination of their ideas, as would have been the case between 1949 and 1976. Instead, enterprising Hong Kong book dealers reprinted their essays in anthologies that were then easily carried into the mainland. At least temporarily, the 1987 criticism of Fang, Wang, and Liu enhanced rather than diminished their influence. Nor has the post-1989 crackdown on intellectuals proved terribly effective in this regard. Travel abroad, conferences in Beijing, Hong Kong contacts, and hand-carried communications and publications are keeping intellectuals in Shanghai and Beijing, at least, attuned to intellectual currents among compatriots abroad. Mainland intellectuals know about the efforts of Tu Wei-ming and his colleagues in Taiwan, Hong Kong, and Singapore to find in traditional Chinese thought the basis for humane answers to some of the perplexing dilemmas of modern society.

Even more intriguing is the likely long-term effect of the substantial dissident community now resident in Western Europe and the United States. Though deeply divided by different beliefs, organizational and personal loyalties, and procedural issues, literally hundreds of Chinese intellectuals in self-imposed exile abroad are now thinking and writing seriously about the future of their country. Many intellectuals in China who, in private, express their unhappiness with their current leaders and the oppressive political climate nonetheless simultaneously voice strong criticism of the dissident émigrés. They complain that those abroad took the easy road by leaving the country; they resent the easy advice offered by people enjoying the shelter of foreign regimes. What influence in the end will the émigré communities have on future developments in China? Have the seeds been planted for the next round of bitter factional strife, to be waged between those who stayed and those who fled? Or in the end, will the ideas that have been nurtured in Paris, Princeton, and elsewhere become influential in the 1990s? One suspects that the answers to these questions will be quite important in determining China's future.

But the oppressive atmosphere on the mainland since 1988–89 has not brought intellectual ferment to an end. A new generation of humanist Marxists and non-Marxists has emerged as creative intellectuals. The political leaders have attacked many of them. But they remain influential, and they are likely to outlast this generation of political figures. Among these social thinkers are Li Zehou, Liu Zaifu, Liu Xiaobo, Chen Zeming, Tang Yijie, Zhang Shiying, Lin Fang, and Su Xiaokang. Some, like Su, are popularizers. Others, such as Zhang and Lin, straddle the boundary between psychology and philosophy. Some are in literary criticism. Some, such as Tang, consciously accept many elements of the Confucian tradition, while others, like Liu Xiaobo or Su, are bitter critics of the Confucian legacy. Many are wrestling with the relationship between the natural and the human worlds. Is society determined by the same kind of immutable, deterministic laws as the material world? What are universalistic human traits? Out of such debates are likely to flow future ideas about governance in China.

In short, not since the May Fourth movement has there been such innovation among Chinese intellectuals both on the mainland and among the diaspora. The events of 1989 were both a consequence of this ferment and a further stimulation of it. It is only a matter of time before the new ideas affect the way China is ruled and the way the populace itself views its condition. A major and indeed urgent task confronting students of contemporary China in the 1990s is to understand the issues gripping the new generation of social critics and to assess their likely political and social implications.

Continuity in Underlying Issues

The trends enumerated above will surely pull mainland China in new directions in the 1990s, and the looming succession to Deng Xiaoping and the other octogenarians will additionally mean that new leaders will seek to mold the country according to their visions—visions that are likely to differ from those of their revolutionary-generation predecessors. But the twilight years of Deng's reign have also amply demonstrated that considerable continuity exists in the agenda of issues confronting China's leaders since the mid-nineteenth century. These include persistent factionalism and the absence of a regularized decisional process at the apex of the system; an inadequate revenue system that plagued the central government with continual budget deficits; a military apparatus in which personal loyalties took precedence over institutional chains-of-command, making armies personal instruments of power; the inability of the articulators of state ideology to make adjustments in its content so that the state could provide the populace with a convincing orientation to its environment and a meaningful guide to action; and a pattern of authority and a national cohesiveness that were fragile and vulnerable to disruption through extensive cultural and economic contact with the outside world.

To many observers both inside and outside China, until the mid-1960s it appeared that Mao Zedong and his associates, through the ideology and organization they had articulated, had reintegrated Chinese society, established a strong central apparatus, and subordinated the military to institutionalized civilian rule. While the Cultural Revolution seriously eroded these accomplishments, most observers thought that Deng and his associates, through their reform program, had not only restored the previous gains of the Mao era but were establishing regular decisional processes at the apex, at last curbing unbridled and unprincipled factional strife, and were demonstrating flexibility in the ideological realm. The purges of Hu Yaobang and Zhao Ziyang, the Beijing tragedy of June 2–4, 1989, and subsequent events, however, have revealed the tenuousness of Deng's institutional reforms. In a profound sense, in short, it now appears that neither the Communist revolution nor Deng's reforms really resolved the underlying crisis in the political order that has enveloped China since the late eighteenth century. To be sure, China's leaders confront their constitutional issues in a significantly altered context from those of the nineteenth and early twentieth centuries, and changes in attitudes and technology permit different solutions. But as elaborated in the concluding section, considerable insight into the current problems is acquired by tracing the evolution of these issues ever since imperial times.

Changes in Chinese Studies

Developments in History, Sociology, Anthropology, and the Humanities

The American study of modern China will change in the coming decade not only because of trends in China but because of certain developments within the China field itself. Foremost among these are the enormous strides in recent years in the American study of Chinese local social, intellectual, and economic history. One thinks, for example, of Benjamin Elman's study of the intellectual community in Yangzhou in the seventeenth to nineteenth centuries, William Rowe's two-volume history of Wuhan, Philip Huang's work on the lower Yangtze, Keith Schoppa's monograph on northwest Zhejiang province, and Joseph Esherick's account of the Boxer rebellion. Historians such as Frederic Wakeman, Philip

Kuhn, and Emily Honig are joining political scientists such as David Strand and Elizabeth Perry to work separately on topics that extend from the Republican to Communist eras: forms of protest and political participation, the working-class movement, the Shanghai underclass, and so on. We will return to the major implications of the explosion in publications on Imperial and Republican China in the concluding section.

The blossoming of studies of modern China literature from the May Fourth period to the present by Leo Ou-fan Lee and Perry Link, among others, as well as the studies of both urban and rural China by sociologists and anthropologists, the result of field research on the mainland, yield a richer sense of Chinese society, its diversity, and the complex patterns of state-society interaction. The net effect of these developments is that anthropologists, historians, sociologists, and scholars of Chinese literature are writing some of the most insightful and revealing monographs on contemporary China, and the field is no longer largely the preserve of economists and political scientists. This development is particularly fortuitous in light of the evolving nature of state-society interaction, and China specialists from these disciplines will be at the forefront in illuminating the change of the 1990s.

The Impact of Émigrés

The influx of scholars and graduate students from the PRC, many of whom will obtain permanent academic appointments in the United States, will considerably enrich American scholarship in the 1990s. Many of the émigrés have a special understanding of their native country. Several were active participants in the high-level policy debates of the 1980s. Some of them remain in contact with relatives and friends, through whom they obtain useful intelligence about current developments in China. They also are able to obtain *neibu* (internal) publications that foreigners are proscribed from purchasing. The United States is clearly the beneficiary in permitting the émigrés to reside and find employment here. As so often in American history, the humanitarian response to the problems of immigrants also enriches the nation.

At the same time, we should recognize some of the difficulties that the influx will present. Some of the émigrés have both scholarly and political interests, and on occasion they seem to subordinate their scholarship to their political objectives. (Of course, the same can be said for Western scholars as well.) The émigré scholars also seem vulnerable to gossip from the mainland; their reporting is not always reliable. Frequently, moreover, their writings are intended for a Chinese rather than American audience. And finally, their American audience must keep in mind that most of the Chinese come from urban, coastal regions; most have very little personal experience in the rural interior.

Despite these difficulties, many of which apply to Western scholars of contemporary China as well, the important point to stress is that a decade hence, a significant portion of the young economists, political scientists, historians, sociologists, and literary critics teaching and writing about China in American universities will be scholars of Chinese ethnicity who immigrated to the United States in the late 1980s and early 1990s. Joining them will be a new generation of American scholars who spent several years studying Chinese language in China, traveling widely throughout the land, and acquiring a grass-roots view of China before embarking on their academic careers. The Chinese language skills of both the émigrés and the Americans will be superb. Their training in their disciplines will be rigorous. Their commitment to achieving rigorous standards of scholarship should be high. Their contacts with the mainland will be extensive. The result will be a much more detailed and extensive understanding of China than was imaginable a decade ago. Indeed, with this expansion in the research manpower, American funders will have to ask another question: How much detail does the United States need to know about contemporary China? At what point will the appetite for knowledge about China be sated? Is it possible that the market will be glutted?

Chinese Studies Outside the United States

Until the 1980s, American scholars set the pace for the worldwide study of contemporary China. The centers established in the 1950s and 1960s in Britain, Australia, and India were created with Ford Foundation support. The Universities Service Centre in Hong Kong, the preeminent locus for documentary research in the 1960s and 1970s, had American funding and leadership. Scholarship in Japan became mired in disputes among liberals, Marxists, and Maoists. The ideological orthodoxies imposed by the Sino-Soviet dispute precluded Soviet sinologists from publishing their insights derived from their extensive exposure to China and their excellent grounding in Chinese language and history. In Sweden, the Netherlands, Germany, and France, strong sinological traditions offered the basis for study of the contemporary era. For complex reasons that differed from country to country but that largely stemmed from inadequate funding, contemporary Chinese studies on the European continent did not flourish. (To be sure, individual scholars such as Lucien Bianco, Marie-Claire Bergère, Marianne Bastid, and Jurgen Domes became quite influential.) Only in Britain, through the entrepreneurial verve of those such as Roderick MacFarquhar, Maurice Freedman, Kenneth Walker, Stuart Schram, and David Wilson, did the field develop momentum.

This situation began to change in the 1980s, and the trends can only accelerate in the 1990s. Useful journals and monographs on contemporary China are published in Canada, Australia, the Netherlands, France, Denmark, Sweden, and Germany. The World Bank and the International Monetary Fund, using their own international civil servants and drawing on scholars throughout the world, publish monographs on the economy to which the Chinese government makes substantial contributions. Because of Japan's extensive and penetrating involvement in China, the Japanese understanding of important facets of contemporary China leads the world. Much of this wisdom remains the proprietary knowledge of Japanese trading companies, but the *China Newsletter,* the English-language publication of the Japanese External Trade Research Organization (JETRO), provides a glimpse of Japanese understanding of political and economic issues on the mainland. The relaxation of tensions between Taiwan and the mainland and democratization of Taiwan itself, coupled with the return of U.S.-trained Ph.D.'s and the rise of a new generation of scholars, have stimulated contemporary Chinese studies on the island, including analysis of Taiwan itself. The relaxation of tensions between China and the former Soviet Union offers promise for scholarly cooperation; economic crisis in Russia and the other republics, however, may preclude its realization.

The rise of European, Japanese, and Taiwanese scholarship reflects their economic prosperity, while such countries as Australia, Britain, and France have also benefited from the influx of mainland Chinese scholars. Scholarship on contemporary China in the 1990s will become a truly global enterprise; as a result, mastery of languages in addition to Chinese will be even more important than in the past. The consequences are likely to be significant. There can be no doubt that Americans—as others—study China through distinctive sets of national lenses. Scholars from other countries will likely bring their own analytical perspectives and research questions to bear. For example, French scholars, influenced by Marxist and neo-Marxist perspectives and less enmeshed in the emotions of the Chinese Communist revolution, never accepted the 1950s American definition of contemporary China; they usually placed post-1949 developments in a broader sociological and historical perspective. Given their desire to advance national commercial interests, both German and Japanese government and corporate-sponsored research institutes are funding detailed studies of specific sectors and locales within keeping of the traditions these countries have for detailed investigation.

In a sense, the challenge confronting the China field in the United States in the 1990s replicates on a small scale the one faced by the entire American people. Can Americans adjust to a situation where they are not at the forefront across the board? Will they be able to appreciate the insights of others and draw on them swiftly? Will they respect the different values that guide the scholarship of other cultures? Or will they expect that the diffusion of democracy will lead increasingly to a scholarship similar to their own and perhaps be resentful when it does not? And how will Americans react as foreign funders from Taiwan, Hong Kong, or Japan, for example, seek to press their agendas on American researchers in perhaps only slightly less subtle fashion than Americans did in the era of dominance by the United States?

New Sources

Perhaps no factor has been as immediately influential in the evolution of Chinese studies as changes in the availability of data. And in this regard, the 1990s could well be extraordinary. Some developments are likely to occur under any circumstances, and the resumption of political liberalization in the post-Deng era could only encourage them.

First, toward the end of the 1980s, the Chinese began to publish documentary collections concerning high-level politics from the inception of the party to the Deng era. These are but the tip of the iceberg, since at all levels in the 1980s, major efforts were made to record local party histories, resulting in extensive publications, many highly classified. The Communist archives are being selectively opened for use by a larger number of Chinese scholars, and journals are being published on party history that, while still constrained by the leaders' whims, enable a deeper and more accurate understanding of elite politics, foreign policy, and economic development strategy. Historians are likely to find the new material sufficiently attractive to move more vigorously into post-1949 studies.

Second, at the local levels, archives are beginning to be opened and control over previously classified data is being loosened. Local gazetteers are again being published. The Chinese University's China Center in Hong Kong and the Academia Sinica in Taipei are making special efforts to collect these materials, and presumably the principal repositories on the mainland, such as the National Library in Beijing and the Shanghai Municipal Library, will assemble their own collections, as will the libraries of the Academy of Social Sciences and the People's University in Guangzhou. While uneven, these publications provide hitherto unavailable information on, for example, party membership figures since 1949 (broken down by gender, age, and education), the changing structure of the county political system and below, data on social order (including, for some counties, murder rates and the number of executions of criminals), reports on illegal activities of Daoist sects, and financial, price, demographic, and production statistics at the county level since 1949. National plans in the cultural sphere call for every one of China's two-thousand-plus counties to publish a gazetteer by the mid-1990s, and if the early products provide a clue as to what is in the offing, a bonanza awaits local social, political, and economic historians, especially if these materials are then used for extensive in situ interviews and combined with the gazetteers of the Qing and Republican eras for careful studies of the long-term evolution of a particular region.

Third, the opportunities for field research and survey research by foreigners are likely to increase. The regime's efforts to curtail such efforts in the 1980s and early 1990s proved feckless, and as China opens to tourism, joint ventures, and research by international financial institutions, its ability to prevent social science research is likely to diminish further. Moreover, Chinese scholars are acquiring the skills to undertake their own social surveys. Several national survey organizations have been established, and they are staffed by scholars knowledgeable in questionnaire construction, survey methodology, sampling procedures, and data analysis. Books by Chinese authors analyzing the contemporary political culture, drawing on social surveys, have already begun to appear. There is likely to be much more accurate information than has ever been available before on values, beliefs, and attitudes of the populace.

Fourth, the collapse of communism in Eastern Europe and the Soviet Union is likely to lead to the release of fascinating materials on the history of the Communist movement and on Sino-Soviet relations. If Russia and the other successors to the Soviet Union prove reluctant to release documents, there still are troves of materials now available in Germany, Poland, Hungary, and Czechoslovakia on the international Communist gatherings from the 1940s through the 1960s that will permit a more precise understanding of those years.

Fifth, despite the efforts to censure literature and the arts, Western ideas of creativity and literary criticism have now penetrated the artistic worlds in the urban areas of coastal China, as well as Taiwan and Hong Kong. The 1990s are likely to be an innovative decade in the arts, if not in Beijing, then in regions less vulnerable to its control.

Sixth, a torrent of statistical information has become available down to the county level. Statistical yearbooks, encyclopedias, compendia, and almanacs of all sorts contain demographic, economic, social, and political statistics. China is now the best recorded of the developing countries, and the accessibility of these data disaggregated to the county level and below provides those social scientists who are enamored with quantitative analytical techniques an unparalleled opportunity to test theories through multivariate analysis.

Finally, the legacy of June 4 and the democracy movement is still alive. Much about what happened during the waning days of the Deng era remains unknown, especially with respect to the removal of Hu Yaobang and the suppression of the demonstrations. Quite possibly, in the post-Deng era, new leaders will seek to establish their legitimacy by reevaluating the Beijing tragedy and attributing blame for it to some of the perpetrators. Significant discontinuities could occur during a succession struggle, which, in turn, could lead to revelations about the Deng era, and perhaps the Mao era as well.

Funding Opportunities

For several reasons, funding opportunities are also likely to induce departures. U.S. government funding is unlikely to be sustained at current levels. Indeed, government funding of CSCPRC (now CSCC, Committee on Scholarly Communication with China) and JCCS activities by the National Science Foundation (NSF), the National Endowment of the Humanities (NEH), and the United States Information Agency has been in gradual decline, especially when inflation is taken into account, since at least the mid-1980s. Further, foundations have placed considerable emphasis on programs to nurture talent in China, such as the Ford Foundation's emphasis on training lawyers, economists, and international relations specialists. They have also turned to active programs, ranging from birth control and environmental protection. Both government and private foundations have also increasingly given priority to collaborative research projects rather than individual research by Americans. Finally, a series of only loosely related developments have on balance heightened funders' interest in the fate of the peoples on the Chinese periphery: the human rights of Tibetans; the alleviation of poverty and environmental protection in Yunnan and Guizhou provinces; the future of Hong Kong; and the democratic evolution of Taiwan. The increased availability of Taiwanese and Hong Kong funding is but one factor directing attention toward the periphery.

The dramatic changes in Eastern Europe and the former Soviet Union are likely to prompt reallocation of funds away from China and toward research on the formation of post-Communist regimes.

Thus American academic China specialists will find less money specifically designated for research on their area. They will have to compete with other scholars for the general funds that the NEH, the NSF, or foundations, such as MacArthur or Rockefeller, award. This will require researchers to defend their topics in terms of their relevance, significance, or relationship to general disciplinary or theoretical interests. The natural result will be research projects that have a comparative dimension and that draw on the particular strengths that Chinese data have to offer, for example, its generally reliable demographic statistics or local statistical series that cover long periods of time. Barring a serious cutback in general funding levels of basic research or Chinese denial of access to mainland data—both of which seem unlikely—American China specialists should do well in this competition.

The Conceptual Opportunities

Not only is the field likely to take advantage of the new sources of information and avail itself of its new talent, but, as before, the conceptual opportunities will also be seized. And those opportunities are powerful. During the past twenty years, without any overarching design, academics have written monographs on various topics that can now be linked together to form coherent analyses of China's evolution, in particular, policy realms from the height of the Qing dynasty in the seventeenth and eighteenth centuries to the present. With additional research that would fill in gaps and permit a systematic historical account, and by drawing on overviews written by Chinese historians on the mainland and Taiwan, scholars can trace the evolution of China's approach to its governance and of continuities and changes in the underlying problems confronting its rulers, as well as the development of particular regions and social groupings.

Put another way, as scholars of contemporary mainland China join other scholars to be students of modern, greater China, a new question will naturally arise: what are the clusterings of specialization within that very large field? Students of modern China at present identify themselves first in terms of their disciplines (historians, economists, sociologists, and so on) or through the narrower time-spans of their research (late Qing and the 1911 Revolution, the war-lord period, the Nanjing decade, and so on), with many scholars having more than one specialty. This, after all, is the way the major journals and newsletters in modern Chinese studies are organized. But the opportunity now presents itself for scholars of modern China to group themselves in two additional, insightful ways: in terms of substantive topics (elite politics, commerce, public health, and so on), and in terms of either the geographic macroregion or level of the hierarchy (center, province, county, or primary marketing area) that interests them. The secondary literature and the number of researchers now permit such a grouping.

A partial listing of such clusterings in modern Chinese studies would include the following topics:

• the political thought of philosophers, social critics, and other intellectuals concerning the nature of Chinese society, the human condition, and the appropriate functions and methods of governance;
• such overlapping sectors of society as women; the urban working class; the bourgeoisie or the urban middle class; ethnic minorities; intellectuals; peasants; scientists, engineers, and technicians; entrepreneurs; and managers;
• social organizations such as religion, family, and secret societies;
• elite and popular cultures and the role of the state in shaping and controlling them;
• local governance, local social control, and political participation;
• civil and criminal law;
• the role of the state in the regulation and management of the economy: commerce, agriculture, water, light industry, transportation, and heavy industry;
• primary, secondary, and higher education;
• health and medicine;
• the mass media;
• science and technology;
• management of currency, the banking system, and the revenue and budgetary system;
• the organization and conduct of foreign trade;
• the recruitment, training, promotion, transfer, discipline, and retirement of bureaucrats;
• the organizational issues and behavior of leaders at the apex of the political system in the Qing, Republican, and Communist eras;
• the formulation and implementation of China's national security policy;
• the structure, doctrine, and role of the military and civil-military relations;
• the communication system within the Chinese bureaucracy, including the gathering, transmission, storage, and retrieval of statistics and documents.

Clearly, some scholars of modern China have already seized the opportunities. Sociologists, anthropologists, and historians have cooperated to explore marriage practices and death practices. Historians, sociologists, political scientists, and humanists have gathered to assess the evolution of popular culture, the media, and the emergence of "public opinion." Many American China specialists in philosophy, history, political science, and the humanities have joined an informal and loose community that has been exploring the evolution of China's intellectual elite in Beijing and Shanghai during the past 150 years. Lawyers, historians, and political scientists have explored Chinese legal practices from a historical perspective. These various efforts have been stimulating and insightful.

But in many areas listed above, the opportunities have yet to be seized. The individuals exist; the sense of community has yet to be established. Three examples illustrate the potential.

The Apex of the System

Several monographs now exist on elite-level politics in the Imperial, Republican, and Communist eras.[2] These include studies of particular emperors—Qianlong, Kangxi, the Empress Dowager Zi Xi—and preeminent leaders of the twentieth century: Yuan Shikai, Mao Zedong, and Deng Xiaoping. (Unfortunately, no decent, extensive monograph on Chiang K'ai-shek yet exists.) There are also good studies of factional strife and the intertwining of power, personality, and policy during several key junctures in modern Chinese history. Succession politics have also been explored, as have the methods through which the preeminent leader sought to obtain accurate information to remain abreast of social and economic conditions.

These studies reveal both the continuities and changes in Chinese approaches to rule. Occasionally, writers portray Mao and Deng as modern emperors, but as Paul Cohen has argued, the roles and structures of the current office have changed enormously.[3] In the past, the emperor ruled over a traditional bureaucratic empire that commanded about 2 percent of the gross national product; the voluntary cooperation of local landed gentry enabled the power of the state to extend below the county level to the village. Today, the rulers command greater resources and on select issues their grasp extends to the village. Their communication network and the flow of information dwarf that of traditional times, and the issues that confront them are far larger in number and more complex in scope. Today's top leader and his court also confront the mass public and are linked directly to citizenry through the media in ways that simply did not exist in traditional times. They command nuclear weapons and are totally enmeshed in international affairs. The imperial institution, in short, has been transformed into a modern office that has at least as much in common with the U.S. presidency, the Japanese premiership and head of the Liberal Democratic Party, or the leader of Russia as with the emperorship.

Yet China's preeminent leader organizes his offices in ways that clearly draw on the practices of the imperial institution. The document flow, for example, clearly reflects the imperial memorial system. Tensions between the inner and outer courts, intrusions of familial considerations into the affairs of state, endemic factionalism, and sordid succession politics mark both imperial and current elite politics. Political scientists would argue that the nature of politics that swirl around the ruler is endemic to the situation. Rulers everywhere are attracted to and survive in the world of power because of their desire to dominate others. The qualities of Chinese monarchs and their courtiers are equally manifest in Hamlet, Macbeth, and King Lear, or in the Bible and the Greek tragedies.

But one also sees in China a repetition of certain patterns of behavior that arise from the culture rather than from the structure of rule, the roles that leaders everywhere must play, or ubiquitous psychological traits of human beings. Recent monographs yield a powerful and attractive interpretation of China's polity. Over the past three centuries, several strong rulers have emerged who established mastery over the political system: the Kangxi emperor; the Qianlong emperor; the Empress Dowager Zi Xi; Chiang K'ai-shek, whose ascendancy was cut short by the war with Japan; Mao Zedong; and Deng Xiaoping. Crucial to modern China's fate, none of these rulers was able to retire. Except for Chiang, each bequeathed a succession crisis. Does this recurring pattern reveal something profound about Chinese attitudes toward authority, society's needs for an ultimate arbiter, and the requisites for political unity? Does China require a single leader, and once he emerges, will his subordinates and the country prevent this preeminent ruler from retiring? So long as he breathes, disputes will be referred to him for resolution. A reading of the long history of Chinese elite politics, in short, reveals that power in China has never been well institutionalized. When the ruler ages and can no longer dominate effectively, the system decays: factionalism, familialism, and indecisiveness in policy plague the apex and permeate the system as a whole. But when a strong ruler is in place, the structure of authority permits the personality and policy preferences of a dynamic ruler to reverberate throughout the land.

The Revenue System

The recent monographic literature also reveals that to focus solely on elite politics is inadequate. It obscures certain longer term trends and underlying institutional continuities. No better example exists than in the realm of government finance, taxation, money, and banking, where a number of books and articles now provide a long-term perspective.[4]

A complex story emerges of continuity and change, with the major developments being the emergence of a national banking system in the Republican era and the dramatic increase in the state's capacity to generate revenue in the Communist era. But the increase in state revenue came from the revenue it earned from enterprises directly under the government's control—state-owned enterprises—rather than from a taxation system.

Ever since the mid-Qing era, the central state apparatus—the national government and ancillary institutions—has had difficulty in securing adequate revenue. The Communists solved this problem in part by placing all major enterprises directly under its control, controlling prices to ensure that these state-owned enterprises would be profitable, and by controlling the marketing of agricultural commodities. But the top leaders developed neither an autonomous central reserve bank nor an independent taxation and revenue system of their own that penetrated to the township and urban ward levels. In the final analysis, as Ministry of Finance officials who designed the system in the 1950s admit, the new regime retained the Qing and Nationalist revenue system; it depended on the lower levels to collect revenue and transmit funds to higher levels. Students of the Qing and earlier will immediately recognize the continuities of this "farming out" system. And as in Imperial and Nationalist times, to provide incentives, the center permitted local governments to retain a percentage of the funds they collected. In the Deng era, some of the revenue reforms represented a reversion to some of the most debilitating and corrupting revenue practices of previous eras, particularly the encouragement of separate functional agencies (such as the police, schools, road-building agencies, or granaries) to raise their own revenues through fees, licenses, and agency-run enterprises.

From this perspective, China retains a primitive revenue system. It has yet to develop an equivalent of the U.S. Internal Revenue Service, which has the ability to collect taxes from corporations and individuals. Accounting systems remain underdeveloped in most firms, and a government auditing system began to be established only in the mid-1980s. The public has yet to acquire a tax-paying ethic. It is therefore only natural that the Deng-era reforms—the transfer of management of state-owned enterprises from central to lower level government units, the expansion of the nonstate sector of the economy, and the loosening of government control over agriculture—have produced huge central government deficits.

Medicine and Public Health

The emerging literature on medicine and public health is an especially interesting example of the insight to be gained from the study of modern instead of contemporary China.[5] One sees the continuity in issues: how to combine and reconcile Chinese and Western medicine; what balance is to be struck between research, advanced training, and attainment of international standards, on the one hand, and the upgrading of existing practitioners for mass rural health care, on the other.

For over a century, in short, Chinese and Western advisers have thought about and planned for a health-care system appropriate to China's size, technological capabilities, rural-based population, income level, and disease prevalence. The Nationalist era (1927–37) saw the formulation of many policies that the government was unable to implement because of its fiscal woes and lack of effective control over much of the country. The Communists, drawing on many of the officials who formulated the plans in the KMT era and deploying the doctors trained in the 1920s and 1930s, then modified and implemented the designs of the previous era.

The medical and health sphere is particularly illuminating of China's dilemmas in its quest for modernity because it embodies two much larger issues. First, medicine and health are intertwined with notions about human beings: the relationship between the mind and the body; the sources of well-being; the healing process; indeed, the defining characteristics of illness itself. Chinese traditional medicine is based on assumptions about the harmonies and balances that exist in a healthy person and the methods for restoring these balances. An intimate relationship exists between Chinese traditional medical practices and Daoist and folk religion. In the West as well, modern medicine grows out of Western philosophical distinctions between the mind and body. (In Chinese thought, the two have been considered more intimately or organically related.) And it is not accidental, I suppose, that Western medicine was first brought to China by Christian missionaries. So, how to design a modern health system that is congruent with Chinese values and elicits popular confidence has been a core issue with which public health specialists have wrestled for a long time, not only on the mainland but in Taiwan and Hong Kong as well.

Second and relatedly, modern medicine is largely synonymous with Western medicine. Binational institutions such as Peking Union Medical College, the Yale-in-China Medical College in Changsha, and German and British institutions in Shanghai and Chengdu, respectively, played important roles in introducing Western medicine to pre-1949 China. In the most recent decade, too, the Rockefeller Foundation, the World Health Organization, the United Nations International Children's Emergency Fund (UNICEF), Japan, Canada, and West European countries have become active in the health area. Given understandable nationalistic sensitivities and the intertwining of health and values, the medical field easily can arouse anti-imperialist and anticolonial sentiment, thereby complicating the process of technology transfer. How to cooperate in the medical sphere without engendering paternalism and patronism has been a recurring problem in modern China. Familiarity with the past enables the observer to see a repetition of past patterns, some of which worked and some of which failed miserably. The Western proclivity in the 1980s and 1990s to proceed in a historical fashion, unaware of the lessons to be derived from previous experience, is particularly striking because the Chinese partners have a keen sense of this history, since many of them were products of it.

Finally, the placing of medicine and health-care policy in a broader time frame enables the student to discover the truly new, the discontinuities, and the departures. Certainly, one departure is the growth of a large community of professional Chinese doctors trained to international standards currently practicing medicine and staffing hospitals not only on the mainland, Taiwan, and Hong Kong, but throughout the world. Many such doctors in Canada, the United States, and Southeast Asia, as well as Taiwan and Hong Kong, now frequently return to the mainland to lecture, demonstrate the latest technologies, and offer advice. The process of technology transfer has a different quality than in the past. (A similar process is also occurring in the sciences and engineering.)

Moreover, China's changing demographic profile and improved standard of living mean that the substantive problems in the health field have also changed. Cardiovascular disease, cancer, and occupational accidents have replaced such eradicable diseases as typhoid fever, malaria, smallpox, and diphtheria as the major health concerns and sources of death. Reduced infant mortality rates, improved diet, and better health care, as well as the vigorous birth control program, are yielding an aging population. In the 1990s, the nature of China's medical and health problems can be expected to change substantially, requiring increasing expenditures and increases in medical personnel.

Conclusion

These examples of elite-level politics, the revenue system, and health provide but a superficial glimpse of the insights that the monographic literature can now yield. The literature on local social control (also involving folk religion, secret societies, and political participation) is now well developed, with a rather refined research agenda. So too are the extensive publications on modern Chinese political thought and social philosophy. And a fascinating series of monographs illuminate the evolution in the state's efforts to regulate and stimulate commerce and industry.

Jonathan Spence's price-winning *In Search of Modern China* and the Cambridge History compendia edited by the late John Fairbank, Albert Feuerwerker, and Roderick MacFarquhar testify to the quality of synthesis that the field can sustain. The potential has only begun to be exploited. And one likely summary conclusion is also apparent: The Communist revolution was a significant departure in some realms but not in others. In some respects, significant breaks occurred in the Qing and early Republican eras, such as in political thought. In many respects, the Nationalist era was innovative, such as in the development of civil law or thinking about a suitable economic development strategy. And in yet other areas, such as methods of raising government revenue, the continuities are more striking than the changes. The rates of development in China, in short, have been uneven not only spatially but substantively, with some policy areas or social sectors changing more rapidly than others.

This more complicated conceptualization of China's modern development raises other questions. What explains the unevenness? Why have some dimensions of the society, culture, economy, and polity changed more quickly than others? And what are the dynamics and consequences unleashed by this uneven development—when, for example, the yearnings for altered life-styles leap ahead of the economy's ability to provide the requisite material goods or when the telecommunications transformation precedes the mechanization of agriculture? As China scholars acquire a detailed map of the differential rates of change in this extraordinarily complex and diverse society, it might even be possible to understand how these separate changes are interrelated and how developments in one sector produce change in other sectors. This is part of the agenda that beckons in the 1990s, as the field expands the shape of its study to the evolution of modern, greater China.

Notes

1. The changing scene is captured in John K. Fairbank and Roderick MacFarquhar, eds., *The Cambridge History of China*, vol. 13, part 1 (Cambridge: Cambridge University Press, 1987); and in Kenneth Lieberthal et al., *Perspectives on Modern China: Four Anniversaries* (Armonk, N.Y.: M.E. Sharpe, 1991).

2. Jonathan Spence, *Ts'ao Yin and the K'ang-hsi Emperor, Bondservant and Master* (New Haven: Yale University Press, 1988); Silas Hsiu-liang Wu, *Passage to Power: K'ang-hsi and His Heir Apparent, 1661–1722* (Cambridge, Mass.: Harvard University Press, 1979); Stephen MacKinnon, *Power and Politics in Late Imperial China: Yuan Shi-kai in Beijing and Tianjin, 1901–1908* (Berkeley: University of California Press, 1980); Ernest Young, *The Presidency of Yuan Shih-k'ai: Liberalism and Dictatorship in Early Republican China* (Ann Arbor: University of Michigan Press, 1977); Roderick MacFarquhar, *The Origins of the Cultural Revolution*, vols. 1 and 2 (New York: Columbia University Press, 1974, 1983); Lucian Pye, *The Dynamics of Chinese Politics* (Cambridge, Mass.: Oelgeschlager, Gunn, Hain, 1981).

3. Paul A. Cohen, "The Post-Mao Reforms in Historical Perspective," *Journal of Asian Studies* 47 (August 1988): 519–41.

4. Madeleine Zelin, *The Magistrate's Tael: Rationalizing Fiscal Reform in Eighteenth-Century Ch'ing China* (Berkeley: University of California Press, 1984); Philip Kuhn, "Comments by Philip Kuhn," in *China in Crisis: China's Heritage and the Communist Political System*, vol. 1, book 1, ed. Ping-ti Ho and Tang Tsou (Chicago: University of Chicago Press, 1987), 194–98; Barry Naughton, "The Decline of Central Control over Investment in Post-Mao China," in *Policy Implementation in the People's Republic of China*, ed. David M. Lampton (Berkeley: University of California Press, 1987); Christine Wong, "Material Allocation and Decentralization: Impact of the Local Sector on Industrial Reform," in *The Political Economy of Reform in Post-Mao China*, ed. Elizabeth J. Perry and Christine Wong (Cambridge: Harvard University, Council on East Asian Studies, 1985), 253–78; Michel Oksenberg and James Tong, "The Evolution of Central-Provincial Fiscal Relations in China, 1971–1986: The Formal System," *China Quarterly*, no. 125 (March 1991): 1–32.

5. Mary Brown Bullock, *An American Transplant: The Rockefeller Foundation and Peking Union Medical College* (Berkeley: University of California Press, 1980); Anelissa Lucas, *Chinese Medical Modernization: Comparative Continuities, 1930s–1980s* (New York: Praeger, 1982).

Contributors

David Shambaugh is senior lecturer in Chinese politics at the School of Oriental and African Studies, University of London, and editor of the *China Quarterly*. He is the author of *Beautiful Imperialist: China Perceives America, 1972–1990* (1991) and *The Making of a Premier: Zhao Ziyang's Provincial Career* (1984) and coeditor, with Thomas W. Robinson, of *Chinese Foreign Policy: Theory and Practice* (1993), and has written extensively on Chinese politics, foreign relations, and military affairs. He was Acting Director, Asia Program, Woodrow Wilson International Center for Scholars during the years 1987 to 1988.

Mary Brown Bullock is director of the Asia Program of the Woodrow Wilson International Center for Scholars and professorial lecturer, School for Advanced International Studies, Johns Hopkins University. Before joining the Woodrow Wilson Center in 1988, she served for more than a decade as director of the Committee on Scholarly Communication with the People's Republic of China. Her publications include *An American Transplant: The Rockefeller Foundation and Peking Union Medical College* (1980) and articles on Sino-American educational and cultural relations.

Thomas Fingar directs the U.S. State Department's Office of Analysis for East Asia and the Pacific in the Bureau of Intelligence and Research (INR/EAP). Before joining INR/EAP in 1986, he held a variety of positions at Stanford University from 1975 to 1986, including senior research associate in the Center for International Security and Arms Control and director of the University's U.S.-China Relations Program. His publications include *China's Quest for Independence* (1981) and numerous articles on politics and policy-making in China.

Paul H.B. Godwin is associate dean of Faculty and Academic Programs and professor of international affairs at the National War College. His research focuses on Chinese security policy and defense modernization. His publications include "Chinese Military Strategy Revised: Local and Limited War," *Annals of the American Academy of Political and Social Science* (January 1992). Other articles have appeared in *Studies in Comparative Communism, Contemporary China, China Quarterly,* and *Armed Forces and Society.*

Thomas B. Gold is associate professor of sociology and chair of the Center for Chinese Studies at the University of California, Berkeley. He is the author of *State and Society in the Taiwan Miracle* (1986) and numerous articles on Chinese affairs. He is currently writing a book on the urban private business sector and the implications for civil society in China.

Nina P. Halpern is assistant professor of political science at Stanford University. She has published articles on many aspects of Chinese economic policy-making, including the role of experts, the politics of economic reform, and lessons from Eastern Europe. Her current research concerns administrative reform and its effect on the relationship between the Chinese state and the economy.

Harry Harding is a senior fellow in the Foreign Policy Studies Program at the Brookings Institution in Washington, D.C. Before joining the Brookings staff in the fall of 1983, he taught for twelve years at Stanford University. His major works include *A Fragile Relationship: The United States and China Since 1972* (1992), *China's Second Revolution: Reform after Mao* (1987), and *Organizing China: The Problem of Bureaucracy, 1949–1976* (1981).

Anthony J. Kane is executive director of the Johns Hopkins University–Nanjing University Center for Chinese and American Studies. He has done research on the Chinese League of Left-Wing Writers and on party-writer relations in contemporary China.

Terrill E. Lautz is vice president and program director for Asia at the Henry Luce Foundation in New York. Prior to joining the Luce Foundation in 1984, he represented the Yale-China Association in China and Hong Kong and taught at the Chinese University of Hong Kong.

Timothy Light is professor of religion and assistant to the president for international affairs at Western Michigan University. He has taught Chinese and Chinese linguistics at the University of Arizona and Ohio State University. A former editor of the *Journal of the Chinese Language Teachers Association,* he has written on Chinese language and linguistics and is the author of *Xiandai Waiyu Jiaoxuefa: lilun yu shijian* (1987) and coauthor (with T.C. Yao) of *The Character Book* (1986).

Richard Madsen is professor of sociology at the University of California, San Diego. His books on Chinese culture include *Morality and Power in a Chinese Village.* He is also coauthor (with Robert Bellah, William Sullivan, Ann Swidler, and Steven Tipton) of three books on American culture, including the *Good Society.*

Jay Mathews is a financial correspondent for the *Washington Post* in New York and a former Hong Kong bureau chief for the *Washington Post* where he covered

China from 1976 until 1980 and Beijing bureau chief from 1980 until 1983. Mathews returned to cover events in Beijing before and after the army crackdown on dissidents in 1989. His book (with Linda Mathews), *One Billion: A China Chronicle,* was published in 1983.

Linda Mathews is senior producer for foreign news on ABC's "World News Tonight." She was the first Beijing bureau chief of the *Los Angeles Times* and is the coauthor (with Jay Mathews) of *One Billion: A China Chronicle* (1983).

Michel C. Oksenberg is president of the East-West Center, Honolulu, Hawaii, and former director of the Center for Chinese Studies and professor of political science, University of Michigan. From 1977 to 1990, Oksenberg served as a senior staff member of the National Security Council with special responsibility for China and Indochina. He is the coeditor of *Beijing Spring, 1989, Confrontation and Conflict: The Basic Documents* (1990) and his research focuses on Chinese domestic affairs, China's foreign policy, and Sino-American relations.

Penelope B. Prime is associate professor of economics at Kennesaw State College in Atlanta, Georgia. She is also an analyst with the China Branch, Center for International Research, U.S. Bureau of the Census. Her current research concerns China's labor market, international trade, and domestic market development.

Thomas W. Robinson is president of American Asian Research Enterprises, Washington, D.C., adjunct professor of National Security at Georgetown University, and course chairperson for China at the Foreign Service Institute. Formerly director of the China and Asia Program at the American Enterprise Institute, he has taught at several colleges and universities, including Georgetown University, the National War College, and the University of Washington. He also served at the Rand Corporation and the Council on Foreign Relations and regularly consults with Washington-area research institutes and federal government agencies. He is the author of more than one hundred articles and five books.

Robert S. Ross is associate professor of political science at Boston College. He is the author of *The Indochina Tangle: China's Vietnam Policy, 1975–1979* (1988) and the editor of *China, the United States, and the Soviet Union: Tripolarity and Policy Making in the Cold War* (1993). He has written numerous articles on U.S.-China relations, Chinese security policy in Asia, and Chinese policymaking. He is currently completing a book on U.S.-China relations during the 1970s and 1980s.

Eugene W. Wu is librarian of the Harvard-Yenching Library, Harvard University, and former curator of the East Asian Collection of the Hoover Institution at Stanford University. He is coeditor (with Peter Berton) of *Contemporary China: A Research Guide* (1967) and coeditor (with Roderick MacFarquhar and Timothy Cheek) of *The Secret Speeches of Chairman Mao: From the Hundred Flowers to the Great Leap Forward* (1989).

Index

J

K